Risk Management:
Problems & Solutions

McGRAW-HILL SERIES IN FINANCE

CONSULTING EDITOR
Charles A. D'Ambrosio, *University of Washington*

Archer and Kerr: Readings and Cases in Corporate Finance
Beaver and Parker: Risk Management: Problems and Solutions
Blake: Financial Market Analysis
Brealey and Myers: Principles of Corporate Finance
Brealey, Myers, and Marcus: Fundamentals of Corporate Finance
Doherty: Corporate Risk Management: A Financial Exposition
Dubofsky: Options and Financial Futures: Valuation and Uses
Edmister: Financial Institutions: Markets and Management
Edwards and Ma: Futures and Options
Francis: Investments: Analysis and Management
Francis: Management of Investments
Fuller and Farrell: Modern Investments and Security Analysis
Garbade: Securities Markets
Gibson: Option Valuation: Analyzing and Pricing Standardized
    Option Contracts
Johnson: Financial Institutions and Markets: A Global Perspective
Kester and Luehrman: Case Problems in International Finance
Kohn: Financial Institutions and Markets
Lang: Strategy for Personal Finance
Levi: International Finance: The Markets and Financial Management of
    Multinational Business
Martin, Petty, and Klock: Personal Financial Management
Peterson: Financial Management and Analysis
Schall and Haley: Introduction to Financial Management
Smith: Case Problems and Readings: A Supplement for Investments and
    Portfolio Management

STANFORD UNIVERSITY
FINANCIAL SERVICES RESEARCH INITIATIVE

Risk Management:
Problems & Solutions

William H. Beaver
George Parker

Editors

McGraw-Hill, Inc.

New York St. Louis San Francisco Auckland Bogotá
Caracas Lisbon London Madrid Mexico City
Milan Montreal New Delhi San Juan
Singapore Sydney Tokyo Toronto

RISK MANAGEMENT: Problems & Solutions

2 3 4 5 6 7 8 9 0 DOC DOC 9 0 9 8 7

ISBN 0-07-048588-7

The editors were Michelle Cox and Judy Howarth;
the production supervisor was Diane Ficarra.
R. R. Donnelley & Sons Company was printer and binder.

Library of Congress Catalog Card Number: 94-74472

The Financial Services Research Initiative is a joint endeavor between the Stanford Graduate School of Business and the following financial services companies.

- Alex Brown & Sons
- Andersen Consulting
- Banc One
- Banco Nacional de Mexico
- Banco Bilbao Vizcaya
- Bangkok Bank
- Bank of America
- Bankers Trust
- Charles Schwab
- Enron Gas Services
- Goldman Sachs
- Industrial Bank of Japan
- Keystone, Inc.
- KPMG Peat Marwick
- Merck & Co.
- Merrill Lynch
- Nikko Securities
- Norwest Corporation
- Reuters America
- Salomon Brothers
- State Farm
- Tong Yang
- Wells Fargo Corporation
- Wells Fargo-Nikko Investment Advisors

Acknowledgments

This edited volume would not have been possible without the assistance of many individuals. The contributions of the chapter authors, of course, are paramount and are acknowledged in the preface. We particularly thank Robert Jaedicke, Dean Emeritus of the Graduate School of Business, who helped us form the Financial Services Research Initiative (FSRI) and obtained the support of the many of the sponsors.

This work could not have been successfully completed without the tireless efforts of Nancy Banks and Ellen O'Connor. Nancy did just about everything except write the chapters. She kept after the authors for their first drafts, coordinated review of the editorial revisions, returned the revised copies to the authors, communicated with the publishers, created the page design and layout, and prepared the entire book in camera-ready form, among numerous other efforts. We are deeply indebted to her. Ellen O'Connor provided invaluable editorial input to ensure consistency among the chapters and to enhance the readability of the entire volume. We also express our gratitude to the members of the FSRI, whose intellectual partnership with us made this possible.

Contents

PREFACE
William H. Beaver, George Parker, and Mark A. Wolfson ix

DIMENSIONS OF RISK MANAGEMENT: DEFINITION AND
IMPLICATIONS FOR FINANCIAL SERVICES
George Parker 1

NUCLEAR FINANCIAL ECONOMICS
William F. Sharpe 17

THE GEOMETRY OF COMMERCIAL BANK BALANCE
SHEET MANAGEMENT
Richard D. Lodge 37

DEBT MANAGEMENT AND INTEREST RATE RISK
Darrell Duffie 57

MANAGING MORTGAGE RISKS
Mark Faris, Richard Kovacevich, and Sonja Rodine 83

ELEMENTS OF QUANTITATIVE RISK MANAGEMENT
Ayman Hindy 107

SHOULD FIRMS USE DERIVATIVES TO MANAGE RISK?
David Fite and Paul Pfleiderer 139

VALUATION RISK AND FINANCIAL REPORTING
Joseph Mauriello and Joseph Erickson 171

RISK MEASUREMENT
William H. Beaver and Mark A. Wolfson 197

OPERATING RISK IN FINANCIAL SERVICES
Joel P. Friedman and Frank Terzuoli 219

RISK MANAGEMENT AND NEW FINANCIAL PRODUCTS
Eff W. Martin and Jan B. Brzeski 239

BANK CAPITAL REQUIREMENTS AND INCENTIVES
FOR LENDING
Charles J. Jacklin 255

COMPARATIVE RISK MANAGEMENT PRACTICES:
JAPAN VERSUS THE U.S.
Yasunori Nagai 279

YIELD CURVE RISK MANAGEMENT FOR GOVERNMENT BOND
PORTFOLIOS: AN INTERNATIONAL COMPARISON
Kenneth J. Singleton 295

THE INTERNAL CALL MARKET: A CLEAN, WELL–LIGHTED
PLACE TO TRADE
Frederick L. A. Grauer and Terrance Odean 323

THE FUTURE OF FUTURES
Myron S. Scholes 349

PREFACE

William Beaver, Professor, Graduate School of Business, Stanford University

George Parker, Professor, Graduate School of Business, Stanford University

Mark Wolfson, Professor, Graduate School of Business, Stanford University

This volume represents a unique combination of essays on the multidimensional aspects of risk management. It is a product of the Financial Services Research Initiative (FSRI), an intellectual partnership formed at Stanford University between members of its faculty and leading financial services organizations.

Because of the importance of risk management to consumers and producers of financial services, the FSRI chose this topic as its inaugural issue. For most of our authors, risks are greater today than they were a generation ago. Risk and risk management now fall under the scrutiny of top management and in the domain of corporate strategy. A review of the popular financial press shows increasing attention to and concern with phenomena as diverse as derivatives, computer models, and technological innovation—all of which simultaneously mitigate against and create new forms of risk. Financial managers may be overwhelmed not only by new risks but also by new ways to manage them. An important objective of this book, then, is to introduce insights and practices that help financial executives conceptualize this complex topic. As many of the authors assert, understanding risk is the first step in managing it.

Like the proverbial elephant surrounded by blindfolded individuals, how you describe risk depends on where you are standing. We have provided various views of risk and of risk management as seen by FSRI academic and practitioner contributors, who have unique and varied perspectives on the subject. These individuals represent institutions, technologies and methods positioned at the forefront of risk management.

George Parker opens the book by defining and illustrating the multidimensional aspects of risk. He outlines two broad categories, product market risk and capital market risk; and he identifies specific risk types in each category. The categories are neither collectively exhaustive nor mutually exclusive. However, they provide an excellent overview of the rest of the volume and a systematic way to think about risk. He concludes by distinguishing between optimal risk management and risk minimization. Parker reminds us that bearing risk "goes with the territory" of the financial services industry.

William Sharpe, Nobel laureate in economics, continues this emphasis on fundamentals. His chapter on nuclear financial economics is a basic yet highly innovative look at financial instruments and the markets that trade and price them. The heart of financial instruments is their derivative nature; that is, they are complex combinations of fundamental building blocks. His chapter sets the foundation for the remaining chapters by underscoring the nature of those building blocks.

Interest rate risk has probably received more attention that any other single dimension of risk management. The volume offers several contributions to addressing interest rate risk management. Richard Lodge illustrates how one financial services organization, BancOne, internationally known for its interest rate risk management, measures interest rate exposure. Lodge offers us ways to "picture" risk. This geometric display of balance sheet exposure becomes the starting point for assessing and managing interest rate risk. By literally "showing" risk, Lodge's approach removes much of the mystery surrounding strictly quantitative representations of risk.

In contrast, Darrell Duffie offers a quantitative approach to interest rate risk. He discusses general principles and then examines models for measuring sensitivity to unexpected changes in interest rates. He captures the essential ingredients of highly complex and state–of–the–art models. His chapter presents them in a concise, accessible manner.

Richard Kovacevich, Mark Faris and Sonja Rodine discuss how another financial services organization, Norwest, a leader in mortgage lending, takes a complex instrument such as a mortgage and analyzes its risk components: interest rate, prepayment, and credit. Their analysis reinforces many points made by the previous two chapters. The chapter demonstrates the interplay among these three components and how understanding it leads to effective management of mortgage risk.

Ayman Hindy generalizes the quantitative approach to interest rate risk and develops the basic elements of quantitative risk management. He distinguishes between the traditional institutional approach versus the broader functional approach. The chapter illustrates why the latter approach is likely to lead to more effective risk management. He identifies basic risk factors and ways to characterize a complex financial instrument in terms of its risk "ID," signature characteristics that capture the relevant aspects. An intriguing implication of his analysis is that such familiar, age–old questions such as "Is it 'debt' or is it 'equity'" may reflect a fundamentally obsolete way of thinking in our modern world of nuclear financial economics. The chapter also outlines the basic steps to follow in developing a risk management system.

In their chapter, David Fite and Paul Pfleiderer raise the basic issue as to whether firms should attempt to manage risk on behalf of the shareholders. They briefly explore three "naive" views of hedging and highlight the limitations of each simplistic approach to risk management. They then explore the necessary conditions for corporate risk management to benefit shareholders. The chapter explores how factors such as financial reporting, corporate taxation, and costs of bankruptcy can create an environment where risk management is beneficial to shareholders. Asymmetrical information, agency costs, and incomplete employee compensation contracts are also discussed as additional factors that can induce a demand for risk management. As the authors clearly point out, the existence of these market imperfections allows risk management to be a value–added activity. The chapter provides incisive analysis to complex questions which are often addressed in simplistic terms

It is axiomatic that you cannot manage risk unless you can measure it. Two chapters are devoted to the key role that risk measurement plays in risk management. Joseph Mauriello of KPMG–Peat Marwick, a leader in providing accounting services to financial sector clients, overviews the major financial reporting disclosures that purport to measure risk exposure. He makes the central point that before one can measure risk, one must first define it. The chapter explains the important role that fair value accounting has played in the measurement of risk. It also suggests that the demand for risk measurement may lead financial reporting away from its historical cost orientation to fair value reporting.

A second chapter on risk measurement by William Beaver and Mark Wolfson takes a conceptual look at risk measurement. Here a key aspect is the divergence between what the accounting system measures as risk (accounting exposure) and actual economic risk (economic exposure). This wedge between the two can lead to a variety of problems and to some anomalous behavior. In particular, it can create a demand for derivative instruments that would not exist if the accounting exposure were equal to the economic exposure. In the more perverse cases, this divergence can lead to instances where a position that reduces accounting exposure actually increases economic exposure and vice versa. In this context, the demand for hedge accounting is examined and evaluated relative to its alternatives. The difficulty of measuring risk exposure so as to effectively communicate it is a recurring theme.

The next three chapters address operational risk, product innovation risk, and regulatory risk. Operational risk is one of the least explored and yet most important aspects of risk management. Joel Friedman and Frank Terzuoli describe the analysis developed at Andersen Consulting, one of the leading consulting organizations to the financial services sector, to address operational risk. Operational risk is subdivided into several manageable subcategories. The key elements of an operational risk management system are identified and include considerations such as technology, product design, transaction and settlement process, human error, and legal and regulatory environments. Each of these is discussed in detail.

Eff Martin and Jan Brzeski describe the importance of product innovation and the risks inherent in pursuing—and failing to pursue—such innovation. They are uniquely positioned to describe the process from the perspective of Goldman, Sachs, a product innovation leader in the financial services sector. Key elements of this risk include market or trading risk, credit risk, liquidity risk, and intangible risk. These are described in detail, and the interrelationships within an entire risk management system are discussed.

Regulatory risk has many dimensions. Charles Jacklin analyzes one major tool of system–wide risk management—capital adequacy requirements by banking regulators. Capital adequacy is of obvious importance to regulators. However, capital adequacy would still be of prime importance to management even if it were not a regulatory requirement. The chapter explores the new capital reporting requirements and the anomalies that are induced by the limitations of the specific measures used. He also discusses the effects that these anomalies are likely to have on bank behavior. The chapter echoes familiar discussions as to the consequences of the divergence between accounting and economic exposure.

The next two chapters address the important global dimensions of risk management. Yasunori Nagai, of the Industrial Bank of Japan, one of the world's leading banks, vividly illustrates the point that risk management is contextual to the economic history and environment of a particular country. In doing so, the chapter makes the important point that what may work in one setting may not in another. He provides numerous examples of historical and economic considerations which form the unique context of risk in the Japanese financial services industry.

Kenneth Singleton continues on this theme in his chapter on interest rate risk management in three different economic settings—the United States, Germany, and Japan. Interest rate risk is decomposed into three elements. Empirically, the relative importance of the three elements varies from country to country. As a result, the optimal hedging instruments and policies are also contextual. However, at the same time, he provides a general framework within which to evaluate yield curve shifts and to manage the associated risks.

The next chapter addresses the use of internal markets to manage risks and reduce transactions costs. Fred Grauer, of Wells Fargo–Nikko, and Terrance Odean, of the University of California at Berkeley, discuss portfolio risk management and the use of index funds. Wells Fargo–Nikko is a world leader in the use of index funds. The chapter illustrates how markets internal to the firm can manage risk in ways that avoid the unnecessary and inefficient transactions costs of outside markets. However, such an internal market requires a formal system to provide many of the safeguards afforded by external markets. The chapter describes the implementation and benefits of such a system. As such, it illustrates a crucial aspect of risk management—organizational design innovation.

The final chapter appropriately closes out the volume by looking ahead and addressing the "future of futures." In this forward–looking approach, Myron Scholes highlights many of the important points made earlier, such as the dual role that market imperfections play in both creating a demand for risk management instruments as well as impeding their development. Scholes eloquently summarizes the central role regulators play in the derivatives markets. In addition, he returns to a key point made by Ayman Hindy—namely, that many practitioners and regulators focus on institutions rather than on functions. The chapter demonstrates how shortsighted the institutional approach can be in markets where innovative, complex instruments can be created by a variety of institutions in a relatively short time. As with our opening chapter by William Sharpe, this closing chapter adopts a primitive, "building–block" approach to financial instruments. It demonstrates that the same function can be accomplished by a unlimited number of substantively equivalent derivative positions. In concluding, the chapter predicts that the pace of product innovations will accelerate. With the prospect of continued explosive growth, regulators and other participants in financial markets must help develop the functions of the financial system rather than focus on simply preserving existing institutions.

Various aspects of risk management are addressed in these chapters; but in many respects, this book is just the beginning. New ways of doing business—electronically, globally, and technologically—have produced new risks. These in turn have sparked the development of risk management concepts and practices. While these chapters reflect some inevitable degree of heterogeneity among the authors, it is our hope that these thoughtful essays will stimulate the readers to continuously develop and structure their own perspectives on, and practices of, risk management. We view this volume as first step and hope that time will prove it a successful one.

Dimensions of Risk Management: Definition and Implications for Financial Services

George Parker, Professor, Graduate School of Business, Stanford University

Introduction

This chapter defines the topography of the expanding area of risk management in financial institutions and services in the 1990s. This topography has evolved from the industry's history, its economics, and the extraordinary change in its environment. Specifically, two broad categories of risk are the basis for classifying financial services risk: (1) product market risk and (2) capital market risk.

Economists have long classified management problems as relating to either the *product markets* or the *capital markets*. Product market decisions relate to the operating revenues and expenses of the firm, those decisions that impact the operating portions of the profit and loss statement. They include decisions about prices, marketing, operating systems, labor costs, technology, quality, channels of distribution, and strategic focus. Product market risks pertain to the risks inherent in the operating side of a financial services firm.

Capital market decisions relate to the financing and financial support of product market activities. They relate most directly to the balance sheet of the firm. The results of product market decisions must be compared to the required rates of return that result from capital market decisions to determine if management is creating or destroying value. If product market returns exceed capital costs, then positive value is being created for the owners (shareholders) of the firm. If product market returns do not meet capital market standards, then value is being eroded or destroyed. In that sense, the entire process of management can be thought of as the achievement of the highest possible value through joint product and capital market decision making.

With product markets and capital markets so defined, it is clear that understanding the risks associated with both categories is integral to the value of any firm. Product market risks relate to variations in the operating cashflows of the firm. Capital market risks relate to variations in value associated with different financing instruments and required rates of return in the economy.

The risks associated with one category have a symbiotic relationship with the other. Product market risks can affect capital market–required rates of return. Similarly, capital market decisions affect the risk tolerance of product market decisions. Ultimately, only when product market risk and capital market risks are combined can the *total risk* of the company be estimated. The following remarks emphasize that product market risks and capital market risks are both separate and interdependent. This makes the analysis of total risk in financial services vastly more complex.

Historical Perspective

During the past decade, even the objective of risk management in financial services companies has been significantly redefined. Many financial services executives recall a time when risk management, while not unimportant, was a reasonably circumscribed process in which midlevel professionals were charged with minimizing losses. Preventing credit losses or other deterioration in asset values topped the risk management agenda. It is only a slight oversimplification to say that the quality of management was defined by the degree to which risk was avoided.

From an organizational perspective, responsibility for risk management was often delegated to staff specialists. Even the best firms seldom considered total firm risk from a stockholder's standpoint. Excellence in risk management did not characterize the best competitors. Most firms used the same approach to risk. The credit policy or lending department managed default risk, auditors managed operational risk, and the insurance department managed risk. Once assured that these departments were adequately budgeted and staffed, most senior executives took little further strategic interest in risk management. Simply put, for many companies, risk was something to be minimized or avoided.

The 1980s and early 1990s brought dramatic, and in some cases, cruel changes in risk exposure. Furthermore, these events changed the objectives of risk management forever. The unwary and ill–informed were caught off guard and paid dearly for it. Bank failures reached the biggest level since the 1930s. Even those that did survive often achieved only a small part of their value and growth potential.

The new risks of doing business in financial services were frequently nontraditional in nature. Interest rate changes—not traditional credit risk—eroded asset value. International business and international expansion caused huge losses for firms that had not been accustomed to these risks. Computer systems replaced manual systems and complicated the audit trail of many transactions. Regulatory changes rearranged the profitability of many traditional financial services franchises. The remaining financial services landscape was nearly unrecognizable to many who had previously coped successfully. For many firms, the entire philosophy of risk management required rethinking and restructuring.

Risk management finally won the attention of senior executives in the 1980s and 1990s. At that time, profits were often impacted as much by risk management as by any other single management variable.

Today, management's understanding and strategic management of risk is an important competitive advantage. Aggressively pursuing the right kind of risk is central to long–term profitability and positive value creation. Finally, risk management provides a powerful means of both defense and offense in today's competitive marketplace for financial services. Those firms who manage risk well will dominate those who do not. However, as is stressed below, managing risk does not mean making it disappear.

An Economic Context

In creating and augmenting economic value, management acts to maximize the aggregate net present value of the firm's cashflow. This objective applies to financial and nonfinancial firms alike. The relevant cashflows in a financial services firm derive from financial (i.e., paper) assets, including investments, loans, contracts and other financial transactions. Positive net present value assets increase the firm's value; negative net present value assets reduce it. In this model, the total value of the firm equals the sum of all the present values—at current required rates of return—of all financial assets.

Although the value of the firm is the sum of the economic worth of all assets of the company, the value can also be disaggregated. For example, one part of value derives from the *size* and *variability* of the cashflows from the product markets. A second part of value derives from the risk–adjusted discount rate used to evaluate those cashflows. At a given level of cashflows, a lower *discount rate* increases value and a higher one reduces value. Conversely, at a given discount rate, a higher level of cashflows increases the firm's value; a lower level of cashflows reduces it.

In organizational terms, the cashflows that come from product markets are sometimes considered the responsibility of the Chief Operating Officer (COO) of the firm, and the discount rates by which they are evaluated are considered the responsibility of the Chief Financial Officer (CFO). The CEO bears responsibility for integrating both product market cashflows and risks and capital market requirements and risks. Figure I diagrams this representation of the firm.

Figure I

Total Financial Services Firm Risk

Together, product market and capital market decisions determine how (and if) the firm competes and prospers.

Distinguishing product market and capital market risks is the first step in managing them. In all firms, but especially financial firms, some categories of risk apply to *both* the product market and capital market categories. Despite this overlap or ambiguity, risks can be assigned to a primary category. The remainder of the chapter refers to this distinction as the "topography" of financial services risk management.

Risk may be defined as danger, volatility of outcomes, or simply uncertainty. Risk is not simply the incidence of adverse outcomes. Unpredictable, favorable outcomes are also a form of risk. Opportunity losses can be as important as actual losses. Foregoing a positive net present value investment conceptually is just as significant as the cost of a negative net present value decision. When wealth maximization is the objective, selling an asset too soon may be as costly as holding it too long.

In capital markets, the firm interacts with owners and lenders. In the product markets, it interacts with customers and suppliers. In both capital markets and product markets, the financial institution functions within legal and regulatory constraints that limit its risk management alternatives. Finally, the economic environment provides the institutional context in which these two markets function.

The following paragraphs describe the most important product market and capital market risks for financial services firms and their owners.

Product Market Risks

Risks in the product markets relate to the operational and strategic aspects of managing operating revenues and expenses. These risks include:

Default (credit) risk: The most basic of all product market risks in a bank or other financial intermediary is the erosion of value due to simple default or nonpayment by the borrower. In nonbank financial institutions, the equivalent of default risk is the risk that a financial asset will become valueless due to the obligor's inability or unwillingness to pay. Credit risk has been around for centuries and is thought by many to be the dominant financial service today. In fact, intermediating the risk of default between borrowers and lenders dates to the origin of banking. If net lenders themselves were willing or able to bear the credit risk of net borrowers, a primary purpose of banking would disappear. Banks intermediate the risk appetite of lenders (depositors) and the essential riskiness of borrowers. Banks manage this risk by: (1) making intelligent lending decisions so that the expected risk of borrowers is both accurately assessed and priced; (2) diversifying across borrowers so that credit losses are not concentrated in time; and (3) purchasing third–party guarantees (credit insurance) so that default risk is entirely or partially shifted away from the lenders. Accepting an appropriate level of credit risk is perhaps the single largest source of "value added" in the banking and financial intermediation business.[1]

Strategic (business) risk: This is the risk that entire lines of business may succumb to competition or obsolescence. An example is the relative disappearance of the traditional market for large, low–risk corporate lending that has been largely replaced by commercial paper. In the language of strategic planners, commercial paper is a "substitute" product for large corporate loans. Those banks that placed great emphasis on large corporate loans (sometimes called wholesale banking) experienced the risk that this business would go away during the 1980s, and a large expense base was built upon a shaky revenue base.

A second example of strategic risk occurs when a bank is not ready or able to compete in a newly developing line of business. Late entry by some banks into credit cards and home equity loans made it difficult for them to achieve a competitive advantage. Early entrants enjoyed a unique advantage over newer entrants. The seemingly conservative act of waiting for the market to develop posed a risk in itself. Business risk accrues from jumping into lines of business but also from staying out too long, a major operating risk of any financial services firm in the 1990s. This explains strategic planning's increasing importance to every financial services firm worldwide.

Regulatory risk: In the highly regulated world of financial services, regulatory risk looms much larger than in many other businesses. Most profit centers of financial services firms are licensed to do business. Two important risks surround such licenses. First, the license to operate may be revoked, which renders significant capital investments worthless. Extreme examples of this may include the nationalization of banks, as has frequently occurred outside the U.S. in the last two decades. Alternatively, banks may be closed in the domestic market due to regulatory rulings on risk and viability.

A second, more subtle regulatory risk occurs when the protected nature of a license is compromised as competitors obtain licenses to do business in a restricted market. Examples of this in commercial banking include the licensing of new competitors in domestic, regional or municipal markets.

While license granting and revocation are perhaps the most conspicuous forms of regulatory risk in financial services, there is the additional risk that regulatory authorities will change their operating policies. For example, usury laws, which limit the interest that lenders can collect, have been both passed and revoked in the 1980s. Many jurisdictions have no usury laws for banks; however, they may have such laws for other lenders. When usury laws come into effect, or when they become binding as in the case of a period of high inflation, they dramatically erode value.[2]

Finally, capital adequacy requirements in financial services allow regulatory authorities to define who may remain and who must leave various financial services businesses. In an unregulated (or less regulated) industrial environment, the market determines who is viable and who is not. In the partially nonmarket environment of regulation, the authorities themselves arbitrate this. Financial services firms that are forced to withdraw from the market often believe that they would have been viable if they had been given more time. In such cases, partially nonmarket variables constitute the regulatory risk of penalties, fines, or closure that threaten firms in the product market.[3]

Operating risk: This is the risk that systems simply do not function properly, resulting in losses of funds or value. In the 1990s, several investment banks reportedly lost significant sums due to trading errors that their systems did not detect. Perhaps no element of the management process has more potential for surprise than systems malfunctions. In an earlier and simpler era when systems were less automated, they were also more visible. Complex, machine–based systems produce what is known as the "black box effect." The inner workings of systems can become opaque to their users. Because developers do not use the system and users often have not developed the system, no one grasps its entirety. This lack of understanding constitutes a significant product market risk. No financial services firm can ignore it.

Certainly, machine–based systems offer essential competitive advantages in reducing costs and improving quality while expanding service and speed. But they also have the subversive effect of rendering their internal workings invisible. The risk of unpredictable malfunction can be extreme and must be anticipated. At the same time, insulating against operational risk can significantly undermine profits. Managing the cost benefit tradeoff in systems malfunctions is no small management challenge in the modern financial services company.

Commodity risk: Commodity prices affect banks and other lenders in complex and often unpredictable ways. For example, the oil price increases in the 1970s were followed by the collapse in the 1980s. In the first instance, the price increases negatively impacted the general economy. They undermined the viability and value of many borrowers, especially major energy consumers. The macro effect of energy price increases on inflation also contributed to a rise in interest rates, which adversely affected the value of many fixed–rate financial assets. The subsequent crash in oil prices sent the process in reverse with nearly equally devastating effects. The value of energy–related stocks and bonds plummeted. Many energy companies declared bankruptcy. The example suggests that prices of primary commodities and agricultural goods can have the same effect either through the fundamental business risk of clients and customers or through interest rate effects.

Human resources risk: Few risks are more complex or difficult to measure than those of personnel policy: recruitment, training, motivation and retention. Risk to the value of financial assets is generally accepted, but risk to the value of the nonfinancial assets as represented by the work force represents a much more subtle form of risk. The departure of an employee with specialized knowledge can bring certain systems to a halt. Of course, protecting against that risk requires paying for multiple individuals with similar knowledge and experience. This human redundancy is conceptually equivalent to safety redundancy in operating systems. It is not inexpensive, but it may well be cheaper than the risk of loss.

Concurrent with the risk of loss of key personnel is the risk of inadequate or misplaced motivation among management personnel. Absence of incentive—or presence of the wrong incentives—can produce disastrous financial results. When incentives are tied to individual performance, they can undermine cooperative effort. Conversely, group incentives can undermine individual motivation. If incentives are tied to short–term results, they can compromise the long term. One observer once noted, "The risk of incentive compensation systems is that they work!" They can be wonderful, or dangerous, or both. It is a risk that demands attention.

"Objective" vs. "subjective" incentive programs represent a different array of risks. Objective programs are based entirely on quantifiable data and are sometimes called formula systems. Formula–based systems may produce unintended results. For example, a financial services officer may concentrate on selling the least profitable products because they are easiest to sell and because they generate the largest commission. The firm does not benefit, but the individual maximizes his compensation. To avoid this, many financial services firms augment formula–based compensation programs with a subjective dimension to penalize individuals whose efforts fail to benefit the firm as a whole. But non-formula–based systems may be viewed as political or subjective in a manner that makes getting along in the firm more important than producing measurable results. Both types of incentives carry personnel risk. The risks and rewards of increased attention to the human resources dimension of management are immense.

Legal risk: This is the risk that the legal system will expropriate value from the shareholders of financial services firms. Legal risks take many forms: (1) lender liability lawsuits when borrowers claim that their bankruptcy was caused by a bank's promises not to foreclose or to grant additional credit; (2) litigation for toxic waste problems on repossessed real estate; and (3) damages for negligence in an "agency" business such as trust accounts. The legal landscape today is full of risks that were simply unimaginable even a few years ago. Moreover, these risks are very hard to anticipate because they are often unrelated to prior events. Who would imagine that a jury could award a borrower several million, including punitive damages, when a bank commented, however casually, "We are your partner." The jury decided that partners are different from lenders, so the bank gave up some of its creditor claim by that remark. Who would have imagined a bank being responsible for the toxic cleanup of a piece of raw land that was repossessed because of a creditor's inability to repay? Risks so difficult to see in the first place are nearly impossible to estimate; but the management of a financial services firm today must have those risks at least in view. They can cost millions.

Product risk: There is a major risk that a financial services product may become obsolete or uncompetitive. Automatic Teller Machines (ATMs) exemplify such risk. Early on, several banks made large investments to develop a competitive advantage in ATM technology. Concurrently, the manufacturers of ATMs were developing their own products for sale to multiple clients. When the manufacturers' machines proved superior to those developed by the banks themselves, the risk of loss in this misplaced R&D investment was not trivial. Product risk is perhaps no more significant in financial services than in other businesses, but it is clearly more significant today than it was in the less innovative, slower, and more regulated environment of the past. Systems to evaluate product risk are, by definition, new and often untried. Those firms that manage this risk well will command investors' attention.

Capital Market Risks

Capital markets and the risks inherent in them affect the value of all companies, but they are particularly significant for financial services firms. Indeed, the distinction between product market risks and capital market risks is blurred in the financial services industry because its products are bought and sold in the capital markets. For example, the interest rate risk connected with fixed–rate borrowing is generally a capital market risk; yet the risk of the same fixed–rate borrowing can cause a weak borrower to default. Thus, interest rate risk may convert to credit risk, which is a product market risk. Financial services firms supply financial products, which carry such risks, to the industrial and consumer markets. But financial services also include risks of their own relating to the capital markets in which they function.

Interest rate risk: In extreme conditions, interest rate fluctuations can create a liquidity crisis. The subject of interest rate risk, however, is much broader than liquidity. The fluctuation in the prices of financial assets due to changes in interest rates can be large enough to make default risk the major threat to a financial services firm's viability. The change in asset values caused by interest rate fluctuations is a function of both the magnitude of change in the rate and the maturity of the asset.

Hindsight shows that many financial services firms did not incorporate adequate interest rate risk assessment in their loan pricing during the 1970s and 1980s. This inadequacy of assessment and consequent mispricing of assets, combined with an accounting system that did not record unrecognized gains and losses in asset values, created a financial crisis for the Federal Deposit Insurance Corporation.[4]

After the recovery from the interest rate risk debacle of the last two decades, it was generally believed that financial executives would be highly reluctant to suffer exposure to interest rate risk. But to the dismay of many observers, they appear to have short memories. Thirty–year, fixed–rate loans, which some observers thought were finished forever after the debacle of the 1980s, have returned. Many of these mortgages are sold primarily to nonbanks, but the specter of huge amounts of interest rate risk remains.

Risk–based capital rules pertaining to banks have done little to mitigate the interest rate risk management problem. Most striking is that the capital required for holding long–term government bonds is so small as to produce large immediate returns on required equity without provision for the considerable interest rate risk of those bonds. If the bond position is monitored constantly and closely, the effect of the risk can be mitigated by selling the securities before they compromise profitability or capital. Yet such monitoring requires huge amounts of organizational discipline primarily because bonds can decrease in market value without affecting reported profits. When the bonds are sold, however, and losses are realized, the income statement reflects the impact immediately. Because reality can be postponed, wishful thinking can ensure it takes the form that what goes down (bond prices) will eventually go up! Such thinking about interest rates has driven several major bank failures—although since 1990, interest rate declines and bond price increases have rewarded those who held their investments.

Interest rate risk management is made at once easier and more difficult with the advent of derivative interest rate contracts which permit banks and other long–term, fixed–rate lenders to pass off this risk. The decision to pass it off, however, is not without large cost, so the cost–benefit tradeoff becomes complex.

Liquidity risk: For experienced financial services professionals, the foremost capital market risk is that of inadequate liquidity to meet financial obligations. The most obvious form is an inability to pay desired withdrawals. Depositors react desperately to the mere prospect of this situation. They can drive a finance intermediary to collapse by withdrawing funds at a rate that exceeds its capacity to pay.

For most of this century, bank failures from illiquidity were caused by individual depositors who lost faith in banks' ability to repay them. In the last decade, however, with $100,000 of deposit insurance behind virtually all individual deposits, the modern "run" on a bank is caused by large institutional investors who deposit funds through the money market. Although called "deposits," they are not deposits in the traditional sense. Large institutional deposits, in the form of Certificates of Deposit, are frequently purchased in arms–length transactions from sources with which the bank has no particular relationship. These sources are often geographically remote and personally unknown. Their funds are deposited primarily as a function of rate. Such funds are called purchased money or "headset funds" as they are frequently bought by employees who work on the money desk quoting rates to institutions that shop for the highest return.

When rumor spreads that a financial institution is illiquid, the purchased fund's market is the first to dry up or rise dramatically in price due to insolvency risk. These funds erode quickly either because they exceed the $100,000 that is insured or because one party lacks confidence in the other.

To check liquidity risk, firms must keep the maturity profile of the liabilities compatible with that of the assets. This balance must be close enough that a reasonable shift in interest rates across the yield curve does not threaten the safety and soundness of the entire firm.

Currency risk: The risk of exchange rate volatility can be described as a form of basis risk among currencies instead of basis risk among interest rates on different securities. Balance sheets comprised of numerous separate currencies contain large, camouflaged risks through financial reporting systems that do not require assets to be marked to market.

Exchange rate risk affects both the product markets and the capital markets. For example, exchange rate volatility can influence the ability of borrowers to repay their loans. During the 1970s, when the price of oil was climbing, Mexican borrowers received an extraordinary amount of credit from U. S. banks that was tied directly to the strength of the Mexican peso. When the peso and oil prices collapsed, borrowers lost the ability to repay. Thus, a capital market phenomenon—exchange rates—converted into the product market phenomenon of default risk. Ways to contain currency risk have developed in today's derivative market through the use of swaps and forward contracts. Thus, this risk is manageable only after the most sophisticated and modern risk management techniques are employed.

Settlement risk: Settlement risk is a particular form of default risk which involves the bank's competitors. Every day, trillions of dollars are exchanged among domestic and international banks. These amounts settle obligations having to do with money transfer, check clearing, loan disbursement and repayment, and all other interbank transfers within the worldwide monetary system. In its annual report for 1992, Chase Manhattan Bank states that this risk is managed closely through sophisticated technology that tracks payments such that netting replaces multiple payments. A single payment is made at the end of the day instead of multiple payments for individual transactions.[5]

Basis risk: Basis risk is a variation on the interest rate risk theme, yet it creates risks that are less easy to observe and understand. To guard against interest rate risk, somewhat noncomparable securities may be used as a hedge. However, the success of this hedging depends on a steady and predictable relationship between the two nonidentical securities. For example, to hedge the interest rate risk of a large U.S. Government bond portfolio, the bank may sell mortgage futures. For that hedge to work, mortgage futures must move opposite to government bonds. Should mortgage futures not move as predicted, the "basis" between the two securities is said to have shifted. This change in basis can negate the hedge partially or entirely, which vastly increases the capital market risk exposure of the firm.

Risk Management—Not Risk Avoidance—Is the Objective

Financial services firms, in addition to managing their own risks, also sell financial risk management to others. For example, they sell their service by bearing customers' financial risks through the products they provide. A financial firm can offer a fixed–rate loan to a borrower with the risk of interest rate movements transferred from the borrower to the bank. The bank, in turn, can carry that risk (presumably with compensation) or pass the risk on (at some expense) in the form of a hedging transaction. Thus, while the risk itself is ultimately unavoidable, the burden of the risk and its costs are both manageable and transferable.

The rapid increase in both product market risk and capital market risk in financial services has sent many executives fleeing for cover. Risk reduction for customers and for financial intermediaries themselves has recently become a big business. The Federal Reserve suggests that its member banks alone held $7 trillion in derivatives (mostly foreign currency and interest rate swaps) during the first quarter of 1993; and even these large numbers may understate derivatives' growth.[6]

Financial innovation has been more concerned with risk reduction than any other subject. Derivatives are the capital markets' way of moving risk around. Swaps, options, futures—all attempt to transfer risk much the way an insurance company can pass off its risks through reinsurance. A company wishing to eliminate nearly all risks can now do so in ways barely conceivable even a generation ago. With the possibility of managing risk near zero, the challenge becomes not how much risk can be removed but rather how much risk *should* be removed. The business of financial services is, in essence, the business of bearing risk for a price. Without risk in the product markets and capital markets of financial institutions, there is much less reason for their existence.

Senior managers in today's deregulated, competitive financial services environment must understand the true value of their services. In a free–market environment for services, customers will not spend their money where they do not perceive value. In financial services, particularly, value is an elusive concept.

Financial services involve the process of intermediation between those who have financial resources and those who need them, either as a principal or as an agent. Thus, value breaks into several distinct functions, and it includes the intermediation of the following:

- Default
- Maturity preference mismatch
- Currency preference mismatch
- Size of transaction
- Market access and information

All these functions assume a degree of risk on the part of the financial intermediary. This risk can either be passed on to another risk bearer through hedging, or it can be carried for a price.

Many financial intermediaries would find life less complicated and management less complex if all risks were shifted away through hedging or maturity matching of assets and liabilities in the capital markets. But an essential part of the intermediation function is to bear some appropriate amount of risk. This, presumably, as in the actuarial insurance business, is the level of risk that does not jeopardize liquidity and solvency. In turn, the acceptable level of risk is the maximum amount that can be compensated without jeopardizing the firm's existence. Any risk which compromises the existence of the firm cannot be adequately compensated since compensation cannot be realized by a firm that is not in business. Even correctly priced assets and liabilities cannot benefit the stockholders if the risk of loss is so great that the institution cannot survive.

It is probably impossible to accurately estimate the excess and survival–threatening risk borne by financial institutions. In 1992, the Federal Reserve Board estimated that "perhaps 20% of the [banking] industry was taking excessive risk."[7] These banks reduce their potential value by mismanaging their risk exposure, i.e., by accepting too much risk. Furthermore, more subtly, some banks may limit their potential value by accepting too little risk—particularly too little correctly priced risk.

A willingness to accept appropriate levels of risk in the financial markets is a fundamental purpose of the financial intermediation process. Risk does not disappear upon transfer to other parties. Precisely because risk has a price, there are costs to transferring it; and the compensation to those that accept risk can be significant. Thus, when banks reduce risk to a minimum, they partially exit the intermediation business.

Establishing which institutions are best positioned to carry risk is part of the market system's efficiency. Since the most efficient risk bearer determines the price of risk, the strategic act of risk management is to identify those institutions best positioned to accept risk. The low–cost risk bearers derive the greatest benefit from the market's compensation for risk.

Understanding the cost of risk requires appreciating the complexity of measuring threats to solvency. The degree to which adverse risks occur concurrently is referred to as the correlation coefficient of the risks. The extent to which they move together is the covariance of the risks. Clearly those institutions with low covariance across risk categories can tolerate a higher level of individual asset risk than those with high covariance. Many banks are presently in the earliest stages of measuring and controlling their risks' covariance, which often is more important than the variance itself. Thus, all banks are not all equally positioned to bear risk. The strategic decisions they make about their assets affect the risks they have and those they can take. Concentrations of correlated risk are the enemy of the institution's risk–bearing capacity.

Derivative securities in the form of options and futures significantly adjust risk concentrations to keep exposures within measurable bounds. Yet financial managers must continually remind themselves that the purpose of these derivatives is not to transfer all risk. Such a policy would defeat an essential aspect of the financial institution and intermediation business.

Conclusion

Risks in financial services are larger in scope and scale than ever before. Many of the risks are of a traditional sort: credit risk, interest rate risk, liquidity risk. However, numerous risks are more recent, such as regulatory risk, currency risk, and human resources risk.

Along with revenue maximization and operational cost minimization, risk management has moved to center stage in defining superior performance. Differences in risk management philosophy and technique can produce prosperity, mediocrity, or failure. No senior management of today's financial institutions can perform its function without a vastly expanded understanding of the dimensions of risk and the various tools to manage it.

Some managements have reacted to this daunting task by pulling back from risk. They decline to accept transactions where the risk is significant (i.e. long–term, fixed–rate loans) or they transfer risk (e.g., hedging). While these techniques have an important place in the risk management process, they can also compromise a financial institution's value through excessive risk avoidance. Placing the firm at the appropriate point between excessive risk acceptance and avoidance will separate the winners from the losers in the years ahead.

Notes

[1] Credit risk management is one area where banking has significantly changed in the past decade. For many years, a primary function of banks was to enhance borrowers' credit by intermediating the relationship between net savers and net borrowers. Thus, banks could borrow more cheaply from lenders than the end users of the money, e.g. corporations. Banks were said to be making a business of "lending their credit" to corporations.

But some of the least risky corporate borrowers came to be perceived as having the same creditworthiness as banks. Some were perceived to have even less credit risk than banks. For example, in 1993, only one bank in the U.S. had a triple-A credit rating while a number of corporate borrowers had this designation. Obviously, the economy derives little value when a single-A–rated bank purchases funds (deposits) in the capital markets and marks them for re-lending to a triple-A–rated borrower.

The net result of a new credit intermediation function is that the most creditworthy debtors borrow directly from savers at a lower cost. Banks get higher credit risk business where their credit is superior to that of borrowers.

[2] Sometimes usury laws are in effect but are nonbinding, that is, the typical market interest rate is below the usury ceiling. For many years, New York had a 12% usury ceiling on some real estate finance. When mortgage rates were 10% or less, the law had no effect. But when inflation forced market rates higher, the usury laws reduced the value of mortgage licenses by up to 100%.

Usury laws have also often applied to credit card balances. Usury rate ceilings on credit cards forced Citibank to move its credit card operation from New York to South Dakota in the 1970s. New York ultimately repealed its most onerous usury laws because the maximum allowable interest rate occasionally fell below the inflation rate. Nonetheless, the risk of loss due to interest rate regulation was significant for Citibank and for many other banks affected by usury laws.

[3] The often–cited reason that regulators close banks is that they are "protecting the Federal Deposit Insurance Corporation ('FDIC')." The underlying assertion is that the holders of bank equity are holders on an option to the bank's returns if it performs well. Otherwise, the FDIC is left with assets worth a fraction of their recorded value. Thus, owners (shareholders) will view their option as expropriated by the FDIC regulators when the business closes.

[4] The extent of their mispricing of assets is variously estimated at between $200–$400 billion (the amount of the FDIC payments to rescue these institutions).

[5] Chase Manhattan National Bank, *Annual Report*, 1992, 9.

[6] "Deriving in the Fast Lane," *The Economist*, 26 June 1993, 88.

[7] "Many Banks Change Strategies to Manage Rate Risk," *Wall Street Journal*, 10 February 1993, 9.

Nuclear Financial Economics

William F. Sharpe, Professor, Graduate School of Business, Stanford University

Introduction

An important subfield of physics—*Nuclear Physics*—deals with the smallest particles of which matter is composed. Constructs developed by Kenneth Arrow[1] and Gerard Debreu[2] provide a similar foundation for financial economics. With a bit of hyperbole, the approach may be termed *nuclear financial economics*.

In pioneering their work, Arrow and Debreu explored aspects of general equilibrium. After dealing with the economists' then–traditional world of certainty, they turned to issues related to *risk*.

Here we show how the Arrow–Debreu approach can be used to analyze risk in the domains of financial engineering, corporate finance, and investment analysis.[3] The simplest possible cases, involving only two time periods (the present and a future date) are employed. While the results are quite general, no attempt is made to prove generality nor to extend the analyses to cover more complex cases. The relatively modest goal of the paper is to interest readers in using "nuclear financial economics" to analyze issues involving risk in financial settings.

Contingent Contracts

To deal with risk, Arrow and Debreu introduced the concept of a *contingent contract*—a contract "for delivery of goods or money contingent on the occurrence of [a] state of affairs,"[4] equivalently: "a contract for the transfer of a commodity [specifying], in addition to its physical properties, its location and date, an event on the occurrence of which transfer is conditional."[5]

A special kind of contingent contract provides one unit of money or some notional commodity at one date if and only if one of the many possible states of the world at that date obtains. This may be termed a "pure" or "primitive" security, or simply a *time–state claim*. A *complete market* is one in which all such claims may be purchased or sold explicitly or synthetically at stated prices.

The *price* of a contingent contract or time–state claim is "…the amount paid…initially by…the agent who commits himself to accept…delivery of one unit of that commodity. Payment is irrevocably made although delivery does not take place if specified events do not obtain."[6]

The concept of a contingent contract allows for the analysis of risk in simple yet powerful ways, as we will show.

Financial Engineering

The International Association of Financial Engineers defines *financial engineering* as "…the development and the creative application of financial technology to solve problems in finance and to exploit financial opportunities."[7]

The Arrow–Debreu approach may seem too far removed from the real world to be used for such purposes. There are hundreds of millions of contingencies for which no specific contingent contracts exist, and it is difficult to imagine a way to synthesize most such contracts from securities that do exist. Nonetheless, the concept is in fact widely used in financial engineering under the assumption that markets are sufficiently complete for the states of the world that affect the securities being analyzed.

Those who employ so–called *binomial models of asset returns*[8] utilize contingent claims[9] explicitly. Those who employ continuous–time models, such as that of Black and Scholes, [10] do so implicitly. Curiously, however, many practitioners of financial engineering are unaware of the intellectual underpinnings of the methods that they employ.

Financial engineering is by no means the only area in which the Arrow–Debreu approach can be employed. In fact, it can address fundamental issues of corporate finance and investment analysis. It allows a very clear distinction between models that require only the assumption that markets are arbitrage–free and those that require additional assumptions about investor preferences and predictions.

In the field of investment analysis, both academics and practitioners tend to favor the *mean–variance* approach introduced by Markowitz[11] over that of Arrow and Debreu. While there are good reasons for doing so, it seems unfortunate that the latter is often entirely omitted from investment courses. A preferred strategy utilizes the Arrow–Debreu model to develop fundamental ideas, then turns to mean–variance analysis and its use in practice.

The Economy

To illustrate the power of the Arrow–Debreu approach, we consider an extremely simple economy in which there is no currency. Apples are the only good and all trades involve apples. There are two time periods—*now* and *next year*. The only source of risk is the uncertainty about next year's weather. More precisely, there are two possible states of the world concerning next year: *good weather* and *bad weather*.

There are three distinct goods available for trade at present: (1) apples now, (2) apples next year if the weather is good, and (3) apples next year if the weather is bad.

Note that the latter two are contingent contracts. For simplicity, we call these goods "present apples," "good–weather apples," and "bad–weather apples."

In this economy, *dealers* stand ready to trade any one of the three goods for any other. Competition is so fierce that bid and ask prices are the same.

Initially, we assume that dealers will *swap* 0.4 present apples for 1.0 good apple. More precisely, if an individual will give up 0.4 apples today, he or she will receive a certificate promising delivery of 1.0 apple next year if (but only if) the weather during the coming year has been good; if the weather has been bad, no apples will be delivered next year.

Dealers will also swap 0.5 present apples for 1.0 bad apple. More precisely, if an individual will give up 0.5 apples today, he or she will receive a certificate promising delivery of 1.0 apple by next year if (but only if) the weather during the coming year has been bad; if the weather has been good, no apples will be delivered next year.

Following convention, we call the terms of trade for swaps involving future and present goods *prices*. Thus the price of a good–weather apple is 0.4 (present apples) and the price of bad–weather apple is 0.5 (present

---

apples). Equivalently, the *present values* of such contingent claims are 0.4 and 0.5, respectively. Note that the term *present value* is simply a convention for stating terms at which market transactions can be made to convert claims for future payments to current payments. Absent competitive markets in which such swaps can be made, the concept has no particular usefulness.

Production in this economy comes from apple trees, each of which will produce 100 apples next year if the weather is good and 70 apples if the weather is bad. This is illustrated (naturally) via a *tree diagram* in Figure 1. For convenience, prices are also shown.

Figure 1

Apple Tree Payoffs and Prices

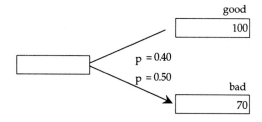

Arbitrage–Free Pricing

The two prices in Figure 1 show the terms of trade for swaps in which a present good is exchanged for a contingent future good. Not shown are the terms for a swap in which one contingent future good is exchanged for another. However, *arbitrage* will insure that such trades are made using terms consistent with those already shown. Consider someone who wishes to trade 1.0 good–weather apple for some number of bad–weather apples. One way to do this is to trade 1.0 good–weather apple for 0.4 present apples while at the same time trading 0.4 present apples for 0.8 bad–weather apples. The net result is to *swap* 1.0 good–weather apple for 0.8 bad–weather apples. Such a swap has zero *net present value* and thus can be said to be "fair." If any dealer were willing to swap good–weather and bad–weather apples at any other terms of trade, an astute individual could exploit the dealers by engaging in combinations of trades that could provide (1) net receipt of apples in at least one time and state and (2) no net payout of apples at any time and state. Such an opportunity, termed an *arbitrage*, is rare in a well–functioning, competitive capital market.

In an arbitrage–free economy with no transactions costs, any given time–state claim will sell for the same price, no matter how obtained. This will also be true for any "package" of time–state claims. This is known as the *law of one price*.

Most transactions involve complex combinations of present and future time–state claims. All are *swaps* in a broad sense. Those involving both present and future payments are often termed *investments*, with the term "swap" reserved for those that involve only future contingent payments. However, such terminology obscures the fact that all reflect trades of one set of valuable claims for another.

Valuation

How much is an apple tree worth? The answer is easily obtained by *valuing* each of the contingent claims that it provides. The 100 good–weather apples can be traded for 40 (0.4 x 100) present apples and the 70 bad–weather apples for 35 (0.5 x 70) present apples. Thus the (present) value of the tree is 75 (present) apples, as shown in Figure 2.

Figure 2

Apple Tree Payoffs and Prices

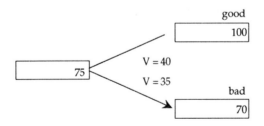

Note that valuation is designed to answer the question: "For how much in present goods (or money) can the asset in question be traded—either directly or indirectly." *In principle, all standard valuation methods rest on the use of market prices to answer such questions.*

Financing

Consider the apple–tree owner who issues two claims. The first promises the holder 60 apples next year. Since the amount promised is fixed, the associated *security* can be termed a *bond*. The other claim promises the holder all the apples left over after the bondholder has been paid. The associated security represents a *residual claim* and can be termed a (common) *stock*.

Table 1 provides the computations required to determine the value of the bond. Note that it is *riskless* since the promised amount can be paid no matter what the state of the world (weather) may be. An equivalent method for valuing a riskless security *discounts* the promised payment using the *riskless discount factor*. For a riskless security, the factor is simply the sum of the prices of all the time–state claims for the date in question; for this is the cost of obtaining one unit at that date, no matter what the state of the world. In this economy, the discount factor is 0.9 (0.4 + 0.5). This is sometimes stated in terms of a *rate of interest*. In this case, the rate of interest is equal to 0.1/0.9, or 11.11%, since 0.9 today can be converted to 1.0 next year (and vice–versa) with certainty.

Table 1

Time	State	Payment	Price	Present Value
1	good	60	0.4	24
1	bad	60	0.5	30
				54

Whichever method is employed, the result is the same. The value of the bond is 54 present apples.

Table 2 provides the computations required to determine the value of the stock. It is *worth* 21 present apples since the same set of contingent payments could be obtained with 21 apples by judiciously making swaps with dealers.

Table 2

Time	State	Payment	Price	Present Value
1	good	40	0.4	16
1	bad	10	0.5	5
				21

Note that the value of the bond plus the value of the stock is 75 present apples. Not surprisingly, this is the value computed earlier for the tree as a whole.

What if the tree had been financed by issuing "risky debt"? Consider a case in which the bondholder has been promised 80 apples next year. In fact, he or she will receive 80 apples if the weather is good but only 70 if the weather is bad. Clearly the bond cannot be valued by discounting the promised payment. Table 3 shows how this should be done. Note that the actual value (67 present apples) is considerably less than the value that the bond would command if the promised payments were guaranteed (0.9 x 80, or 72 present apples).

Table 3

Time	State	Payment	Price	Present Value
1	good	80	0.4	32
1	bad	70	0.5	35
				67

With this sort of financing (high leverage), the stock is risky indeed—it will pay 20 apples if the weather is good but nothing if the weather is bad (i.e., the firm will be bankrupt). Such a stock will be worth 8 apples, as shown in Table 4.

Table 4

Time	State	Payment	Price	Present Value
1	good	20	0.4	8
1	bad	0	0.5	0
				8

Note that the sum of the values remains the same as before (67 + 8 = 75). This reflects the *principle of value additivity*. In a complete market with no transactions costs, the value of the sum of the claim will be the same, no matter how those claims are structured. In this setting, "financing doesn't matter." This is the essence of the famous Modigliani–Miller Proposition Number I.[12]

In the real world, of course, transactions costs (broadly construed) do matter. Nonetheless, the principle of value additivity remains useful if a broad-enough view is taken of the set of claimants on a firm's prospects. In particular, governments (which impose taxes on firms and on those who receive income from firms) must be included, as must lawyers, accountants, investment bankers and others who may be more likely to absorb some of a firm's cashflows under certain financial arrangements than under others.

In a sense, the questions to be asked concerning alternative financing procedures have more to do with the division of the pie than with its overall size. The latter tends to be determined more by nonfinancial decisions than by financial ones. However, there are cases in which financial decisions can significantly alter incentives for those charged with "corporate governance" to maximize the size of the pie.

Synthetic Securities

In the real world, people rarely make explicit agreements for payments to be made if one and only state of the world obtains. Most traded securities represent patterns of payments over many states. Equivalently, they may be thought of as packages of pure time–state claims.

To illustrate this, we return to the case of a firm that has issued a riskless bond promising a payment of 60 apples (as described in Table 1) and a stock representing a claim for the remaining apples (as described in Table 2).

Consider an economy in which the only traded goods are this firm's bond and stock. We assume each can be divided into smaller holdings and that dealers are willing to trade the bond for 54 present apples and the stock for 21 present apples. No other markets exist.

Given the current price of a security and the payments it will provide in each state of the world, it is possible to determine the *value–relative*, or future payment per unit invested, that will be received if that state obtains. Tables 5 and 6 show these computations for the bond and stock, respectively. Note that the percentage *realized return* associated with a given state of the world is simply 100 times [the value–relative minus 1.0].

Table 5

Time	State	Bond Payment	Price	Value Relative	% Return
1	good	60	54	1.1111	11.11
1	bad	60	54	1.1111	11.11

Table 6

Time	Stock State	Payment	Price	Value Relative	% Return
1	good	40	21	1.9048	90.48
1	bad	10	21	0.4762	-52.38

Figure 3 plots the value–relatives for the two securities. Since the bond is riskless, it lies on a 45–degree line from the origin—indicating that the payoff per unit invested is the same, no matter what happens in the future. Any security that plots at a point not falling on such a line is *risky*—the payments differ in different states of the world, and hence the amount to be received is not fully predictable in advance. In this case, the stock is risky and the bond is not.

Figure 3

Payments from a 1–Unit Investment

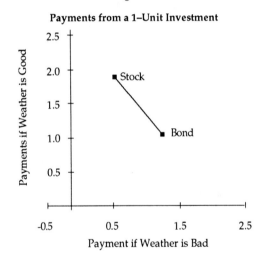

An *investor* may prefer the bond over the stock or vice versa. However, these are by no means the only alternatives. By choosing a *portfolio* that includes proportionate shares of the bond and the stock with a total present value of 1 (apple), an investor can obtain any point on the line connecting the two points in Figure 3.

It is helpful to write the relationships among portfolio *holdings*, payments in the two states of the world and portfolio *value*. Letting N_s and N_b represent the number of stocks and bonds held, P_G and P_B the payments received in good and bad weather, and V the present value of the portfolio:

$$40N_s + 60N_b = P_G$$
$$10N_s + 60N_b = P_B$$
$$21N_s + 54N_b = V$$

The equation of the line in Figure 3 is obtained by setting V equal to 1 and then varying N_s and N_b over the range in which neither is negative.

But these are not the alternatives in a well–functioning capital market. Directly or indirectly, it should be possible to take a *negative* position in a security (e.g. "sell it short") as long as an investor's overall portfolio does not involve commitments that would lead to obligations involving negative *net* payments in any state of the world. By judicious use of such positions, an investor should be able to obtain any point on the line through the two points extended to the axes, as shown in Figure 4.

Figure 4

Payments from a 1–Unit Investment

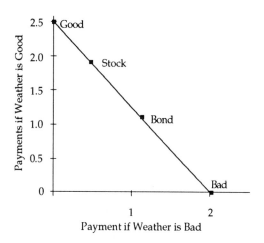

In practice, such arrangements require procedures to guarantee "counterparty creditworthiness." Frequent marking of positions to market, the use of impound accounts, the guaranteeing of credit, and the reliance on credit ratings made by outside agencies represent institutional approaches to this issue.

Note that by combining a "long" position in the stock with a short position in the bond in precisely the right proportions, one can *construct* a (pure) "good–weather claim." This is represented by the point labeled *good* in

Figure 4. Not surprisingly, it provides 2.5 good–weather apples per 1.0 present apple. Equivalently, the price of 1.0 good–weather apple, obtained in this manner, is 0.4 present apples (as in our earlier example). By combining *existing securities* (the bond and the stock), one can *synthesize* a security that does not exist (a good–weather security). The result is often termed a *derivative security* since it is derived from existing securities.

The point labeled "bad" shows the payments received from a synthetic bad–weather security with a present value of 1. Not surprisingly, the associated price of 1.0 bad–weather apple is 0.5 (again, as in our earlier example).

In principle, any desired set of payments in the two states of the world can be created using only the two "standard" securities. Given desired payments P_G and P_B, one simply solves the set of simultaneous equations:

$$40N_s + 60N_b = P_G$$

$$10N_s + 60N_b = P_B$$

The value (cost) of obtaining the payments can then be determined by "pricing out the portfolio" with the final equation:

$$21N_s + 54N_b = V$$

In financial engineering terms, the portfolio (N_s and N_b) is sometimes termed a *replicating strategy*.[13]

It is a simple matter to determine the prices of pure time–state claims implicit in a set of existing securities. First, the cost of a strategy for which $P_G = 1$ and $P_B = 0$ is determined. This is the price of a claim to receive 1 unit if and only if the "G" state obtains. In this economy it is 0.4. Then the cost of a strategy for which $P_G = 0$ and $P_B = 1$ is determined. This is the price of a claim to receive 1 unit if and only if the "B" state obtains. In this economy it is 0.5. Henceforth, any desired set of payments can be "priced" by simply multiplying the amounts to be paid by these prices and then summing. In this case:

$$V = 0.40P_G + 0.50P_B$$

Only when a replicating strategy needs to be employed will it be necessary to solve the original set of simultaneous equations.[14]

Forward Prices

A *forward price* can be defined as a price to be paid *with certainty* at a specified future date for delivery of one or more goods, where the amount delivered may be contingent on events occurring on or before that date. An important special case is the *forward price of a (pure) time–state claim*.

In our economy, the expenditure of 0.4 apples today will purchase a security promising delivery of 1.0 apple tomorrow if the weather during the forthcoming year is good. A forward contract for the same security would promise the payment of some amount f_G next year, *no matter what*. For example, one party might promise to pay 0.4444 apples next year (no matter what) in exchange for a promise from a counterparty that the latter will deliver 1.0 apple if the weather has been good and nothing if it has been bad. Equivalently, after netting, if the weather has been good, the counterparty will deliver 0.5556 apples; on the other hand, if the weather has been bad, the original party will deliver 0.4444 apples.

In the absence of any payments or receipts during the year (as in our example), a very simple relationship should hold between the present price and the associated forward price. The forward price will simply equal the present price plus associated interest. Equivalently, the present price will equal the forward price divided by the discount factor for the payment date. In this case:

$$0.4444 = 0.40 / 0.90$$

If this relationship does not hold, clever arbitrageurs can exploit others in the market. They literally "make something for nothing." Such opportunities are fleeting at best.

Forward prices for pure time–state claims can also be used to value desired payments. First, the *forward value* (F) for the set of payments is determined. Here:

$$F = f_G P_G + f_B P_B$$

This is the amount that one should be willing to commit to pay next year for the set of payments in question.

To find the present value, the forward value is simply discounted. Here:

$$V = .90F$$

This two–step procedure is widely used by financial engineers. Unfortunately, the underlying economics is obscured by the use of terms that are at best confusing and at worst misleading. Forward prices of time–state claims are termed *risk–neutral probabilities* (or just *probabilities*). The forward value of the set of payments is called the *expected future value*, and the present value is the *discounted expected future value*.

While the procedures employed by those who use such terms provide correct answers, it is dangerous to confuse forward prices with probabilities and forward values with expected values. In a world of risk–averse investors, probabilities and forward prices will generally differ, as will forward and expected values.

There is every reason to believe that investors are risk averse. This, in turn, gives rise to differences in expected returns. To construct an appropriate investment strategy, one must attempt to understand such differences.

Investment Choice

The astute reader will have noted that none of the conclusions reached thus far used the concept of *probability* in any way! Issues of valuation, replication, the construction of swaps, and so on, can in principle be addressed without assuming or measuring probabilities associated with various states of the world. All that is required is a sufficiently complete market and price information for enough securities to allow purchase of pure time–state claims, either directly or synthetically.[15]

In effect, once a tree representing the payments provided by a sufficient set of existing securities has been drawn, further analysis proceeds from the sole assumption that markets are arbitrage–free. This is the proper domain of financial engineering.[16]

Investment choice deals with the selection of a *portfolio* of investments. Fundamentally, it is concerned with choosing an appropriate combination of time–state claims given the investor's overall wealth. In the Arrow–Debreu framework, wealth (including potential future earnings from human capital) can be stated in present–value terms. The *consumption–investment* decision is to select the best combination of present and state–contingent future goods (for example, apples) from among all combinations that can be obtained given overall wealth. Letting P_N represent the payment now (that is, consumption of present apples), $EU()$ the investor's "expected utility" function, and W his or her wealth, the goal is to:

maximize: $\qquad\qquad EU\left(P_N, P_G, P_B\right)$

subject to: $\qquad 1.00P_N + 0.50P_G + 0.40P_B \leq W$.

Clearly, the utility that an investor expects to receive from holdings of contingent claims on future consumption will depend on his or her assessment of the probabilities that the associated state of the world will actually come about. Hence, investment choice must deal with probabilities.

Moreover, while the financial engineer may be able to take security prices as given, investors will wish to consider their determinants, including productive opportunities and the opinions and preferences of others. In a sense, the current price of a time–state claim reflects a consensus of all investors' *predictions* of the *probability* of the associated state and their *feelings* about the *desirability* of obtaining goods in that state. A specific investor will, in the first instance, compare his or her own assessment of the probability of a state and the desirability of obtaining goods in it with the price that must be paid for the associated contingent contract. At a deeper level, however, the investor is comparing his or her own probability assessment and utility with that of the consensus of other investors.

Space precludes a detailed analysis of these relationships here. Instead we focus on two central aspects of investment analysis: the existence of *risk premiums* and *type* of risk that is likely to be rewarded with such premiums.

Consensus Probabilities

There is no reason to believe that individuals agree on the probabilities associated with various future states of the world. Thus the very notion of, say, "the probability" of good weather is ill defined. As a practical matter, it is frequently assumed that markets are "efficient" in a particular sense. A market can be said to be *efficient relative to a given set of information* if security prices are the same as they would be if all investors had carefully analyzed that information. The set of probabilities assessed by a "careful analyst" after having processed a body of information can be termed "fully informed" relative to that set of information. Theorists sometimes assume, for example, that prices "incorporate all publicly available information."

Roughly, this is equivalent to assuming that prices "reflect" probabilities that would be assigned by a sophisticated analyst after having studied all such information.

A modest set of assumptions holds that security prices reflect a set of "consensus probabilities" representing weighted averages of investors' predictions. In this process, the predictions of those with large amounts of wealth are generally weighted more heavily than the predictions of those with small amounts of wealth.

Formal models of investment behavior generally assume that all investors hold the same set of opinions concerning probabilities. Results are then derived concerning security prices, expected returns, and the like. Such results can be compared with the opinions of a particular investor who may assign different probabilities either due to the use of a different information set or a different analysis of the same information. Recommended consumption and investment decisions can arise from any of the three types of differences between the investor and "average investor": differences in *preferences*, in *circumstances*, or in *predictions*.

For the purposes of this paper, we assume that there are no differences of opinion concerning the probabilities of possible states of the world. More precisely, everyone agrees that the probability of good weather is 0.5, as is the probability of bad weather.

Forward Prices, Probabilities, and Expected Returns

Properly constructed probabilities have two well–known properties: they are non–negative and sum to 1.0 when all possible states of the world are included.

Forward prices for pure time–state claims have precisely the same properties. As long as the goods in question are indeed "good," each forward price will be non–negative. Moreover, as argued earlier, the sum of all such forward prices will be 1.0 when all possible states of the world are included.

These two facts imply that either (1) every pure time–state claim forward price will equal its probability or (2) some forward prices will be greater and others less than the associated probabilities.

The *expected payment* from a pure time–state claim is simply the probability that the associated state will occur since an expected value is obtained by multiplying a payment (here, 1.0) by a probability. The ratio of the expected payment to the current price will equal the *expected value relative*, or [1 + the *expected return*] for the time–state claim in question.

Table 7 shows the calculations for our economy. The expected return for a good–weather apple contact is 25%; that for a bad–weather apple contract is 0%. Note that the former exceeds the riskless rate of interest (11.11%) while the latter falls below it.

Table 7

Time	State	Price	Payment	1 + Exp. Return
1	good	40	0.5	1.25
1	bad	50	0.5	1.00

Recall that arbitrage insures that a forward price will equal the present price times $(1+i)$, where i is the riskless rate of interest. It follows that if the probability of a state equals the forward price of a claim to receive one unit in that state, then the expected return on the claim will equal the riskless rate of interest. Using this as a watershed, we can easily conclude that for any pure time–state claim:

```
Probability  >  Forward Price  <==>  Expected Return  >  Riskless Rate
Probability  =  Forward Price  <==>  Expected Return  =  Riskless Rate
Probability  <  Forward Price  <==>  Expected Return  <  Riskless Rate
```

In our economy, the good–weather state represents a case of the first type, and the bad–weather state represents a case of the third type.

If all forward prices equaled probabilities, all time–state claims would have expected returns equal to the riskless rate of interest. But then, so would all securities! In such a world, there would be no reason to expect to do better with stocks, for example, than with Treasury securities.

We can define a *risk premium* as the difference between the expected return on a security and the riskless rate of interest. In a society in which all time–state claim forward prices equaled probabilities, there would be no risk premiums.

Simple experience, introspection and many empirical studies suggest that in actual economies, prices will be set so that some securities should be *expected* to outperform others. In the vernacular, such securities should provide better "long–term performance."

To offer a superior expected return, a security must provide disproportionate amounts of payments in the states of the world for which the probability exceeds the forward price of the associated time–

state claim. Such a security will have a *risk* for which there is a *reward* (risk premium). Our good–weather–apple security provides an example.

But, as we have argued, if there are states for which the probability exceeds the forward price, there must be states for which the reverse holds. Securities providing disproportionate amounts of payments in such states will produce what may be termed a *risk discount*—their expected returns will be less than the riskless rate. Such securities will have a risk for which there is a *penalty* rather than a reward. Our bad–weather–apple security provides an example.

The Societal Risk Premium

In our economy, good–weather apples are cheap—their forward price is less than the expected payment. Conversely, bad–weather apples are expensive—their forward price is greater than the expected payment. This is perfectly plausible. If the weather is bad, there will be fewer apples. In general, the greater the value of an additional apple, the fewer there are to consume. Investors will reduce present consumption to provide more "for a rainy day" than they will to provide for a sunny day. More to the point, an additional unit of a commodity is likely to be worth more in a *state of scarcity* than in a *state of plenty.*

In well–functioning economies, bad news generally accompanies good news. If there is good news about a security (high expected returns), there is likely to be bad news as well (very bad returns in states of scarcity). Securities with high expected returns are likely to be "fair–weather friends"; those with low expected returns are likely to be "foul–weather friends."

What of the *market portfolio*—made up of all securities representing claims for future goods and services? What will be the *societal risk premium* associated with investment in a portfolio that includes proportional shares of all securities?

Given the fact that some time–state claims must provide risk discounts if others are to provide risk premiums, one might erroneously conclude that the societal risk premium would equal zero. However, this is unlikely to be the case. The expected return on a portfolio will be a value–weighted average of the expected returns on the underlying securities. More fundamentally, it will equal a value–weighted average of the expected returns on the underlying time–state claims. In general, a greater amount of value will be associated with "states of plenty" than with "states of scarcity." Since the former provide risk premiums and the latter risk discounts, the value–weighted average expected return is likely to exceed the riskless rate of interest. There will be a societal risk premium to compensate those who hold proportionate shares in the market as a whole for their willingness to take on the risk of doing badly in bad times.

Conclusion

The main goal of this paper was to show the power of using contingent claims analysis to analyze the impact of risk on financial decisions. In the process, we reached some conclusions concerning a simple economy—conclusions that can be shown to hold for far more general economies.

Risk can usefully be characterized in terms of the pattern of payments obtained over different future states of the world. If markets are sufficiently complete, it is possible to transform any such set of payments into any other set that has the same present value. Moreover, the cost of obtaining any desired set of payments can be computed directly, and a strategy that will replicate the payments using existing securities can be constructed. The technology for doing this provides the backbone of the profession of financial engineering. The creation and valuation of derivative securities represent direct applications of the methods discussed here.

It is not enough, however, to know how to construct and value sets of payments. Ultimately, someone must select the best feasible payment set for a given investor. In general, one can expect to earn higher returns in the long run from certain strategies than from others. However, it is not risk *per se* that is likely to be rewarded in well–functioning capital market—only *the risk of doing badly in bad times*.

Financial engineers can reshape future contingencies into many different patterns. Investors are thus faced with larger and larger menus from which to choose. More than ever, it is important that they understand the determinants of security prices, which form the inputs for financial engineering. Nuclear financial economics, concerned as it is with "first principles," can provide a solid base for such an understanding.

Notes

1 Arrow, K. J. "The Role of Securities in the Optimal Allocation of Risk–bearing." *The Review of Economic Studies*, XXXI(2):86 (April 1964): 91–96.

2 Debreu, G. *Theory of Value*. The Cowles Foundation Monograph 17, 1959.

3 This chapter is intended to be incorporated into the author's work-in-progress, tentatively titled *Financial Economics and the Management of Investments*. The comments and suggestions of Professors William Beaver, Ayman Hindy, and Paul Pfleiderer at the Stanford Graduate School of Business are gratefully acknowledged.

4 Arrow, K. J. in William Breit and Roger W. Spencer, *Lives of the Laureates: Ten Nobel Economists*, Second Edition, Cambridge, Mass.: MIT Press, 1990, p. 55.

5 Debreu, *Theory of Value, op. cit.*

6 Debreu, *Theory of Value, op. cit.*

7 *The Journal of Financial Engineering*, 1, 1 (June 1992).

8 This concept was introduced in William F. Sharpe, *Investments*, First Edition, Prentice–Hall, Englewood Cliffs, N.J., 1978, 7:3, pp. 366–71, then expanded upon in John C. Cox, S. A. Ross and M. Rubenstein, "Option Pricing: A Simplified Approach," *Journal of Financial Economics*, September 1979, pp. 229–263.

9 Some use the term *time–state claim* instead of *contingent claim*.

10 Black, F. and M. Scholes, "The Pricing of Options and Corporate Liabilities." *Journal of Political Economy* (May–June 1973): 141–183.

11 Markowitz, H. M. "Portfolio Selection." *Journal of Finance*, 7:2 (March 1952): 77–91.

12 Modigliani, F. and M. H. Miller, "The Cost of Capital, Corporation Finance and the Theory of Investment." *American Economic Review* (June 1958): 261–297.

13 This terminology is more appropriate when multiple time periods are involved. In such a situation, some of the decision variables represent investments that are programmed to take place at various dates in specific circumstances. The solution then determines not only the current set of investments but also investments to be undertaken over time. While such problems can be solved by determining the solution to a set of simultaneous equations, it is generally preferable to take advantage of special aspects of the structure of an assumed payment tree to reduce the computational burden.

14 Alternatively, the solutions for the pure time–state claim replicating strategies can be mixed in the appropriate propositions.

15 In general, as many "independent" securities as there are states of the world will suffice. In our economy, with two states of the world, only two are required. Formally, it must be possible to invert the matrix of payments from the securities in the various states of the world. This will not be possible, if, for example, the payments from one of the securities can be obtained from some combination of one or more of the others.

16 In practice, the distinction is not this precise. Financial engineers usually construct payment trees based on assumptions about security attributes (for example, standard deviations of returns) that incorporate probabilities. In many cases, additional assumptions are employed (e.g., that each branch of a binomial tree is equally probable). If the collective set of such assumptions is in error, the resulting valuation and replication strategies may be incorrect. The potential magnitudes of such errors are basically empirical issues. In any event, the subject is beyond the scope of this paper.

The Geometry of Commercial Bank Balance Sheet Management

Richard D. Lodge, Senior Vice President, Banc One

Introduction

Most medium and probably all large commercial banks employ modeling techniques to measure the degree to which earnings are at risk through interest rate changes. However, bank executives tend to distrust computer modeling for several reasons, including: its distant removal from the process of amalgamating the asset and liability information, the often haphazard reconciliation of predictions to results, the lack of understanding of model dynamics and methodology, and the misunderstanding of option dynamics in the balance sheet. This chapter describes the use of geometric forms in visualizing balance sheet mismatches as well as in constructing derivative instruments to "manage" the mismatches. The use of geometric shapes helps the bank executive rapidly see the macro implications of balance sheet management. Moreover, it removes some of the mystery associated with asset and liability modeling.

The Rectangularization in Asset/Liability Management

In a financial sense, a goal of a commercial bank is to produce the widest and most consistent net interest margin (NIM) possible over the longest possible time. Theoretical perfection would be an infinite NIM in perpetuity. Bank stock values should favorably track those institutions that garner wide and predictable net interest margins over long periods. Rendering this concept into a geometric shape produces a rectangular form as depicted below.

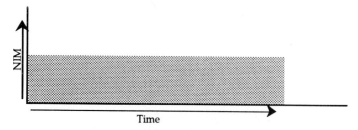

Because the net interest margin in dollars is calculated by subtracting the product of liability interest rates and liability balances from the product of asset yields and asset balances, this same rectangular form applies to NIM in dollars as depicted below.

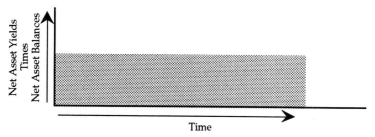

The two–dimension concept (plane geometry) applied to most assets and liabilities in a commercial bank, however, will produce non–rectangular (and therefore less desirable) shapes for the two sides of the balance sheet.

Constructing Individual Asset/Liability Geometries

Every loan, investment, deposit, and borrowing has an intrinsic plane geometric shape associated with it. Associated solid geometric shapes and three–dimensional shapes will be addressed later. Consider the two–dimensional shape of a 3–month, prime–based loan with a principal of $100,000, depicted below. The vertical or x–axis represents revenues (balances times rate) while the y–axis represents time (maturity or repricing) of the loan.

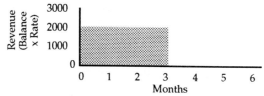

The example produces a rectangle represented by interest earnings of $2,000 over 3 months (6% x $100,000 x 1/4 year).

A mortgage loan with an expected prepayment might take the following plane geometric form:

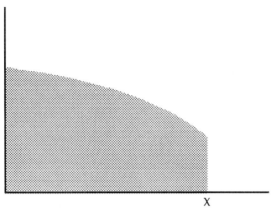

Because the principal of the loan amortizes over time, the interest revenue (balances x interest rate) declines. Additionally, most mortgages prepay before the contractual term of the loan, which is represented by the truncation of the geometric form at the time period "X."

A short–tranche collateralized mortgage obligation (CMO) would look like this:

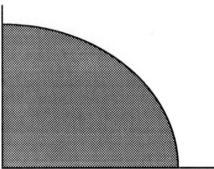

CMOs consist of several individual mortgage loans pooled such that the principal and the interest payments are collectively passed along to the investor. The short–tranche aspect of the security results from channeling *all* principal payments on a larger mortgage loan pool into the principal reduction of a security representing a fraction of the pool.

A zero–coupon investment might look like this:

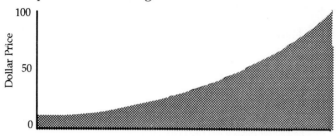

Zero–coupon investments accrue interest in the form of an increase in the principal value of the security. A 9% zero coupon accrues more rapidly than a 6% zero coupon although each accrues to an ultimate value of 100.

On the liability side of the balance sheet, other geometric shapes take form. For instance, time–deposit accounts and portfolios of time deposits grow as interest is credited. The geometric shape associated with savings and other forms of time–open accounts might look like the following:

Certificates of deposit, federal funds borrowing, or repurchase agreements will tend to be rectangular because their balances do not ordinarily amortize or accrete; and the height and the breadth of the rectangle is a function of the interest rate and the terms of the liability.

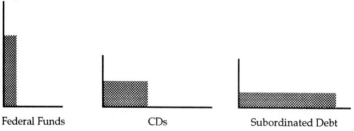

Amalgamating Asset and Liability Geometrics

Generally speaking, banks face only three asset/liability situations. Short–duration liabilities funding long–duration assets is a *short–funded* bank. Long–duration liabilities funding short–duration assets is a *long–funded* bank. A bank where the duration of the liabilities is similar to the duration of the assets is a *match–funded* bank. There are degrees of short and long funding as well as combinations of short, long, and matched funding. We explore these concepts below.

First, the degree of mismatched funding, either short or long, has to do with the amount of time the bank is subject to the mismatch. Examples of mismatches are as follows: Overnight federal funds borrowings funding 30–year, fixed–rate mortgages represent a high degree of short funding. Three–month certificates of deposit funding 1–year, fixed–rate consumer loans represent a low degree of short funding. An example of a high degree of long funding is 10–year, fixed–rate subordinated debt funding prime–based, variable–rate home equity loans. A low degree of long funding is 2–year, fixed–rate certificates of deposit funding 1–year, fixed–rate construction loans.

Second, a bank usually experiences combinations of short, long, and matched funding aggregating its asset/liability mix. For example, a bank having subordinated debt, federal funds, and 2–year CDs in its liability structure; and 6–month Treasury bills, 2–year, fixed–rate commercial loans, and 5–year, average life mortgage–backed securities in its asset structure would be characterized as having segments of its balance sheet short funded (federal funds purchased versus 6–month T–bills), long funded (subordinated debt versus 5–year, mortgage–backed securities) and match funded (2–year CDs versus 2–year commercial loans).

Actual commercial bank balance sheets are much more complicated because their asset and liability products are many and varied. Nevertheless, basic assets and liabilities can be depicted by plane geometric forms.

Consider a bank that has a preponderance of fixed–rate CDs which fund mostly variable–rate assets and some fixed–rate investments. The bank also has capital as a liability, which exacerbates the institution's long funding nature. Assume an upward–sloping yield curve (short durations equal low yields, long durations equal high yields), which suggests a low net interest margin (i.e., the loan asset is variable rate and thus priced on the short end of the yield curve; the liabilities have longer maturities and fixed rates priced further out on the yield curve). Table 1 illustrates this scenario.

Table 1

Assets	Yield	Liabilities	Cost
80% Variable–rate loans	@ 8.00%	90% Fixed–rate CDs	@4.00%
20% Fixed–rate investment	@ 6.00%	10% Fixed–rate capital	@0.00%
100%	7.60%	100%	3.60%

This bank generates a current net interest margin of 4.00%, or the difference between its earning asset yield (7.60%) and its funding liability cost (3.60%). The weakness in this balance sheet structure is the lack of stability in the NIM because it is a long–funded bank: in other words, the amalgamated assets and liabilities do not form a rectangle.

Earnings Volatility—A Function of Non–Rectangularity

The asset/liability structure illustrated above makes the bank vulnerable to declining interest rates, what practitioners call "asset sensitive." As interest rates fall, the yield on the assets of the bank declines more rapidly than the cost of the liabilities, resulting in compression of the net interest margin. Table 1 illustrates the impact of a 1% decline in interest rates on this hypothetical bank:

Table 2

Before Change in Rates

Assets	Yield	Liabilities	Cost
80% Variable–rate loans	@ 8.00%	90% Fixed–rate CDs	@ 4.00%
20% Fixed–rate investments	@ 6.00%	10% Fixed–rate capital	@ 0.00%
100% Total assets	@ 7.60%	100% Total liabilities	@ 3.60%

After 1% Decline in Rates

Assets	Yield	Liabilities	Cost
80% Variable–rate loans	@ 7.00%	90% Fixed–rate CDs	@ 4.00%
20% Fixed–rate investments	@ 6.00%	10% Fixed–rate capital	@ 0.00%
100% Total assets	@ 6.80%	100% Total liabilities	@ 3.60%

Since the only balance sheet item vulnerable to change is variable rate loans, which represent 80% of total assets, a 1% decline in interest rates translates into an 80– basis–point reduction in net interest margin (3.20%

versus 4.00%). In this case, a sufficient amount of additional fixed–rate assets funded by variable–rate liabilities is required to stabilize net interest margin. We could call this a balance sheet hedge. The amount and duration of the hedge are problematic but simplified by conceptualizing the hedge as the conversion of a nonrectangular configuration of assets and liabilities into a rectangular one.

For example, the duration of total assets is calculated by summing the weight of each asset times its duration and dividing by total assets. Assuming the commercial loans are 90 days to maturity, the fixed rate investments are 3 years to maturity, and they are weighted 80% and 20%, respectively, then the weighted duration of total assets equals 0.8% years or [(.25 years x 80%) + (3.0 years x 20%)] + 100% = 0.8 years.

Applying the same methodology to the liability side, where the CDs are 2 years to maturity and capital is 10 years to maturity (in theory, equity capital has perpetual maturity; but to simplify the examples, we assume 10 years), the total duration of liabilities and capital equals 2.80 years.

The hedge amount is determined by the amount of the assets or liabilities contributing to the sensitivity problem. In our case, the variable–rate loans create margin variability in the short run, and the CDs and investments create long–run margin variability. Depicting geometric shapes of net assets and liabilities makes rectangularization much easier to achieve. We will construct the hedge shape by combining the duration of the assets with the dollar–unit contribution to NIM together with the duration of the liabilities, including their dollar–unit contribution to NIM.

On the asset side, we have loans and investments comprising 80% and 20% of the balance sheet, respectively, as shown below.

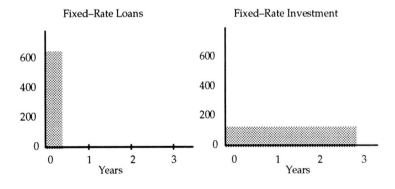

The rate on the loans is assumed to be fixed for 90 days. An 8% yield times 80% of assets generates 640 units of interest earnings. The fixed–rate investments are assumed to be 3 years to maturity with a 6% fixed yield. At 20% of assets, the investment produces 120 units of interest earnings. The combination of the two geometries produces the configuration of total earnings assets shown below:

Total Earnings Assets

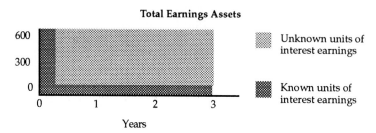

That is, 760 units of interest earnings for 1/4 year (640 units, loans + 120 units, investments) fall to 120 units of interest earnings for 3 3/4 years. At the end of 90 days, the loan will mature and be reinvested or repriced at an unknown rate. Remember, it is the very uncertainty of the repricing rate or the unknown reinvestment which leads to nonrectangular geometries given maturity or repricing mismatches. The lighter–shaded area in the above graphic represents the *unknown* units of interest earnings because the assets will have variable rates associated with them in the future.

On the liability side of the balance sheet, we have fixed–rate CDs in combination with fixed–rate capital. Because capital is assumed to be at zero cost, its geometry is the y–axis out to 10 years.

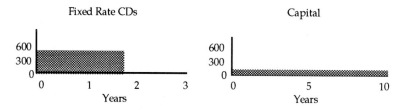

A 4% liability cost times 90% of liabilities generates 400 units of interest expense for an assumed 2–year period to maturity of the CD. Equity capital with an accounting cost of 0% times 10% of liabilities lowers total liability cost to 360 units of combined interest expense for 100% of the liabilities:

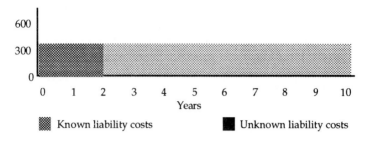

Total Liabilities (Including Capital Priced at 0%)

Known liability costs · Unknown liability costs

Again, the lighter–shaded area represents uncertain liability costs in the future. The rectangularization concept means that fixed–rate assets funded with fixed–rate liabilities *or* variable–rate assets funded with variable–rate liabilities are superior to other combinations of risk. In fact, the combination of funding fixed–rate assets with variable–rate liabilities and vice versa creates nonrectangularization and thus the potential volatility in the net interest margin.

We now align the asset/liability geometrics of our theoretical commercial bank to determine how well we have achieved a rectangular configuration. Aligning the asset coordinates with the liability coordinates and shading the geometrics for fixed (or certain) rates and variable (or uncertain) rates, we get the following schematic:

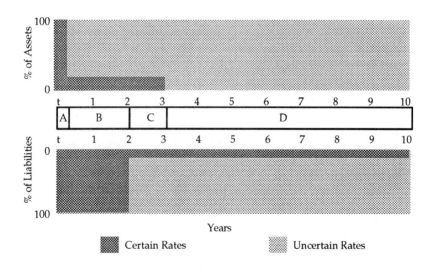

Certain Rates · Uncertain Rates

The alignment of these geometrics highlights net interest margin "holes," periods when variable–rate assets are funded by fixed–rate liabilities or fixed–rate assets are funded by variable–rate assets. Period A, $t+1/4$, represents 3 months when 100% of the bank's assets are fixed and funded by 100% fixed–rate liabilities (a period contributing to rectangularization). Period B, $t+1/4$ year to $t+2$ years, represents a net interest margin "hole"— i.e., 100% of the liabilities are fixed or at a certain cost, but only 20% of the assets are fixed (investments), with 80% of the asset variable (the 90–day loan matured into an uncertain earning rate). Period C, $t+2$ years to $t+3$ years, is still another NIM "hole" because 20% of the assets are earning a fixed or certain rate (investments) while only 10% of the liabilities (capital) are at a fixed rate. Period D, $t+3$ years to $t+10$ years, is yet another NIM "hole" because all of the assets are now earning uncertain rates while 10% of the liabilities are still costing fixed or certain rates (capital).

If we now combine the asset/liability coordinates, we observe the asymmetry of the fixed and variable assets and liabilities:

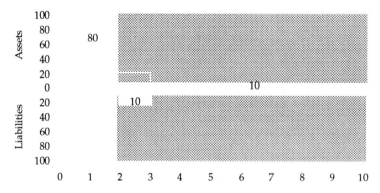

Rectangularization is achieved when equal rate–certain and rate–uncertain areas exist in each time period. As is obvious from the above schematic, equal rate–certain and rate–uncertain areas do not exist in each time period except for the period $t+$ to $t+1/4$. For example, additional rate–certain assets need to be created for 80% of the balance sheet from period $t+1/4$ to the period $t+2$. Additional rate–certain liabilities need to be created for 10% of the balance sheet for period $t+2$ to period $t+3$, and additional rate–certain assets need to be created for 10% of assets for period $t+3$ to period $t+10$.

The geometry of the instrument to fill the NIM "hole" in the above example should resemble the following:

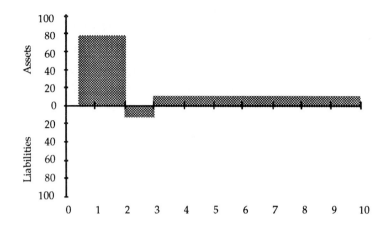

Creating the Desired Geometry

In this example, rectangularization is more desirable than non–rectangularization. That is, matched maturities of rate–certain assets and liabilities and rate–uncertain assets and liabilities are more desirable than mismatches. Of course, there are earnings tradeoffs associated with assuming rate risk. Moreover, while the goal in rectangularization is high and enduring NIM, the reality is that the marketplace may not offer opportunities to achieve *consistently* high margins. In a more practical sense, then, the rectangularization concept suggests that it is better to have *predictable*, albeit variable, net interest margins than unpredictable and variable net interest margins. Moreover, the process of developing the geometry of the instrument(s) to achieve rectangularization reveals opportunities to maximize net interest margin and to reduce overall institutional interest rate risk.

At Banc One, the process of reducing interest rate risk includes filling the NIM "hole" during the current accounting period, projecting expected future "holes," and creating financial instrument geometry to fill those "holes." Our orientation toward managing interest rate risk far into the future focuses attention not only on the forward financial markets but also on derivatives as substitutes for cash securities to create desirable geometry. We emphasize the interchangeability of securities and off–balance–sheet derivative products such as interest rate swaps. Whether the institution utilizes interest rate swaps (where it receives a fixed rate and pays a variable rate, or vice versa), or it purchases securities (which earn a fixed rate but are financed by paying a floating rate, such as the repo rate or federal funds), the institution's risk position can be equally well managed. However, the interplay among liquidity, capital and returns determines the final mix of cash securities and swaps (or other derivatives) to manage the institution's structural net interest margin "holes." For these reasons, cash securities and swaps function in similar ways to create the appropriate geometry.

Returning to the previous schematic, we now explore ways to create the geometry depicted there.

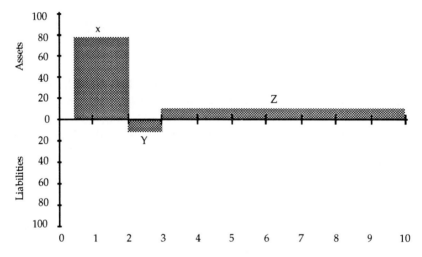

Starting in period $t+1/4$, or 90 days from the start date, this institution might enter into forward interest rate swaps on 80% of its assets, where the institution receives a fixed or certain rate and pays a variable or uncertain rate for 1.75 years, represented by the segment X. In essence, this action converts the uncertain rate associated with the maturity of 80% of the institution's assets into a fixed and certain rate because the variable (and uncertain) rate on the assets received will be offset by the variable (and uncertain) rate paid on the interest rate swap, leaving the institution with a fixed rate on 80% of the assets. When added to 20% of the assets that are already fixed for this period (investments), the entire period t to $t+2$ is matched with assets and liabilities at certain rates.

For the period $t+2$ to $t+3$, we need to enter into a 1–year interest rate swap, 2 years forward, where the institution pays a fixed rate and receives a variable rate for 10% of the liabilities. This action converts the variable rate associated with 10% of the liabilities into a fixed rate for 1 year because the variable (and uncertain) rate paid on the liabilities (matured CDs) will be offset by the variable (and uncertain) rate received on the interest rate swap, leaving the institution with a fixed rate paid on 10% of the liabilities. At this juncture, period $t+2$ to $t+3$ has 20% fixed–rate liabilities (10% capital + 10% pay fixed interest rate swap) funding 20% fixed–rate investment and 80% variable–rate assets (matured receive fixed interest rate swap) funded by 80% variable–rate liabilities (matured CDs).

For the period $t+3$ to $t+10$, we need to enter into a 7–year interest rate swap, 3 years forward, where the institution receives a fixed rate and pays a variable rate for 10% of the assets of the institution. This will convert the variable rate associated with 10% of the assets into a fixed rate for 7 years because the variable (and uncertain) rate received on the assets (matured investments) will be offset by the variable (and uncertain) rate paid on the interest rate swap, leaving the institution with a fixed rate received on 10% of the assets. Period $t+3$ to $t+10$ now has 90% variable–rate liabilities (matured loans and investments and receive fixed interest rate swaps) funded by 90% variable–rate liabilities (matured CDs) and 10% fixed–rate assets (receive fixed interest rate swaps) funded by 10% fixed–rate liabilities (capital).

The resulting rectangularization is depicted below:

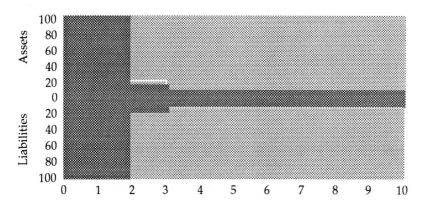

To repeat, whether an institution chooses to rectangularize will depend upon several considerations, including (1) attractiveness of the current and forward rates *vis-à-vis* the institution's current book yields (assets) and costs (liabilities); (2) the breadth and depth of the forward markets; (3) the accounting treatment of hedging vehicles; and, of course, (4) the sophistication of the institution's modeling capability and management. The important element in this exercise is not so much the financial results of rectangularization but rather the *illusion* of the risks, which highlights market opportunities.

Conclusion

This chapter has applied strictly *plane* geometry concepts to asset and liability management in commercial banks although *solid* geometry would be more suitable, albeit more complicated. In the derivative market, where products are being developed with intrinsic optionality, two–dimensional (or plane geometric) thinking is too simple. Three dimensions include the interplay of outstanding balances, maturity or duration; and the level of interest rates applies to *solid* geometry, undoubtedly a more elegant approach for further discussions.

Executives develop methods to simplify their understanding of complex issues. Asset and liability problems in commercial banks are extremely complex. They result from the interplay of the duration risk of assets and liabilities, basis risk, yield curve risk, and option–based prepayment risk. Many large and intermediate commercial banks use simulations to better quantify interest rate risks. As bankers have experienced undesirable volatility in earnings, their solutions have become more esoteric.

The use of geometric shapes focuses management attention on risk reduction efficiency and facilitates creative applications of derivative knowledge and experience to risk–taking activity. Some oversimplicity associated with geometric concepts as they relate to asset/liabilities is evident. Simplicity is sometimes rejected in favor of quantitative techniques because intellectual substance is perceived in one and not the other. The most elegant solutions are often the most simple. And, because they're more easily understood and communicated, simple solutions promote better and more timely decisions.

Appendix

Examples of Specific Geometries Used at Banc One

Transactions involving interest rate swaps and other derivatives have facilitated the use of geometry because derivatives allow risk customization unavailable in the cash markets. The following pages describe geometric shapes used to assess risk/return tradeoffs and acceptability.

Geometry 1

Generic Interest Rate Swap (IRS)

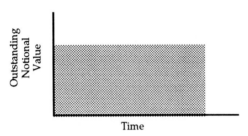

A generic interest rate swap where the bank receives a fixed rate and pays a variable rate is virtually identical in rate–risk profile to purchasing a fixed–rate security funded by short–term, variable–rate liabilities (fed funds, repos, etc.). The notional value (or principal value in bond terms) is certain and the maturity is fixed. This geometry is useful when fixed–rate assets (or when entered in reverse, liabilities) are required immediately and lack of variability in notional value and maturity is desired.

Geometry 2

Forward Interest Rate Swap

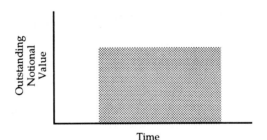

This shape is identical to Geometry 1 except for the future start date. This geometry is useful when the NIM "hole" is in the future and the forward interest rate swap curve is steep *vis–à–vis* expectations.

Geometry 3

Strip of Forward Generic Interest Rate Swaps

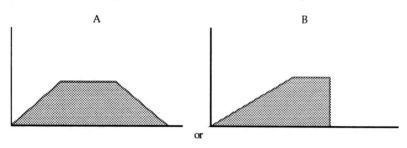

A   B

or

By layering in both current and forward generic swaps, we can achieve a trapezoidal geometry (A) if all the generic swaps have similar maturity periods. A truncated trapezoidal geometry (B) can be achieved by layering in successive forward swaps that have successively shorter maturities. These shapes are useful in achieving objectives associated with a combination of Geometry 1 and 2. Moreover, these geometries facilitate earnings distribution management.

Geometry 4

Amortizing Interest Rate Swaps (AIRS)

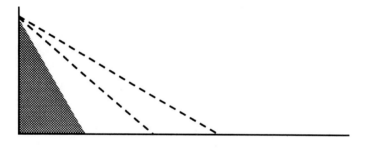

These swaps have many of the rate–risk behavioral characteristics of mortgage–backed securities or collateralized mortgage obligations in that their notional values and ultimate maturities (dotted lines) depend on the future level of some selected interest rate index (i.e., LIBOR, CMT, mortgage pool prepayments, etc.). The geometry is useful and generally more profitable if (1) predictable notional values are not critical, (2) the geometry offsets another similarly shaped but opposite risk, or (3) the option component is attractive compared to nonoption instruments. These swaps generally require a higher level of sophistication because of their optionality and the commensurate unpredictability of notional value and maturity.

Forward Amortizing Interest Rate Swaps

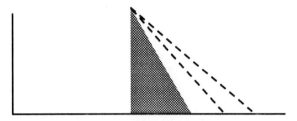

This geometry applies in circumstances similar to Geometry 4 except where the "hole" is in the future and the forward yield curve and volatility curve are steep *vis–à–vis* current levels.

Geometry 6

Strip of Forward Amortizing Interest Rate Swaps

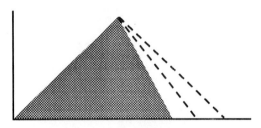

By successfully layering forward amortizing interest rate swaps, we add symmetry to Geometry 5 and achieve specialized problem solving such as offsetting similarly shaped but opposite risks.

Geometry 7

Amortizing Interest Rate Swaps with Lockouts

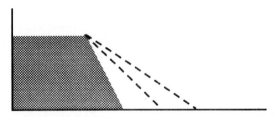

This is the reverse geometric configuration of Geometry 3(B), where a strip of forward generic swaps is entered into with progressively shorter maturity dates such that they mature together. This geometry features a "lockout" period that resembles a generic interest rate swap where no amortization occurs. It achieves the benefits of generic swaps during the lockout period and offers predictability of notional value outstanding in addition to the benefits and shortcomings of amortizing swaps—i.e., enhanced yield with variable maturity and outstanding notional values after the lockout.

Geometry 8

Forward Amortizing Interest Rate Swaps with Lockouts

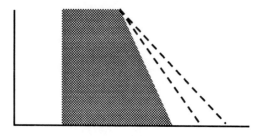

This geometry is simply Geometry 7 with forward start dates. Like all geometrics with forward start dates, it addresses NIM "holes" in the future and takes advantage of "cheap" forward yield curves.

Geometry 9

Strip of Forward Amortizing Interest Rate Swaps with Lockout

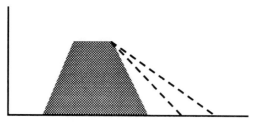

This shape resembles Geometry 4 but with enhanced yield and uncertain amortization of notional value.

Geometry 10

Combination of a Generic and Amortizing Interest Rate Swap

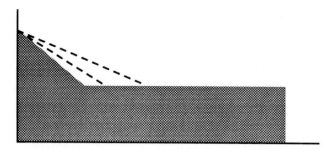

This geometry applies to situations where unpredictability is more acceptable at the front end of a longer transaction.

Geometry 11

Generic Swaps and Forward Strip of Amortizing Swap with Lockouts

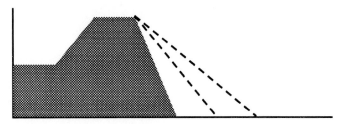

This geometry back–end–loads the risks as well as the benefits of amortizing interest rate swaps.

Debt Management and Interest Rate Risk

Darrell Duffie, Professor, Graduate School of Business, Stanford University

Introduction

This chapter reviews some considerations involved in managing the interest rate risk of corporate debt.[1] After discussing general principles, we examine quantitative methods for debt management, such as Monte Carlo simulation of interest rate risks and term structure modeling of derivative prices.

Corporations prefer stable financial environments in which to maximize long–term returns on investment. Interest rate risk may affect a firm's ability to meet this objective.

What is the firm's current exposure to unexpected changes in interest rates? Should the firms issue long– or short–term debt? More specifically, what maturity mix for its new issues is appropriate, and how should that mix be adjusted by derivatives that convert fixed–rate debt to floating rate or vice versa? This chapter presents some of the relevant considerations and tools that help with these questions.

We address the motives and basic structure of an interest rate risk management system, including quantitative models. We also deal with the Monte Carlo simulation of whole yield curves and the basic concepts and applications of term structure derivatives models. The appendix describes the extraction of zero–coupon yield curves (or forward rate curves) from historical data and related quantitative issues.

Why Worry About It?

Principles of finance tell us only "imperfections" in capital markets make it important to manage a firm's debt structure. More importantly, however, the Nobel–prize–winning "financial irrelevance" theories of Modigliani and Miller provide a basis for developing risk management policies that take advantage of these imperfections.

In perfect capital markets, shareholder welfare is maximized by the debt management policy that minimizes the market value of liabilities for the given stream of funding requirements. This policy maximizes the market value of equity (assets minus liabilities) and thus gives each shareholder the maximum possible disposable wealth. In perfect capital markets, all possible portfolios of liabilities that generate the same given stream of funding requirements have the same present market value and are therefore equally good.[2]

Functioning markets differ from this ideal world because of some fundamental market imperfections such as:

1. Taxes. The present value of tax shields varies from one financing strategy to another. Even if all debt issues receive identical tax treatment, a mere reduction in the volatility of taxable earnings can increase the market value of the firm by reducing the present value of the extra tax costs of net operating loss carryforwards.[3] In general, nonlinearities in the tax code imply potential benefits from financial risk management.

2. Issuing and transaction costs. Funding with shorter maturity issues, or trading more, can increase costs. Transactions costs is a broad category that includes the costs of the debt management function itself. These costs can easily vary by policy.

3. Security innovation profits. New financial products may enter the marketplace and generate "innovation" profits from investors who need these products, for example, potential buyers of tax shields.

4. Trading profits. Firms realize attractive returns on capital by identifying profitable security trades or by providing intermediation services to financial markets. (These two profit sources are sometimes difficult to separate.) To the extent that the capital markets group of a large corporation

combines its responsibilities for raising capital with an ability to generate appropriately hedged trading profits, it adds value to the firm.

5. Financial distress costs. Higher–risk firms have a greater probability of incurring the costs of reorganization, which are discounted into the current market value of the firm. Hedging can therefore reduce the present value of financial distress costs.[4]

6. Managerial incentives. Managerial performance depends on the environment in which managers operate, including financial risk. Given the ability to control financial risk, a manager may more aggressively pursue profits.

7. Monitoring of managerial quality. It is sometimes difficult to separate the effects of managerial performance from effects outside the manager's control. The "signal–to–noise ratio" may be improved by reducing financial risk. Here, we speak more in terms of managing the core business than of managing the acquisition of capital. One may ask, "Did we do well this year because of superior management or because we were heavily exposed to short–term interest rates, which ultimately moved in our favor?" Reducing interest rate risk makes this question easier to answer but perhaps at a cost.[5]

8. Underinvestment. A highly levered firm may avoid new projects that add to its market value unless risk management policies and practices ensure that debtholders do not reap the majority of the upside potential payoffs.[6]

9. Reduction of borrowing costs. If a firm knows more about its ability to pay off debt than outside investors in the bond market, then its cost of debt capital may, on average, be above that of retained earnings. Funding new projects from retained earnings is more likely with risk management.[7]

10. Lowering of the firm's risk premium. Other things equal, investors pay more for a firm with lower undiversifiable risk provided that the reduction of risk cannot be achieved by shareholders trading on their own accounts. For example, if the firm is aware of hedgeable risks associated with proprietary information unavailable to shareholders, then all shareholders may benefit from financial hedging by the firm.[8]

Since there are many tradeoffs involved, exploiting these market imperfections to the firm's benefit makes for a challenging problem. In some cases, the challenge can be met without changing the net financial risk. For example, an internal banking operation may be able to handle issues (6) and (7), which can allow different divisions of a firm to transfer risk without incurring the trading costs of outside capital markets (2).

Objectives of a Debt Management Strategy

Given the above description of why and how a financial policy adds value, the optimal debt management strategy thus maximizes the net present value of the firm's after–tax cashflows while accounting for all capital market imperfections. Many of these imperfections are difficult to model. Aside from taxes, suppose that one would not attempt to measure each imperfection's impact on total market value. This does not mean that impacts should be ignored. For example, a corporation may be far from financial distress, but certain "obviously–too–risky" debt management policies are ruled out immediately because they could jeopardize the firm. (An "A" credit rating, for example, reflects the market's perception that the default is small but above zero.)

Instead, one could apply reasonable judgment and modern quantitative methods to monitor and limit risk exposures, possibly of several types, bearing in mind the varied role of risk management in these imperfections.

Of course, one must first select a measure of the profits (or costs) associated with a given debt strategy. For example, a standard adopted by many investment banks is direct trading profits on a mark–to–market basis. This provides solid discipline to the trading function, allows quick identification of potential problems, and gives a current view of profitability and risk. Unfortunately, in managing a corporation's liability portfolio, the funds received for a new issue are not invested in securities for potential retrade. Instead, they are invested in the core business, where they provide returns that are difficult to measure directly and which are outside the control of those managing the debt. Total trading profits therefore do not represent a suitable measure for evaluating debt management policy or performance.

In the best of worlds, the debt manager eliminates risk by matching the cashflows from assets to those required by liabilities. This ideal situation can seldom be achieved. For example, the assets of a large industrial corporation generate cashflows that are difficult to predict beyond a short time and depend on future decisions regarding capital investment projects. The following discussion assumes that the manager has only a general idea of the maturity structure of the firm's assets.

In some ways, the debt management function mirrors mutual fund management. A mutual fund manager takes in funds and measures performance in terms of returns to investors—the higher, the better. In this computation, the fund manager does not consider the cost of funds to the investor. Similarly, a debt manager provides funds to the firm and can measure performance in terms of total interest cost on that debt—the lower the cost, the better.

A fund manager measures returns *relative to funds under management*, that is, in terms of profits (dividends plus mark–to–market capital appreciation) divided by funds under management. It also makes good sense to treat a debt manager's performance in terms of total costs (current interest expense plus mark–to–market change in liabilities) divided by total initial liabilities. For example, if

a.   liabilities at the close yesterday were $1 billion (mark–to–market value, including derivatives), and

b.   today $6 million in coupons are paid to bond holders, generating a reduction in taxes payable to $2 million, and $1 million was received in net cashflows on derivative positions (including swap payments and exercise options), and

c.   at the close today, liabilities are marked to market at $997.2 million, then

d.   the total effective interest rate paid in liabilities (simple daily interest annualized) is

$$\frac{997.2+6.0-2.0-1.0-1000}{1000}\times\frac{365}{100}=7.3\%$$

Interest Expense Versus Mark–to–Market

We have discussed the performance of a debt manager based on all–in–cost, the interest expense in the current period as well as the change in value ("mark–to–market") of the liability portfolio. This all–in–cost flows into the balance sheet and, thorough the interest expense component, into the income statement. Management pays close attention to both income statement and balance sheet and sometimes places independent importance on each. This is natural despite the fact that in perfect capital markets, shareholders only care about the firm's total market value. Apparently, and perhaps for some of the reasons described earlier, capital markets are imperfect.

The income statement typically reflects interest expense directly; each additional dollar of interest expense in the current quarter reduces income by one dollar (before tax) for that quarter. Although a mark–to–market of the liability portfolio must appear in supplementary accounting notes under the new GAAP requirements of FASB 107, it need not appear in the firm's accounts at present.[9]

It is therefore natural to separate the effects of interest expense and marks–to–market for debt management. The ability to separately assess and control the risks associated with each allows management to pursue profits with greater control.

For short planning intervals, such as quarters, mark–to–market risk may dominate. The near–horizon, risk–minimizing strategy is then to fund all liabilities with short–term ("floating rate") borrowing. With an upward–sloping yield curve (the usual case) and a short planning horizon, short–term issues are also the most cost efficient. Over a 10–year period, however, the total risk associated with issuing 10–year fixed–rate bonds is of course zero, but floating rate risk can be dramatic. This distinction between short– and long–term planning horizons shows that "efficient" debt management strategies need not exist. The firm is not like a individual investor, whose risk attitudes lead directly to an "optimal" investment policy. Instead, a large corporation has complex and often conflicting goals.

Debt Management Measurement System

Ideally, one could envision a system that allows an immediate screen readout of many value and risk measures for each of a number of positions or strategies, such as:

a. Default (or "benchmark") liability strategies, such as some fixed maturity profile.

b. Past and current strategies.

c. Candidate strategies, which include static policies (e.g., "We issue everything in 7–year par straight bonds") or dynamic strategies ("If and when the slope of the yield curve reaches 600 basis points, we issue only short–term debt" or "We continually rebalance our portfolio so as to maintain a duration of 5 years"). (These are not serious proposals but rather illustrations of the innumerable ways that dynamic strategies can be contingent on future events.) In principle, the system can treat a "default" or "benchmark" strategy like any other strategy redefined on a dynamic basis.

d. Particular instruments, such as an option, an existing or proposed 10–year callable bond, a swap, and so on.

e. Particular groups of instruments, such as "all current derivatives," "all current debt issues," "all instruments of duration 2 years or less in candidate strategy A5," and so on.

The ability to select objects for study along these lines requires a database of existing instruments as well as the ability to enter a number of "paper" positions for comparison purposes.

Given any particular position or debt management strategy, one might wish to estimate a number of attributes such as:

1. Current market value
2. Duration
3. Convexity
4. Present value of tax shields
5. Issuing costs
6. Transactions costs
7. Total effective interest rate, or cost
8. Vega (sensitivity of total cost to volatility)
9. Exposure to (named index)
10. Risk (standard deviation of total effective interest rate, or cost)
11. Expected effective total interest rate, or cost
12. Worst case (e.g., 95–percentile) effective total interest costs or expense

13. Expected interest expense, by quarter, and associated standard deviation of changes to this expectation over a given period.

This list is by no means exhaustive. The "exposure" to an index can be thought of as the expected change (or percentage change) in total interest costs given a unit change in the named index. For linear responses, this can be estimated using statistical regression. Otherwise, some form of modeling may be required. The simplest and most common exposure measure is duration, which can be thought of as the percentage change in the market value of bond portfolio per unit–parallel downward shift in the zero–coupon yield curve.

Such a debt management system requires inputs such as current market conditions (yield curves, volatilities, correlations, and so on), a fixed–income derivatives pricing model, and price data (including current market quotation feeds).

Ideally, for any type of position such as (a)–(e) above, a request for an attribute such as (1)–(13) would prompt queries from the system to meet the request. For example, if the request were for effective total interest costs, the system would ask for the pair of dates over which to make the computation, for example, "year–to–date." For a particular candidate policy, the system would generate the total costs that would have been realized had the candidate policy been chosen over the indicated period. (Looking back over long periods, total costs are misleading unless corrected for present–value effects. For example, a coupon payment at the beginning of the year should be treated differently from one at the end of the year. Rules for discounting may be needed for retrospective total cost analysis.)

Duration, volatility, convexity, and other current risk measures would provide the indicated current exposure. A request for the risk (standard deviation) or expected value of total interest costs (or effective interest rate) would generate a query for the time period over which to compute these measures as well as the basis for the measurements (historical data, model type, and so on). A request for "exposure to (named index)" would generate a query for the user's desired index and provide an estimate of the expected change in total costs per unit change in the named index. For volatility changes and parallel shifts in the yield curve, these sensitivities are already effectively available from the duration (2) and "vega" (8) measures. One could specify, for example, nonparallel shifts in the yield curve of various kinds, credit spreads, counterparty default probabilities, or "events" such as a doubling of volatility combined with a parallel downward shift of the yield curve of 100 basis points. Value changes are not necessarily additive across instruments (mainly for tax reasons) nor across "shocks," and the ability to test sensitivity to different shocks simultaneously could be important.

Probability distributions (plots, or deciles, showing the likelihood of costs above or below a given level) could be based on Monte Carlo models that derive scenarios either from historical data or from statistical models for generating random price and interest rate changes, as explained below.

The system should also include the ability to input and monitor exposure limits and to parallel the outputs above with GAAP accounting versions.

Practically speaking, it would require many thousands of expert programming hours to develop such a system. To whatever limited extent this is done, one can stay with prioritized essentials and then build over time.

Simulation of Interest Rate Risk

This section describes techniques to simulate the risks associated with interest rate changes in the market value or interest expense of a portfolio of fixed–income liabilities. We suggest the resources required for each alternative and their relative advantages.

Simulating the Changes in Value of a Fixed–Income Portfolio

A liability portfolio of fixed–income instruments has a market value at time t that depends on the current forward rate curve, which we will treat as a list

$$f_t = \left(f_t(T_1), f_t(T_2), \cdots, f_t(T_n) \right).$$

Here, $f_t(T_1)$ is the forward rate (continuously compounding) contracted at time t for loans to be made at time $t + T_{i-1}$ and maturing at time $t + T_1$. We could take $T_0 = 0$ and T_1 to be one month, T_2 to be 3 months, T_3 to be 6 months, and so on, out to a last maturity T_n of, say, 30 years. The specific maturities are not important. Instead, we emphasize the idea of expressing the value of the portfolio as a function of the current forward rate curve. From its definition, the forward rate $f_t(T_1)$ is given by

$$f_t(T_1) = \frac{-1}{T_i - T_{i-1}} \left[\log D_t(T_i) - \log D_t(T_{i-1}) \right],$$

where $D_t(T_i)$ is the discount at time t for loans maturing at T_i. Conversely, discounts can be computed from the forward rates by the formula

$$D_t(T_i) = exp\left[-f_t(T_1)m_1 - f_t(T_2)m_2 - \cdots - f_t(T_i)m_i \right],$$

where $m_i = T_i - T_{i-1}$.

For discussion purposes, we view the forward rate curve f_t as that of a particular credit rating. Of course, if some of the portfolio's components are derivatives, such as Treasury futures or options, we must adjust for credit spreads. If all of the instruments are straight bonds, then the portfolio value can be computed directly from the forward rates by the usual discounting of coupons and principal. If, on the other hand, some of the instruments are derivatives such as caps, or if some, such as callable bonds, have embedded options whose payoffs depend on future forward rate curves, then we need a term structure derivative pricing model (described below) to compute the market value $P_t(f_t)$ as a function of the current forward rate curve f_t. For our purposes here, we suppose that this value $P_t(f_t)$ can be computed for any possible forward rate curve.

We are interested in estimating the risk associated with changes in the portfolio's market value due to unpredictable changes in the forward rate curve. By "risk," we could mean the standard deviation of the new portfolio value $V = P_{t+1}(f_{t+1})$ or any other measures of risk associated with the probability distribution of this random variable, such as the 95–percentile worst case (the value of V which is exceeded with only 5% probability). We assume no risk of changes in the credit rating of the instruments between t and $t+1$ (taking, for instance, a weekly interval). Thus, all of the risk is due to unpredictable changes in the forward rate curve, including changes in credit spreads. (Remember, however, that we always evaluate the portfolio with a reduced maturity corresponding to the passage of time between t and $t+1$. Sometimes it is useful to measure the change in value due solely to maturity reduction, $P_{t+1}(f_t) - P_t(f_t)$, that is, holding the forward rate curve fixed.)

Generating a large number N (say 1000) of possible new forward rate curves is a useful method for evaluating the portfolio's forward rate curve risk. We call these possible forward rate curves $F_1, F_2, \cdots, F_N$. Each is a plausible candidate for f_{t+1}. (Below, we describe alternative methods for generating these N possible forward rate curves.) Then we can compute the associated portfolio market values $V_1, V_2, \cdots, V_N$, where $V_i = P_{t+1}(F_i)$ for each i. We think of these N possible values as independent "draws" from the probability distribution associated with $P_{t+1}(f_{t+1})$. Now we can estimate any summary statistic, such as mean, standard deviation, percentiles, and so on.

For example, the estimated mean is

$$\overline{V} = \frac{V_1 + \cdots + V_N}{N}.$$

The usual estimate of risk (standard deviation) is

$$\sigma_V = \frac{1}{\sqrt{N-1}} \sqrt{\left(V_1 - \overline{V}\right)^2 + \cdots + \left(V_N - \overline{V}\right)^2}.$$

The estimated 95–percentile is the number exceeded by 5% of the N outcomes $V_1, V_2, \cdots, V_N$. Many other summary statistics or a plot of the frequency distribution (histogram of $V_1, \cdots, V_N$) may be useful.

The interest expense between t and $t+1$ can be treated separately from the total volume or combined with it.

We now turn to alternative methods for generating the forward rate curves $F_1, \cdots, F_N$.

Historical Forward Rate Curves

To generate candidate forward rate curves from historical data, one must obtain the historical forward rate curves from the available data, including coupon bond prices, swap rates, future indices, and so on. As explained in the appendix, cubic spline methods, nonlinear least squares estimation of forward rates, and other curve–fitting techniques produce estimates of the government or corporate forward rate curve for a particular rating. While changes in the spread due to credit risk are much less volatile than changes in the government curve itself, changes in credit spreads for investment–grade corporate bonds are correlated with changes in government bond forward rates.[10] The credit spread is typically an increasing function of maturity. Thus, if one's strategy is to begin with a government curve and add a spread for credit quality, one must carefully model the spread.[11]

Direct estimation of a credit–sensitive forward rate curve can also be obtained from Eurodollar futures prices and swap prices. One must still get a corporate forward rate curve from the Eurodollar curves by some spread estimation. Swap input data are not likely to be rich going back further than a few years.

Simulating from Historical Data

Given historical forward rate curves $f_1, \cdots, f_{t-1}$ for the previous t periods, one might simply compute the value of the current portfolio at each past date and examine the resulting path of portfolio values over the sample period. One may reduce the maturity of the portfolio as one passes through history in order to simulate the results of holding that portfolio at various points. One might call this a "bootstrap" simulation. Generally, the quality of such a simulation is better if the statistical behavior of interest rates is stationary. This is unlikely to be the case in reality.

One way to help with this "nonstationarity" problem is as follows. Compute, for each historical period k, the change $\Delta f_k = f_k - f_{k-1}$ in the forward rate curve from the previous period. That is, $\Delta f_k(T_1)$ is the change in forward rate at the shortest maturity, $\Delta f_k(T_2)$ is the change in forward rate at the next shortest maturity, and so on. The changes in the forward rate curve are likely to be more "stationary" than the forward rate curves themselves and will be a better source for the bootstrap process. A candidate draw for the new forward rate curve f_{t+1} could then be $f_t + \Delta f_k$, where Δf_k is a random choice of one of the historical forward rate curve changes from $\Delta f_1, \cdots, \Delta f_t$.

This bootstrap experiment differs from the "what–would–have–happened" exercise described earlier. It is, instead, a "what–might–happen" experiment (assuming that the change from the current to the next forward rate curve statistically resembles prior changes). Even this more sophisticated approach, however, is subject to nonstationarity problems. For example, there is definite persistence in forward rate curve volatility, i.e., if recent changes in the forward rate curve are more volatile (larger in magnitude) than average, then the next change in the forward rate curve is typically larger in magnitude than average. Recent history may therefore be a better guide than more distant history.

To account for this further nonstationarity problem, one can develop a time–series model for volatility (say, garch) or turn to the volatilities implied by the current prices of option–embedded assets. Both of these alternatives fall outside the scope of the bootstrap approach to historical data.

Monte Carlo Simulation of Forward Rates Using Statistics

For a somewhat different approach, suppose that unexpected changes in forward rates from now to the next period are given by a vector $g = (g_1, \cdots, g_n)$ of random variables that are normally distributed and that we have an estimate Σ of the covariance matrix of g from historical data. We can simulate g on a computer repeatedly and independently N times. By adding each simulation of g to the forward rate curve $\hat{f}_{t+1}$ expected for the next time period, we obtain a series $F_1, \cdots, F_N$ of simulated forward rate curves.

To estimate the forward rate curve expected for the next time period and the covariance matrix Σ of unexpected changes in forward rates, we make some simplifying assumptions. The "expectations hypothesis" is that forward bond prices are unbiased predictors of spot bond prices. (This assumption applies, for example, if there are any risk–neutral investors in the market.) Let us assume for ease of calculation that $T_i - T_{i-1} = 1$ for all i. The calculations below can easily be adjusted otherwise. If we follow the expectations hypothesis, the forward price for maturity T_i at time t is an unbiased predictor for the forward price for maturity T_{i-1} at time $t+1$ given that both are unbiased predictors for the spot price of one–period loans at time $t + T_i$. Following this line of reasoning, and using a normality assumption on forward rates, an unbiased predictor at time t for the forward rate $f_{t+1}(T_{i-1})$ is given by

$$\hat{f}(T_{i-1}) = f_t(T_i) - \frac{1}{2} var[f_{t+1}(T_{i-1}) - f_t(T_{i-1})], \qquad (2.1)$$

where this variance is conditional on information available at time t and may be estimated by several methods. (One could simply use the sample variance of changes in forward rates at T_{i-1}.) This handles all but the last maturity T_n, for which we might substitute the biased estimator $\hat{f}_{t+1}(T_n) = f_t(T_n)$.

For each period in the historical data base, we can now take the differences between forward rates and expected forward rates from the prior period. That is, the data at period s is of the form $g_s(T_i) = f_s(T_i) - \hat{f}_s(T_i)$. Under stationarity assumptions, the sample covariance from this data set can be used to simulate the new unexpected shift from the anticipated forward rates expected to apply in the next period, which can themselves be estimated by (2.1). The sample covariance between two time series $X_1, X_2, \cdots, X_t$ and $Y_1, Y_2, \cdots, Y_t$ is

$$C_{XY} = \frac{1}{t}\sum_{i=1}^{t}\left(X_i - \overline{X}\right)\left(Y_i - \overline{Y}\right).$$

In our application, $X_1, X_2,...$ could be the unexpected forward rate changes at the 1–year maturity point; and $Y_1, Y_2,...$ could be the unexpected forward rate changes at the 10–year maturity point. Over all n maturities, we thus obtain an $n \times n$ covariance matrix Σ, from which we can simulate g. Once again, the simulated change g is added to the current forecast f_{t+1} of the new forward rate curve.

Incidentally, if the sample means of the modeled unexpected changes in forward rates are significantly different from zero, we may be skeptical of the expectations hypothesis (or our distributional assumptions). If the volatility of forward rate changes is not constant over the data base, we may pursue corrective measures.[12]

Forward Rate Curve Components

It is often said that the majority of changes in the forward rate curve from one period to the next typically take the form of a parallel shift and change in slope. What does this mean, and how can this information help?

Let us think of certain types of standardized changes in the forward rate curve, say Δ_1 and Δ_2. For example, we could take Δ_1 to be a parallel shift of 100 basis points so that

$$\Delta_1(T_1) = \Delta_1(T_2) = \cdots = \Delta_1(T_n) = 0.100.$$

We could take Δ_2 to be a particular steepening of the forward rate curve, for example, a change of -30 basis points at 1 month, -20 basis points at 3 months, 0 basis points at 6 months, 10 basis points at 1 year, out to a specified shift at 30 years. These standardized forward rate curve shifts Δ_1 and Δ_2 are sometimes called "factors." For results superior to those based on *ad hoc* factors, we can estimate factors [13] from the data. They could be chosen using multivariate statistical theory, such as principal component analysis, to minimize the proportion of unexplained changes in forward rate curves that cannot be represented as linear combinations of the factors.

For example, for December 1987 through July 1992, weekly forward rate curve changes for the U.S. Treasuries have the estimated principal components shown in Table 1. The first principal component is a roughly parallel shift of the forward rate curve. Also shown are the R^2 coefficients for a regression of the changes in each forward rate on the first ("parallel") principal component. This "parallel" component explains a reasonably large fraction of forward rate changes. Adding a second principal component to the regression, as shown, increases the R^2 substantially. The second estimated component is roughly a change in the slope of the forward rate curve.

There are two major differences between this analysis and that of Litterman and Scheinkman (1989), which shows that parallel changes account for most of the interest rate risk in a bond portfolio. The former uses weekly periods; the latter, monthly. Changes over weekly periods involve more "noise" relative to the basic factors driving interest rate changes. Additionally, Litterman and Scheinkman study the factors that best explain the excess returns of bonds rather than the principal components of forward rate changes.

Table 1

Principal Components of Weekly Forward Rate Changes								
Component	Maturity	0.25	0.5	1	2	5	10	20
"parallel"	shift (b.p.)	27.1	40.6	42.3	49.5	40.5	28.8	31.2
(Δ_1)	R^2	0.36	.064	0.75	0.85	0.82	0.37	0.39
"slope"	shift (b.p.)	-32.2	-27.5	-27.3	-17.6	12.8	55.6	62.3
(Δ_2)	Total R^2	0.51	0.73	0.84	0.88	0.84	0.79	0.83

Fixing two standard changes Δ_1 and Δ_2 (whether derived from principal components analysis or by some other means), the change Δf_k in the forward rate curve at period k may be described as a combination of the two standardized changes plus an "error" e_k in that, for some weights w_{1k} and w_{2k},

$$\Delta f_k = w_{1k}\Delta_1 + w_{2k}\Delta_2 + e_k,$$

where e_k is the residual. Although there are various ways to choose the weights w_{1k} and w_{2k}, they are typically chosen to minimize the size of the residual vector e_k, where "size" refers to the sum of squared errors. That is, we could take $w_k = (w_{1k}, w_{2k})$ to minimize $e_k(T_1)^2 + e_k(T_2)^2 + \cdots + e_k(T_n)^2$. This is simply a multiple regression of Δf_k on Δ_1 and Δ_2 with estimated coefficients w_{1k} and w_{2k}.

This weighting vector w_k for each historical period k produces a sample $w_1, w_2, \cdots, w_t$ of weight vectors for statistical analysis. For example, the sample mean weight vector $\bar{w} = (\bar{w}_1, \bar{w}_2)$ and covariance matrix[14] C provide an historically based model for generating new weight vectors at random. For example, we can draw a random sample $w(1), \cdots, w(N)$ of weight vectors from a Monte Carlo simulator using a normal distribution with $\bar{w}$ and covariance matrix C. With any draw $w(i)$ from this randomly generated sample, we can create the associated forward rate curve change $\Delta f(i) = w_1(i)\Delta_1 + w_2(i)\Delta_2$. Finally, we can generate N candidate new forward rate curves, $F_1, \cdots, F_N$ by taking $F_i = f_t + \Delta f(i)$.

Although this procedure for simulating forward rate changes is less accurate in a stationary setting than drawing directly from the historical data base of forward rate curve changes, it has some advantages:

1. *Data handling*: To generate data in this fashion, one need only store the mean vector $\bar{w}$ and the covariance matrix C rather than all of the forward rate curve changes $\Delta f_1, \cdots, \Delta f_t$.

2. *Statistical analysis and updating*: It is natural to account for changes in the random behavior of interest rates by updating $\bar{w}$ and C. For example, one can develop a time series model (such as garch) for the variance in the weights that accounts for changes in the volatility structure. This represents a promising compromise between maintaining historical reality and keeping the volatility structure current.

3. *Discussion purposes*: Although it may be difficult to discuss the random behavior of interest rates directly in terms of the entire data base of forward rate curves, it is quite natural to speak in terms of the covariance structure C. For example, assume that the standard deviation of the parallel shift of a forward rate curve has historically been 25 basis points per week. This number, 25 basis points, would be computed as the standard deviation $\sqrt{C_{11}}$ of the parallel weights, multiplied by the size, 100 basis points, of the standard parallel move. One could continue by exploring how increasing this standard deviation from 25 basis points to 40 basis points would affect the portfolio's risk. Assuming the correlation between the slope change and parallel change is held constant, it is easy to adjust C accordingly. Likewise, one can describe the risks associated with changes in slope and correlations between slope changes and parallel changes.

One can expand this approach to incorporate international forward rate curve factors and covariance among them (credit spreads) to manage the risks associated with multiple yield curves.

Risk Management

A reasonable approach to risk management of a fixed–income portfolio is the immunization of the portfolio against various types of shocks. For example, an obviously important shock is a change in the forward rate curve given by the first principal component as described above. In order to immunize a portfolio to a given form of shock with a given hedging instrument (such as a swap or option), we can first measure the change in market value, say Δ_P, of one's portfolio to the given shock. Then we can also measure the change in value, Δ_H, of the hedging instrument to the same shock. The number of units of the hedging instrument necessary to neutralize the shock in question is then

$$x = -\frac{\Delta_P}{\Delta_H}.$$

By adding x units of the hedging instrument to the portfolio, the net change in value due to the given shock is then

$$\Delta_P + x\Delta_H = 0$$

as desired. While one may not always want to choose hedges in this manner, knowledge of the principal components of changes in the forward rate curve clearly gives one an advantage in measuring and controlling the risk of a given portfolio.

When controlling n sources of risk simultaneously using n hedging instruments, the above immunization approach can be extended to give immunizing positions in each of the hedging instruments by solving n linear equations in n unknowns. With embedded optionalities or other nonlinear value responses, one must use a term structure model, as described below, to measure the changes in value of the portfolio and hedging instruments induced by a given shock. The same approach nevertheless applies provided that the shocks are not too large and that one rehedges with each change in the interest rate environment (see Chapter Six, "Elements of Quantitative Risk Management," by Ayman Hindy, for more details).

Term Structure Derivatives Modeling

This section reviews fixed–income derivative pricing models with applications in portfolio risk management.

What Is an Interest Rate Model?

The key component of a fixed–income derivative pricing model is the "interest rate model," which specifies how the short–term interest rate evolves randomly over time. For example, using r_t to represent the overnight interest rate that applies on a given future day t, the Ho–Lee[15] model takes

$$r_t = r_{t-1} + a_t + b_t z_t ,\qquad (3.1)$$

where a_t and b_t are coefficients supplied by the user in a manner described below and where z_t has outcomes +1 and -1 only, each with 50% probability. In the Ho–Lee model, the coefficients $a_1, a_2, \cdots$ serve mainly to control the level of interest rates at each maturity, and the coefficients $b_1, b_2, \cdots$ explain the volatility of interest rates at each maturity. Another simple example, the Black–Derman–Toy[16] model, follows a dynamic equation similar to (3.1). It is obtained merely by replacing r_t with $\log r_t$ for suitable coefficients a_t and b_t.

Most of the available models are based on "continuous time," which means that the difference equation (3.1) is theoretically based on a stochastic differential equation of the form

$$dr_t = a_t dt + b_t dZ_t ,\qquad (3.2)$$

where Z_t defines a Brownian motion. The difference between (3.1) and (3.2) is a theoretical nicety that we shall avoid. In any case, for computational purposes, one often replaces the continuous–time model (3.2) with the difference equation (3.1).

An interest rate model, such as the Ho–Lee model (3.1), provides the ability to estimate the market value of any fixed–income security, such as bonds, options, caps, floors, and swaptions. Suppose, for example, that it is currently day t and that an asset to be priced pays the amount Y at some

---

future day T. (If the asset is a zero–coupon bond maturing at T, for example, then $Y = 1$.) The price of this asset today, according to the model, is simply

$$p_{t,T} = E\left(\frac{Y}{(1+r_t)(1+r_{t+1})\cdots(1+r_{T-1})}\right). \qquad (3.3)$$

This is merely the discounted expected value of the payoff, where the discount factor is the rolled–over value of investing at the short rate.

This pricing formula (3.3) may seem strange at first in that there is no correction for any risk associated with the payoff Y or the interest rate process r. A major advance in modern derivative pricing methods, following the development of the Black–Scholes option pricing model, shows that one can always account for risk by choosing the coefficients of the model (a_t and b_t in this case) in a "risk–corrected" manner.[17]

Suppose we want to price a bond option, specifically, the price of an option on a zero–coupon bond. The bond matures at day T; the option, a European call, expires at day $S < T$, with an exercise price K. The payoff of the call option is thus $Y = max(p_{S,T} - K, 0)$, where the price $p_{S,T}$ of the bond at the option–expiration day S is computed as in (3.3); and it depends on the interest rate r_S prevailing on that day. From (3.3), the modeled price of the bond option is then

$$O_{t,S} = E\left(\frac{max(p_{S,T} - K, 0}{(1+r_t)(1+r_{t+1})\cdots(1+r_{S-1})}\right). \qquad (3.4)$$

The Ho–Lee model (3.1) is one of many interest rate models. All work in the same way; they price term–structure assets as in (3.3) or (3.4). Some models are "multi–factor" in that the evolution of the short–term interest rate r_t depends not only on its past behavior but also on additional "factors" or "state variables." (See Duffie and Kan [18] for a list of commonly used single– and multi–factor term structure models.)

Incidentally, it is not conceptually important whether one takes daily, weekly, or even varying time intervals for the model. Results are generally more accurate as the length of a time period decreases. There is a key tradeoff, however, between accuracy and computational speed.

The expectations above are typically computed using "tree" methods, finite–difference methods, or Monte Carlo simulation. The details[19] of these computations are elaborate, particularly in the more complicated multi–factor models, but the basic idea is fairly simple.

Calibration of the Model

For each of the available models, the user must supply coefficients, such as a_t and b_t, in the Ho–Lee model. These are usually determined by "calibration," a process of selecting the model coefficients so that the modeled prices of selected bonds and bond options (or other volatility–sensitive securities) equal the quoted market prices. Black and Karasinski[20] extend calibration procedures to cover the prices of caps, securities that periodically pay the excess of a short–term floating interest rate over a given level for some future period.

An interest rate model can only be used effectively if accurately calibrated. Rarely is an effective calibration algorithm published with the model. The user must obtain such an algorithm or ensure that the model is supplied in a calibrated form. An interest rate model should be calibrated daily to maintain accuracy.

What Can Be Done with a Term Structure Model?

Interest–rate models have numerous applications:

a. Pricing fixed–income securities. The pricing application is obvious. Whether for accounting, planning, or trading, it is important to estimate the price of an instrument or portfolio of instruments. Each model has inaccuracies that limit this application. In particular, a "winner's curse" is associated with any model used to identify "good" buys. If an investor finds that the modeled price exceeds the actual market price, he might well conclude, "This is a profitable buy." In fact, however, the model may overestimate the value of the security. If one consistently identifies trades with a model that is less accurate than that used by others to set offer prices, then one will systematically lose money while executing apparently "profitable" trades. Since the models that set market prices for option–embedded instruments are often sophisticated and carefully calibrated, it is wise to trade exclusively with sophisticated, carefully tested, and proven models.

b. Evaluating risk. One may need to know the sensitivity of the value of one's fixed–income portfolio to various types of interest rate shocks, such as a shift in the level of interest rates or a change in the volatility of interest rates. A term structure model can be used for this purpose. The model, calibrated to today's market, prices the portfolio before the hypothetical shock. Then one recalibrates the model to reflect the shock, and this gives the "shocked" value of the portfolio. The difference between the before– and after–shock values is the sensitivity of the portfolio value to a wide range of shocks, including parallel and various types of nonparallel shifts of the yield curve and changes in volatility at various maturities.

c. Managing risk. If one's term structure model can measure the sensitivity, Δ_P, of one's portfolio to a given shock, then one can also measure the sensitivity Δ_H of a potential hedging instrument to the same shock. As mentioned earlier, the number of units of the hedging instrument necessary to neutralize the shock in question is then

$$x = -\frac{\Delta_P}{\Delta_H}.$$

While one may not always want to choose hedges in this manner, access to a term structure model clearly gives one an advantage in measuring and controlling the risk associated with a given strategy. The more accurate the model, the better the measurement and control. A term structure model is particularly valuable for measuring the sensitivity of option–embedded instruments to changes in volatility. For example, with two hedging instruments, say an option and a swap, one can determine the positions in these two instruments necessary to simultaneously immunize one's portfolio to a specific change in the forward rate curve and a specific change in volatility. The resulting positions are accurate only "locally," that is, for small changes in markets.

Conclusion

There are many models in use and many ways to classify these models. The most useful breakdown is multi–factor versus single–factor. In the single–factor models, changes in yields at all maturities are perfectly correlated over short intervals. Multi–factor models allow for imperfect correlation and for the incorporation of more information to estimate coefficients. Multi–factor models are typically more difficult to understand, calibrate, and use. They also may require significantly more computation time. The tradeoff, of course, is that they are more accurate when calibrated accurately and used properly.

One can start with a simple model and build in sophistication over time. As one gains a sense of a model's workings, the choice of a more complicated and accurate model can be made on a more informed basis. The term structure model is only one component—albeit a key one—of a debt management system. It can be easily replaced if the system is thoughtfully designed.

For many purposes, single–factor models produce accurate, useful measures of risk exposure and hedging ratios. They are not sufficiently accurate to identify mispriced securities for trading purposes unless used by a skillful bond trader familiar with the model's idiosyncrasies. They can be implemented fairly easily (for example, on a spreadsheet)— significantly more so than any of the multi–factor models. Finally, they are frequently used by trading firms, most of whom are only now beginning to switch over to various multi–factor models for special tasks.

Appendix: The Zero–Coupon Curve

This appendix describes how to extract zero–coupon bond prices from price data on coupon bonds and derivatives.

We consider only the government yield curve since credit–sensitive bonds of a homogeneous credit class can be treated by the same method. To incorporate bonds from heterogeneous credit classes, we must estimate differential credit spreads in order to estimate the yield curve of a given creditor.

A *zero–coupon* bond is a bond guaranteeing a payment of $1 at its maturity. The price $D(T)$ for zero–coupon bond maturing in T years is also called the T–year discount, and the schedule assigning discounts to each possible maturity is called the discount function. While the U.S. Treasury has begun issuing zero–coupon bonds ("strips") for selected maturities, there may not be enough of such maturities, nor enough liquidity in the strips market, to obtain an accurate discount function directly from strips prices alone. Instead, practitioners often estimate the discount function from over 200 different coupon and zero–coupon instruments, including bills (zero coupons of maturity less than 2 years), notes (coupon instruments of maturities ranging from 2 through 10 years at issue), and bonds (coupon instruments of maturities over 10 years, and currently running up to 30 years, at issue).

Suppose there are currently N (200, for example) such Treasuries trading at prices $P_1, \cdots P_N$. The associated coupon rates are $C_1, \cdots, C_N$. These coupons are paid semi–annually from the date of issue with detailed rules governing exact payment dates that we ignore here. Of course, if instrument i is a bill, we have $C_i = 0$. In practice, one should make special allowances for the following characteristics:

a. Some bonds are callable and have prices that are reduced to reflect the value of the call option held by the Treasury.

b. Some bonds are "flower" bonds and convey special inheritance tax privileges.

c. Treasury bills are typically exempt from state taxes.

d. Certain Treasuries, particularly current issues (the latest issue of a given maturity) are in high demand as collateral in repurchase agreements and have an elevated price that reflects the "special" low interest rate[21] charged for loans in repurchase agreements collateralized by such bonds. For this reason, some models use only current issues while others use only off–the–run issues.

At a given hypothetical discount function D, it is easy to compute the present value of the i–th instrument: simply the sum of the coupons and principal, each discounted according to its payment date. The price of a 1–year Treasury bill at issue is thus $D(1)$; and the price at issue, per dollar of principal, of a 30–year bond of coupon rate C, is

$$D(0.5)C + D(1)C + \cdots + D(29.5)C + D(30)(1+C).$$

Here, we ignore slight variations from exact payment dates that would normally be carefully accounted for in practice. For example, a particular "1–year" bill might actually have a maturity of 362 days at issue. With accurate accounting for maturities of coupons and principal, let $\hat{P}_i(D)$ denote the discounted present value of the i–th instrument, given the discount function D. The pricing error $e_i(D) = P_i - \hat{P}_i(D)$ can be made close to or equal to zero by adjusting the discount function accordingly. More importantly, one could choose the discount function D that minimizes the weighted sum of squared errors across all bonds to pick one of the many possible fitting criteria

$$S(D) = w_1 e_1(D)^2 + \cdots + w_N e_N(D)^2,$$

with a weight w_i associated with i often chosen as the reciprocal of the square root of duration of that bond or some other volatility–related factor.

If one is free to choose $D(T)$ for each and every maturity T, one could typically make the fitting error $S(D)$ very small or even zero, but that would result in a very erratic discount function. Instead, one wants a reasonably smooth discount function, bearing in mind that an erratic discount function can be caused mainly by measurement error.

In practice, the estimated implied discount function is obtained from sophisticated fitting routines such as "cubic splines," "tension splines,"[22] "weighted non–linear least squares," and other methods outside the scope of this chapter. Such an exercise produces an "implied discount function" D, that is, a discount function that is implied by the prices of all available Treasuries. (Indeed, there are reasons not to restrict oneself to straight Treasuries, but that is another story.)

Table 2 presents a sample of such fitted discounts using Federal Reserve Treasuries price data and a weighted nonlinear least squares criterion suggested by Coleman, Fisher, and Ibbotson[23] with coding and computational work by Robert Ashcroft and Ping Jiang. The column headed "No." shows the number of bonds for which price data are available on the given date.

From the discount function, one can compute the forward rates or the (continuously compounding) zero–coupon yield, $Y(T) = -log(D(T))/T$ at each maturity T. The schedule of yields for each maturity is the zero–coupon *yield curve*.

Table 2

Example of Estimate Discount Function

Date	Bonds	0.25 yr.	0.5 yr.	1 yr.	2 yr.	5 yr.	10 yr.	20 yr.
06/19/92	221	99.061	98.077	95.796	90.724	72.548	47.196	19.238
07/01/92	222	99.082	98.133	96.003	91.073	73.138	47.635	19.410
07/02/92	222	99.131	98.251	96.274	91.507	73.952	48.350	19.841
07/06/92	222	99.159	98.290	96.347	91.689	74.134	48.399	19.863
07/07/92	223	99.163	98.305	96.371	91.834	74.365	48.555	19.793
07/08/92	222	99.163	98.310	96.383	91.848	74.312	48.302	19.832
07/09/92	223	99.168	98.319	96.383	91.828	74.332	48.268	19.874
07/10/92	223	99.148	98.312	96.367	91.859	74.387	48.166	19.598
07/13/92	223	99.161	98.331	96.382	91.866	74.327	48.013	19.402
07/14/92	222	99.166	98.350	96.419	91.990	74.501	47.904	19.342
07/15/92	221	99.174	98.364	96.497	92.117	74.940	48.112	19.550
07/16/92	221	99.174	98.362	96.481	92.124	74.932	48.351	19.735
07/17/92	221	99.151	98.342	96.459	92.088	74.838	48.172	19.385
07/20/92	221	99.171	98.367	96.487	92.098	74.823	48.249	19.576
07/21/92	222	99.168	98.361	96.450	92.022	74.856	48.332	19.518
07/22/92	221	99.174	98.369	96.467	92.063	75.030	48.573	19.740
07/23/92	221	99.182	98.374	96.478	92.198	75.596	49.152	20.053

Debt Management and Interest Rate Risk

Notes

1. I am grateful for conversations with Ayman Hindy, George Parker, and Bill Beaver of Stanford University; to Will Bogaty, Elizabeth Glaeser, Mike Burger, and Ken Knowles of Mobil Corporation; and to Scott Richard of Miller, Anderson, Sherrard. I am also grateful for support from the Financial Services Research Initiative at the Graduate School of Business, Stanford University; for computation research assistance from Robert Ashcroft, Ping Jiang, Qiang Dai, and Chris Mueller; and for editing from Ellen O'Connor. All opinions expressed here are those of the author.

2. If this were not true, and two portfolios "A" and "B" of liabilities generated the same cashflows, but the market value V_A of portfolio A exceeded the value V_B of portfolio B, then an arbitrageur could buy portfolio B, sell portfolio A, and generate an arbitrage profit of $V_A - V_B$ with zero risk.

3. See, for example, S. Mayers and C. Smith, "On Corporate Demand for Insurance," *Journal of Business*, 55 (1982): 281–296 and C. Smith and R. Stulz, "The Determinants of Firms' Hedging Policies," *Journal of Financial Quantitative Analysis* 20 (1985): 391–405. For a general overview of the role of taxes in capital structure and dividend decisions, see M. Scholes and M. Wolfson, *Taxes and Business Strategy: A Planning Approach* (Englewood Cliffs, NJ: Prentice–Hall, 1992).

4. See, for example, S. Mayers and C. Smith (1982) and C. Smith and R. Stulz (1985), *op. cit.*

5. For a model, see P. DeMarzo and D. Duffie, "Corporate Incentives for Hedging and Hedge Accounting," Working Paper, Northwestern University, 1993.

6. This is also known as the problem of "debt overhang," pointed out by Stuart Myers, in the "The Determinants of Corporate Borrowing," *Journal of Financial Economics* 5 (1977): 147–175. Some empirical evidence that debt overhang plays a role in risk management is offered by D. Nance, C. Smith, and C. Smithson, "On the Determinants of Corporate Hedging," *Journal of Finance* 48 (1993): 267–284.

7. See K. Froot, D. Scharfstein, and J. Stein, "Coordinating Corporate Investment and Financing Policies," forthcoming, *Journal of Finance*.

8. See P. DeMarzo and D. Duffie, "Corporate Financial Hedging with Proprietary Information," *Journal of Economic Theory* 53 (1991): 261–286.

9. See the Statement of Financial Accounting Standard Number 107, "Disclosures About Fair Value of Financial Instruments," Financial Accounting Standards Board, (December 1991).

10. Longstaff and Schwartz (1992), in "Valuing Risky Debt: A New Approach," (UCLA Working Paper), show a significant relationship in a regression of changes in credit spreads for AA industrials on changes in 30–year U.S. bond yields as well as S&P 500 index returns.

11. See Litterman and Iben, "Corporate Bond Valuation and the Term Structure of Credit Spreads," Goldman Sachs Financial Strategies Group Report (1992).

12. Consider, for example, a test of the null hypothesis that the variance of weekly forward rate changes at a given maturity is constant over the first and second halves of the period December 1987 and July 1992. At the 99–percent confidence level, this hypothesis cannot be rejected for the following forward rate periods: 0.5 to 1 year, 1

---

year to 2 year, 2 year to 5 year, 5 year to 10 year, and 10 year to 20 year. It can be rejected, however, for the 0–to–90 day maturity range and the 90–day to 180–day maturity range. This is based on a database of all noncallable, nonflower U.S. Treasuries and a zero–coupon forward rate curve extractor based on nonlinear least squares written by Robert Ashcroft under the author's direction.

[13] See R. Litterman and J. Scheinkman, "Common Factors Affecting Bond Returns," Goldman Sachs Financial Strategies Group (1988), and P. Knez, R. Litterman, and J. Scheinkman, "Explorations into Factors Explaining Money Market Returns," Working Paper, The University of Chicago (1989).

[14] As usual, C_{ij} is the sample covariance between the i-th and j-th and weights.

[15] See T. Ho and S. Lee, "Term Structure Movements and Pricing Interest Rate Contingent Claims," *Journal of Finance* 41 (1986): 1011–1029. This is an extension of the original model of Robert Merton, "A Theory of Rational Option Pricing," *Bell Journal of Economics and Management Science* 4 (1974): 141–183.

[16] See F. Black, E. Derman, and W. Toy, "A One-Factor Model of Interest Rates and Its Application to Treasury Bond Options," *Financial Analysts Journal* 46:1 (January–February 1990): 33–39.

[17] See, for example, J. Hull, *Options, Futures, and Other Derivative Securities,* Second Edition (Englewood Cliffs: Prentice Hall, 1993), or D. Duffie, *Dynamic Asset Pricing Theory* (Princeton University Press, 1992).

[18] Please refer to D. Duffie and R. Kan, "Multi–Factor Term Structure Models," forthcoming in *Philosophical Transactions of the Royal Society*, Series A (1993).

[19] See Hull (1993) or Duffie (1992), *op. cit.*, for details.

[20] See F. Black and P. Karasinski, "Bond and Option Pricing When Short Rates are Log–normal," *Financial Analysts Journal* 47:4 (July–August 1991):52–59.

[21] See D. Duffie, "Special Repo Rates," Working Paper, Graduate School of Business, Stanford University (1992).

[22] See M. Fisher, D. Nychka, and D. Zervos, "Fitting the Term Structure of Interest Rates with Smoothing Splines," Working Paper, Federal Reserve Board, Washington D.C., (1994).

[23] See T. Coleman, L. Fisher, and R. Ibbotson, "Estimating the Term Structure of Interest Rates from Data That Include the Prices of Coupon Bonds," *The Journal of Fixed Income* (September 1992): 85–116.

Managing Mortgage Risks

Mark Faris, Senior Vice President,
Norwest Mortgage

Richard Kovacevich, President and Chief Operating
Officer, Norwest Corporation

Sonja Rodine, Vice President/Portfolio Manager,
Norwest Corporation

Introduction

The housing finance market, in which funds are borrowed to purchase a home, is the largest sector of the debt market in the world. Originators of mortgage debt have continually developed new mortgage product that better appeals to both borrowers and institutional investors. Financial intermediaries are pooling a greater array of financial assets and using them as collateral securities purchased by institutional investors. These investors have increasingly demanded more sophisticated financial engineering to redirect cashflows and thus satisfy balance sheet needs. These massive changes, coupled with the mortgage market's increased efficiency, have required both the originator and investor to fully understand and hedge the complex options embedded in mortgages and their components. To understand the risk and rewards in the mortgage market is to prepare for a future in which other loan markets are securitized and cashflows are engineered to meet investor needs.

This chapter describes the interest rate and credit risks involved in the transfer of capital to meet the needs of the residential mortgage market. We examine the risks faced by institutions that create, sell and invest in mortgages and mortgage–backed securities (MBS) and the techniques they use to manage these risks.

The first section addresses risks associated with the origination and securitization process, and the second section addresses interest rate and credit risks. We begin with an overview of the dimensions of this extremely large segment of the U.S. debt market and its institutional participants.

Background

The mortgage market is often perceived as just another debt market where some mortgages are held, some are sold and some assume a security format. In fact, the mortgage market is one of the most pervasive and far–reaching success stories of the free market system. Residential mortgage debt outstanding at the end of 1991 was $4.05 trillion. This amount surpasses all other capital markets. Mortgage debt outstanding exceeds the outstanding debt of the U.S. government.

Capital provides financing for residences in many ways. In the '50s, '60s and '70s, the traditional portfolio lender, typified by Savings & Loan (S & L) institutions, filled this need. Community based, they gathered together the small savings accounts of local residents. By aggregating these funds, even small institutions could loan to at least a few customers. The loans made up the asset side of the balance sheet and provided income to pay interest on savings.

The advent of the money market fund, the mutual fund, jumbo CDs, and other new products increased the competition for deposit funds. As rates rose on deposits, loan rates on the assets they supported could not go up since the loans were primarily fixed rate and long term. The cost to maintain the liability side of the balance sheet exceeded the value that could be derived by the asset side. The resulting adjustment ultimately led to the S & L crisis. As this method of capital accumulation and transfer lost favor, it was replaced by another method of capital transfer for the residential mortgage market. If savings institutions could not fill residential borrowers' needs by portfolio holdings, then mortgage loans would be placed with institutions better suited to holding mortgage loans.

In fact, savings institutions had sold loans to each other and other loan sellers had sold to savings institutions for some time. It was a natural, although not painless, transition into capital transfer through the mortgage intermediaries prevalent today.

Mortgage Originator

Mortgage Intermediaries

We divide the current mortgage intermediary industry into three major categories by function: mortgage banker, mortgage broker, and wholesale or conduit. These categories include several types of institutions such as commercial banks, savings and loans, and mortgage companies. In fact, a single institution may operate in several functional categories.

The mortgage banker originates loans by taking applications from borrowers, closing the loans in the name of the institution, and selling the loan. The mortgage broker originates and sells loans by taking applications from borrowers closing in the name of another institution. The wholesaler or conduit originates loans by purchasing from other institutions and reselling the mortgages. This list is not intended to be exclusive, but it covers most institutions operating in today's mortgage market.

Interest Rate Risk

Many issues associated with interest rate risk in mortgage banking apply equally to mortgage brokers and wholesalers–conduits.

The first step in examining the interest rate risk faced by mortgage bankers is to thoroughly understand the loan origination process. Each loan transaction is unique, but a standard pattern characterizes most organizations.

The loan transaction begins with the borrower's initial contact, which often results from a real estate agent's referral to the mortgage banker. The application process consists of information exchange between the borrower and the mortgage banker. The borrower gives financial data and information about the property being financed. The lender gives information on the entire process, makes disclosures required by law, and describes the anticipated interest rate and fees. Important information about the borrower is verified in writing. An appraisal of the subject property verifies that the value is sufficient to provide security for the loan owner. A credit report ascertains the borrower's credit history.

When the documentation is complete, the loan is approved or denied. This decision is usually made by an individual not involved in the preparation of the file. Upon approval, a title search ascertains that the title is clear and that the mortgage supporting the loan will be in a first lien position.

At this point, most lenders establish a closing date and advance funds in exchange for a note. For most loans, the time from application to closing is 30 to 60 days. When the closing occurs, the lender advances the full loan amount of the note. The lender collects fees from the borrower (or the property seller), such as origination fee and discount points. The origination fee is usually 1% of the loan amount although that ranges by loan type and geographic location. Discount points are used along with the interest rate to adjust the effective yield of the loan by discounting the sale price. In return, the borrower makes monthly payments to the lender based on the agreed–upon interest rate and the amortization schedule.

Once the loan is closed, it must be prepared and delivered to the loan buyer. After some form of review, the buyer remits the funds to remove the loan assent from the lender's balance sheet. This process frequently takes 15 to 30 days.

So far the process is simple. The borrower makes an application, the lender processes the paperwork, a decision is made, and the loan closes 30 to 60 days later. It is then shipped to the loan buyer and funds are received 15 to 30 days later. From our interest rate risk perspective, it is easy to close the loan and send it to the loan buyer except for the decision as to what rate to charge.

When we think of mortgage loans as one of a group of investment vehicles competing for the loan buyer's capital, we see that the required effective yield will change moment by moment just as the stock market or other debt markets change. Therefore it is possible to close a loan at a rate which the buyer will not accept. This could require unexpected discounting to raise the yield to acceptable levels, resulting in the lender's loss. To protect against this occurrence, the lender must sell forward—that is, arrange a price for future delivery of loans. These arrangements are often mandatory, meaning the lender must deliver as agreed or face a market buyout of the commitment.

When we view the application process as a competitive activity against the backdrop of constantly changing rates and prices, it is obvious that borrowers want to know their rate and terms at the time of application. To provide the rate quote, the lender must sell forward from the time of application for future delivery. A forward sale helps repair the process. We can presell the loans to our buyer and then loan to borrowers at the agreed–upon rate. The simultaneous execution of these transactions is easily done. Then when the loans close, they can be delivered and the appropriate rate is assured. The lender must provide rate and price quotes to the borrower at application. These quotes hold until the loan closes. The lender must make sure the loan is delivered to the loan buyer consistent with the requirements necessary to receive the agreed–upon price.

Almost all mortgage loans made by mortgage bankers are sold to another party. There are many loan buyers and methods for selling loans. This discussion concentrates on mortgage–backed security (MBS) delivery. Almost all Federal Housing Administration (FHA) and Veterans Administration (VA) loans are delivered by the MBS method. Also, the vast majority of conventional loans eligible for agency guarantee are delivered using the MBS method. Security markets that trade MBS's are some of the largest and most liquid in the world.

A MBS entitles the holder to an undivided interest in a pool of mortgages. Prepayments are distributed evenly among the security holders. In addition, the MBS usually carries a credit enhancement or guarantee of some sort. The MBS is characterized by declining prices for each month of delivery into the future. The further into the future an MBS is sold, the lower the price.

The major factors of risk are now established. They are as follows: (1) the lender must sell the loans it creates without a loss of value; (2 a rate and price must be available to the borrower at application which holds through closure; and (3) until the loan is closed, borrowers may cancel their loan applications.

Factors Affecting Fallout. A prudent mortgage banker wants to know how many loans will ultimately close. For each group of applications, how can we predict that number so that we can sell that amount forward and have loans available to meet delivery needs?

There are as many ways to determine this as there are mortgage bankers. Many of these ways are just elaborate cover for market predictions underlying a trading bias. We assume that if a mortgage banker could profitably trade an MBS by predicting market movement, there would be no need to burden the operation with the overhead necessary to originate mortgages—in fact, only telephones would be necessary. Following this assumption, one must be as precise as possible when predicting fallout.

The components of fallout can be grouped into three categories: (1) rejection of poor–quality loans; (2) failure of the underlying real estate transactions; and (3) cancellation of the loan transaction at borrower request.

The first two causes of fallout represent a random occurrence and are generally constant over time and interest rate environment. The third, however, is the exercise of the borrower's option to cancel a loan when rates are more attractive. This illustrates the position of mortgage lenders. Every borrower has a free option to cancel the loan application when rates have improved over those at application.

Ample evidence indicates that the borrower is not completely efficient in exercising the option to cancel and reapply. While most mortgage bankers know this intuitively, they have no basis for estimating the level of borrower cancellation. Some method must be employed to measure the cancellation percentage against another factor such as the difference between the agreed–upon rate and the current rate. Such a method must assess borrower gains as a result of exercising the option to cancel.

The Northwest Mortgage Model. The Norwest Mortgage Model predicts borrower cancellation by tracking the value in points (each point equals 1% of the loan amount) that the borrower gains or loses if he cancels and reapplies. Table 1 shows a simplified version of this model.

Each cell in the center is the total amount of loans with the same interest rate and discount points. Loans are compared to the current market rate and points and then are added to the cells representing the appropriate difference. The column labeled "Difference" is the amount in points to be gained or lost if a loan in that category cancels and reapplies at current market. The columns marked "total" and "cumulative total" reveal the bulk of the pipeline in relation to current market. The column marked "closing percentage" is the percent of each cell that will close. This estimates how efficiently consumers will exercise their option. At Norwest, this number was originally an average of estimates from several senior managers. Subsequently, we tracked fallout within various groups of loans. We now use that data to modify and validate our percentages.

The numbers here are examples only. We believe the numbers are affected by factors such as geographic mix and relock procedures which differ among lenders. This information also provides a basis for constant adjustments. The amount in each cell multiplied by the closing percentage gives a weighted average closing percent. This number represents the estimate of closings which will come from this particular group of loan applications if the market stays constant until the closing date of all loans.

Since we all know that the market will change, the single–point estimate of closing is of limited value. We need a way to look at the changes in the expected closings of this group of applications over a range of market conditions. To this effect, we use a graphic depiction of what we term the "function" of a group of loans. Since we can calculate a weighted–average closing number in the current market, we should also be able to calculate a weighted–average closing number for a market 1/4 point higher, 1/2 point higher, 3/4 higher, and so on.

Figure 1 shows the closing function of the loan applications used in Table 1. It extends from four points lower than current market to four points higher than current market along the x-axis. The y–axis shows the closing percentage. Not surprisingly, the higher the potential gain to the borrower (current market improves), the less likely the borrower is to close. Conversely, the greater the potential loss to the borrower (market declines), the more likely the borrower will close. Based on the prior assumptions and our confidence in the accuracy of the closing percentages, we now have a predictive model of closings based on future interest rates. Now we need to hedge this set of closings given the various market conditions.

Figure 1

The Closing Function

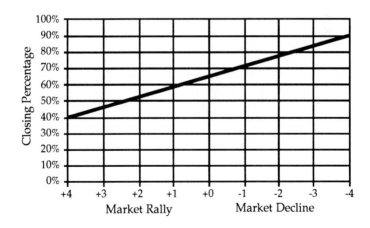

From Figure 1, we know that the amount of loans to be delivered from our group of applications will change as the market changes. The prices on the loans are constant; therefore, the changes in the amount closing are adverse to the mortgage banker. In a higher price environment (lower borrower rate), there are fewer loans to deliver. If the mortgage lender has previously sold these loans, there will be a shortfall in deliverable loans. With mandatory sales, the only alternative is to repurchase the shortfall at a price above the original sale price. Conversely, if the price environment is lower (higher borrower rates), then more loans than expected will close, exceeding those initially sold. The only alternative is to sell loans with previously agreed–to rates and prices in the current higher rate (lower price) environment. Once again, the mortgage banker has bought high (by closing the loan at the original price) and sold low in the current environment.

The answer to this problem is clear: The mortgage banker cannot offer an option to borrowers and then give mandatory commitments to sell those loans. Even if borrowers are inefficient in exercising this option, the results are too damaging. The mortgage banker may employ several forms of options. They are all different, but some features apply to most of them—notably that the choice to deliver belongs to the mortgage banker. The fees involved make this method of delivery more costly than mandatory delivery.

Extensive literature discusses option theory, both academic and practical. The scope of this chapter does not allow a detailed analysis of the function of options. We look at options in a simplistic fashion. They are valuable as a delivery mechanism ("in the money") or not valuable for delivery ("out of the money").

Options are structured such that both parties agree to an interest rate and a delivery price (strike price). This price will be paid upon delivery of the MBS. The party buying the right to make delivery pays a fee for that right. The more attractive the strike price, the higher the fee. For example, a mortgage banker could purchase an option as follows:

Rate:	7.0%
Strike Price:	98.16/32 (98.50)
Amount:	$1,000,000
Fee:	1.0 points
Delivery:	120 days

After paying the fee, the mortgage banker has the option to deliver into the transaction as if it were a mandatory sale. A mortgage banker may choose not to deliver. In no event is the fee returned. If, in our example, the current market price on a 7.0% MBS after 120 days was 96.0/32 (96.00), the mortgage banker would exercise the option and make delivery. But if the market price at the end of 120 days was 100.0/32 (100.00), the mortgage banker would not deliver but would instead sell the loans into a new, immediate MBS sale at 100.0/32 (100.00). Of course, if there were no loans to deliver, there would be no buyout of a commitment since it is the mortgage banker's option to deliver.

Figure 2 represents the delivery preference on options. If the option in the money is more valuable than current market, the mortgage banker will deliver. If the current market is more advantageous, there is no delivery. We now have all the pieces necessary to match sales to pipeline. Figure 3 combines Figures 1 and 2. Mandatory coverage is shown by a solid area and the levels of optional coverage as indicated. Connecting the uppermost points of this figure, which represents the maximum desirable deliveries considering various market changes, gives a line that looks like a match for the expected closing line in Figure 1.

Figure 2

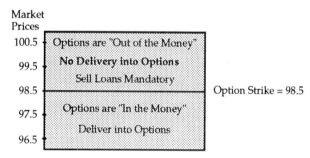

Figure 3

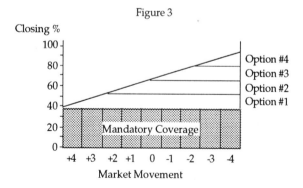

From here, it is a simple task to arrange the strike prices and option amounts to match any expected closing line. Various options can be sold at different strike prices to "stack" above mandatory sales. With this initial estimate of the closing function and the corresponding sale structure, constant feedback about actual closing experience validates and refines the model.

The Mortgage Investor

This discussion uses the commercial banking community to illustrate the challenges associated with holding mortgages on a balance sheet. We describe the risks and risk reduction aspects of various mortgage structures after briefly reviewing the origin and development of this complex asset class.

Mortgage-backed securities have increasingly become an investment choice for commercial banks. For the top 150 U.S. banks, mortgage securities as a percentage of the securities portfolio increased from 27% in 1987 to 52% in 1991 and 48% in 1992. This growth of MBS as an investment is rooted in two events — weak loan demand and new tax laws.

Commercial banks face growing competition for business loans from nonbank financial intermediaries. Corporations continue the trend that began in the late 1980s of bypassing banks through commercial paper issuance or through financing from new sources such as foreign banks, investment banks, and insurance companies. Commercial banks' loan-to-deposit ratios have consequently declined.

Sources of strong loan growth during the previous two decades—energy, foreign, agricultural, commercial real estate—continue to be weak and will not support sustained growth. Banks have sought to replace lost loans with higher–yielding investment securities. U.S. Treasuries, credit–risk–free and embedded option–risk–free investments have not provided sufficient yields for bank portfolios. Lengthening the maturity of the portfolio to increase the yield has not been prudent (as evidenced by the thrift industry) due to the changes in the interest rate risk profile. Instead, banks have taken advantage of the steep yield–curve environment and favorable regulatory capital rules by investing in the high–quality, higher–yielding MBS sector and funding their purchases with low–cost, short–term liabilities.

Furthermore, as the "bar gets higher" with respect to rating agencies, banks with profitability, good management, capital adequacy, and low troubled loans as a percent of assets will continue investing in mortgage-backed securities. The MBS market can be characterized by the crosscurrents generated by Treasury market volatility and the subsequent uncertainty regarding MBS cashflows. These factors cause the MBS to trade at higher yields than Treasuries. The relative malleability of mortgage cashflows for virtually any investment objective (fixed, variable, short or long term) explains the explosive growth of MBS in bank portfolios.

The Tax Reform Act of 1986 essentially eliminated leveraged purchases of newly acquired tax-exempt municipal bonds—an investment that afforded banks the highest after-tax yield. Under the old law, banks could deduct 80% of interest expense on indebtedness incurred or continued to purchase or carry tax–exempt obligations. The tax law change denied banks an interest expense deduction in direct proportion to their tax–exempt holdings, effectively placing banks on an equal footing with nonbank taxpayers.

The 1986 act also introduced a new type of trust device known as a Real Estate Mortgage Investment Conduit, or REMIC, a classification of the U.S. tax code designed to facilitate the marketing of multiple–class mortgage securities. REMICs are "pass–through" tax entities which hold mortgage collateral secured by real property and through which multiple classes of ownership interest can be issued under various legal forms. REMIC collateral includes whole loans, participating certificates, mortgage pass-throughs, STRIPS, streams of interest in a mortgage, senior/subordinated participations in mortgage pools, classes from other REMICs, CMO (collateralized mortgage obligations) debt, and other interests representing real estate debt.

REMIC legislation removed the federal tax obstacles to creating securities which were optimal from an accounting, regulatory, and economic standpoint. However, it did not amend the federal and state securities laws, state and local tax rules applying to investment entities, ERISA rules, or accounting conventions for MBS. REMIC legislation enhanced efficiency in the secondary mortgage market because of the tremendous flexibility it gave issuers to tailor mortgage securities to diverse investor needs. Seemingly similar MBS may have radically different performance profiles and intrinsic values. This is because of the single characteristic that distinguishes mortgage securities, Treasuries, municipals, and corporates from one another—the degree of uncertainty of the cashflow pattern. Treasuries, except for callable bonds, have certain cashflows. The cashflows of long-term corporates and municipals, however, are not known with certainty. These securities are not callable until a specified future date. With some degree of certainty, the investor can expect that the issuer will not irrationally exercise the call options (e.g., by calling the issues when the coupon rates fall below current market rates).

The uncertainty about the timing of cashflows for mortgage loans exists because the investor has granted the borrower/homeowner the option to prepay, or call, part or all of the mortgage at any time at par. The exercise of the option is a function not only of the current market rate, as is the case with corporates and municipals, but also of individual circumstances.

Characteristics

Pass-through securities are created when mortgages are pooled and undivided interests or participations in the pool are sold. Mortgage originators continue to service the underlying mortgages and to collect payments and "pass-through" principal and interest (less servicing, guarantee and other fees). The security holders receive pro–rata shares of resultant cashflows. By the end of 1992, pass-throughs, which are the predominant form of collateral for structured MBS, totaled $1.5 trillion.

A major advantage of agency MBS is their strong credit quality. Government National Mortgage Association (GNMA), Federal National Mortgage Association (FNMA), and Federal Home Loan Mortgage Corporation (FHLMC) pass–throughs and REMICs carry the guarantees of U.S. government agencies or government-sponsored enterprises and account for 90% of MBS. Nonagency mortgage securities are issued by thrifts, commercial banks, and private conduits. Their credit is enhanced by pool insurance, letters of credit, or subordinated interests. A subordinate MBS is fundamentally an asset with leveraged credit risk. The credit risk has been reduced by segmenting the subordination into a hierarchy of loss positions. The resulting variety of cashflows and credit structures offers a spectrum of risk alternatives, which range from AAA-rated, publicly offered securities to high–yielding, unrated private placements.

Since mortgage payments are made in arrears, payment delay also affects price. Delay decreases the current value of the stream of payments. The greater the delay, the lower the price for a given cashflow yield. GNMA pass–throughs with shorter delays trade at higher prices than FNMAs, which trade higher than FHLMCs. But while pass-throughs trade at spreads over Treasuries because they are less liquid and have more credit risk, the greatest contributor to the premium is option risk. The prepayment option in pass-throughs is comprised of both call (or contraction) risk and extension risk. The former is the risk that in a declining interest rate environment, the embedded call option granted to the borrower will be exercised (prepayment) and the investor will be forced to reinvest the cashflows at rates lower than the MBS coupon rates. Extension risk results when prepayments slow as interest rates rise and the investor is prevented from reinvesting cashflows at rates above the MBS coupon rates.

Factors affecting prepayment behavior include the prevailing mortgage rate, the characteristics underlying the mortgage pool, seasonality and the overall economic conditions.

The greater the difference between the current mortgage rates and the contract rate, the greater the incentive to refinance. It is questionable whether the basis point or percentage difference best explains recent behavior. The path and level of mortgage rates influence prepayment behavior and lead to "burnout," the slowing of prepayments when interest rates have not increased. Historically, if mortgage rates fall 200 basis points or more from their current levels, mortgagors who have +200 basis point premium mortgages will prepay. Premium burnout occurs after the interest–rate–sensitive mortgagors exit the pool, leaving only those who are less inclined to refinance. Burnout describes the path of prepayments holding interest rates constant. Path dependence relates to the impact of the path of previous interest rates on future prepayments.

Numerous characteristics of the underlying mortgage loans affect prepayments, including the contract rate; status (whether the loans are FHA/VA guaranteed or conventional); seasoning (conventionals season faster than GNMAS; and premiums season faster than current coupons, which season faster than discounts); rate terms (ARMs take longer to fully season; and the annual coupon, caps, and floors affect repayments); the pool factor (remaining mortgage balance outstanding relative to the original mortgage balance); and the geographics of the underlying properties (specified versus generic pools).

The seasonal pattern in prepayments is fairly constant and parallels the primary housing market, rising in the spring and peaking in late summer. General economic activity affects prepayment behavior through its effect on housing turnover. Prepayment uncertainty is compounded by social, economic, and institutional factors. These include the high cost of refinancing, the period of residence after refinancing needed to recoup the upfront costs, limited appreciation in regional housing prices, tightening of mortgage underwriting criteria, and reduced mortgage insurance activity of government agencies.

The relationship between prepayment behavior and interest rates is more difficult to project. Clearly, however, the slope of the yield curve strongly influences prepayment behavior. Housing activity in 1992 disproved the often-stated rule that an interest rate differential of 150 to 200 basis points is required to make refinancing attractive. With the yield curve at historically steep levels, mortgage product priced off the shorter end (15–year mortgages, balloons, ARMs) offers homeowners significantly lower interest rates than traditional 30–year mortgages. In this steep yield curve environment, mortgage bankers have made refinancing easier and cheaper to preserve their servicing rights. This has been very positive for the mortgage bankers and homeowners but very detrimental for the MBS investor. Changes in the yield curve affect the valuation of a security and the forecasted prepayments, which influence the security's cashflows.

Valuation

All MBS valuation methods revolve around the treatment of prepayment uncertainty. The relationship between interest rates and MBS prepayment rates directly influences MBS pricing. In a bond market rally, prepayment rates rise, reducing the price gains of mortgage-backed securities. However, in a bear market or rising rate environment, prepayment rates slow down and prices fall. This price movement pattern is referred to as "negative convexity" (Figure 4). An investor who is long a mortgage or MBS can view the position as a combination of two assets—long a noncallable bond, which has a convex price yield curve, and short a prepayment option, which the borrower owns. The option premium is basically the yield spread of MBS to Treasuries. The value of the investor's composite asset equals the value of the bond (which is a long) minus the value of the option (which is a potential short).

When current market rates are high relative to the mortgage coupon, the borrower's prepayment option is virtually worthless. A deeply out-of-the-money option will not gain appreciably in value as rates start to drop. Thus, for deep–discount MBS, the price yield curve resembles the Treasury curve. As rates continue to drop, however, the prepayment option increases in value. Since the investor is short the option, the increase in option value is subtracted from the increase in bond value. As rates continue to fall, the increase in option value overwhelms the increase in bond value at some point, and the decrease in market yield produces a decrease in price performance. This is a fact of life for premium MBS. An investor who considers an MBS product for $105 and knows that a further drop in market rates could result in borrowers prepaying at par will reduce the bid if rates continue to fall.

The recent and prolonged refinancing boom suggests that the weighted–average outstanding coupon of the universe of mortgage products is declining. That is, the embedded convexity risk in the outstanding mortgage sector is being reduced, with significant long-term consequences. The single most important reason to be concerned about investing in MBS—negative convexity—is diminished.

Furthermore, investors encounter fewer implied absolute dollars and cashflow. A downward coupon trend may diminish the investment universe by several percentage points. The dependence of prepayment rates on interest rates affects not only MBS returns but also their interest rate risk. Modified duration, a traditional measure of the price sensitivity of fixed–income securities, gives the percent change in price caused by a 100–basis–point shift in the yield curve. Modified duration is a reasonable price sensitivity measure for securities with constant cashflows. It is often inadequate for MBS because, again, prepayment rates vary as interest rates change; and 100 basis points may bring the MBS to the prepayment threshold. Mortgage–to–Treasury spreads have served well as past indicators of the relative value of mortgage securities.

A mortgage security has value if its current yield spread over a comparable Treasury is considered wide by historical standards. However, a true relative–value analysis has to incorporate projected future returns on mortgage pass-throughs. Mortgage securities will only have true value when they have the potential to outperform comparable Treasuries under various interest rate scenarios.

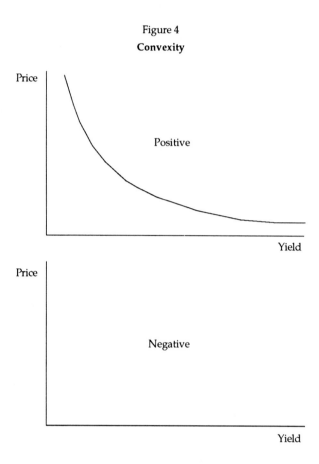

Figure 4

Convexity

Multiple approaches to valuing MBS exist because no single methodology completely explains their price performance. Although static cashflow–yield analysis ignores many critical factors of MBS valuation, it provides a historical perspective on the MBS market. Total–rate–of–return scenario analysis is a valuable extension of the static cashflow yield analysis because it assesses the relative attractiveness of different MBS coupons in a holding period. The option– adjusted spread (OAS) Monte Carlo models further extend total–rate– of–return scenario analysis by simulating MBS performance over many interest rate paths.

Additionally, assuming the relationship between interest rates and prepayment rates is correctly specified, such models provide MBS risk and return measures. The refinancing threshold pricing model differs from the OAS approach by directly modeling the refinancing decision of the individual mortgage holder instead of specifying aggregate MBS prepayment rates as a function of interest rates. However, both the OAS and the refinancing threshold pricing models are black boxes into which an investor puts assumptions and out of which come risk and return measures. An investor must determine the sensitivity of these models' results to the accuracy of the assumptions used.

In managing a portfolio, the investor analyzes, predicts, and protects (1) the economic value of the interest rate spread on mortgage securities and (2) the market value of the securities themselves as interest rates vary. The investor in MBS seeks to minimize negative convexity by equating the convexities of MBS to those of liabilities.

For example, a duration-matched but convexity–mismatched balance sheet is thought to be hedged against interest rate risk. A portfolio of GNMA 9% mortgages has negative convexity while liabilities with fixed cashflows have positive convexity; that is, they become less price sensitive (shorter in duration) when rates rise and more price sensitive (longer in duration) when rates fall. When interest rates rise, the hedge deteriorates as the MBS increases in price sensitivity; liabilities do the opposite (Figure 5). Rebalancing such a portfolio produces a loss to spread income and/or capital values. If rates decline, there is a net capital loss, and income falls below expectations as average assets roll over for reinvestment before the liabilities funding them. All else equal, returns on a portfolio with higher convexity are expected to exceed those on one with lower convexity.

Figure 5

Convexity in Asset/Liability Management

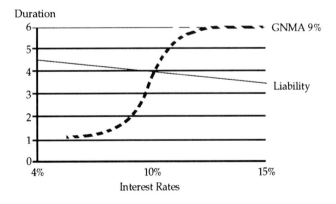

Structured MBS

Pass-throughs lack "call protection," meaning that rapid prepayments may shorten the average life of a mortgage pool. They also have "extension risk," meaning that a slowdown in prepayments lengthens average life. Portfolio managers who invest in pass-throughs must tailor their portfolios to reflect not only the desired duration but also required convexity and exposure to prepayment trends. The creation of securities backed by mortgage loans resolved this dilemma by offering increased call protection and decreased extension risk. Such securities trade at tighter spreads to Treasuries than pass-throughs and increase the investor base for mortgage-backed products by appealing to a broader, more risk-averse class of investors.

Collateralized mortgage obligations (CMO) resulted from using the cashflows of long-maturity, monthly pay collateral to create securities with short, intermediate, and long final maturities and expected average lives. The Tax Reform Act of 1986 permitted the election of REMIC status and provided tax and accounting advantages to CMO investors. By segmenting the components of mortgage cash flows—principal, interest, and embedded options—issuers of these multiclass securities created serially maturing bonds from the collateral with varying degrees of call protection. CMOs are bonds that are collateralized by whole-loan mortgages, mortgage pass-through securities, or stripped mortgage-backed securities. In addition to the security afforded by the fully dedicated collateral, some CMO issues also have a minimum reinvestment rate and minimum sinking fund guarantees. The cashflows generated by the assets in the collateral pool are first used to pay interest and then to pay principal to the CMO bondholders.

CMOs are distinguished from traditional pass-throughs by the principal payment process. In a pass-through, each investor receives a pro–rata distribution of any principal and interest payments (net of servicing); and because mortgages are self-amortizing assets, a pass-through investor also receives some return of principal each month. Complete return of principal and the final maturity of the pass-through occur when the final mortgage in the pool is fully paid. This results not only in a great deal of uncertainty with regard to the timing of principal return but also in a large difference between average life (when one half of the original principal has been repaid) and final maturity.

The CMO substitutes a principal paydown priority schedule among tranches (classes of bonds) for the pro–rata process found in pass-throughs, which redistributes the prepayment risk. CMO bonds vary significantly from the underlying mortgage collateral in average life, duration, convexity, prepayment risk, pay period and final maturity. The only constraint is that the cashflow from the CMO collateral meet the aggregate payment requirements of the individual bonds. The first structures were sequentials or "plain vanilla" CMOs in which only one class of bondholders at a time received principal until it was paid off. To further reduce prepayment risk for some classes of bonds, tranches with a specified principal repayment schedule were introduced. The repayment schedule was guaranteed as long as the actual prepayment speeds were within a designated range. These classes of bonds, called planned amortization class bonds (PACs), protect against both call and extension risk and provide a structure similar to sinking fund corporate bonds. Structures with PAC bonds carry lower yields and lesser average life variability than collateral, but PAC support bonds (non-PACs in the same deal) have wider yield spreads to Treasuries and greater average life variability than collateral.

Moreover, some subordinated MBS have among the most stable principal cashflows because of a prepayment lockout feature required by the credit rating agencies. The prepayment lockout keeps the dollar value of the subordinate essentially fixed, and the dollar value of the pool as a whole declines as a function of prepayment rates. Fixed-rate mortgages commonly have a full lockout on prepayments for the first five years and a partial lockout for another four years. Such a structure shifts the interest in the pool's prepayments from the subordinate class to the senior class (and only later back to the subordinate class). Although there is extension risk, the prepayment lockout's call protection puts subordinates in a similar category as PACs and other CMO tranches with protected cashflows. The emphasis on the subordinate's credit risk sometimes obscures this benefit.

Many variations in coupon structure have been developed, including fixed–rate bonds with the coupon paid currently over the life of the bond, structures allowing for the accrual of interest, floating coupon levels and zero coupons. These recent "alphabet-soup" innovations in CMOs are best described as a set of rules which determine the order and nature of principal bond redemption and the type and level of the coupons.

The CMO floating–rate bond further expanded an investor base for MBS and CMOs by attracting overseas investors. This market depends not only on the features of the CMO floater but also on the demand for residuals from these deals. The floating–rate bonds have coupons which periodically reset over an index, most commonly the London Interbank Offering Rate (LIBOR), the 11th District Cost of Funds (COFI), the 1–year Treasury rate (CMT), or the Certificate of Deposit (CD) rate. Investors use such CMO floaters as passive substitutes for shorter–term money market holdings. Investors save on the cost of constantly rolling over short–term investments as they mature, and the floating–rate instruments provide slightly higher coupons. Floaters are defensive instruments. They offer lower interest rate risk than fixed–rate debt, lower price volatility than fixed–rate bonds, and closer pricing to par. Floaters allow better asset/liability matching for institutions with floating–rate liabilities and liabilities with low interest rate volatilities.

Because fixed–rate mortgages generally serve as collateral to support floating–rate CMO bonds, the bonds must be capped to ensure that the weighted–average coupon (WAC) of all the classes, including the floating–rate bonds with their coupons set at their caps, does not exceed the WAC of the underlying collateral. This requirement has led to a variety of structures. While the embedded cap in a floater decreases the value of the bond because market rates may rise above the cap during the bond's lifetime, the margin over the index can compensate for the cap rate since the bonds without the cap could presumably be sold at a rate equal to or less than the index. This feature brings the floater back to earth—when interest rates approach the caps, the floater's negative convexity shows itself. Evaluating fixed–rate CMOs is primarily an analysis of how prepayments affect the security value. Evaluation of floating–rate bonds concentrates on the index and life cap.

Adjustable–rate mortgages are a hybrid of floating–rate notes, interest rate options, and fixed–rate mortgages. ARMs have coupon rates that reset at a spread over an index at specified intervals. However, they also have embedded interest rate options—periodic and life-of-loan caps, floors, and maximum payment changes that restrict the level of the mortgage rate when it resets. A floating-rate note maintains a constant spread to an underlying index on reset dates, but the restrictions of mortgage rate movements in an ARM may vary the spread between the mortgage rate and the index.

Periodic caps denote the maximum change in the mortgage rate at each reset date. Life-of-loan caps limit the mortgage rate to a certain range above its origination level. These caps can present interest rate risk to the investor by making the floating-rate mortgage act like a fixed-rate mortgage. Caps shift some interest rate risk from borrowers to lenders. If interest rates rise and the caps become binding, the lender protects the borrower from "payment shock" by providing funds at the capped rate rather than the market rate. Floors limit downward adjustments in the mortgage rate. When reached, they may increase prepayment speeds. Like fixed-rate mortgages, ARMs are amortizing assets with 30-year final maturities subject to prepayments. To value an ARM, the investor must understand both the floating– and fixed-rate characteristics. ARMs usually originate at below market ("teaser") rates to attract and/or qualify home buyers. As the teaser period ends, the ARM coupon adjusts toward its fully-indexed rate, which equals the index value plus a spread (net margin). "Gross margin" refers to the spread of the ARM loan above its index. "Net margin" is the spread over the index received by investors and is equal to gross margin less servicing fees and securitization expenses.

Commercial banks' increased interest in the short-duration sector of the mortgage market is partly a result of FASB 115, the accounting rule change which moves financial institutions closer to mark-to-market accounting. This change will likely produce a continuing shift in bank assets to ARMs and floating-rate CMOs because of their low price volatility and modulated interest rate risk. Other products used to neutralize interest rate risk and price volatility are derivative MBS.

Traditional derivative products such as futures contracts can also hedge interest rate risk. MBS investors, however, are concerned with hedging both interest rate risk and prepayment risk. Stripped MBS can hedge these two risks at the same time. Hedging involves creating a position with a zero duration, i.e., a position that quells the price volatility of an interest-sensitive security. The price of a security with positive duration moves opposite to interest rates; the price of a security with negative duration parallels interest rates. While a pass-through assigns the cash flow from the underlying pool of mortgages on a pro–rata basis to security holders, a stripped MBS is created by altering the distribution from pro–rata to unequal. Consequently, the price/yield relationship of stripped MBS differs from that of the underlying mortgage pool. Stripped MBS include synthetic coupon pass–throughs, interest only (IO)/principal only (PO) securities, and CMO strips.

A PO has positive duration and affords leveraging potential for hedging because it can be bought at a discount. A PO can hedge mortgage product with negative duration, such as mortgage serving and pass–throughs selling at a premium.

IO has negative duration because it moves in the same direction as interest rate changes when mortgages are declining. IO investors want prepayments to be slow because they receive interest on the outstanding principal only. If this amount declines and less dollar interest is received, the amount paid for the IO may not be recovered if prepayments are too fast. An instrument with IO characteristics should be used to hedge the interest rate and prepayment risk for a portfolio of discount pass-throughs. IOs and POs are high–risk securities because of their price volatility. However, mortgage product with IO or PO characteristics can be used to effectively hedge a portfolio's interest rate and prepayment risk (Figure 6).

Figure 6

Relationship Between Price and Mortgage Rates for a Pass–through, PO and IO

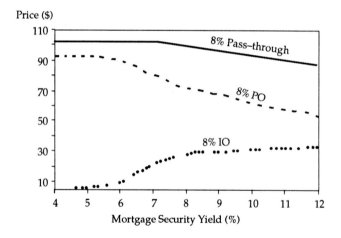

Conclusion

The diversity and complexity of MBS offer substantial opportunities for the experienced and pitfalls for the novice. Failure to keep abreast of the ever-expanding menu of exotic MBS instruments can mean forfeiting profits and risking losses. MBS engineers want to create products that increase call protection and decrease extension risk.

Understanding the interplay between interest rate risk, prepayment risk, and credit risk that results from these various structures is the key to successfully accomplishing investment objectives with MBS.

Portfolio management strategies should be designed to protect the economic value of the interest rate spread on mortgage securities as well as the market value over various interest rate scenarios. Portfolio management strategies should be balance sheet management strategies. Recent regulatory and accounting directives mandate this objective by segregating the portfolio based on risk and intent. Portfolios that institutions have positive intent and ability to hold to maturity are classified as held–to–maturity securities and reported at amortized cost. Securities that are bought and held principally for selling in the near term are classified as trading securities and reported at fair value with unrealized gains and losses included in earnings. Securities not classified as either held–to–maturity securities or trading securities are available–for–sale securities and reported at fair value with unrealized gains and losses excluded from earnings and reported separately in shareholders' equity.

Obviously, anything other than an investment designation may inject significant fluctuations into a financial institution's earnings and capital ratios. From regulatory and accounting perspectives, the "trading versus investment" rules prohibit transactions in which gains are recognized, losses are deferred or embedded, and capital is overstated. The choice between active and passive portfolio strategies is based on knowing the risk/reward relationships of various aspects of MBS. Understanding the optimum balance sheet construct and using MBS to reduce income sensitivity to fluctuations in interest rates, the MBS investor maintains adequate capitalization and achieves a greater net interest margin.

Elements of Quantitative Risk Management

Ayman Hindy, Professor, Graduate School of Business, Stanford University

Introduction

Using derivative securities for risk management purposes has increased dramatically over the past decade. Volatility of interest rates, exchange rates, and prices of major commodities stimulated the demand for risk management tools. Advances in the theory and practice of creating and pricing derivatives facilitate the supply of new securities. This chapter provides a framework for managing price risk with derivative securities.[1]

There are three major themes in this chapter. The first stresses a functional approach to risk management. In a functional approach, a few basic risk factors are identified; and all assets are described mainly in terms of exposure to these factors. This contrasts with the institutional approach in which the name or legal attributes of an asset are given primary consideration in its uses. The second theme is the treatment of risk factors and securities as an integrated portfolio. In particular, special attention is paid to the correlation among changes in the risk factors.[2] The third theme is the observation that many ideas of quantitative risk management can be utilized in other strategic, nonquantitative, decision–making situations.

A Simple Framework for Risk Management

Assuming and managing risk is the essence of business decision making. Investing in a new technology, hiring a new employee, choosing a pension plan, or launching a marketing campaign are all decisions with uncertain outcomes. Risk is unavoidable as long as we do not know what the future brings. As a result, all major management decisions are choices of how much risk to take and how to manage those risks.

Risk management is fairly simple to describe. The risks of a proposed action may be as simple as buying a single security or as complex as building a new factory in eastern Europe. Understanding the risks means grasping the range and likelihood of the possible outcomes of the intended action. The trader who purchases a security understands the risk when he knows the possible movements of its price over the intended holding period. Similarly, the board of a multinational corporation planning a new venture in eastern Europe understands the risks when it knows how the outcome of the project is linked to the economic and political environment in the host country. Some assessment of the likelihood of possible changes in the foreign investment climate is required to understand the risks. We use the term "exposure measurement" to describe this first step of the risk management process.

The second step in the process is tool analysis. This step involves analyzing various tools that can alter risk exposure. The important characteristic of any risk management tool is its risk–cost tradeoff. For example, the trader who is about to purchase a security might consider hedging: purchasing a derivative security such that the combined position is close to risk free. The trader should be able to analyze whether the price of the derivative security is commensurate with the benefits of risk reduction. Similarly, the board of the multinational firm might consider engaging in a joint venture with a local firm in the host country. The costs of such an action must be understood relative to the perceived benefits.

Exposure management is a third step. The alternatives range from no exposure, to a selective exposure with some benefits traded for some protection in unfavorable events, to a magnified exposure in which potential gains and potential losses are deliberately increased. For example, the multinational firm might decide to scrap its plans to invest in a particular country, or the trader might decide to purchase a security and utilize a particular hedge. The trader may alternatively decide to magnify his exposure to the price of the security by taking a highly leveraged position.

New information about subsequent events affects risk exposure. For example, the trader learns about new prices and the board of directors learns about constitutional crises in the host country. Effort is expended in responding to changes in exposure. Effective exposure management results from preparedness for different future outcomes. Managers who anticipate a range of contingencies and plan corresponding actions are ready to respond. Failure to anticipate and plan adversely affects the quality of the response.

The final step in the risk management process is performance evaluation. How accurate was diagnosis and exposure measurement? How useful were the risk management tools used? Were risk–cost tradeoffs properly estimated? Were events a surprise? What can be learned from the experience, and how can the quality of risk management be improved?

The implementation of each step varies from business to business, from one management style to another, and from one time to another. Risk management in the financial services industry is not the same as in the electronics business. Circumstances, institutions and managers are different. A position in a well–understood derivative security whose payoff depends on the value of a widely observed index, for example a call option on S&P 500, offers a very clear measurement of risk exposure. On the other hand, an investment decision in a foreign country with no recent history of legal and political stability may involve few, if any, insights into the potential hazards and opportunities.

Similarly, risk management tools vary considerably. Some markets offer a large menu of risk management tools for quick, effective use. Other situations offer very limited possibilities for exposure management. Finally, some businesses cannot survive without formal risk management programs that are constantly evaluated and developed— successful investment banks, for example. Other businesses have a different culture and pay little attention to risk management.

Such arrangements notwithstanding, it is productive to outline a simple framework that highlights the important features of risk management. The four–step mode described above captures the essence of the process. Although many risk management situations differ materially in the implementation of each step, our description generally accommodates these differences. Thus we may compare risk management situations and adopt implementation features from one program to another.

Many risks are managed quantitatively. Risk exposure is measured by some numerical index. Risk–cost tradeoffs of many tools are described by numerical valuation formulas. Exposure can be managed and performance analyzed using quantitative algorithms on computers. The model described above corresponds well to quantitative methods. Quantitative risk management (QRM) is a growing industry. Many situations that were once managed based on judgment and experience can be better analyzed quantitatively. Furthermore, new problems arise that can only be analyzed with QRM techniques. The following sections describe QRM when it works best: managing risk in a portfolio of financial securities. In this domain, the problem is well understood; and many powerful techniques have been successfully applied. A subsequent section argues that the techniques of QRM are likely to emerge as powerful and useful concepts in their domains.

Exposure Measurement

This section discusses exposure measurement. We limit the focus to financial and commodity markets. We discuss decisions on how to allocate funds to different securities and commodities and how to use risk management tools, particularly derivative securities, in this context. We explain how risk can be measured using a small number of indices, or risk factors, that reflect the changes in major sectors of the financial markets. We also describe the historical behavior of these risk factors.

A Functional Approach to Risk Management

Financial securities include the following: common stock in all listed corporations in the U.S., Europe, Japan and emerging markets; fixed–income obligations of the U.S. and other governments; money market instruments; corporate bonds of different investment grades; municipal bonds and mortgage–backed securities; exchange–traded and over–the–counter derivative securities such as options, forward contracts, future contracts and swaps; hybrid securities such as commodity–linked bonds; and investment commodities such as gold and silver. There are many differences among these securities. For example, stocks, bonds and options differ in their legal, accounting, and tax treatment and according to the structure of the markets where they are traded. These distinctions are important—they establish property rights and corporate control. However, for an investor who cares only about returns, such distinctions may be meaningless and even misleading.

Consider, for example, a manager of a Canadian pension fund who is prohibited by law from investing more than a certain fraction of the pension fund assets in foreign securities but who would like to diversify by investing a higher fraction in the U.S. equity market. This manager can effectively invest in the U.S. equity market by purchasing a Canadian bond whose coupon payment is linked to the return on the S&P 500. Such a bond, or synthetic U.S. equity instrument, can be issued by the Canadian subsidiary of a U.S. investment bank. Although such a security is legally a Canadian bond, it is effectively a U.S. equity instrument.

This simple example shows that any financial institution could, in principle, issue a synthetic security in one market and link payment to an index, such as equity return or foreign currency rates in another market. As long as investors are not concerned about issues such as corporate control, the synthetic security substitutes perfectly for a direct investment in the underlying index. The synthetic security can be packaged in any convenient legal form without changing its nature as a claim to the returns on the chosen index. In many circumstances, the synthetic security may even be preferred to the direct investment. This arises, for example, when the synthetic security reduces transactions costs or withholding taxes. In such cases, the synthetic security reduces the trading frictions and restrictions created by jurisdictional differences in accounting and tax treatment.

The concept of a synthetic security whose payoff is linked to one or more indices forces us to examine the traditional classification of financial assets into stocks and bonds. It behooves us to abandon this view, which is based on legal and institutional conventions, in favor of a more functional approach. We should think of any security as a claim to some future cashflows, the amount of which will be determined by the value of one or more basic indices or risk factors. For example, the synthetic Canadian bond is a package of quarterly cashflows whose amount is related to the return on the S&P 500 index.

A mortgage–backed security provides another example. It is a sequence of cashflows whose timing and amount is related to the level of mortgage interest rates, among other things. A third example is a yen–dominated futures contract on the Nikkei index. For a U.S. investor, the payoffs of such a contract are related to the level of the index in yen and the yen/U.S. dollar exchange rate.

A change from the institutional to the functional view means that in thinking about holdings in different securities, one should consider the risk factors that affect the value of the portfolio rather than the particular legal form of the securities. Although a share of IBM and a bond whose coupon payments are linked to the returns on IBM are two legally distinct securities, they are both exposed to the same risk factor: the performance of IBM. With the functional point of view, any investment or risk management decision is a choice of how to expose funds to the movements of the basic risk factors. This choice of exposure is obtained by taking positions in some securities whose values are tied to the risk factors. We may also think of securities as legal containers of different combinations of exposures to the basic risk factors. Risk management may thus be viewed as a process of analyzing financial securities to determine the magnitude of exposure of their values to the basic risk factors and combining these securities in a portfolio to achieve a target exposure.

The functional approach is a powerful idea and a useful practice. Conceptually, investors need to consider the risk factors, which are far fewer in number than all the varieties of traded securities. The approach allows investment strategies to be designed and risk management to be analyzed clearly and consistently. It also makes different portfolios and investment strategies easy to compare by isolating their basic risk elements. The approach also emphasizes the separation between form and function. After deciding on the required risk exposure to the basic factors, or the content of the strategy, an investor may choose the specific securities to implement this exposure. There are typically many ways to implement any particular exposure. For example, one may choose a direct investment in an index, a derivative security based on the index, or a swap. This conceptual and operational separation between risk exposures and their implementation in the form of specific securities are the major advantages of the functional approach.

Dynamics of Risk Factors

What are the basic risk factors? No "standard" risk factors are unanimously accepted by the financial community. There is, however, agreement that any list of risk factors should include those that (1) affect the equity markets in the major industrialized countries; (2) determine the short–, medium–, and long–term interest rates; (3) shape the exchange rates between major currencies; and (4) drive the prices of major commodities such as oil and gold.

Some simple indices measure these risk factors. For example, the risk factors in the U.S., Japanese and British equity markets can be measured, among other ways, by the S&P 500, Nikkei, and FTSE indices, respectively. The risk factor in the U.S. short– and long–term bond markets can be measured by the prices of 1–year and 30–year bonds, respectively. Investors choose indices that best reflect the risk factors of their investments. Furthermore, indices vary in quality and accuracy. The U.S. Treasury bills index, for example, is based on accurate trading prices in liquid markets. Other indices are based on sporadic prices in rather illiquid markets.

Although all indices change randomly over time, they differ in the statistical properties of their random movement. Some indices (e.g., the return on U.S. Treasury bills) move in a rather narrow range; others (e.g., the returns on U.S. growth stocks) exhibit large swings from one month to the next. This variability, which we express using the standard deviation of monthly returns, is one measure of the volatility of the underlying risk factor. Risk factors and their representative indices also vary in the size and direction of average movement. We will measure the size of the expected returns for any factor by the average historical monthly return. Table 1 summarizes the sample average and standard deviation for the monthly returns on a variety of indices.

Table 1

Mean and Standard Deviation of Annual Returns on the Basic Indices

Risk Factor	Average Annual Return	Standard Deviation
U.S. T–bills	08.23	00.94
U.S. long–term bonds	13.08	12.64
U.S. corporate bonds	12.72	09.08
U.S. mortgages	12.84	09.94
Foreign bonds	11.76	12.47
U.S. value stocks	15.60	15.14
U.S. growth stocks	15.72	17.42
European stocks	12.48	17.74
Japanese stocks	17.40	25.39
European currencies	08.04	10.63
Japanese yen	11.28	12.40
U.S. real estate	10.56	15.73
U.S. venture capital	13.20	14.13

The table shows that expected returns and volatility of returns vary among the risk factors. However, some of the risk factors tend to move together. For example, all equity markets fell in October 1987. We can capture such a tendency by computing the correlation coefficients among different risk factors. For example, the correlation coefficient between the returns on U.S. long–term Treasury bonds and U.S. corporate bonds is 0.94, but the correlation between U.S. mortgages and U.S. value stocks is only 0.29. Understanding the correlations among risk factors is essential for developing successful risk management strategies. Table 2 documents the correlation coefficients among the risk factors in Table 1 from January 1980 to December 1992.

The statistics in Tables 1 and 2 crudely describe the movement of the risk factors at any time. These statistics are computed from historical records of risk factor movements. There is no reason to believe that history will repeat itself and that past patterns of movement will continue in the future. The behavior of the risk factors and their correlations change as a result of monetary policy changes, economic contraction and growth, and political events. Historical estimates should be considered only as a point of departure. Statistical analysis confirms that movements of the indices from January 1980 to December 1992 were not the same at all times. For example, volatility of all equity indices increased from July 1987 to June 1988 relative to earlier periods. Similarly, the correlations among the movements of the major European currencies changed suddenly in September 1992 when England and Italy withdrew from the European Monetary System.

Table 2

Correlations Among Annual Returns on the Basic Indices

	Treasury bills	Long-term T–bonds	Corporate bonds	Mortgages	Foreign bonds	Value stocks	Growth stocks
T–bills	1.00	0.16	0.21	0.21	0.01	-0.70	-.11
Long T-bonds		1.00	0.94	0.89	0.43	0.33	0.33
Corporate bonds			1.00	0.95	0.42	0.35	0.31
Mortgages				1.00	0.39	0.29	0.25
Foreign banks					1.00	0.07	0.60
Value stocks						1..00	0.91
Growth stocks							1.00

	European stocks	Japanese stocks	European currencies	Japanese yen	Real estate	Venture capital
T–bills	0.12	0.00	-0.40	0.00	-0.2	-.11
Long T–bonds	0.24	0.16	0.18	0.19	0.27	0.07
Corporate bonds	0.25	0.15	0.19	0.20	0.05	0.10
Mortgages	0.22	0.11	0.20	0.74	0.23	0.05
Foreign bonds	0.51	0.56	0.83	0.85	0.09	0.10
Value stocks	0.60	0.27	-.03	-.05	0.74	0.52
Growth stocks	0.58	0.26	0.01	-.02	0.68	0.56

	European stocks	Japanese stocks	European currencies	Japanese yen	Real estate	Venture capital
European stocks	1.00	0.52	0.47	0.36	0.54	0.41
Japanese stocks		1.00	0.35	0.62	0.24	0.20
European currencies			1.00	0.67	-.09	-.01
Japanese yen				1.00	-.06	0.09
Real estate					1.00	0.58
Venture capital						1.00

Statistics computed from the history of any index should be treated only as preliminary estimates of the future behavior of that index. These estimates should be modified using all available information about changes in the environment and their likely impact on the risk factors. Successful risk management requires constant monitoring of the risk factors and continual adjustment of the expectations of their future behavior. In particular, special attention should be given to exogenous events that might change the volatility of the risk factors and their correlations. Such events include actions by central banks, announcements by key policy makers in the industrial economies, and changes in regulations and tax laws.

In summary, the basic risk factors affecting the portfolio of invested funds over the relevant investment horizon should be identified. These factors should be measured using reliable and accurate indices of traded securities. The nature of the random movement of the factors over the relevant decision horizon must be understood. In particular, it is important to have a good estimate of the volatility of each basic index and the correlation among the indices. Many sources can provide such estimates. They should be augmented by an analysis of all events that might affect the volatility and correlation of the indices. The probability of "significant events" that lead to sudden, large changes in the value of the risk factors should be estimated. A sudden cut in key interest rates or devaluation of a major currency are examples of such events. This process includes the following key elements:

1. A list of major risk factors and the indices used to measure them. There are N such factors measured by N indices, denoted by $x_1, x_2, \cdots, x_N$.

2. An estimate of the volatility of the changes in each index and the correlation among the changes in the indices. We record this information in the $N \times N$ variance–covariance matrix V. We also use the term "volatility matrix" to refer to V. The element $v_{ij} \in V$, in the ith row and j^{th} column of the matrix, is an estimate of the covariance between the changes of the indices x_i and x_j over the decision horizon. As usual, v_{ii} is an estimate of the variance of changes in x_i for $i = 1, 2, \cdots, N$.

3. A description of major events that lead to sudden, large changes in each index and estimates of the probability of such events over the relevant horizon.

The statistics presented in Tables 1 and 2 are preliminary estimates of the volatility matrix V corresponding to the chosen risk indices.

Major financial institutions organize their trading and risk management activities along market lines, with traders specializing in a small number of securities in a single market. Naturally, such specialists focus on the risk factors they face in their own markets. Division–wide or firm–wide risk management should analyze the risk factors as an integrated portfolio. In particular, correlations among individual risk factors should be carefully studied. The portfolio approach is far superior to approaches that do not utilize the correlations among the risk factors. Additionally, it can lead to better allocation of capital among the different trading groups within an institution.

Tool Analysis

This section discusses the risk–cost tradeoffs for derivative securities, the major risk management tools in financial markets. In particular, we show how to describe any derivative security as a contingent claim whose cashflows vary with the basic risk factors. We then explain the basic arbitrage pricing ideas used to compute the prices of contingent claims. For example, we compute the famous Black–Scholes option pricing formula based on these ideas. We also discuss the dynamic trading strategies that can be used to manufacture, or hedge, a position in a derivative security. Finally, we show how one can organize all the relevant information about a derivative security in a convenient "risk profile."

After identifying the basic risk factors and the associated indices, $\{x_1, x_2, \cdots x_N\}$, together with the volatility matrix V, one can analyze any security whose payoffs are linked to the values of the basic indices. For such a security, one should ask the following questions:

1. What are the values and timing of the cashflows? How do they vary with the future value of the indices $\{x_1, x_2, \cdots x_N\}$?

2. What is the price of the security? How does it depend on the current value of $\{x_1, x_2, \cdots x_N\}$ and volatility matrix V?

3. How does the value of the security change when the risk factors or their volatility matrix change?

Contingent Payoffs

Answers to the first question describe the cashflows and their variation with the value of the risk factors. This information helps develop a portfolio of securities that meet specific cashflow requirements such as guaranteed minimum available cashflow. In addition, understanding the timing of the cashflows and their correlation with the value of the risk factors is essential for computing the price of the security.

There are many different types of contingent cashflows. Some cashflows are easily described. For example, a Treasury bill is a claim to a fixed amount of U.S. dollars at its maturity. A forward contract on Deutsche marks is a claim to the difference between the forward price and spot price of Deutsche marks at maturity. In a slight variation, a futures contract is a claim to daily cashflows, until maturity, equal to daily changes in the settlement price. A simple interest rate swap is a claim to quarterly or semiannual cashflows equal to the difference between a fixed rate and variable rate on some notional amount. These simple payoffs are "linear" in that the claimholder gets a proportional amount, positive or negative, of the change in the underlying index.

Options of different types provide "nonlinear" payoffs. The simplest option, a European call on a non–dividend–paying stock, is a claim to the excess of the stock price at maturity over the exercise price. Since the option holder does not have any obligation if the stock price at maturity is lower than the exercise price, the resulting payoff is nonlinear or asymmetric. Using different combinations of options, in spreads, straddles, and strangles, one can manufacture a variety of nonlinear payoffs from the value of the stock.

Some payoffs are rather hard to predict in both timing and amount. For example, the payoffs from a mortgage–backed security depend on the refinancing decisions of the mortgage borrowers. Such refinancing decisions are partly linked to the general level of mortgage rates. Additionally, there is an independent prepayment component because of job changes, relocations, and other idiosyncratic factors. A sophisticated statistical model is needed to predict the timing and amount of cashflows on mortgage–backed and other asset-backed securities.

In principle, it is possible to design any desired pattern of cashflows through either a custom–made contract with an investment bank or an exchange–traded security. For example, U.S.–based investors who wish to participate in the gains of the Japanese equity markets without being exposed to the dollar/yen exchange rate risk may buy a futures contract whose futures price is denominated in U.S. dollars. The futures price is based on the level of the Nikkei index multiplied by a fixed U.S. dollar/yen exchange rate. Investors might also be interested in a contract that pays quarterly the maximum of the return on two equity indices in two different countries. Such a contract can be further modified by fixing the minimum quarterly payment. The possibilities for generating different patterns of contingent cashflows are limited only by investors' demand and the ability of financial institutions to evaluate and manage the risks of supplying these cashflows.

Arbitrage Pricing

Computing the price of the security is the next important step. We use P and A to denote the price and the attributes, respectively (any value–relevant parameters), of the security. A includes such characteristics as the maturity of the security, exercise price (if any), minimum and maximum cashflows, and the formulas that describe how the cashflows depend on the future values of the risk factors. To price the security, one needs to understand the relationship between the price and the current values of the risk factors, the current estimate of the volatility matrix, and the attributes of the security. Ideally, one would express this relationship in the form:

$$P = F(x_1, x_2, \cdots, x_N, V, A),$$ (1)

where F is some algebraic expression or a tabular representation of the relationship between $P, \{x_1, x_2, \cdots, x_N\}$, V, and A.

Systematic development of pricing relationships as in (1) began with Black and Scholes[3] and with Merton's[4] analysis of stock options. Although many pricing models have been developed subsequently, the basic idea of Black and Scholes is fundamental to all models. Black, Scholes, and Merton argue as follows: In many circumstances, it is possible to duplicate the cashflows of the contingent security by trading in the underlying index and borrowing or lending. Typically, such duplication requires frequent trading and dynamic adjustment of the portfolio holdings as the value of the risk factors changes. Markets which are theoretically rich enough to permit duplication of all contingent claims are said to be dynamically complete. Of course, actual markets can only approximate such ideal constructs.

The duplication strategies used by Black, Scholes, and Merton require some initial funds to buy the replicating portfolio, but all subsequent adjustments can be financed by borrowing or lending at the riskless rate. In an ideal, frictionless market with no trading costs and unlimited adjustments of portfolio holdings, the duplicating portfolio and the contingent claim produce exactly the same cashflows. As a result, the price of the contingent claim should equal the initial amount required to purchase the duplicating portfolio. Otherwise, arbitrage opportunities can be exploited to create a riskless, unlimited profit.

In actual markets with costly trading, the duplicating portfolio only approximates the payoffs of the contingent claim. In other words, the contingent claim and the duplicating portfolio will be close but not exact substitutes. In this case, the price difference between the security and the approximating portfolio will be determined by the risk aversion and trading costs of the most efficient "producer" of contingent claims. As competition increases and trading costs decline, the price of the contingent claim approaches that of the approximating portfolio.

Dynamic arbitrage analysis produces dynamic trading strategies required to manufacture contingent claims with high accuracy. This allows financial institutions to manage the risks of custom–made contingent claims they produce for their clients. By dynamically trading in the underlying index, or in a futures contract on the index, the financial institution can manufacture a contingent claim similar to the one sold to the client. The institution is thus protected from changes in the price of a claim. Such changes will be offset by equal and opposite changes in the value of the dynamic trading strategies. The institution is exposed only to the possibility of default by its client.

Cox and Ross[5] illuminate the elegance of the arbitrage pricing ideas of Black, Scholes, and Merton. They observe that since prices are determined by arbitrage between a contingent claim and its duplicating portfolio, attitudes towards risk are not a factor in pricing. Two individuals with different risk tolerance definitely agree that the price of the claim should equal the price of the duplicating portfolio. In particular, a risk–neutral individual will come to the same conclusion. We can then compute the price of the contingent claim as if it were determined by a risk–neutral trader who may represent any other trader.

It is convenient to choose a risk–neutral trader to price securities because risk–neutral traders do not adjust for risk. A risk–neutral trader computes the price of any security by discounting its expected cash flows using the riskless interest rates. To price contingent claims, we can assume that expected returns on *all* securities equal the riskless rate. The price of a contingent claim is just its expected discounted cashflow under this assumption. This technique is known as the "risk–neutral" pricing approach.

Risk–neutral pricing does not imply that attitudes towards risk do not affect prices of contingent claims. The degree of risk aversion of individuals in the economy determines the prices of the underlying, primitive risk factors. The higher the risk aversion, the higher the required expected return for the same level of risk. However, prices of contingent claims *relative* to prices of primitive risk factors are determined independent of risk aversion in society. In other words, the degree of risk aversion determines the prices of contingent claims *indirectly* through its effect on the prices of the primitive securities. If, however, one knows the prices of the primitive securities, there is no need to know the risk–return tradeoff in the economy. Such tradeoff is unnecessary for pricing derivatives since they are priced by comparison to the duplicating portfolios.

We can apply the risk–neutral pricing approach to compute the prices of many derivative securities. Consider a forward contract with maturity T on a non–dividend–paying stock whose current price is S. Let the interest rate be r and the forward price be f. A long position in a forward contract is a commitment to take delivery of the stock at time T in exchange for f dollars. Recall that no money changes hands at the inception of the contract. Put differently, a long position in a forward contract is a long position in a stock and a short position in f dollars, both at time T. Furthermore, the present value of these combined long and short positions is zero.

The present value of the long position in the stock at time T and the short position in $\$f$ at time T are $\$S$ and $-\$fe^{-rT}$, respectively. Since the combined position is of zero net present value, we conclude that $f = \$Se^{rT}$. This expression is known as the *cost–of–carry* formula, which can be written in general as $f = Se^{qT}$. The cost to carry q is the sum of the financing rate r plus any storage costs minus any dividends or convenience yield that the carried asset provides. By constructing trading strategies in the underlying asset combined with borrowing, we can easily verify that violations of the cost–of–carry formula lead to arbitrage opportunities.

The same arbitrage pricing techniques can be used to compute the futures price. Futures contracts differ from forward contracts because they are marked to market every day. A trader with a long position in a futures contract receives the difference between the daily settlement prices of the contract. Of course, if the settlement price declines from one day to the next, such a trader pays the amount of change. When daily interest rates are deterministic over the life of a futures contract, the futures price equals the forward price calculated from the cost–of–carry formula. In the case of random daily borrowing rates, the futures price and forward price differ by a quantity related to the covariance between changes in the futures price and the daily interest rate.

Derivation of the Black–Scholes Formula: An Illustration of Arbitrage Pricing

We can also use risk–neutral valuation to derive the celebrated Black and Scholes option pricing formula. Consider a non–dividend–paying stock with current price S. Assume that the returns on the stock over a period T are normally distributed with a variance of $v^2 T$. This assumption implies that the variance of returns is proportional to the duration of the holding period. For example, the variance of annual returns is four times the variance of quarterly returns. The variance of returns on this stock is independent of the level of the stock price. Many researchers have documented that the variance of returns on stocks declines as the stock price increases. This can be partly attributed to a leverage effect in which an increase in stock price, for a given level of debt, reduces the leverage in the stockholders' equity and thus reduces the uncertainty about the returns.

This evidence notwithstanding, we proceed with this simple model of stock price movement. For a risk–neutral trader, the expected return on the stock over any period should be rT, where r is the constant riskless rate. The expected return and the variance of return together imply that the stock price at time T, denoted $S(T)$, is given by the random variable:

$$S(T) - S \, exp\left\{\left(r - \frac{v^2}{2}\right)T + v\sqrt{T}Z\right\}, \qquad (2)$$

where Z is a standard, zero–mean–and–unit–variance, normal random variable.

Now consider a European call option on the stock with maturity T, exercise price K, and price C. The holder of this option has a claim, at time T, to the maximum of $S(T) - K$ and zero. We denote this quantity by $(S(T) - K)^+$. The price of this option is simply the expectation of

---

$e^{-rT}(S(T)-K)^{+}$. Computing this expectation and using the properties of the normal random variable Z, we obtain the Black–Scholes pricing formula

$$C = SN(d_1) - KN(d_2),$$

$$d_1 = \frac{\ln(S/K) + (r + v^2/2)T}{v\sqrt{T}}, \tag{3}$$

$$d_2 = d_1 - v\sqrt{T},$$

where $N(x)$ is the cumulative probability distribution for a standard normal variable. Other formulas, for example Cox's constant elasticity of variance model, have been developed for pricing options on stocks with richer descriptions of random returns.

It is rather rare to find a closed–form pricing equation similar to the Black–Scholes formula. Numerical computation algorithms are needed to develop pricing relations as in (1). One of the basic algorithms is Sharpe's binomial pricing model. As mentioned earlier, pricing a contingent claim requires producing a dynamic trading strategy that duplicates its cashflows. To specify such a duplicating strategy, one must anticipate all possible values of the stock price at all future dates. These anticipated future values should be consistent with our knowledge about the volatility of returns on the stock. The range of prices for a stock with high volatility should be wider than that for a stock with lower volatility. In addition, anticipated future values of the stock should conform to the anticipated relationship between the stock price and its volatility.

After reasonably describing all anticipated values of a future stock price, one can specify the duplicating strategy at each time and in each contingency. The original funds required to initiate the duplicating strategy are equal, by the law of one price, to the value of the contingent claim. Sharpe's binomial model describes all possible movements in the stock price by constructing a binomial tree. A binomial tree depicts very simple dynamics. The stock can move only at prespecified times, the number of which can be arbitrarily large. At each time, the stock price can only take two values, the sizes of which are related to the volatility of the return on the stock. As Figure 1 reveals, these simple rules combine to produce a large number of possibilities for the stock price upon the maturity of the contingent claim.

Figure 2 outlines the dynamic trading strategy, specified for every contingency, that duplicates the payoff of a call option. Of course, the stock price will only follow a single path on the tree. However, our policy anticipates every conceivable path and plans ahead for a trading strategy to duplicate the option payoff should the stock price follow that path. In fact, the binomial tree displays a key feature of all risk management programs. The program should anticipate and plan for *all* possible contingencies even though only one will materialize. Dynamic arbitrage analysis performs this function systematically in its search for duplicating strategies and values of contingent claims.

The binomial tree incorporates a wide range of possible movements in the stock price. For example, it can accommodate dividend payments, changes in volatility, and sudden jumps in stock price. The idea also accommodates more than one risk factor. A multidimensional lattice can be constructed to model all anticipated movements of two or more basic indices. The sizes of the possible movements are governed by the volatility and correlation of the returns on the risk factors. A variety of multiple–factor pricing models is found in the literature and in the arsenals of many investment banks. In particular, such models are used to analyze interest rate–contingent securities such as mortgage–backed securities and swaps.

Figure 1

Possible Movement of the Stock Price until the Option Matures

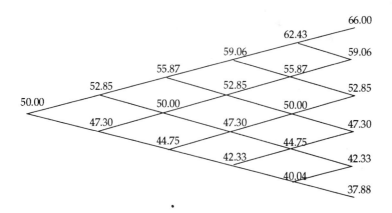

Figure 2

Dynamic Duplication of the Option

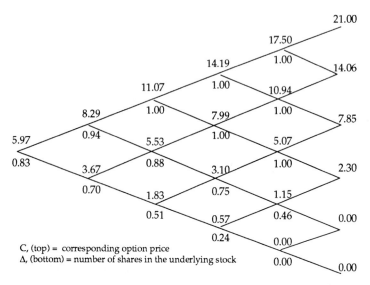

C, (top) = corresponding option price
Δ, (bottom) = number of shares in the underlying stock

In addition to the practical utility of the "tree–type" pricing models, many theoretical arguments support their use. For a fixed maturity, the price and trading strategy obtained from a binomial tree for a stock price converge—as the tree grows through finer subdivisions—to the corresponding price and trading strategies in a world with continuous trading. In addition, Black and Scholes show that the price of any contingent claim, as a function of the underlying stock price and time, satisfies a partial differential equation. Such an equation is known as the fundamental pricing equation. The binomial tree model represents one of many finite–difference schemes that numerically solve the fundamental pricing equation.

The accuracy of the pricing model depends on the accuracy of the duplicating trading strategy. The closer the payoff from the duplicating strategy to the payoff of the contingent claim, the more accurate the price and the more effective the risk management program. The accuracy of the duplicating strategy, in turn, depends on the accuracy of anticipated future values of the underlying index. If a model does not anticipate some plausible future behavior in the index, then the payoff of the contingent claim will not be accurately reproduced; and the manufacturer of the claim will be exposed to the discrepancy between the claim and the manufacturing strategy. Much of the effort of financial engineers aims to develop algorithms that better anticipate the behavior of the risk factors. Of course, pricing models will never precisely capture *all* possible future values of the risk factors. Financial engineers improve their algorithms incrementally and seek to relax the limitations of each class of models.

Risk Profiles

The risk profile of a security is the response of its price to changes in the value of underlying indices. Such a response is simple to describe. Recall the pricing equation (1). By Taylor's expansion theorem, we can write:

$$F(x_1 + \Delta x_1, \dots x_N + \Delta x_N, V, A) \approx F(x_1, \dots, x_N, V, A) \tag{4}$$

$$+ \sum_{i=1}^{i=N} F_i \Delta x_i + \sum_{i,j=1}^{i,j=N} F_{i,j} \Delta x_i \Delta xj$$

where F_i and F_{ij} denote the first and second derivatives, respectively, of F with respect to x_i and x_j. For very small changes in the value of the state variables, such as overnight movements in a calm environment, we can compute the change in the price by further approximation as:

$$F(x_1 + \Delta x_1, \dots, x_N + \Delta x_N, V, A) \approx F(x_1, \dots x_N, V, A) + \sum_{i=1}^{i=N} F_i \Delta x_i . \tag{5}$$

When there is a closed–form solution for the pricing relationship, one can compute the first and second derivatives analytically. Otherwise, these derivatives can be computed numerically. In any case, it is important to note that the values of the first and second derivatives change as the value of the underlying indices change. Consider, for example, the case of the European call option on a non–dividend–paying stock whoe price is given by (3). The first derivative,

$$\frac{\partial C}{\partial S},$$

is low for low values of the stock price S and increases as S increases. On the other hand, the second derivative,

$$\frac{\partial^2 C}{\partial S^2},$$

is highest when the stock price is close to the exercise price K and declines as the stock price moves away in either direction from K.

Options traders use the terminology Δ and Γ to describe

$$\frac{\partial C}{\partial S}$$

and

$$\frac{\partial^2 C}{\partial S^2},$$

respectively. Δ is typically known as the hedge ratio, and Γ is known as the convexity of the option. We generalize this terminology and use Δ_i and Γ_{ij} to denote the first and second partial derivatives F_i and F_{ij}, respectively, in (4).

For contingent claims with "linear payoff" structures such as forward contracts, futures contracts and simple swaps, Γ_{ij} is always zero. This is easily verified from the cost–of–carry formula or by direct inspection of a linear payoff diagram. In this case, the response of the price of the linear claim is given exactly by (5) for all changes in the underlying index. That is not the case for claims with nonlinear payoffs such as options, caps, floors, and collars. For such claims, the change in the price given by (5) is a good approximation for small changes in the underlying index. Larger changes require an adjustment that takes into account the convexity Γ as given in (4).

It is also important to understand how the price of a contingent security changes when the volatility and correlation among the basic indices change. Such changes in the volatilities and correlations of risk factors are common. Understanding the reactions of security prices to such changes is vital for effective risk management. From (1), we can measure the reaction of the price to a change in v_{ij}, the covariance between the changes in x_i and x_j, by computing

$$\frac{\partial P}{\partial v_{ij}}.$$

In the world of options on a single stock, the derivative of the price with respect to volatility is called *vega* and is denoted by Λ. We generalize this terminology and use Λ_{ij} to denote

$$\frac{\partial P}{\partial v_{ij}}$$

for any contingent security.

Contingent securities with linear payoffs, such as forward contracts, are not sensitive to changes in the volatility and correlation of the underlying indices. For such securities, $\Lambda_{ij} = 0$ for all indices i and j. An increase in the volatility of an index increases the likelihood of large changes in that index, which implies a higher likelihood of a large payoff to the security holder. But this favorable outcome is counterbalanced by a higher likelihood of a small or even negative payoff because payoffs are symmetric, or linear, in the value of the index. As a result, the price of the security does not respond to changes in volatility.

This neutrality to changes in volatility contrasts with the reaction of securities with nonlinear payoffs. Consider a European call option. Similar to a forward contract, an increase in volatility implies an increase in the likelihood of favorable outcomes to the option holder. In contrast to a forward contract, the accompanying increase in the likelihood of low values of the index does not affect the option holder, who is guaranteed a minimum payoff of zero. As a result, the option price increases as volatility increases. Sensitivity of the option price to changes in volatility is highest when the stock price is close to the exercise price, in which case the option is said to be "at the money." As the stock price moves away in either direction from the exercise price, the sensitivity of the option price to changes in volatility declines. This is a common phenomenon. Γ_{ij} and Λ_{ij} tend to attain their maximum values at roughly the same values of the underlying index.

American and European options of the call and put variety on a single index increase in price as the volatility of the underlying index increases. In contrast, an option on two indices might behave differently. A spread option grants its buyer the right to buy or sell the difference between two indices at a fixed strike price. Such indices may be the prices of two grades of the same commodity or of two bonds in different European countries. Typically, the two underlying indices are highly correlated. The price of some spread options *declines* as the volatility of one or both indices increases. Recall that the variance of the change in the difference between two indices, x_1 and x_2, is given as

$v_{11} + v_{22} - 2v_{12}$. We write v_{12} as $\rho\sqrt{v_{11}v_{22}}$, where ρ is the correlation coefficient between changes in x_1 and x_2. For high enough positive correlation, an increase in v_{11}, *ceteris paribus*, decreases the volatility of the spread and hence the value of the spread option.

It is useful to summarize all information about a derivative security in a summary sheet or a risk profile. Such a profile should contain the following information:

1. Underlying indices.
2. Description of the contingent cashflow.
3. Arbitrage price of the security.
4. Sensitivity of the price to changes in the underlying state variables as given by the vector $\{\Delta_1, \cdots, \Delta_N\}$.
5. Convexity coefficients as given by the parameters Γ_{ij} for $i, j = 1, \cdots, N$.
6. Coefficients of sensitivity to changes in variance and correlation of the underlying indices as given by the parameters Λ_{ij} for $i, j = 1, \cdots, N$.

Items 3 to 6 should be computed from an adequate pricing model and updated as the values of the underlying indices change. Table 3 presents an example of a risk profile for a contingent claim. Risk profiles of securities are the hallmark of the functional approach to risk management. From a risk management perspective, all relevant information is contained in the continually updated risk profiles of securities. Two securities that have the same risk profile for a certain period can be considered identical for risk management during that period. For example, a mortgage loan and a position in a long–term Treasury bond coupled with an amortizing swap can have the same risk profile for some period. A commercial bank can substitute the Treasury bond/swap portfolio for the mortgage loan without any change in its overall risk profile. The Treasury bond/swap portfolio could be more attractive for the bank because of more favorable accounting treatment or lower capital requirements. The construction of portfolios with specific risk profiles is discussed in the next section.

Exposure Management

This section describes how to formulate and implement an exposure management program. We first discuss how to construct the risk profile of a portfolio of securities from the individual risk profiles of those securities. We then describe how to express the desired risk exposure and how to achieve it by trading in derivative securities. We also explain how to describe the performance of the managed portfolio under different scenarios. This type of scenario analysis effectively communicates the results of the exposure management step.

Table 3

Risk Profile for an Option on the Slope of the Yield Curve

1 – Underlying Indices	x_1	Yield on 2–year Treasury bond in bp.
	x_2	Yield on 10–year Treasury bond in bp.
2 – Security Characteristics	Maturity	Six Months
	Exercise Spread	40 bp
	Payoff	$(x_2 - x_1 - 40)^+ \times 0.01 \times \$1,000,000$
3 – Price	15 bp	Per $100,000 face value
4 – Delta	Δ_1	-0.67
	Δ_2	+0.73
5 – Convexity	Γ_{11}	-0.011
	Γ_{22}	+0.015
	Γ_{12}	-0.008
6 – Vega	Λ_{11}	+0.12
	Λ_{22}	+0.08
	Λ_{11}	-0.06

Ends and Means

Exposure management aims to combine different securities to produce a portfolio with a specific risk profile. For example, an investor might be interested in constructing a portfolio whose value is immune to small changes in short–term interest rates or one whose value increases significantly when the volatility of the Deutsche mark–U.S. dollar exchange rate increases but not when the level of the exchange rate changes. The latter is known as a long position in the volatility of the DM/US$ exchange rate. A commercial bank might seek to construct a portfolio that behaves like an option on the spread between long–term and short–term interest rates. The bank wants to benefit from an increase in the spread while avoiding declines below a certain critical value.

Exposure management can achieve these goals. In the first example, we must construct a portfolio with $\Delta_r = 0$, where Δ_r is the derivative of the portfolio value with respect to the short–term rate. Such a portfolio can be termed "short–term rate delta–neutral." In the second instance, we must construct a portfolio with a large derivative with respect to the volatility of the DM/US$ exchange rate and a very small derivative with respect to its level. Such a portfolio can be termed a "high DM/US$ vega, delta–neutral position." The commercial bank can achieve its objective by constructing a portfolio with a risk profile (Δ's, Γ's, and Λ's) similar to that of a call option on the spread between the long– and short–term interest rates.

The risk characteristics of a portfolio of securities can be easily computed from those of the individual securities. For a portfolio of securities, the following relationships hold:

Value of portfolio= sum of(number of shares of each security $\times$ corresponding value)

Δ_i of portfolio = sum of(number of shares of each security $\times$ corresponding Δ_i)

Γ_{ij} of portfolio = sum of(number of shares of each security $\times$ corresponding Γ_{ij})

Λ_{ij} of portfolio = sum of(number of shares of each security $\times$ corresponding Λ_{ij})

With these relationships, exposure management is formulated as an optimization problem. Given the risk characteristics of each security, we can choose trading positions which closely match the target risk profile. We can also incorporate institutional or legal constraints such as limitations on short positions or self–imposed limits on the funds allocated to certain classes of securities. Furthermore, we can assign different weights to different risk characteristics of the target portfolio to reflect the style and philosophy of the risk management program. For example, we can assign higher importance to achieving certain levels of sensitivity to correlations between two indices, with lower emphasis on the degree of convexity relative to some other index.

A convenient formulation of the risk management problem is as follows. Suppose that there are M basic securities exposed to N risk factors. Risk analysis of security m, where $m = 1, \cdots, M$, produces a profile summarized by the numbers $P^m, \Delta_i^m, \Gamma_{ij}^m, \Lambda_{ij}^m$, for $i, j, = 1, \cdots, N$. Suppose that a portfolio of these securities has α^m shares of security m. A risk manager aims for a portfolio with target risk profile $P^*, \Delta_i^*, \Gamma_{ij}^*, \Lambda_{ij}^*$, for $i, j = 1, \cdots, N$. Furthermore, suppose that the risk manager assigns the weights w_{Δ_i}, $w_{\Gamma_{ij}}$, and $w_{\Lambda_{ij}}$ to the different risk characteristics of the portfolio.

The risk management problem can be written as:

$$\text{Minimize } \sum_{ij}\left[w_{\Delta_i}\left(\Delta_i^P - \Delta_i^*\right)^2 + w_{\Gamma_{ij}}\left(\Gamma_{ij}^P - \Gamma_{ij}^*\right)^2 + w_{\Lambda_{ij}}\left(\Lambda_{ij}^P - \Lambda_{ij}^*\right)^2\right],$$

by choosing $\alpha^1, \cdots, \alpha^M$, where

$$\Delta_i^P = \sum_{m=1}^{m=M} \alpha^m \Delta_i^m$$

$$\Gamma_{ij}^P = \sum_{m=1}^{m=M} \alpha^m \Gamma_{ij}^m$$

$$\Lambda_{ij}^P = \sum_{m=1}^{m=M} \alpha^m \Lambda_{ij}^m$$

subject to the constraints that

$$\sum_{m=1}^{m=M} \alpha^m P^m = W \text{ and}$$

$$\underline{\alpha}^m \le \alpha^m \le \overline{\alpha}^m, \text{ for } m = 1, \cdots, M.$$

In this formulation, W and P^m denote the value of the portfolio and individual securities, respectively. The constants $\underline{\alpha}^m$ and $\overline{\alpha}^m$ represent the constraints on holdings of different assets. Any standard optimization algorithm can solve the risk allocation problem. Many commercial programs implement a wide variety of solution techniques.

Risk management is a dynamic problem. As the values of risk factors change, the risk profiles of securities change. The risk manager needs to solve the optimization problem again and to adjust for changes in the environment. In addition, the risk manager needs to adjust the risk profile of his portfolio when his emphasis on different risk characteristics changes. Frequency of adjustment of the risk profile depends on the nature of the business for which the risk management program is used. A pension fund manager might revise the risk profile monthly; a trading group might revise it many times a day.

Presentation of Risk Profiles

The risk manager has to present the risk profile of the managed portfolio to different constituencies both within and outside the organization. Describing the risk profile in simple, intuitive terms enhances communication and decision making.

To communicate the overall risk exposure of a portfolio, the risk manager should present the variance of changes in the portfolio value over the relevant horizon. We use Λ^* to denote the vector of sensitivities, of $\Lambda_1^*,...,\Lambda_N^*$, of the portfolio as described earlier. The variance of changes in the portfolio, v^{*2}, is approximately $\Lambda^*V\Lambda^{*T}$, where T denotes the transposition of a vector. The standard deviation of changes in the portfolio value, v^*, is the square root of v^{*2}.

In the case of a portfolio exposed to more than one source of risk, correlation among changes in the risk factors is an important determinant of the portfolio's variance. For example, consider the case of two risk factors with the volatility matrix

$$V = \begin{bmatrix} v_1^2 & pv_1v_2 \\ pv_1v_2 & v_2^2 \end{bmatrix},$$

where p is the correlation between changes in x_1 and x_2. The variance of changes in the value of the managed portfolio is $v^{*2} = \Lambda_1^{*2}v_1^2 + 2\Lambda_1^*\Lambda_2^*pv_1v_2 + \Lambda_2^{*2}v_2^2$. When both Λ_1^* and Λ_2^* are positive, the total variance of changes in the value of the portfolio declines as the value of the correlation coefficient declines, *ceteris paribus*. For this reason, it is very important to understand the correlation among the basic risk factors to accurately estimate the total risk in a portfolio.

For convenience, we assume that the random changes in the portfolio value are normally distributed. The risk profile can be presented using the properties of normal random variables. In particular, there is 0.68 probability, or roughly two chances in three, that the value of the portfolio will differ from its expected value by an amount between $-v^*$ and $+v^*$ over the decision horizon. Furthermore, there is 0.95 probability that the change will be between $-2v^*$ and $+2v^*$. Of course, both the manager and the recipients of such information recognize that these estimates are tentative. Further analysis of the distribution of random changes is advised to determine the appropriateness of the assumption that changes are normally distributed. Any skewness in the distribution of changes in the portfolio value should be presented as part of the risk profile.

It is also useful to explain the sources of volatility in the portfolio using some scenario analysis. We can represent possible future changes for each risk factor, x_i, by a few events together with their associated probabilities. The values of the risk factor in these possible events and the corresponding probabilities should reflect the volatility of the risk factor. The higher the volatility, the larger the dispersion in possible future realizations. Suppose we represent possible changes in the state variable x_i by the K numbers, $\varepsilon_i^1, \cdots, \varepsilon_i^K$, with corresponding probabilities $p_i^1, \cdots, p_i^K$. For example, possible changes in the short–term interest rate over a week might be (-20bp, -10bp, 0bp, +10bp, +20bp) with corresponding probabilities (0.1, 0.2, 0.4, 0.2, 0.1). This would represent a weekly volatility of about 11bp.

We should augment the presentation of these numbers with an analysis of the events that correspond to such changes. For example, in the case of the short–term rate, we could discuss Federal Reserve Policy and link each possible change to corresponding Fed actions. Such an analysis facilitates communication among users of the risk management system and adds to its credibility. We can then present scenarios in which each factor, x_i, changes by some possible value ε_i. The corresponding change in the value of the portfolio is $\Delta_1^* \varepsilon_1 + \Delta_2^* \varepsilon_2 + \cdots + \Delta_N^* \varepsilon_N$. This decomposition of the possible change in the value of the portfolio to its basic elements provides better insight into the nature of the portfolio risk.

A good example of such scenario analysis is the study of the risk in fixed–income securities. The basic risk factors are the yields on short–, medium–, and long–term Treasury securities. An arbitrage pricing model can determine the price of a fixed–income security such as a mortgage–backed security or an interest rate swap as a function of the values of the three yields. Such a model also produces the sensitivity of the price to changes in the three yields. We can then specify scenarios for the joint movement of the three yields and compute the corresponding reaction of the security's price.

The proposed scenarios should accurately portray the volatility and correlation among the three basic yields. This contrasts with the widely used idea of *duration* as a measure of price sensitivity to changes in the term structure. The duration of a security measures its sensitivity to a parallel shift in the term structure. In other words, the duration measure presumes that the typical event affects all yields equally. Such a presumption is inaccurate because it does not take into account the different volatilities of different maturity yields.

A complete scenario analysis should also estimate the likelihood of different future scenarios. When the risk factors are independent, the probability of a joint movement is the product of the corresponding probabilities of each individual movement. Such is not the case when the risk factors are correlated. A movement of one risk factor in one direction affects the likelihood of other factors moving in the same direction. Factor analysis, a statistical technique that produces *uncorrelated* linear combinations from correlated risk factors, handles this complication. For example, in the case of the three–factor term structure model, the average of the three yields, the difference between the long–term and short–term yields, and the value of the medium–term yield relative to the average of the short– and long–term yields appear uncorrelated. These new variables can be interpreted as level, slope, and curvature of the term structure, respectively.

We can present the scenario analysis using the new, transformed variable. The advantage of such a transformation is that the movements in the transformed variables are uncorrelated. As a result, it is easy to compute and communicate the probabilities of their joint movements. Of course, factor analysis does not alter the dynamics of the prices or the risk profile. It does, however, present the risk profile in a more convenient and intuitive way.

Risk Management Systems

The different stages of quantitative risk management can be integrated into a risk management system whose major components are displayed in Figure 3. Such a system can be utilized to manage the trading position of a single trader, a small specialized division, or an entire financial institution. The modules of the system can be implemented with different degrees of accuracy and sophistication. The dynamics of the risk factors can be described by simple approximate numbers or by sophisticated, multi–factor econometric models.

Arbitrage pricing models range from simple equations to large–scale, numerically sophisticated computational algorithms. Cashflow generators also vary from a single formula (as in the case of a simple option) to a sophisticated simulator that accounts for the dependence of cashflows on the history of the risk factors (as in the case of mortgage–

backed securities). Similarly, risk optimizers can vary from the small–scale programs that handle a handful of securities to large programs that allocate funds among hundreds of securities.

Financial engineers are continuously incorporating advances in econometric techniques, asset pricing models, simulation techniques, and optimization algorithms to produce better risk management systems. This trend is magnified by the continuous improvement of price/performance characteristics of computer hardware. In particular, many sophisticated pricing problems can be solved on speedy hardware in real time to meet the demands of traders in fast–changing markets. Furthermore, advances in development software such as object–oriented programming increase the productivity of system developers. In addition, attractive and user–friendly interfaces to risk management systems can be developed quickly. This promotes rapid proliferation of automated risk management systems. Finally, basic knowledge about pricing and managing derivative securities is available to a large audience through many excellent professional and academic publications. All these trends encourage the development and utilization of accurate, comprehensive quantitative risk management systems.

Figure 3

Risk Management System

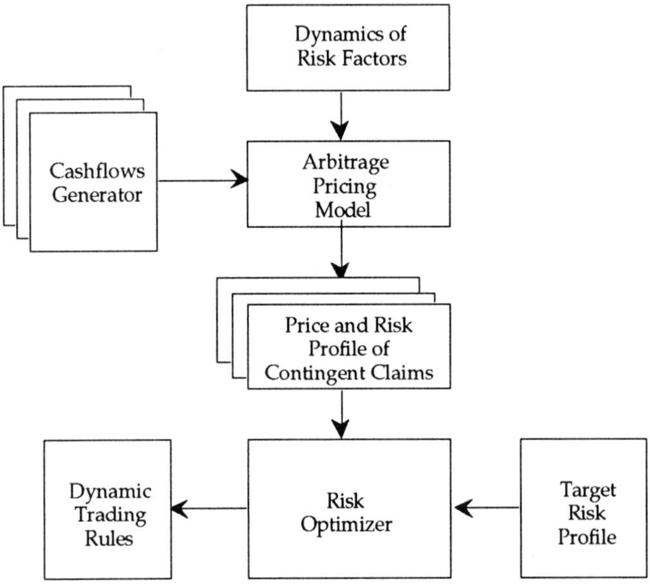

Lessons from Quantitative Risk Management

The quantitative risk management model presented in this chapter is facilitated by the following components:

- Accurate, up–to–date indices that reflect the basic risk factors facing the entity.
- Accurate description of the dynamic behavior of the risk indices.
- Arbitrage pricing models.
- Ability to change the risk profile of a portfolio quickly and inexpensively by trading in a large variety of derivative securities in liquid markets.
- Sophisticated computer hardware and software systems for implementing the pricing and exposure management functions.

These features limit the applicability of quantitative risk management systems to institutions trading liquid securities in well–developed financial markets. However, important concepts of the approach can be useful in other risk management situations even without the above features. In particular, the functional perspective and the portfolio approach to risk management can analyze any business and provide insights that might shape U. S. strategy.

The functional approach identifies a few basic factors and describes each asset in terms of the exposure to these factors. The name or the legal attributes of the asset are irrelevant for risk management. This approach generates insights into the nature of any business. A senior executive adopting the functional perspective perceives the organization as a portfolio of risks. The strategic analysis of any organization should penetrate the specific legal and institutional package in which the risk factors are assembled.

The change in perspective promotes effective strategic decision making. In particular, executives can decide which risks to assume and manage. Other risk factors can be contracted away via a variety of operational and financial arrangements. Of course, executives have to function within the legal and institutional constraints of their environment. However, an abstract view of the organization as a package of risks, some to be assumed and others to be contracted away, encourages innovative, effective organizational structures and strategies.

The second important ingredient in the risk management approach of this chapter is the treatment of risk factors and securities as an integrated portfolio. Specifically, special attention is paid to the *correlation* among the risk factors, which translates to correlation among the values of securities. Identifying the correlation among the basic risk factors leads to more effective risk management. The risk profile can be assessed more accurately, and the correlation can be exploited to reduce the trading required to attain a target risk profile.

The portfolio perspective can also be used for strategic analysis of any business. Analyzing the correlation among the real, financial and strategic assets of an organization leads to a clear understanding of its risk exposure. For example, a securities firm might be exposed to interest rate risk in a financial sense as the value of currently held securities moves with interest rates. The firm could also be exposed to interest rate risk in a strategic sense because changes in interest rates affect the flow of business to the firm as consumers look for alternative investments. Understanding this correlation between the financial and strategic exposure might lead the firm to change the composition of its balance sheet for better control of the combined risk.

Conclusion

Strategic risk management can benefit from borrowing the functional and portfolio perspectives of quantitative risk management systems discussed in this chapter. The increasing volatility of many markets is forcing many organizations to decide which risks to assume as their core business and which to transfer elsewhere. As a result, there is a growing trend towards more focused organizations which rely on market–based transactions to purchase the services needed for managing their core risks. This trend is also creating high demand for standard "indices" to measure and price the risks and for liquid financial securities to manage these risks. This is evident in the introduction of indices on such factors as the value of real estate, electrical power, pollution rights, DRAM microchips and a host of commodities and industrial products. The increasing pace of securitization of illiquid assets of many financial intermediaries, such as mortgages, consumer loans, and credit card loans, also illustrates the demand for higher liquidity and better risk management tools.

These trends indicate that quantitative risk management techniques will gradually extend to more risk factors as better indices, more accurate pricing techniques, and more liquid derivative securities are developed. Furthermore, basic ideas of quantitative risk management have an increasing impact on the strategic thinking of many business leaders as they realize the relationships between strategic decision making and quantitative risk management. This chapter is presented as a contribution to this process.

Notes

[1] I am grateful to Bill Sharpe for his time, ideas and data; to Herbert Allison, Robert Ashcroft, William Beaver, Darrell Duffie, Charles Jacklin, Paul Pfleiderer, Ken Singleton, and Guy Weyns for useful discussions.

[2] The technical material in this chapter requires familiarity with the statistical notions of variance, covariance, and correlation together with elementary calculus. The reader, however, can skip the technical discussion with no significant loss.

[3] F. Black and M. Scholes, The Pricing of Options and Corporate Liabilities, *Journal of Political Economy*, 81 (1973): 637–659.

[4] R. Merton, Theory of Rational Option Pricing, *Bell Journal of Economics and Management Science*, 4 (1973): 141–183.

[5] J. Cox and S. Ross, The Valuation of Options for Alternative Stochastic Processes, *Journal of Financial Economics*, 3 (1976): 145-166.

Should Firms Use Derivatives to Manage Risk?

David Fite, Vice President, Bankers Trust*

Paul Pfleiderer, Professor, Graduate School of Business, Stanford University

*Introduction***

Over the past few decades, the performance of financial markets has been greatly improved by the development of new technologies in communications and information processing. Some argue that financial market performance has also been improved by the creation of new types of securities, especially the financial instruments known as derivatives. The creation and widespread use of derivatives has been brought about in large measure by conceptual advances that have allowed various financial institutions to value and hedge these complex instruments. While the use of derivatives has become widespread, it has also become controversial. Some question the value of derivatives and call for restrictions on their use and new regulations. In this article we consider the economic role played by derivatives. We focus in particular on the use of derivatives by corporations to hedge risks. Should corporations hedge risks; and if so, which ones and why?

Before addressing the issue of corporate hedging, it is useful to consider the general role derivatives can play in financial markets. Financial markets create value in free market economies by performing a number of important functions. One is the allocation of scarce capital to its most productive uses. Should a billion–dollar electric power plant be built, or should the billion dollars be spent instead on the development of a new commercial aircraft? Any elementary textbook on finance or economics shows that financial markets, by establishing the cost of capital for different types of projects, help direct investment to its most productive applications. Financial markets also create value by facilitating an efficient distribution of risks among risk bearers. If the power plant is built and the demand for electricity falls, who should suffer the consequences? Should this be the same party that bears the risk of increases in the price of the coal that fuels the plant? These functions of allocating capital and risks are obviously closely related. In general, the optimal allocation of capital depends on how efficiently risks can be shared among investors. In particular, if the risks created by a given investment can be more efficiently allocated among risk bearers, then the cost of capital for that investment may be reduced and the investment becomes more attractive.

Derivatives have generally lowered the cost and increased the precision with which the market is able to unbundle and distribute risks among risk bearers. However, from this it does not immediately follow that corporations should use derivatives to hedge risks. After all, it might be argued that the ultimate bearers of risk are individuals and not corporations. Corporations can trade risks among themselves, but would such trading have any consequences for how these risks affect individual investors? Since individual investors typically hold positions in many corporations and can themselves alter their risk exposure by trading in derivatives, the case for corporate hedging is not immediately obvious.

We argue below that various "market imperfections" create a solid case for corporate hedging. It is not correct to view corporations as simply passing risks through the corporate structure to individuals who then adjust their positions to attain their optimal risk exposure. Some risks affect corporate earnings in ways that individual investors cannot offset by altering their own financial positions. Because of this, there are several valid reasons for corporations to hedge risks. At the same time, there are some reasons that have been given for corporate hedging that do not make economic sense. We do not intend to provide an exhaustive list of valid reasons for hedging. Undoubtedly many readers can think of specific cases for hedging that do not fall neatly in the taxonomy we present. Our hope is that we have identified most of the major justifications for corporate hedging as well as some of the more dubious ones.

The question as to whether or not a corporation should hedge is not well posed. To have a meaningful discussion, we must specify an objective for the corporation and then ask if and how hedging advances the corporation toward this objective. The standard objective used in a context such as this one is the maximization of shareholder value or shareholder wealth. For most of the following discussion, we assume this is the goal; but in some cases this is problematical — especially where significant differences exist among a firm's shareholders. For example, if some shareholders hold diversified portfolios while others have concentrated holdings in a firm, the two groups will not necessarily agree on the value of a hedging program. In such a case there will not be a clear, unambiguous measure of shareholder value.

Three Views of Corporate Hedging

To frame our discussion of corporate hedging, we begin by examining three frequently encountered views about the value of hedging programs. Our arguments against these lead us to conclude that the only valid justifications for hedging on corporate account are those based on "market imperfections."

Hedging, since it reduces risk, is good.

Financial markets provide a wealth of evidence supporting the notion that investors are risk averse and demand a premium (in terms of a higher expected return) when they hold risky positions.[1] Hedging, it might be argued, reduces the volatility of a firm's earnings and by doing so makes the cashflow stream delivered by a company to its investors less volatile and therefore more valuable. According to this line of argument, the firm reduces volatility through hedging, which reduces the risk premium investors demand to hold its stock and bonds. This, in turn, raises the value of the future cashflows delivered by the firm since they will be discounted at a lower rate, and this increases the value of the firm and shareholders' wealth.

Hedging, since it reduces risk, is bad.

This polar view of hedging is based on the argument that value is generally created by taking on risk and not by avoiding it. A firm that wants to reduce risk can always do so by not investing in risky projects. In the extreme, it can reduce all risk by investing only in short–term government securities. Obviously this course of action produces no value for the shareholders. Thus it is argued that a firm must take on reasonable risks to create value; and if it avoids or transfers these risks, it gives up this value.

Both these arguments are based on incorrect views of how the market "prices" risk. Some risks are priced in the financial markets in the sense that investors require a higher rate of expected return to bear those risks. Other risks are not priced in the sense that investors require no adjustment in expected return. A firm generates value for its investors only when it makes an investment that has a higher expected return than investors require as compensation for the risk.

Hedging is neither good nor bad; it is irrelevant.

Unlike the first two views which rely on simplistic notions of the relations between risk and value, this view is based on a more subtle understanding of the alternatives available to investors and how these investors view various risks.

Part of this argument for the irrelevancy of hedging is based on the fact that many sources of volatility within a firm are not risks that investors care about since these risks nearly vanish in a diversified portfolio.[2] In particular, an investor who holds a diversified portfolio is not affected in any significant way by sources of volatility that affect only one or a few firms. Such "idiosyncratic" risks are inconsequential for investors. Consider a well–diversified investor who holds stock in Ford. Even though Ford is a large firm with a market capitalization of $18.854 billion (as of December 1992), its capitalization is only 0.47% of the total value of NYSE stocks and an even smaller fraction of the total value of all U. S. stocks.

Assume there is a risk that affects only Ford and that this risk either adds 10% to Ford's return or subtracts 10% from it. Then a diversified investor who holds Ford in same proportion as its value in the NYSE stock portfolio will see his return vary by at most 0.047% due to this risk. To put this into perspective, note that a diversified investor with a total investment of $100,000 loses only $4.70 as a result of a 10% decline in Ford stock. Such an investor would see little value in Ford's removing this risk and would oppose its removal if there were a significant cost involved. The diversified investor is only concerned with *pervasive* risks, i.e., risks that affect a large number of firms. The idiosyncratic risk at Ford has virtually no effect on any investor who has allocated his wealth across many firms.

Even when we consider pervasive risks, it is not immediately clear that a firm can gain by hedging these risks. Oil price shocks are good examples of pervasive risks that affect many firms. Note, however, that unexpected changes in the price of oil affect firms in different ways.

An increase in the price of oil will generally increase the earnings of the oil companies but will decrease those of the airlines. A diversified investor who holds both oil and airline stocks is therefore at least partially hedged in his portfolio against oil price shocks. Such a diversified investor's risk exposure is essentially unchanged if the airlines take long positions in oil futures contracts and obtain them from the oil companies who take the offsetting short sides. Of course, there are pervasive risks that affect most firms in the same way. These risks do not "cancel out" in a diversified portfolio, and it is reasonable to assume that diversified investors will be sensitive to them. Does this mean that a firm is better off if it reduces these risks? Not necessarily.

Assume that an unexpected increase in energy costs affects almost all firms adversely. This, then, is a pervasive risk that does not cancel out in diversified portfolios.[3] Assume that because energy cost risk cannot be diversified away, diversified investors require a higher expected return on securities with a high sensitivity to energy costs than they do for securities with lower sensitivity. If a firm could change its real operations in some costless way that reduced its exposure to energy costs, then its value would increase. However, if that firm reduced its energy cost exposure by hedging, then it would pass energy risk on to some counterparty who would demand compensation for bearing this risk. In an efficient market, that compensation is precisely equal to the increase in the value of the firm's cashflows due to the energy risk reduction. The shareholders will be neither better nor worse off. Thus it is irrelevant what the firm does to "manage" this risk.

Even if one is unwilling to accept the arguments made above for the irrelevancy of corporate hedging policies, one still must contend with another argument for irrelevancy, this one based on the well–known and important insights contained in Modigliani and Miller's analysis of a firm's capital structure.[4] Modigliani and Miller considered changes in a firm's financing policy that do not alter the firm's investment policy. They showed that such changes neither increase nor decrease the firm's value when there are no transactions costs, no taxes, and no information asymmetries. Their argument was based on the observation that any financial position that the firm can achieve by altering the set of claims it issues can also be achieved by holders of the firm's debt and equity if they adjust their "own account" positions. At the same time, any investors unhappy with the change can undo it by trading on their own accounts.

In their original analysis, Modigliani and Miller focused on the corporation's debt/equity ratio (i.e., its use of leverage), but their arguments clearly apply with equal force to a firm's hedging strategy. Under the assumptions made by Modigliani and Miller, there is no reason for a firm to hedge since investors can do it on their own accounts if this is something they desire. For example, a U. S. export firm that sells in Germany can reduce its exposure to exchange risk by taking a position in the $/DM forward market. However, any of the firm's shareholders who value this risk reduction can achieve the same result without the firm's hedging by taking a similar (but smaller) position in the forward market on their own account. However, some of the shareholders might actually prefer the export firm's exposure to exchange risk — perhaps because they are importers of German goods and their risk is offset to some extent by the exporter's position. If the exporter does hedge its exposure, these shareholders can undo the result by taking the opposite and offsetting position on their own accounts. In all cases, it makes no difference what the exporter does as long as the shareholders know the exporter's hedging positions and can trade in the same instruments.

The General Conditions for Corporate Hedging to Benefit Shareholders

If value is created by altering risk exposure through derivatives, it must be because one or more of the assumptions used by Modigliani and Miller do not hold. It is clear that at least two conditions must be met by any worthwhile corporate hedging strategy: (1) It must change the firm's cash flows in a way that shareholders' value and the benefit to shareholders must be greater than the cost of hedging; and (2) Hedging on corporate account must be the least expensive way to bring about the beneficial change in cashflows. In particular, the firm must be at least as efficient in adjusting the risk exposure and creating the improvement as shareholders would be if they hedged on their own account.

One might think that the second condition hardy merits serious attention. Doesn't the firm always have a cost advantage over individual shareholders since it can take advantage of scale economies and therefore pay lower transactions costs? In fact, there are many situations where shareholders have a distinct advantage over firms in controlling risk exposure. For example, in the 1960s, a large number of conglomerate mergers occurred in the U. S. At the time, one of the justifications given for these mergers was that by creating a diversified company, a conglomerate merger lowered the risk experienced by shareholders. While there may have been good reasons for the formation of conglomerates, this almost certainly was not one of them. Individual shareholders could on their own accounts achieve the benefits of diversification simply by buying shares in a number of companies in different industries. This could be accomplished at far lower cost (especially if it were done through mutual funds) than the cost of "physically" merging several companies. Corporations are *high–cost* producers of diversification, at least when they do it through mergers. It is therefore reasonable for us to ask whether the second condition is met by corporate hedging strategies. As we show below, for many of the benefits produced by hedging, the corporation is likely to be the lowest–cost producer. In fact, we argue that several benefits of hedging cannot be produced at all by the shareholders' hedging on their own accounts and that only corporate hedging can bring about these gains.

Since we measure the value of corporate hedging in terms of the effects hedging has on shareholder wealth, we must now consider how shareholders value the cashflows produced by a firm. Many approaches break the problem of valuing a firm's shares into two parts. In the first step, future cashflows that will be produced by the firm and paid to shareholders are forecasted. In the second step, these expected cashflows are discounted to the present using the appropriate risk–adjusted discount rate. This discount rate is the rate of return shareholders require as compensation for the riskiness of the firm's cashflows. It follows that hedging can affect the firm's value by changing the expectation of its future cashflows, by changing the discount rate shareholders use to discount these cashflows, or by doing both. Since corporate hedging policies alter the firm's risk exposure, it would seem that the most profound effects of hedging would be felt through changes in the firm's risk–adjusted discount rate.

Paradoxically, we argue below that most of the gains produced by corporate hedging for shareholders are due to increases in expected cashflows and not to reductions in the discount rate. Along these lines, we divide the remaining discussion into two parts. First we discuss the effects of corporate hedging on the risks shareholders actually bear. This relates mainly to the discount rate. Then we discuss how risk actually affects the firm and more specifically how corporate hedging affects the expected cashflows the firm can generate and deliver to shareholders.

Risks Shareholders Bear and Benefits of Corporate Hedging

Does corporate hedging produce any gain to shareholders by changing the risk they experience? Much of the foregoing discussion leads one to be skeptical that it does. Since shareholders tend to hold well–diversified portfolios through intermediaries such as mutual funds and pension funds, many corporate risks are diversified away in the typical shareholder's portfolio. In addition, the Modigliani–Miller argument reminds us that shareholders have the ability to control their risk exposure on their own account and do not necessarily require that corporations do it for them. Do these arguments for the irrelevance of corporate hedging hold up after we explicitly consider transactions costs and other market imperfections?

First, note that not all shareholders hold well–diversified portfolios. Many U. S. corporations have shareholders who own fairly large stakes in the firm and for whom this stake is a large portion of their net worth. In many cases, these are founders or others who for control reasons have acquired a significant number of shares. These undiversified shareholders will quite likely differ from diversified shareholders in the way they view the risks faced by the corporation. We have already noted that in this case it is somewhat problematic to talk about the affects of hedging on shareholder value. Shareholders will not value corporate hedging in the same way.

For example, assume that a firm has one large shareholder who holds 30% of the firm's shares and that this stake represents almost all of his wealth. The remaining shares (70%) are held by diversified investors. Now assume that the firm faces foreign exchange risk since it is a net importer from Canada, but also assume that the diversified shareholders *on net* have no foreign exchange exposure. This can come about if the diversified shareholders hold stock in both exporters to and importers from Canada. In terms of their risk exposure, the diversified shareholders will not benefit if the corporation hedges the exchange rate risk, but clearly the undiversified shareholder will see his risk reduced. Should the firm hedge?

Assume that the firm can *costlessly* eliminate the foreign exchange risk by trading a futures contract with a firm that exports to Canada but that the cost of the undiversified shareholder's hedging on his own account is greater than zero. An argument can be made for the firm to hedge since the diversified shareholders are no worse off and the large shareholder is better off.[5] Now assume that it is somewhat costly for the firm to hedge the exchange rate risk due to transactions costs, but that this cost is less than the cost the undiversified shareholder pays if he hedges on his own account. Should the firm hedge? If it does, the diversified shareholders are worse off since they pay 70% of the cost of hedging but receive no gain. The diversified shareholder potentially gains, however, since he only pays 30% of the costs of hedging but benefits from the lower risk exposure. Given the assumptions we have made, it is clear that if we put the matter to a shareholder vote and everyone votes in his or her own interest, the vote will go against hedging.

Before concluding that hedging will always be rejected by shareholders when the majority of shareholders are diversified, we should ask if the large shareholder's presence in any way benefits the diversified shareholders. Several arguments have been made to support the notion that the presence of a large shareholder does benefit the other shareholders. Many of these are based on "free-rider" problems that occur when shareholding is widely diversified. It is clear that when each shareholder holds a very small stake in each firm, none has much of an incentive to monitor the performance of the firm or to pressure its management into making value-improving changes. A diversified shareholder who pays the substantial costs of time and effort involved in monitoring and lobbying for changes receives only a tiny fraction of the gain. He prefers that others pay these costs and that he "free ride" on their efforts. Of course, the free–rider problem exists even when there is a shareholder who holds a stake of, say, 30%, but in this case it is not as severe. A shareholder with a 30% stake has some incentive to monitor since he receives 30% of the gains rather than the minuscule part a diversified investor receives. In fact, the larger the stake, the greater the incentive to monitor.

Since this monitoring produces a gain for all of the shareholders, diversified shareholders may want to encourage a few shareholders to maintain large positions in the firm. One way to do this is to lower the costs paid by those investors who take large stakes. Obviously one of the major costs borne by these investors is the added risk exposure due to the loss of diversification. A corporate hedging program reduces this cost and encourages the undiversified investors to maintain larger stakes than they otherwise would. Ultimately this increases expected cashflows since with more concentrated ownership, more monitoring occurs.[6]

Now we turn to the diversified investors' exposure to risks. Again, diversified investors include a large number of securities in their portfolios and put a small weight on each. Although investors who hold well-diversified portfolios are hardly affected by risks that are felt by only one or two firms, they generally have reason to be concerned with risks that are pervasive, i.e., risks that are felt by many firms. Pervasive risks typically do not vanish in diversified portfolios.[7] Diversified investors will therefore prefer that firms hedge pervasive risks rather than nonpervasive risks.[8] It must be emphasized, however, that diversified investors as a class gain only if the pervasive risks are transferred "out of the system." This means that when corporation A hedges a risk, it is not absorbed by corporation B, a company in which the diversified shareholders also hold stock. If risk is not transferred out of the system, the risk exposure of the *average* diversified investor remains the same. If, however, corporation A hedges the risk by transferring it to a privately held company or to a foreign company in which the diversified investors do not hold shares, then the average diversified shareholder may gain.

Hedging that transfers risk "out of the system" is one way to expand the set of securities over which investors diversify. Consider international diversification. The gains to international diversification appear to be quite large, yet most investors continue to concentrate their portfolio holdings in their domestic markets. Under certain circumstances, hedging can provide a way for these investors to realize some (but by no means all) of the gains of international diversification. For example, if the average firm in the country of Sellpetrol has positive exposure to the risk of changes in oil prices (returns increase when oil prices rise) while the average firm in the country of Buypetrol has negative exposure, the inhabitants of both countries can reduce the variance of their portfolios' returns by buying diversified portfolios consisting of shares in Sellpetrol *and* Buypetrol. If, for some reason, the inhabitants of each country do not diversify in this fashion but instead hold only portfolios diversified over their domestic stocks, then risk can still be reduced if the companies in each country hedge their risk of oil price exposure. This might be done by having the companies in Sellpetrol take short positions in oil futures and the companies in Buypetrol take the offsetting long positions. It could also be done if the investors of Sellpetrol issue short futures contracts to the investors of Buypetrol.

Given resistance or impediments to international diversification, hedging is potentially valuable to the shareholders of each country; but at this point there is no reason for it to be done at the corporate level. The obvious justification for corporate-level hedging is the savings in transactions costs. The potential sources of these savings are obvious. If fixed costs are associated with a hedge, it is better for a firm to pay these costs once on behalf of all shareholders than for each shareholder to pay these costs individually. A major component of these fixed costs is the cost of acquiring the information about the firm's risk exposure. Clearly there are also possibilities of reducing trading costs, legal costs, and so on, when hedging is done at the corporate level.

It would seem that the transactions cost advantages that firms possess would always decide in favor of hedging on corporate account. Surprisingly, this is not always true. The question of who should hedge — the corporation or shareholders — becomes much more complicated once we acknowledge that not all diversified investors are alike. This is because diversified investors are exposed to risks that affect them outside of their investment portfolios.

An airline pilot, for example, is exposed to oil price risk by virtue of his occupation.[9] If the pilot is a savvy investor, he skews his investment portfolio away from stocks that are negatively affected by oil price risk (i.e., have low returns when oil prices increase) and toward those that are positively affected. This reduces his overall exposure to oil price risk. If the pilot holds a stock in a firm that has a *negative* exposure to oil price risks, he prefers that the firm hedge the risk if it is not too costly to do so. At the same time, an Exxon employee who holds stock in a company with a *negative* exposure to oil price risk prefers that the company bear this risk. The negative exposure to oil price risk is a valuable hedge for the Exxon employee since it tends to offset his positive exposure to oil price risk resulting from his employment in the oil industry. Thus even shareholders who hold diversified portfolios may disagree over what a particular firm's hedging policy should be.

This disagreement among shareholders may mean that the best policy for the firm is not to hedge even if a majority of its shareholders benefit and if the firm's transactions costs are lower than those of its shareholders. For example, consider a firm with 100 shares and assume that it has a negative exposure to oil prices. Suppose that 60 of its shares are held by airline pilots and the remaining 40 by oil company employees.[10] Finally, assume that it costs twice as much for shareholders to hedge a unit exposure to oil price risk as it does for the company to hedge the same unit of exposure. If the company hedges its negative exposure to oil price risk, it pays $100c$, where c is the cost the company pays *per share* to hedge. The oil company employees are, however, worse off than they were before since they have lost the risk reduction produced by the company's negative exposure to oil price risk. As a consequence, they must unwind the hedge on their own accounts. This costs them $40(2c) = 80c$. (Recall that individual shareholders pay twice the transactions costs that the firm pays). Thus the total transactions cost spent when the firm hedges is $180c$. If the firm does not hedge, then the airline pilots must hedge on their own. This will cost $60(2c) = 120c$, which is less than $180c$.

Of course this is only a partial analysis of the problem. If the company does hedge, then it becomes more attractive to airline pilots and less attractive to oil company employees. The mix of shareholders may change from the 60/40 mix we assumed. The point remains that if shareholders have differing risk exposures due to such factors as their occupations (their human capital) and their undiversified real estate holdings, they will have conflicting preferences about corporate hedging programs. Hedging to meet some of the shareholders' needs may be worse than not hedging at all.

This brings us to the final consideration concerning shareholder risk exposure. Since shareholders have differing risk exposures outside of their security market portfolios (again consider the pilot and the oil company worker), they form "clienteles" for various stocks that serve as good hedges for these nonmarket risks. These shareholders want the risk exposure of the stocks they are buying to remain relatively constant over time. If the risk exposures of firms' shares were subject to frequent and major changes, then investors would need to closely follow the firms in which they invest. If exposures were changing significantly, these investors would often find it necessary to trade their shares to reestablish their optimal positions. This places a burden on the shareholders that can be avoided if companies follow a hedging policy that keeps the exposure of their shares relatively constant even if their operational exposure to risks is changing. This argument for stabilizing a stock's risk exposure in the interest of a clientele resembles arguments made concerning dividend policy. It is suggested that some investors desire dividends and form a natural clientele for high-yield stocks; others prefer "growth" and seek low-yield stocks. Firms do not necessarily gain by following a high-yield or low-yield strategy. What is important is that the firm not vary its payout significantly quarter to quarter or even year to year.

We have argued that there are justifiable reasons for corporate hedging based on its effects on shareholder risk bearing. However, in all of these cases, the gain is probably modest (at least for investors that hold well-diversified portfolios). The biggest gains may come when hedging substitutes (partially) for international diversification or allows shareholders to share risk with privately held firms or other firms in which diversified shareholders cannot trade. The issue is complicated by the fact that there are cases where a hedging program might benefit some shareholders but make others worse off.

Even if the gains created by corporate hedging and the lowering of shareholders' risk are typically small, this does not mean that hedging is not worthwhile. After all, the costs of hedging are often also small. We could attempt to quantify these gains and costs in particular situations, but this would not be easy — nor is it necessary. Most of the value of corporate hedging is not due to how it alters the risks experienced by shareholders but rather to how it alters the risks experienced by the firm itself. We now turn to this issue.

The Effects of Risk on the Firm and the Benefits of Corporate Hedging

In considering the effects of risk on the firm itself, we do not want to fall into the trap of assuming the firm should be treated as a separate individual with preferences of its own. We recognize that the firm is owned by the shareholders and that the firm's behavior is determined by the interaction of a number of individuals who may have conflicting interests. It has been argued that since the firm is not an individual with preferences, it is inappropriate to characterize the firm as risk averse. In some cases, this has been interpreted to mean that the firm should be considered "risk neutral." Discussions along these lines are generally not very fruitful and are often misleading. Nevertheless, we argue that often the firm should, from the perspective of its shareholders, behave as if it is risk averse. This risk aversion on the firm level creates the demand for corporate hedging and risk management.

Individuals are risk averse if they value the gain of any given dollar amount less than they value the loss of the same dollar amount. A risk-averse individual rejects a gamble that gives an equal chance of winning and losing $10,000; the 50% chance of having an extra $10,000 does not make up for the 50% chance of having $10,000 less. Now consider a firm that accepts the following gamble: with 50% probability, its earnings (before interest and taxes) will be $20 million higher than otherwise; and with 50% probability they will be $20 million lower. Does this gamble increase, decrease or leave unchanged the *expected* amount the firm can deliver to its investors? Suppose that the increase of $20 million results in only $13 million in additional cash for the investors but the investors feel the full effect of the $20–million loss; when the company loses $20 million, the investors receive $20 million less cash than they would have received if the company had not gambled. In this case, the investors are clearly worse off with the gamble than they are without it.

We emphasize that the investors are worse off *not* because this gamble added risk to their portfolios. The gamble could be decided by the flip of a coin, in which case it would be purely diversifiable risk. A diversified investor essentially would not care about this risk as it affects the risk of his portfolio holdings. Rather, the investors lose because the gamble reduces the expected amount of cash the firm delivers to them. From an investor's perspective, the value of the extra $20 million in corporate earnings measured *in terms of the extra cash delivered to the investors* is less than the value of the $20 million loss in corporate earnings *measured in terms of cash lost to the investors*. This means that even if an investor were risk neutral, he would want the firm to behave as if it were risk averse when it considered this gamble.

This raises the key question: do a firm's investors lose more when a dollar of earnings is lost than they gain when an extra dollar is earned? Note that this asymmetry does not occur when investors buy shares in an open-end mutual fund. Within a mutual fund, gains and losses are generally symmetric. A dollar earned is one more dollar available to the fund's investors, and a dollar lost is one less dollar. The amount the mutual fund can distribute to its investors is a linear function of the amount it earns.[11] If there are asymmetries in gains and losses within a corporation, it will be because of some *nonlinear* relation between earnings and what investors receive. We now explore some of these, starting with taxes.

Corporate Taxation and Hedging

Consider a firm with a corporate tax rate of 40%. Assume that if this firm does not hedge any of its operating risks, it will each year either earn $250 million with probability 75% or lose $50 million with probability 25%. Given these probabilities, the firm's expected earnings each year are $175 million. Assume that the company has the opportunity to fully and costlessly hedge its risks away. This means that the company will receive $175 million per year for certain. Should this company hedge?

Assume that it does not. Then when the firm earns $250 million, it will have $150 million after taxes to distribute to shareholders. (To simplify matters, we assume that the company has no debt so that all after–tax earnings are paid to shareholders.) When the company loses $50 million, it pays no taxes. If we assume that it can carry these losses forward (with interest) and use them fully to offset future taxes, then the loss to shareholders is not $50 million but only $30 million since future tax liability is reduced by $20 million. Thus the expected cash available to shareholders is 0.25 x (-$30,000,000) + 0.75 x ($150,000,000) = $105,000,000. If the company hedges, the cash available is also $105,000,000 since this is 60% of $175,000,000. Hedging has not changed the expected amount of cash available to shareholders.

Hedging did not have any effect because we assumed a uniform tax structure which treats losses and gains symmetrically by allowing the firm to take full advantage of losses carried forward or backward. In actuality, most tax structures are not linear. Tax rates often rise as income increases, and corporations cannot fully realize the tax benefits of losses as we assumed. This creates a role for hedging. Assume that when a $50 million loss is incurred, future tax liability is only reduced by $10 million, not by $20 million as we assumed above. This could be due to limitations on the ability to carry losses forward or backward, reductions in value of these offsets due to the time value of money, and so on. If the firm does not hedge, the expected amount available to shareholders is only 0.25 x (-$40,000,000) + 0.75 x ($150,000,000) = $102,500,000. This is $2.5 million less than the amount available to shareholders when the firm hedges. Even if hedging is costly, as long as the cost is under $2.5 million, shareholders are better off with corporate hedging. Hedging is valuable here because with the asymmetric tax structure, shareholders lose more when the company's before-tax income falls by a given amount than they gain when it rises by an equal amount. In a sense, the tax structure makes the corporation risk averse.[12]

Finally and importantly, this gain can *only* be produced by hedging on the corporate level; shareholders cannot hedge on their own accounts and reduce the corporation's tax liability in the manner shown above.[13]

Hedging and the Costs of Bankruptcy and Financial Distress

Any good corporate finance textbook has a long disquisition on the costs of bankruptcy and financial distress. These costs are usually cited as one of the reasons why firms do not fully exploit the tax advantages of increasing leverage. Since these costs are described in such detail elsewhere (Brealey and Myers 1991; Ross, Westerfield and Jaffe 1993; and Van Horne 1992), we summarize them briefly here and then discuss the obvious role hedging plays in reducing these costs. When a levered firm defaults on its debt or enters bankruptcy proceedings, direct costs are incurred through the increased need for legal, accounting and other professional services. While these direct costs are not necessarily trivial, it is usually claimed that the *indirect* costs of financial distress and bankruptcy are the most significant. These indirect costs take many forms.

For example, in situations of financial distress, the attention of upper management may be diverted from managing the firm's operations. This generally results in a loss of value. Due to uncertainties in how bankruptcy proceedings will be resolved, customers may be more reluctant to buy and suppliers may be more reluctant to make costly supply commitments when the value of these transactions depends on how long and in what form the firm remains in business.[14] Conflicts among various claimholders may cause the firm to pass up profitable investment opportunities. These conflicts occur when a firm is near bankruptcy and any new investment by shareholders will mainly benefit the bondholders. The simple solution to this problem is to reorganize the firm in such a way that the conflict no longer exists and then raise the funds necessary to undertake the profitable investment. In practice, such reorganization takes time and may not be achievable. These are just a few examples of indirect costs.

While some of the costs of bankruptcy and financial distress are subtle, the role hedging can play in reducing these costs is obvious. Hedging generally lowers the probability of financial distress and bankruptcy. By lowering the probability, hedging lowers the expected costs of distress and increases the expected cashflows available for shareholders. Again, the gain produced by hedging is due to an asymmetry. If earnings are low or negative, the shareholders must pay the costs of financial distress and perhaps bankruptcy.[15] If earnings are high, the shareholders do not get any extra bonus (e.g., a reverse payment from bankruptcy lawyers) to make up for the costs on the downside. Finally, note that when hedging reduces the cost of financial distress, it also increases debt capacity. Thus the gain due to hedging may show up through the firm's ability to increase its degree of leverage and realize the tax advantages or other benefits of a higher debt-to-equity ratio.[16]

Hedging and the Cost of Funding New Investment

The simple rule often given for choosing investment projects is the net present value rule: choose those and only those projects with *positive* net present values (NPVs). A project has a positive NPV if the present value of the cashflows it produces is greater than the investment required to undertake the project. Value is left lying on the table whenever a positive net present value project is not undertaken.[17] Unfortunately, a firm's current shareholders may find that they are better off passing up a positive NPV project. This occurs when the project cannot be funded out of retained earnings and outside financing is required.[18] Consider a firm that has 100 shareholders, each of which owns one share. The firm's management knows that the total value of the firm's assets is $1,000,000. Thus each shareholder currently has a claim worth $10,000. Now assume that the firm can undertake an investment project which costs $500,000 but which will produce cashflows worth $700,000. The net present value of this project is therefore $200,000. The firm, however, has no retained earnings to fund the project, so it must issue new shares to raise the capital. The firm's problem is that the outside market only values the assets the firm has in place at $500,000, not $1,000,000.

What could give rise to this discrepancy in valuations? Those who firmly believe in efficient markets would probably conclude that the management is mistaken and that it overestimates the value of the firm by $500,000. This, of course, is possible. But it is also possible that the management has information about the value of assets in place that the market does not have. For example, the company might be a biotech firm which is developing an experimental drug. The management could have some information relating to the prospects for success that cannot be quantified and is not subject to disclosure requirements. Indeed, the management may have compelling strategic reasons to keep the information secret. Thus, even if the management could voluntarily disclose the information, it might find it too costly to do so.

Assume that the management's valuation of $1,000,000 is correct, and consider what happens if the management raises capital to undertake the project. To do this, an additional 100 shares must be issued to raise $500,000. This means that each of the original shareholders will own 1/200 of the firm. The true value of the firm will be $1,000,000 + $700,000 = $1,700,000. Each of the original shareholder's stakes thus falls in value to $8,500. Recall that if the project is not undertaken, the value of each stake is $10,000. Quite simply, the dilution that occurs when shares are issued at prices below their true value overwhelms the increase in value brought about by the positive NPV project. The shareholders are forced to leave money on the table.

This problem would not have occurred had the firm possessed sufficient internal funds to undertake the project without raising capital on the outside. For example, if the firm had $500,000 in retained earnings in addition to its $1,000,000 in fixed assets, it could undertake the project and increase its value from $1,500,000 to $1,700,000. The original shareholders would not be hurt by dilution and would capture the full $200,000 increase created by the positive NPV project. All of this points to another valid reason for hedging on corporate account. Consider a firm that will over the years have a sequence of valuable investment projects to undertake, and assume that in a typical year it will have sufficient internal funds to finance the projects available that year. However, in those years when earnings fall to very low levels, the firm will not have sufficient internal funds to undertake positive NPV projects and may find itself in the predicament described above. A hedging strategy that stabilizes earnings and lowers the likelihood of the firm's needing outside capital is valuable since it reduces the chance that profitable investment projects will be foregone. In fact, any additional cost associated with outside financing (underwriters' fees, market price impact, etc.) creates a rationale for stabilizing earnings through hedging.[19]

Hedging and Agency Costs

We have shown that in many circumstances, reducing the volatility of earnings increases the expected amount of cash shareholders will receive. One should not conclude from this that shareholders always desire lower volatility. In fact, when the firm has substantial leverage (i.e., a high debt-to-equity ratio), shareholders have strong incentives to increase volatility. Additional risk or volatility tends to raise the value of the shareholders' position in a levered firm whenever the shareholders receive the benefits of the "upside" while the debtholders suffer the consequences of the "downside."

The possibility of the shareholders' taking advantage of the debtholders with a "heads I win, tails you lose" gamble is one of the sources of what has come to be termed "the agency costs of debt." The following example illustrates these agency costs and shows how hedging might be used to reduce these costs. Assume a firm has a single debt liability of $700 million which is due in one year. Suppose that if the firm continues to operate in its current manner, it will have assets worth $600 million when the debt comes due. This means that the firm will be bankrupt, shareholders will receive nothing, and debtholders will receive only $600 million of the $700 million owed to them.

Now assume that the company can change its operations and follow a risky strategy. If the risky strategy pays off, the firm will be worth $800 million; if the strategy fails, the firm will only be worth $400 million. If these two outcomes (success and failure) are equally likely, the expected payout to shareholders will be $50 million (50% chance of receiving $100 million — which is the residual from the $800 million once the $700 million in debt is paid — and 50% chance of receiving zero). The expected payout to bondholders is $550 million (50% chance at $400 million and 50% at $700 million). The risky strategy has not increased the expected value of the firm's assets (this remains $600 million), but it has transferred $50 million in expected payout from the bondholders to the shareholders. Of course, the bondholders are well aware of this possibility when they purchase the bonds and use bond covenants to restrict shareholders from following risky strategies.

Assume that the shareholders are prevented by covenants from taking a risky strategy of the sort described above. Is this a problem? Consider again the above example but with one change: assume that if the risky strategy pays off, the value of the firm is $1,200 million, not $800 million. The risky strategy has now increased the expected value of the firm from $600 million to $800 million (the average of $400 million and $1,200 million). This strategy is clearly worth pursuing.[20] However, unless the terms of the debt are renegotiated, the debtholders will not favor the strategy and will be unwilling to waive the covenants even though doing so would increase the firm's value. This is because the debtholders continue to have a claim that pays either $400 million or $700 million with equal probability. Since the expectation of this claim is $550 million, they will prefer that the company do nothing since this gives them $600 million for sure. The problem is solved if the terms of the debt contract can be easily renegotiated; but in many cases, especially those of publicly placed debt, this may be costly or impossible. Can hedging solve this problem?

Assume that the risk of the proposed risky strategy can be hedged away. For example, it may be that the risky strategy involves the firm's selling in a foreign market and that much of the risk is due to foreign exchange uncertainties. Assume that when this risk is hedged away, the 50/50 gamble of $400 million or $1,200 million becomes $800 million with certainty. Then, without the debt being renegotiated, the debtholders will receive $700 million instead of $600 million, and the shareholders will receive $100 million instead of nothing. By hedging the risk, the firm captures the value of the risky strategy; if the risk had not been hedged and the debt could not be renegotiated, the bondholders would have blocked the firm from obtaining the increase in value.

The example is admittedly simplistic, but the point it illustrates carries over to more realistic and complicated settings. When the capital structure includes debt, shareholders and debtholders may take opposite positions as to the firm's operations since such matters affect the riskiness of the firm's value. Hedging allows risks to be controlled and thus gives the shareholders more flexibility in altering the firm's operations without substantially changing the firm's overall risk. As we have shown, this added flexibility may mean that the firm can make value-improving changes in the way the firm operates — changes which otherwise would have been blocked by the bondholders.[21]

Hedging, Incentives and Employee Compensation

In most cases, the compensation of employees is positively related to the performance of the firms that employ them. If a firm does well, its employees generally receive higher levels of compensation than if the firm does badly. There are at least three reasons that justify this positive relation: risk sharing, constraints on the firm, and incentives.

First, we consider risk sharing. A small shopkeeper with a single employee would probably find it advantageous to pay the employee more when business is good and less when it is bad. This is because the shopowner absorbs all of the risk if the employee is paid a wage that is independent of the level of business in the shop. Unless the shopowner is risk neutral, it is generally better for the owner and the employee to share the risk. This means that *on average*, the employee must be paid more since the employee must be compensated for bearing some of the risk. However, a risk-averse shopowner will gladly pay a little more to the employee (on average) for bearing some risk since this reduces the shopowner's risk. The employee's variable compensation is basically a hedge for the shopowner.

While risk sharing along these lines makes sense in a small business, it is a less compelling reason for the variable compensation of employees in large corporations with diversified shareholders. The risk of a large corporation is shared extensively among its shareholders and other financial claimholders; there is minuscule advantage in employees' bearing a portion of the risk.[22] In fact, if risk sharing is the only consideration, a substantial loss occurs when employees bear significant risk since they must be compensated for it through higher average compensation. This increased cost is worth much less than the meager benefit the shareholders receive when risk is shifted to the employees.[23]

This brings us to the second reason employee compensation might vary with the firm's fortunes: in bad times, the firm may be constrained to pay employees less because of market imperfections. Consider a firm that has a wage bill of $50 million and revenues which vary between $25 and $100 million. We have argued that from a risk-sharing point of view, it is generally optimal for the shareholders to absorb most of the risk of variations in revenues or earnings. If the firm has several bad years of revenues at the $25-million level, the shareholders should contribute to make up the shortfall between the wage bill and revenue. If the money is not available in retained earnings, then the firm should raise more capital. But this may be excessively costly if it is even possible. Recall our discussion about hedging and the cost of funding new investment where the issuance of new shares involved substantial dilution. In such a situation, the company may cut back on employee compensation rather than raise funds externally. The employees are forced to bear a risk created by the company's funding constraints. Obviously, hedging can play a role here. If the risk of the revenue stream can be reduced, the company is less likely to have to reduce employee compensation. This means that employees will have more stable incomes and will not require additional compensation for risk. This savings in the wage bill accrues to the shareholders.

The third and final reason for employee compensation to be tied to the firm's performance concerns incentives, especially those for upper management. Over the last two decades, economists have extensively studied incentive contracting issues. This research considers the problems faced by a principal who hires an agent to act on the principal's behalf. It is generally assumed that the principal cannot observe all the agent's actions and in particular cannot observe the agent's level of effort. The optimal incentive contract for a principal to offer an agent can be quite complicated. Among other things, it depends on what the principal can observe, how the agent can affect the principal's welfare, and what degree of risk the principal and the agent can tolerate. In the context of our discussion, the principals are the shareholders of a firm and the agents are the firm's managers. As we have pointed out above, the shareholders are generally well-diversified investors and are much better able than the employees to bear the firm's risks. A number of results in the incentive contracting research concern cases where the principal is risk neutral (or nearly so) and the agent is risk averse. In these cases, the optimal incentive contract for the agent does not expose the agent to a risk unless it creates an incentive for the agent to work harder.

For example, assume that in January, a U. S. company sends an employee to negotiate a one-year supply contract with a French company. Assume that the contract will specify the quantity to be delivered each month and that the monthly payment will be denominated in French francs and fixed up front. Clearly, it is not sensible for the company to pay the employee a bonus in December that is inversely related to the *dollar* cost of the goods purchased over the year. If the French franc unexpectedly appreciates relative to the dollar over the year, the dollar cost of the good will increase; but it is not sensible to penalize the employee for this since the exchange rate is completely outside of his control. Of course, if the French franc depreciates instead, the dollar cost falls and the employee is rewarded. But again there is no reason for this since the gain was due to an exchange rate change and not to the employee's efforts. Exposing the employee to the risk of exchange rate movements that occur after the contract is negotiated serves no purpose at all in motivating the employee at the beginning of the year to negotiate a better price in French francs.

It would seem that these incentive contracting considerations provide another rationale for hedging on the corporate level. The compensation of the upper-level managers of a corporation is typically tied to various measures of corporate performance such as earnings and stock price appreciation. Stock options, for example, provide an obvious incentive for managers to increase shareholder value since many things affecting the stock price are under the managers' control. However, for almost every company, many determinants of the stock price are beyond the managers' control. If the company is a multinational corporation, *unexpected* changes in exchange rates can affect the company's profitability and its stock price; but just as in our example above, these typically fall outside the control of managers. It would seem that corporate hedging, since it removes some of these risks, makes stock options more effective in motivating the manager. If exchange rate fluctuations, oil price changes and similar risks are hedged, then changes in the stock price are less likely to arise from factors not under management control and more likely to result from actions taken by the management.

There is a problem with this incentive-based argument for corporate hedging. It provides a reason for hedging certain risks insofar as they affect the amount paid to managers, but it provides no reason for hedging to be done for the entire firm. Assume a multinational firm faces exchange rate risk beyond the control of management. One way to establish the appropriate incentives for managers is to base their compensation on the firm's future stock price performance and then hedge the exchange rate risk for the entire company. Call this Plan A. The same effect, however, can be achieved by Plan B. Under Plan B, the company does not hedge the exchange rate risk but instead adjusts the manager's compensation to remove the effects of unexpected exchange rate movements. Doing this involves determining what the stock price would have been had the company hedged and what the manager's compensation would have been had this been the stock price and had the company adopted Plan A. The manager could then receive this amount. The company would not need to hedge its entire risk to remove this risk from the managers' compensation. (Note that Plan B involves no trading at all by the firm in outside markets. All hedging is done internally by adjusting accounts.)

One could argue that the compensation committee of the board of directors would not have all of the information needed to make these adjustments. The risk exposure of the company might frequently change, and at any time of the year the managers would be the best informed about the need for hedging. It could be argued that managers should be given the opportunity to take the appropriate hedging positions on corporate account throughout the year as opposed to letting a committee guess an appropriate year-end adjustment. While this might seem to justify using Plan A and hedging for the entire corporation, it does not. Plan B can still be implemented if during the year the managers report daily the hedging they would do under Plan A. These reports can then be used at the end of the year to make the appropriate adjustments.

Is there any reason to adopt Plan A over Plan B? One possible justification for the use of corporate-wide hedging over hedging only for the managers is more "political" than economic. Consider what might happen if plan B is used and the company experiences a large loss due to a risk beyond the managers' control. Even though the shareholders suffer this major loss, the compensation required for the managers under Plan B might be quite high. This would be true if the managers had performed quite well in terms of those things under their control. In other words, losses would have been even higher had the managers not performed so well. In such a circumstance, managerial compensation (under Plan B) might be higher than it typically is in years when earnings are high. This outcome might seem perverse to shareholders who do not fully understand the incentive considerations behind the compensation contract. Under plan A, the compensation of managers would appear to be more closely tied to shareholder wealth and would perhaps generate less controversy.

Hedging and the Market's Signal Extraction Problem

As noted earlier, a firm can be hurt if the market undervalues its assets. This occurs, for example, when the firm has a valuable investment opportunity and needs to raise external funds. Corporate hedging has the potential to reduce these "information asymmetries" existing between the firm's managers and the market by improving the "signal-to-noise" ratio in corporate earnings. This can be illustrated by a rather fanciful example. Imagine that a charitable organization hires a fundraiser to solicit donations but is unsure of the fundraiser's ability. Assume that all the organization observes is the amount of money the fundraiser turns in each day. Over time, the organization will gather data to help it resolve the uncertainty concerning the fundraiser's ability. Obviously, a good fundraiser will on average turn in more than a poor one.

Now imagine that each day the fundraiser, before turning in the money, goes to the track and wagers some of the day's proceeds on the horses. The fundraiser then turns in the amount raised plus or minus the winnings or losses at the track. The betting has clearly made it more difficult for the charitable organization to determine the fundraiser's ability. For several days, a good fundraiser could turn in little due to losses at the track while a poor fundraiser might look good due to some lucky bets. In making its assessment of the fundraiser's ability, the organization will put less weight on the daily amounts turned in when these are influenced by the noise of the wagers at the track. A fundraiser who knows he is good and who wants to have this revealed as soon as possible has a clear incentive to avoid the noise added by gambling.

Hedging, to the extent that it removes noise, seems to allow security analysts and others in the market to obtain more precise estimates of the value of a firm's assets. Of course, a key assumption here is that the security analysts do not know all of the risk exposures the firm would face if it did not hedge. If the charitable organization in the example above knows all of the bets placed by the fundraiser at the track and the outcome of each race, then the gambling does not produce noise. Similarly, if the analysts know precisely the foreign exchange exposure, interest rate risk exposure and oil price risk exposure of the company at each moment, then the company gains nothing in terms of eliminating noise by hedging these risks. Of course, if the analysts do not know the company's exposure, the firm's management has the alternative strategy of removing the noise—not by hedging but by publicly disclosing the firm's exposure. In a similar manner, the fundraiser need not avoid the track altogether to remove the noise; instead, he could give the charitable organization his track receipts and disclose his betting for the day. The hedging approach might be preferred to the disclosure approach since it puts less of a burden on the market. For many investors, it may be difficult to process all of the information necessary to describe the risk exposures of a large company.[24]

Rewards for Supplying Hedging Services

Our final reason for hedging on corporate account is based on all the above reasons for hedging. These show that corporations can gain by hedging and should in many circumstances be willing to pay another firm or institution to take the counterparty position if necessary. Consider a company, Company A, that is exposed to a particular risk which it has no compelling reason to hedge. This company is in a natural position to provide a hedging contract to another firm, Company B, that is exposed to the same risk but in the opposite way. If Company B derives significant benefit from hedging its exposure, then Company A may be in a position to demand favorable terms of the contract. Whether it can depends on whether there are other potential suppliers of the hedging contract that can compete on the same terms as Company A. The simple point here is that even if the firm has no demand for hedging, its operating exposures may place it in a privileged position to supply hedging services and to receive value for doing so.

Conclusion

We have shown a number of ways in which hedging on corporate account can increase shareholder value. While a firm that hedges on corporate account can change the risk borne by shareholders in their portfolios, the gains from this are likely to be small. The substantial gains produced by hedging are due to the fact that risk affects the expected cashflows corporations can deliver to their shareholders because of taxes, bankruptcy costs, flotation costs for externally generated funds, and other "market imperfections." These considerations make the firm behave as if it were risk averse when it acts in the interest of shareholders and creates a need for hedging. Moreover, for most of these market imperfections, hedging on shareholders' accounts does not substitute for hedging on corporate account. A shareholder's hedging on his own account cannot lower the firm's expected costs of bankruptcy or financial distress. Nor can a shareholder take a position in a futures market and change the firm's expected tax liability. The firm itself must hedge to capture these advantages of risk reduction. We have not described in any detail how derivatives can be used to hedge since this is done elsewhere. Instead of looking at how derivatives can be used by corporations, we have asked the prior questions of whether they should be used at all and why. The justifications given above for hedging on corporate account show that corporations have a legitimate demand for instruments such as derivatives that they can use to control risk.

References

Brealey, R. A. and S. Myers. *Principles of Corporate Finance*. New York, NY: McGraw–Hill, 1991.

Breeden, D. and S. Viswanathan. "Why Do Firms Hedge? An Asymmetric Information Model," working paper, Duke University, 1990.

DeMarzo, P. and D. Duffie. "Corporate Incentives For Hedging and Hedge Accounting," Working Paper, Northwestern University, 1992.

Froot, K. A., D. S. Scharfstein, and Jeremy C. Stein. "Risk Management: Coordinating Corporate Investment and Financing Policies." *Journal of Finance* 48,5 (1993): 1629-1658.

Modigliani, F. and M. H. Miller, "The Cost of Capital, Corporation Finance, and the Theory of Investment." *American Economic Review* 48 (1958): 261-297.

Myers, S. and N. Majluf, "Corporate Financing and Investment Decisions When Firms Have Information That Investors Do Not Have." *Journal of Financial Economics* 13,2 (1984): 187-221.

Ross, S. A., R. W. Westerfield and J. F. Jaffe. *Corporate Finance.* Homewood, IL: Irwin, 1993.

Smith, C. W., and R. M. Stulz. "The Determinants of a Firm's Hedging Policies." *Journal of Financial and Quantitative Analysis* 20,4 (1985): 391-405.

Stulz, R. M. 1984. "Optimal Hedging Policies." *Journal of Financial and Quantitative Analysis* 19,2 (1984): 127-140.

___, "Managerial Discretion and Optimal Financing Policies," *Journal of Financial Economics* 26 (1990): 3-27.

Van Horne, J. C. *Financial Management and Policy.* Englewood Cliffs, NJ: Prentice Hall, 1992.

Notes

* Since writing this chapter David Fite has left Bankers Trust.

** We thank Anat Admati and Howard Mason for helpful comments.

[1] For example, Ibbotson and Sinquefield report that from 1926 to 1991, the average return on common stocks was 8.5% higher than the return on U. S. Treasury bills. This is an estimate of the risk premium that investors require to hold risky common stocks. The estimated risk premium for small company stocks over this period is even higher: 14.6%.

[2] A diversified portfolio is one that is composed of many securities. Moreover, the value of each security in a diversified portfolio is a small portion of the total value of the portfolio. With the growth of large institutional investors such as pension funds and mutual funds, a large portion of corporate liabilities is now held by diversified investors.

[3] It is possible for some investors to hold some stocks long and others short in such a way that energy cost risk disappears. The average investor, however, must hold a portfolio that is sensitive to energy cost risk.

[4] See Modigliani and Miller (1958).

[5] We assume that the diversified shareholders also hold shares in the firm that exports to Canada and that took the other side of the futures contract. If this is true, the diversified shareholders' exposure to foreign exchange risk remains neutral.

[6] We have not provided a full argument for why large shareholders exist. Corporate hedging lowers the cost of a large shareholder's taking an undiversified position, but it does not remove that cost entirely. Some other explanation must be provided for large shareholders. It is often suggested that there are benefits to holding controlling stakes in a corporation beyond the cashflows paid out to shares and that this compensates the large shareholder for the disadvantages of a large position. Another explanation is that large shareholders are caught in undiversified positions by historical circumstances and it is too costly for them to sell their shares and diversify. This is because large shareholders who sell out might be required to pay significant

capital gains taxes. It is also possible that the sale of their shares might have a large negative impact on the market price due in part to the market's recognition that they will no longer monitor the firm as closely. Note also that if the diversified shareholders use corporate hedging to lower the cost of a large shareholder's taking a larger position in the firm, there must be some way that the firm can commit to maintaining a hedging policy in the future. An exploration of these issues is beyond the scope of this article.

[7] As we mentioned above, it is possible to construct portfolios that are unaffected by pervasive risks. This is done by carefully choosing portfolio weights so that those securities having positive exposures to the pervasive risk exactly offset those having negative exposures. For example, one balances the positive exposure of oil companies to oil price risk with the negative exposure of airlines. If all securities have the same exposure (e.g., they are all affected positively), then this is still possible if one is willing to take short positions. The point is that diversification alone is not sufficient to remove pervasive risks. Moreover, although any individual investor can construct a portfolio that removes a pervasive risk, not all investors can do so.

[8] One might think that from a *diversified* investor's point of view, it makes no difference whether a particular firm hedges away a pervasive risk or a nonpervasive risk. It would seem that in both cases the effect on the diversified investor's portfolio is roughly proportional to the weight the firm's stock receives in the portfolio, and in a diversified portfolio this weight is small. This intuition is not correct. Assume, for example, that an investor holds 100 stocks and puts 1% of his wealth in each. (Dividing the investment equally among the 100 firms is generally not the optimal way to diversify. We make this assumption only to simplify the illustration.) Assume that firm i's return is equal to $\tilde{F} + \tilde{e}_i$ where $\tilde{F}$ measures the effect of the pervasive risk on returns (in this case, the pervasive risk affects all of the firms in the same way), and $\tilde{e}_i$ captures the risk that affects only firm i. For simplicity, assume that the variance of each of the $\tilde{e}_i$'s is equal to V and the variance of the pervasive risk is equal to W. Then if no firm hedges any of its risks, the variance of the diversified investor's portfolio is $W + V / 100$. If the first firm hedges its nonpervasive risk component (i.e., $\tilde{e}_1$) the variance of the diversified investor's portfolio falls to $W + 99V / 100$. If instead the first firm hedges its exposure to the pervasive risk $\left(\tilde{F}\right)$ and this risk is not transferred to any of the other 99 firms in the diversified investor's portfolio, then the variance of the diversified investor's portfolio falls to $(99 / 100)^2 W + V / 100$. If W is roughly equal to V (the variances of the pervasive and the nonpervasive risks are roughly equal), the hedging of the pervasive risk reduces the variance of the diversified investor's portfolio by *199 times* the amount hedging the nonpervasive risk does. As N (the number of stocks in the diversified investors portfolio) grows, so does the difference between the effects of hedging pervasive and nonpervasive risks.

[9] We implicitly assume that the pilot's employer is not fully hedged against oil price risk and that when oil prices increase, the pilot's compensation falls. This occurs, for example, if the pilot is temporarily laid off due to a decline in air travel. Issues concerning employee compensation and corporate hedging are discussed below.

[10] The reader may object that we have assumed that the majority of shareholders are pilots and not oil company employees. After all, pilots are the ones who should shy

away from companies with negative exposure to oil price risk. Even though this seems perverse, it could occur if there are many more pilots in the economy than oil industry employees or, more to the point, if pilots have greater wealth to invest.

[11] We ignore transactions costs and other fees associated with the mutual fund since these are generally small. Moreover, these only invalidate our assertion about the symmetry of gains and losses in a mutual fund if these costs have a nonlinear relation to the fund's returns.

[12] For more discussion on the effects of a convex tax structure on the value of corporate hedging, see Smith and Stulz (1985) .

[13] Of course, given the progressive nature of personal taxation in many countries, individual taxpayers who have volatile incomes might reduce their expected tax liability by hedging on personal account. This does not in any way reduce the need for the corporation to hedge on corporate account as a way of reducing corporate tax liability.

[14] Note that we need to distinguish between what is caused directly by bankruptcy or financial distress and what is caused by general market conditions. The proverbial firm that manufactured buggy whips in the 1920s went out of business because the market for its product changed — not because of its financial structure. Even if the buggy whip firm had no debt at all, it still would go out of business. We are concerned here with what happens when a firm has debt; and because of the failure of the firm's creditors to reorganize the firm quickly and efficiently, the firm follows a different (and lower-value) trajectory than it would have followed if it had no debt.

[15] It might be argued that the shareholders do not completely absorb the costs of bankruptcy and financial distress but instead that they share them with the bondholders. After all, the bondholders have expenses; and even if these are paid out of the firm's assets, this is money they might otherwise have received. This argument is wrong because it focuses only on what occurs at the time of financial distress. At the time the bonds are issued, the price is set to compensate bondholders for their expected losses due to these costs. The shareholders thus receive less from the bond issue, and the shareholders pay the expected costs of the bondholders at the time of issuance.

[16] Some additional discussion of the ability of hedging to increase debt capacity can be found in Smith and Stulz (1985) .

[17] This statement is a bit too strong. The NPV rule looks at investment in a "static" environment where investing in a project is a take-it-or-leave-it matter. In a more dynamic context, firms may find it optimal to delay initiating a project with a positive net present value since over time more information becomes available. In this sense, investment projects are like call options for which early exercise is not necessarily optimal. Even if we consider investment in a dynamic context, the story we tell below does not change in any major way.

[18] This example is based on Myers and Majluf (1984).

[19] For a more detailed discussion of this rationale for hedging, see Froot, Scharfstein

and Stein (1993).

[20] We implicitly assume here that the risk of success or failure is diversifiable risk, so it is appropriate to consider only the expected outcome. In other words, we assume no need to adjust for risk.

[21] Some additional discussion on the ability of hedging to reduce agency problems can be found in Stulz (1990).

[22] See Stulz (1984) for a discussion of the differences between the diversified position of shareholders and the undiversified position of managers and other employees. Stulz argues that this creates an incentive for the managers to hedge on corporate account if they are free to do so.

[23] If all investors in the economy are equally averse to risk, then for optimal risk sharing, each employee of a company should bear a fraction of the company's risk that is equal to the fraction of his wealth to the total wealth in the economy. To illustrate in a *very rough* way the magnitude of this amount, we consider an employee of a company who has $100,000 to invest. Since the total value of the U. S. stock market is approximately $4 trillion, the investor should bear something on the order of 1/4,000,000 of the company's risk. (This fraction actually overestimates the exposure the employee should face if risk is shared completely since we ignore international diversification and investment in bonds. Since the total value of the world capital market is estimated to be well over $20 trillion, complete risk sharing would put the fraction closer to 1/20,000,000. However, if we also account for noninvestable wealth such as human capital, the employee's wealth increases as does world wealth. Since we only want to establish a rough order of magnitude here, we do not consider these other factors and take the lower value of 1/4,000,000 to obtain a conservative estimate.) Now assume that the company is a $500–million company and suppose that it loses 10% of its value. If risk is efficiently shared, the employee should suffer a loss of only $12.50 (= $50,000,000/4,000,000). This means that a 10% loss for the company is only a 0.0125% loss for the employee. It might be argued that it makes no difference how much risk the employee faces in his compensation since the employee can always hedge on his own account to remove this risk. Here we must again distinguish between pervasive risks and company-specific risks. For the former, the employee can potentially make adjustments in his portfolio to balance his exposure. For example, the Exxon employee who is exposed to oil price risk through his compensation can adjust by holding very little investment in stocks that have positive exposure to oil prices and by increasing his holdings in those that have negative exposure. In some cases, the employee can also use derivatives and other hedging instruments to control these risks, but for many employees this is costly. If employees are forced to do this, then efficient risk sharing is in all likelihood not being achieved in the least costly manner. While the employee has some ability to manage his exposure to pervasive risks, he has much less ability to control his exposure to company-specific risks. The only effective way for the employee to remove a significant exposure to these risks is through shortselling his employer's stock. When this is allowed, it is generally quite costly for the employee. Of course, the shareholders of a company clearly have legitimate concerns about employees' taking short-sale positions

in the stock, especially if these employees are upper-level managers. This means that employees will face restrictions on shortselling. When these restrictions are enforced, employees cannot hedge exposures to company-specific risk in their compensation.

[24] For models of the use of hedging in improving the outside market's signal extraction problem, see Breeden and Viswanathan (1990) and Demarzo and Duffie (1992).

Valuation Risk and Financial Reporting

Joseph Mauriello, Partner and National Director —
     Banking and Finance, KPMG Peat Marwick
Joseph Erickson, Partner,
     KPMG Peat Marwick

Introduction

The manner in which risk is measured and reported influences behavior in dramatic ways. This chapter considers how financial institutions measure and report the value of their portfolios. We examine the issue of fair value accounting in order to consider the broader consequences of economic and accounting exposure.

Specifically, this chapter:

- Defines valuation risk and clarifies its relationship to financial reporting;
- Provides relevant background information concerning the changing risk profile of financial institutions and their risk management methodology;
- Discusses the results of market studies on valuation; and
- Advances beyond mark–to–market issues to focus on behavioral, institutional and competitive implications.

Although written from an accountant's perspective, the chapter is not intended to recommend any particular valuation or reporting methodology. Rather, we consider the market context in which the debates over fair value reporting have evolved. We explore how reporting methodology affects management's behavior in pursuing competitive advantage. With respect to mark–to–market accounting, we discuss the nature and important elements of the debate. A synopsis of recent pronouncements of the Financial Accounting Standards Board (FASB) and the ramifications for institutional and market behavior are also included.

Risk Management and Financial Institutions

Like other for–profit entities, financial institutions seek to maximize cash receipts over disbursements, acting as financial intermediaries or brokers of funds by acquiring funds from depositors or providers and investing funds with users or borrowers. Generally speaking, the more the interest earned on invested funds exceeds interest paid to acquire funds, the more profitable the financial institution—and the more likely that, in the long run, its cash receipts will indeed exceed disbursements. Maximizing interest earned over interest paid (also known as net interest margin or spread) is a primary objective.

When interest rates were less volatile, there were limited risks in acquiring and investing funds. The primary risk was credit risk, which the financial institution typically managed through lending limits and collateralization and by pricing credit risk into the lending rate. As the volatility of markets increased, however, financial institutions had to manage such risks. Because of their access to the markets, they became the natural brokers for the risks of other institutions.

Since then, distinctions and services of different types of financial institutions have blurred and competition has increased. The risk manager or financial risk insurer fulfills a primary function in many financial institutions. In addition, many insurers of physical risks have entered the financial risk arena, which further reduces the ability to distinguish among different types of financial institutions.

An institution's position on risk–taking is a function of management's propensity to accept or reject varying risk levels. Management may be risk averse, protecting depositors or avoiding a negative balance sheet impact by investing conservatively and strictly limiting exposure to fluctuations. Or management may adopt an aggressive investment strategy, striving to maximize profits while assuming greater risk. While the degree to which management assumes risk may indicate profit and growth potential, it also suggests potential volatility and losses.

Risk management includes the buying and selling of a variety of financial exposures as well as the management of all risks inherent in the environment. Exposures to changes in interest rates, foreign exchange rates, prices of securities, liquidity, and credit status must be actively managed. Managing these risks while attempting to maximize net interest margin requires the anticipation of future economic conditions and their impact on the institution's funding and investment alternatives. Consequently, to maximize profitability and limit risk, institutions seek to (1) limit and diversify exposure and (2) maintain more privileged access to a broader range of financial markets than their customers have.

As the market sought ways to manage new risks, Wall Street became more proficient at segregating specific economic risks and devising risk–management products with prices derived from the markets for cash securities (derivative products). These products are designed to improve management's flexibility in buying and selling risks and to reduce transactions costs by providing for future settlement dates without using valuable working capital. Some products that are traded on exchanges improve liquidity by standardizing transactions and inviting speculators to trade in specific risks. They also reduce transaction–specific credit risk by market–regulated collateralization. While this has greatly enhanced the risk management flexibility of financial institutions, it also has increased competition. Commercial enterprises often manage risks through derivative products that they previously could manage only through cash instruments offered by financial institutions. Now, they opt for complex and sophisticated financial instruments that may cost less.

Valuation Risk and Financial Reporting

Financial institutions hold large portfolios of financial instruments, including many that are carried off the balance sheet. Their values are sensitive to movements and expected movements in interest rates or market prices. If interest rate risk is the exposure to changes in market interest rates and resulting fluctuations in the value of net assets,[1] valuation risk is the exposure to a change between the market fair value assigned to a financial instrument and the amount realized upon sale or settlement.

Institutions often maintain a trading portfolio (actively traded instruments) and an investment securities portfolio (instruments held for investment). Historically, traded portfolio instruments are carried at market value and investment securities are carried at amortized cost. This policy assumes that the amount currently realized in the market is the most relevant measure unless the security can be held to maturity. Management and regulators have been concerned with the financial reporting impact of these classifications.

Valuation risk management represents a critical institutional activity because of increasing regulatory requirements, volatile capital markets and an overall loss of consumer confidence. Managing valuation risk becomes more important as a larger percentage of the institution's portfolio is required to be marked to market. This is especially true to the extent that regulators adopt mark–to–market valuations in measuring capital adequacy. While some risks have been managed in a reactionary fashion, valuation risk management involves proactively identifying and controlling risk.

The markets underlying financial risks have become more volatile, and the financial instruments used to manage exposure and volatility have become more complex. However, financial reporting requirements have not kept pace with these changes. As the focus of financial institutions has shifted from liquidity management to risk management, there is increasing concern that financial statements have not provided sufficient information on the risks assumed and the methods used to mitigate them. Consequently, as market changes adversely affected the financial condition of many financial institutions, existing reporting standards failed to capture the full impact of those changes.

The shift in focus from liquidity to risk management, the inadequacy of existing financial reporting standards, and permissive regulatory oversight are often cited as reasons for the failure of many financial institutions. Failures in the past decade have raised questions about the complexity of risk management transactions, concerns about the implications of risk management decisions, and uncertainty about the relevance of historical cost information in volatile markets.

Although today's financial statements do not communicate the risk of market volatility, measurement and recognition on a fair–value basis also fail to address this risk. Market values express the value of assets or liabilities at a single point in time and do not communicate the degree of risk that the value will change. Consequently, many believe that market values are only marginally more relevant than historical costs.

Moreover, determining such relevance requires an understanding of the institution's operations. Does the portfolio contain investments that can and will be held to maturity? Is the portfolio funded by liabilities that are equally sensitive to market fluctuations, thereby resulting in little or no net exposure to the institution? Market value information does not communicate the risks and uncertainties underlying many concerns about existing financial reporting. Consequently, the usefulness of market value information has been extensively debated.

Valuation Methodology: A Source of Debate and Scrutiny

Background

There has always been a direct relationship between accounting and risk management behavior. Given the competitive economic environment and growing regulatory scrutiny, managers increasingly seek to reduce the risk of volatility in their accounting methodology. Valuation risk management has been associated with a lack of consistent accounting methodology. This is attributable to the growing number of complex financial instruments, the slow development of accounting standards, and a lack of discipline and consistency in applying and enforcing standards.

The debate over the appropriate accounting methodology for financial institutions began in the 1930s. The Department of the Treasury forced a change from fair value accounting to historical cost accounting as a result of confidence issues raised by the Great Depression. The debate intensified in recent years as problems in savings and loan and banking industries raised concerns about the soundness of financial institutions and markets. Those concerns, along with the rapid growth of securitization, derivative products, mutual funds and commercial paper, have in turn raised new doubts about the adequacy and rationale of historical cost accounting.

Market value supporters at both the Securities and Exchange Commission (SEC) and the General Accounting Office (GAO) advised Congress that market value concepts would be necessary to avoid further unanticipated failures. To institute market or fair value accounting, the SEC first applied pressure to standard setters (the American Institute of Certified Public Accountants, or AICPA) and then to the FASB.

In Support of Fair Value Accounting

Proponents of fair value accounting highlight a number of real or perceived problems with historical cost accounting. They note the regularity with which financial institutions engaged in gains trading ("cherry picking"), the selling of investment securities with unrealized gains while carrying those with realized losses as historical costs. This allowed management to report earnings or reduce losses during periods of economic stress while waiting for markets to recover. Advocates of fair value accounting criticize the inconstancy with which securities were designated as investments versus trading. They question the objectivity and reliability of accounting that is based on management's intent. They also raise related questions about the use of hedge accounting rules to defer losses, the use of asset securitization rules to dress balance sheets and generate gains, and the inconsistency among financial institutions in establishing loan loss reserves. These issues have led to claims that financial institutions have not identified and managed risk effectively.

Proponents of fair value accounting argue that historical cost information is misleading and is not based on true economic principles. They argue that where markets exist, the market—not financial institutions or their regulators—should control valuations of assets and liabilities.[2] Only then will more accurate results of the institution's risk management policies be reported. Proponents also assert that owners of financial institutions need market value reporting to properly value their institutions and evaluate their management teams.

In Opposition to Fair Value Accounting

Opponents of fair value reporting generally argue that such information only meets the needs of users interested in estimated liquidation value. Fair value may provide useful information for regulators, but it can mislead users who focus on short–term market fluctuation effects and disregard the overall risk management practices of the institution. Fair value opponents argue that regulators' information needs should not be met through general–

purpose financial statements. If fair value information does not serve users of general–purpose financial statements, then the significant costs of producing the information are unjustified.

Fair value opponents also contend that the information is highly subjective, resulting in unreliable and incomparable information. They are concerned that the volatility in reported earnings and equity from fair value accounting unnecessarily weakens market and public confidence. This is especially true for depository institutions functioning as financial intermediaries where short–term fluctuations have limited, if any, effect on long–term exposure. Some opponents argue that this results in management's focus on short–term exposure, which further constricts the availability of intermediate and long–term credit.

Like historical accounting, fair value information portrays a transaction or balance sheet at a point in time and says little about future prospects. Since the information is, in part, more subjective than historical cost data, an even greater opportunity may exist for manipulation of reported values, earnings and capital. Auditors and regulators will depend on information provided by the institution to evaluate or challenge market value estimates.

Developments in Fair Value Reporting

The rate of change in financial markets and instruments has strained the resources of the accounting profession as well as those of standard setters who keep pace with changes. The demands of this rapidly changing environment were a major factor in the 1984 formation of the Emerging Issues Task Force (EITF), a group created to assist the FASB in the early identification of emerging financial reporting issues and problems in implementing policy. A vast majority of the issues brought to the EITF addressed financial instruments.

In 1986, the FASB launched a project to more broadly address the issues in the recognition and measurement of financial instruments. To date, that project has produced two statements addressing disclosure, two addressing accounting, and several preliminary research and discussion documents. The Board continues to grapple with the challenge of hedge accounting while pursuing the broader recognition and measurement project.

The four major, authoritative FASB pronouncements resulting from the financial instruments project are as follows:

SFAS 105. *Disclosure of Information about Financial Instruments with Off–Balance–Sheet Risk and Financial Instruments with Concentrations of Credit Risk*, originally was part of a pronouncement intended to address both credit risk and the disclosure of fair value information. The opposition to the breadth of the proposal and particularly to the proposed market value disclosures was so strong that the FASB made fair value disclosures a separate project.

SFAS 105 requires all entities to disclose contractual and quantitative information about financial instruments not currently recognized in the balance sheet. The disclosure should address the nature of the credit and market risks, the cash requirements, and the potential accounting loss upon failure of counterparties to meet contractual terms, including the accounting and collateralization policies of such instruments. SFAS 105 also requires disclosures about significant concentration of credit risk with an individual counterparty or similar groups of counterparties.

SFAS 105 was an important first step in improving disclosures about complex financial instruments. It provided information not readily available to users of financial statements. The implementation of SFAS 105 highlighted the significance of the gross exposures in off–balance–sheet financial instruments. FASB Interpretation No. 39, *Offsetting Amounts Related to Certain Contracts*, clarified that off–balance–sheet positions should not be netted for disclosure purposes unless those positions can legally be settled by offsetting. While a financial institution may net those positions internally for risk management purposes, there are still underlying concerns about exposure to credit risk, systemic risk (how a major counterparty's failure to perform affects the system's liquidity), and the fact that such obligations cannot be discharged by offsetting under bankruptcy or liquidation.

SFAS 107. After issuing SFAS 105, the FASB returned to researching and developing an approach for fair value information disclosure. SFAS 107, *Disclosures about Fair Values of Financial Instruments*, requires the disclosure of fair value information for all financial instruments— both recognized assets and liabilities and off–balance–sheet—for which it is practicable to estimate fair value.

According to SFAS 107, fair value disclosures should be based on a quoted market value as of the reporting date if such amounts are available. If not, the institution must estimate fair value based on the market–quoted price of similar financial instruments or on valuation techniques. If it is not practicable to estimate fair values, disclosures of fair value estimates should include an explanation.

SFAS 107 prohibits including the long–term relationships associated with deposit–type liabilities as part of the deposit's value and, absent a maturity date, requires disclosure of the fair value as the amount due upon demand. Such intangible relationships, as well as other intangible and tangible assets and nonfinancial liabilities, can be valued and disclosed separately. The FASB staff is currently researching the valuation of deposit liabilities to assess the feasibility of including various liabilities in a fair value recognition model.

The public expectations and reactions to these disclosure requirements are discussed in the following summary of recent surveys.

SFAS 114. Despite the FASB's desire to broadly address recognition and measurement of financial instruments, external pressures have accelerated various parts of the financial instruments project. SFAS 114, *Accounting by Creditors for Impairment of a Loan*, applies to all creditors. The FASB accelerated this part of the financial instruments project to address concerns about the inconsistencies among different types of financial institutions and their accounting for impaired loans. The Accounting Standards Executive Committee (AcSEC) of the AICPA and several regulators urged the FASB to undertake this project when AcSEC failed to reach consensus in reconciling the various existing AICPA industry guides. The most significant inconsistency in the existing guidance was the treatment of interest, specifically whether or not to include it when valuing troubled loans.

SFAS 114 requires that impaired loans be measured based on the present value of expected cash flows discounted at the loan's effective interest rate. As a practical alternative, the loans may be valued at their observable market price or the fair value of the underlying collateral. Under SFAS 114, the collectibility of both contractual interest and principal should be evaluated when assessing the impairment of a loan. SFAS 114 also allows aggregation of loans with common risk characteristics when past experience with similar loans indicates the expected future cashflows. Also, total loan investment subject to

SFAS 114 accounting must be disclosed together with the gross activity in allowance for credit losses and the institution's income recognition policy.

SFAS 114 may increase the consistency with which loans are valued in relation to anticipated credit losses, but such valuations still require significant subjective judgments. Additionally, SFAS 114 does not specify how to identify those loans to be evaluated for collectibility. Consequently, financial institutions will continue to approach loan loss evaluations inconsistently. Based on the surveys summarized below, the disclosure requirements do not sufficiently provide the credit–related information that users want.

SFAS 115. This pronouncement, *Accounting for Certain Investments in Debt and Equity Securities*, also responded to regulators' concerns about inconsistencies between accounting literature and practice. Specifically, the pronouncement assessed the appropriateness of accounting for debt securities investments at amortized cost and the effect of gains trading activity. Regulators believed that sales of securities out of the investment portfolio indicated that such securities were not being held to maturity. Instead, they were available for sale and thus subject to the lower of cost or market (LOCOM) or market–value accounting. AcSEC concluded that the FASB could more effectively deal with the project. Along with regulators, it encouraged the FASB to account for debt and equity securities uniformly.

SFAS 115 applies to (1) investments in equity securities traded either on a SEC–registered exchange or in the over–the–counter market and quoted nationally and (2) debt securities. It does not apply to restricted stock, investments in subsidiaries, or investments accounted for under the equity method. It also excludes entities whose specialized industry practices include accounting for virtually all investments at market or fair value.

SFAS 115 addresses both the classification of securities and the subsequent accounting. At acquisition and each subsequent reporting date, all debt and equity securities must be classified as held–to–maturity, available–for–sale, or trading. The subsequent accounting for each category is different: transfers between categories, also limited by SFAS 115 rules, must be made at fair value. By specifying the criteria for classification, the FASB sought to reduce the opportunities to manage income effects.

To classify securities as held–to–maturity, the investing entity must have both the positive intent and ability to hold them to maturity. The pronouncement also identifies certain events that may result in the sale or change in classification of such securities without questioning the entity's intent to hold them to maturity. Securities bought with the intent to sell in the near term are classified as trading securities. Securities neither qualifying as held–to–maturity nor purchased for trading are classified as available–for–sale.

Securities that qualify as held–to–maturity continue to be accounted for at their amortized cost. Trading securities are accounted for at their fair value with unrealized holdings gains and losses included in earnings. Available–for–sale securities also are recorded at their fair value, and the unrealized holding gains and losses are excluded from earnings and recorded as a net amount in a separate component of shareholders' equity until realized. For securities classified as held–to–maturity or available–for–sale, permanent declines in value below amortized cost are recognized as earnings.

Disclosure of fair value, cost basis, and unrealized holding gains and losses are required for securities classified as held–to–maturity or available–for–sale. These disclosures are to be provided by major security types, and separate disclosure of maturity information is required for investments in debt securities. SFAS 115 also requires transaction–related disclosures for various types of sales and transfers between categories.

SFAS 115 is a significant first step toward fair value recognition in financial statements. One major concern is that SFAS 155 is a one–sided fair–value model and does not require or even allow fair valuation of liabilities. Opponents of this approach maintain that it improperly reports the effects of interest–rate and market changes on only the asset side of the balance sheet. If properly matched, changes in the values of the reporting entity's liabilities will mitigate or fully offset any unrealized gain or loss in its assets.

Critics of SFAS 115 accuse the FASB of succumbing to regulators' pressure rather than taking the time to assess the impact of fair value information disclosed under SFAS 107. The FASB began by pursuing a two–sided fair value reporting requirement and could not gain consensus among Board members on some controversial issues. The completion of SFAS 115 prior to an assessment of the costs and benefits of SFAS 107 indicates the strong regulatory influence on standard setting. The information provided by SFAS 115 pertains more to regulatory users of financial statements than to others. The important unanswered question is whether fair value recognition, especially one–sided recognition, provides sufficient incremental benefit to justify the costs of the system. Recent surveys indicate that users other than regulators are not anxious to abandon the historical cost model. Although interested in fair value information, they have other disclosure priorities that are unheeded in favor of regulatory interests.

Implications and Behavioral Changes

By issuing SFAS 107, the FASB has mandated fair value disclosures with 1992 reports. SFAS 115 required an increased level of fair value recognition in 1994. In a broad sense, it began an experiment in fair value accounting. The effects of this new information will be apparent only as the information is scrutinized and publicly discussed in the markets. For many financial institutions, these estimates will represent a first attempt to quantify information that is, to some extent, inherently subjective and judgmental. Estimation techniques, assumptions, and observable facts will affect fair value estimates.

Financial statement users must realize that fair value estimates are made at a discrete point in time. Changes in assumptions can significantly change the estimates. In that regard, fair value estimates may be only marginally more useful than historical cost information. Users must be careful not to draw incorrect conclusions from the information disclosed. Furthermore, fair value disclosures under SFAS 107 are limited to financial instruments, do not include many tangible and intangible assets, do not consider tax implications, and cannot be used to derive an institution's economic value.

The subjectivity of fair value disclosures places a significant burden of responsibility on preparers. They must select from subjective criteria and determine what level of disclosure makes the information meaningful. It could take several years for comparable and sufficiently useful fair value disclosures to evolve. The initial inclinations to provide minimal information and avoid user reactions to any unexpected information will inhibit the evolution of the disclosures. Both preparers and users, respectively, should exercise care in their explanation and interpretation of disclosed fair value information.

Regulators of financial institutions will need to be especially cautious in using value information. Earnings and capital under a one–sided SFAS 115 model could be volatile enough to place the institution in and out of capital compliance. The regulatory side will need to address what the FASB could not—the fair valuation of liabilities and determination of net market value. Perhaps a supplemental fair value balance sheet will be mandatory and include some of the more subjective fair value estimates required by SFAS 107. So much estimating is involved, and rates and market values are so volatile and subjective that regulators must resist the temptation to overreact to fair value fluctuations without fully understanding an institution's risk structure and risk management policies. Fluctuations in fair value may shed little, if any, light on earnings potential and long–term risk structure.

Although fair value information may provide new insights into an institution's operations and financial condition, management will have the same incentives to manage or manipulate a fair value accounting or disclosure standard as it would a historical accounting standard. Some argue that this may occur to a greater extent under fair value accounting. Without regulatory or market pressures to provide meaningful fair value information, fair value disclosures will not necessarily change behavior. Regulatory and/or market incentives must be sufficiently strong for fair value information to affect the basic business and reporting strategies of financial institutions.

The movement to reliable fair value information may be prompted by internal rather than external information needs. Financial institutions recognized as leaders in risk management are rapidly changing internal attitudes toward risk and the pricing of risk. The internal changes at many financial institutions to risk–based capital allocations, risk pricing models, and total risk management programs are years ahead of regulators' interest in and understanding of these issues.

Valuation Risk and Financial Reporting: Market Research

Recent market research provides insight into of preparers', regulators', and other users' attitudes toward fair value information. KPMG Peat Marwick has completed three major studies on fair value reporting since the FASB issued SFAS 107 in December 1991.

One study, *Estimating Fair Values for Financial Instruments—Disclosure and Beyond*, was performed for the Association of Reserve City Bankers (ARCB) to consider practical issues relating to fair value reporting. The second study, *Fair Value of Financial Instruments—An Insurance Industry Survey*, was conducted in November 1992 to determine the views of users and preparers of insurance company financial statements on fair value disclosures and fair value accounting. The third study, *Fair Value of Financial Instruments—Disclosure and Reaction*, was issued in September 1993. It reviewed actual fair value disclosures under SFAS 107 in order to gauge public reaction to such disclosures.

The objective, methodology and results of these studies are summarized below.

Association of Reserve City Bankers Study

With the issuance of FASB 107, the theoretical debate over the relative merits of fair value information versus historical costs shifted to the issue of practical implementation. The 1992 study conducted by KPMG was commissioned by the Trustees of the Banking Research Fund of the ARCB to consider practical issues relating to the generation and use of fair value information. The primary objectives of the study were to:

- Determine the perceived ability of banks and others to obtain reliable, consistent estimates of fair value;
- Consider the manner and extent to which management, investors, and regulators are likely to rely on fair value information;
- Explore the likely changes in behavior resulting from the availability of fair value information; and
- Assess the sensitivity of valuation procedures and fair value estimates to changes in assumptions and parameters.

These objectives were designed to capture informed judgments about the expected relevance and reliability of fair value information and its likely impact on management, investors, and regulators. The study consisted of written surveys, focus group meetings, and direct interviews to better understand the views of the institutions that will provide fair value information (preparers) and the expectations of analysts, investors, managers, and government agencies that will use it (users).

In general, the survey revealed a significant gap between users' expectations in receiving reliable, comparable fair value information and preparers' intentions in providing information. Key questions raised in the survey results included:

- Would fair value information prove too subjective to users?
- Would a lack of comparability among institutions limit the usefulness of fair value disclosures?
- Would time lags cause information to become outdated before users could receive and interpret it?

Respondents indicated that, at least initially, these issues could reduce the usefulness of fair value disclosures. Users overwhelmingly opposed fair value accounting as the primary basis for preparing financial statements. They were more favorably inclined to supplement existing financial statements with fair value disclosures but remained concerned about the reliability, comparability, and timeliness of fair value disclosures.

Preparers agreed that fair value accounting should not replace historical cost as the primary basis of financial statements and were pessimistic about the usefulness of fair value disclosures. Most preparers indicated that historical cost accounting supplemented with fair value disclosures would not provide useful, understandable information. They were concerned about the subjectivity of the information and whether sufficient detail would be available and considered by users to ensure that the disclosures were understood.

Respondents indicated that information on credit quality and problem assets was considered both the item of greatest interest and the item most inadequately disclosed. Users indicated that existing financial statements and disclosures were adequate for most types of information; but they sought improved disclosure on potential problem loans, off–balance–sheet instruments, loan concentration, and general credit quality.

Investors and analysts expressed strong reservations about the subjectivity involved in calculating fair value information and thus its usefulness. There was wide support for the notion that financial institutions should provide detailed information to help investors and analysts make fair value estimates and formulate comparable information. However, when asked which additional items they would like to have disclosed, the institutions focused on details pertaining to credit quality and problem assets.

The survey revealed a significant disparity between the amount of measurement error in fair value estimates that users were willing to tolerate and the amount of precision that preparers expected to provide. The largest divergence occurred in items such as loans and guarantees that typically are characterized by unique facts and circumstances, including relatively greater credit risk.

Preparers expected that the cost of obtaining the estimates would significantly affect the level of measurement precision. For example, when asked to ignore costs, preparers expected measurement errors closer to user expectations than when costs were considered. Users were asked to indicate error tolerances assuming that fair value estimates served as the basis for recognition in the balance sheet. The result: a more narrow tolerance for error than that of the preparers, even when cost was not a consideration.

In general, respondents agreed that the usefulness of fair value disclosures would diminish over time. A majority of users believed that fair value information would be marginally diminished over just one month; more than one third believed such disclosures would be greatly diminished over two or three months.

Users emphasized the need for practices to ensure comparable fair value estimates. They supported uniform methodologies, assumptions, and presentation. Despite the importance of comparable results to users, preparers indicated that a range of methodologies and assumptions was likely to be used when determining fair value estimates. They also indicated that comparability would most likely fall short of user expectations, at least initially.

When asked to identify the methodology to determine the fair value of particular nontraded, on–balance–sheet financial instruments, preparers often indicated that they would use discounted cashflow analysis. However, several other approaches were cited, including the quoted market prices of similar loans, independent valuations, and the carrying value of the instruments. For off–balance–sheet financial instruments, quoted market prices of similar instruments and the replacement or close–out approach were the most frequently listed valuation approaches. Pricing models and discounted cashflow analysis were also frequently mentioned.

In addition to varying methodologies, preparers indicated a range of different assumptions. For example, although most preparers indicated that credit risk would be incorporated into fair value estimates, a small percentage indicated that it would not. For those who would consider credit risk, the means of incorporating it in the cashflows, the discount rate, or the allowance for loan losses would differ, as would the application to either individual loans or loan pools.

If preparers were to follow through on the expectations reported in the survey, there would be considerable diversity in methodologies and in the underlying assumptions used to estimate fair values. This would result in very limited comparability.

Users identified several descriptive items that they considered essential in understanding fair value estimates, e.g., discount rates, methodology, sensitivity of estimates to assumptions, sources of market prices, and estimates of amount and timing of cashflows. Preparers had mixed expectations regarding disclosure of these items, but few expected to disclose either cashflow estimates or the sensitivity of fair value estimates to the underlying assumptions.

The majority of preparers believed that investors and regulators would be influenced by fair value disclosures although approximately only one third believed that stock prices would be affected. They were almost evenly split on whether fair value information would drive business strategies to a short–term focus. No preparers indicated the likelihood of a change in focus toward longer–term goals.

Interviews conducted with staff of the federal bank regulatory agencies confirmed stated public positions: they opposed comprehensive fair value accounting but generally supported fair value disclosures. Regulators expressed concern about the relevance of fair value information given the subjectivity of the estimation process and the reporting institutions' unique knowledge of the instruments.

As a step toward the broader use of fair value in financial reporting, the SEC and GAO staffs reiterated established agency positions in favor of fair value disclosures. Comparability among institutions was cited as an important consideration. The SEC considered the judgments that management must make versus those required to establish loan loss allowances.

The survey results suggest that the range of different methodologies and assumptions likely to determine fair value may well squelch users' strong interest in comparable and reliable information. The second part of the ARCB study documented those differences, discussed alternative valuation methods, and considered the subjective judgments required to calculate fair value estimates for certain instruments. The effects of subjective judgments were tested to illustrate the sensitivity of fair value estimates to changes in assumptions for various instruments.

Financial institutions face numerous implementation issues in preparing fair value disclosures under SFAS 107. Although fair value estimates for instruments with quoted market prices are straightforward, SFAS 107 provides limited guidance for calculating fair value estimates when quoted market prices are unavailable. For certain instruments that are relatively homogenous and for which active markets exist—residential mortgages, consumer loans, swaps or options—quoted market prices of similar instruments represent viable alternatives. Adjustments may be necessary to reflect differences in credit quality, servicing fees or other unique characteristics.

Alternative approaches include discounted cashflow analysis (DCF), independent valuation, price modeling, or replacement costing. The survey results suggest that preparers will most frequently use DCF or pricing models to determine fair value information for instruments without quoted market prices. Theoretical concepts underlying DCF are not difficult, but they require subjective judgments in estimating timing, cashflow amounts, and discount rates. Additionally, the approach involves other subjective questions:

- Will a fair value estimate be prepared on an individual instrument or portfolio basis?
- How will portfolios be segmented?
- Will credit quality factors be reflected? If so, will they be incorporated into the cashflows or the discount rate?
- Will a single discount rate or yield curve approach be used?

The answers must be determined for each type of financial instrument. In turn, they influence the comparability, reliability, and precision of fair value estimates.

The ARCB study concludes that SFAS 107 represents an interim step in the evolution of the fair value reporting. It projects that it will take several years for users to obtain sufficiently reliable and comparable fair value information and for such information to influence capital allocation. The study also predicts that the pressure from government agencies and regulators for fair value disclosure and accounting will continue. It emphasizes that while regulators focus on fair value information, other users seek more detailed disclosures in areas where market information is not readily available: credit quality, problem assets, and certain off–balance–sheet items. Such disclosures would be more factual in nature than some estimates of fair value and would permit financial statement users to make their own judgments.

Insurance Industry Survey

KPMG Peat Marwick issued *Fair Value of Financial Instruments—An Insurance Industry Survey* in November 1992. The survey was conducted to determine how users and preparers of insurance company financial statements viewed the reliability, comparability, and relevance of fair value disclosures and fair value accounting. The majority of the responding preparers represented the largest insurance companies, those with total assets over $1 billion. These preparers represent a diverse group of companies that write both property/casualty and life/health coverage.

In addition to FASB implementation considerations, the survey covered expectations of financial statement users. Specifically, it explored (1) what they hoped to gain and (2) how they expected managers, investors, policyholders, creditors, and regulators to behave as a result of fair value disclosures.

Although their opinions about fair value disclosures differed, the majority of preparers and users did not favor a change from historical cost accounting to fair value accounting. If the fair value basis were required, 69 percent of the preparers and 75 percent of the users believed that both assets and liabilities should be recorded at fair value. When asked what additional piece of information outside of basic financial statements could be obtained, respondents overwhelmingly favored the amount and timing of future cashflows rather than fair value information.

Seventy percent of the users believed that historical financial statements supplemented by fair value disclosures are more meaningful than either historical cost financial statements alone or financial statements prepared on a fair value basis. As a second choice, they favored two separate financial statement presentations, one based on historical cost accounting and one based on fair value accounting.

Users believed that fair value disclosures will improve historical cost financial statements; but preparers were divided on the issue. They believed that consistency and comparability of financial statements will be compromised to achieve the additional disclosures.

Almost half the preparers currently used fair value estimations in some manner to manage companies. Approximately 70 percent of the preparers did not see a change in business strategies as a result of the fair value disclosure requirements of SFAS 107. Of those who did see a change in focus, the most frequently perceived change was a focus on shorter– rather than longer–term goals.

Preparers believed that fair value disclosures vary in usefulness among users, as follows:

Figure 1

Preparers' Assessment of Usefulness of Fair Value Disclosures

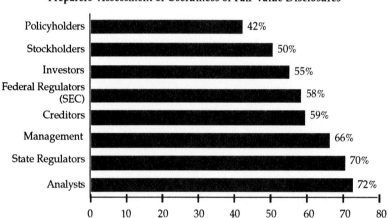

Generally, the insurance survey responses agree with the ARCB study. The majority of both users and preparers favor fair value disclosures rather than a change in the underlying historical cost recognition model. Notably, there is very little support for the type of one–sided recognition required by SFAS 115.

Follow–up to ARCB Study: Disclosures and Reactions to Disclosures

In 1993, KPMG undertook a follow–up study of the ARCB report to review the actual fair value disclosures of banking institutions and the reactions to such disclosures. This study, *Fair Value of Financial Instruments: Disclosure and Reaction*, was released in September 1993.

The primary objectives of the study were to:

- Determine the extent of fair value disclosures;
- Determine the degree of reliance on fair value estimates;
- Identify the methods used to calculate fair values; and
- Identify changes or enhancements to fair value estimates and disclosures.

Annual reports and fair value disclosures were reviewed. Then financial statement preparers and users were surveyed and interviewed to determine their attitudes toward the disclosures and the methodologies used to ascertain fair value.

Written surveys were sent to two groups: bank financial reporting managers responsible for developing fair value information (preparers) and banking investors and analysts dependent on fair value information for analysis and decision making (users). In general, the survey results and interviews revealed a gap. Users inclined toward continued presentation of fair value information, and preparers desired to downplay or eliminate such disclosure. As predicted by the expectation gap reported in the 1992 ARCB study, users were not satisfied with the extent and depth of information provided; consequently, they did not seem to be influenced by the disclosures. However, they supported the experiment and freely provided suggestions for improvement. In contrast, preparers indicated that the information was not useful and did not warrant the compliance costs.

The predominant style of presentation was footnote disclosures with side–by–side tabular presentation of carrying values and fair values. Less than 20 percent of the annual reports addressed fair value estimates in management's discussion and analysis. Nearly all institutions commented on the subjectivity of fair value estimates and the inability to actually realize such values. None of the institutions reviewed chose to exclude fair value information on the basis that it was "not practicable" to provide, but some indicated that materiality affected the level of disclosure.

When quoted market prices were not available, discounted cash flow was the most frequently cited method to estimate fair value. However, fewer than 20 percent of the annual reports disclosed specific assumptions used in the calculations. The rate used was often the current interest rate for similar instruments; preparers seldom disclosed the actual discount rate.

Many of the early concerns about estimating fair value centered around treatment of the loan portfolio and allowance for loan losses. Preparers' responses in this survey generally conformed to the anticipated methodologies for estimating fair values of loans as discussed in the initial 1992 ARCB study. However, users were disappointed by the level of detail in annual reports. Of those reports reviewed, over 80 percent presented the fair value of loans as a net amount.

Preparers and users rated the usefulness and quality of fair value disclosures as either fair, poor, of no value. Given the 1992 survey results, preparers' attitudes toward usefulness were not unexpected. Users were disappointed that relatively broad disclosures did not meet their high expectations. Over 80 percent of responding users indicated that they learned nothing new from the disclosures; preparers reported receiving few if any questions about the fair value disclosures.

Users did not support eliminating the information. However, they did recommend several ways to improve the quality of fair value estimates and disclosures. Standardization of methodologies and assumptions were frequently cited as the most likely improvement. Users were equally divided between voluntary standardization by preparers and mandatory action by the FASB. There was little support for action by the SEC or AICPA to improve standardization. Although preparers generally agreed that fair value disclosures should be discounted, they felt strongly that standardization, if required, should only be brought about by the FASB.

Fair value as an accounting concept will continue. Financial reporting standards such as SFAS 107, SFAS 114, and SFAS 113 will further fair value measurement, disclosure, and recognition processes. Users of such information, including regulators, will be influenced by the diligence in estimating and reporting fair values. The ultimate role of these steps in the evolution of the accounting model will depend on the usefulness of the information.

The follow–up study noted that the issuance of SFAS 114 triggered an SEC initiative to review the Securities Act Industry Guide 3, *Statistical Disclosure by Bank Holding Companies*. This review is expected to focus on impaired loans; however, it could lead to a broader effect to improve asset quality and credit quality disclosures in bank holding companies' annual reports. The study cited concern that regulators may address the standardization issues without the benefit of the FASB's more intensive due process.

Conclusion: Opportunities and Threats in a Changing Marketplace

The general opposition of many financial institutions to fair value accounting has received a great deal of exposure in the press and has been the subject of many surveys. While we do not presume the conclusions of a decades–long debate, we note a clear trend toward increased interest in fair value information. These pressures will move financial institutions, as well as other enterprises, to disclose more about their operations and decision making.

Public companies understandably fear the forced disclosure of any information that may assist competitors. Each new disclosure represents an opportunity for a competitor to mimic a strength or to exploit a weakness. However, the market wants to know more about how risk and uncertainties are being managed and how risks are being brokered. Financial institutions can view increased fair value reporting both as an opportunity and as a threat.

Fair value reporting—and the resulting valuation risk and volatility— will likely result in new opportunities to standardize and package risk. Commercial enterprises will be subject to the same disclosure and accounting standards as financial institutions. They will have to deal with the volatility created by their own financial structure. A shift to fair value disclosures and accounting increases volatility in financial reporting. Many industries will choose to mitigate this effect. This will improve the business prospects for financial institutions specializing in brokering financial risks.

This introduction of new products and greater risks to broker also may threaten the preferential access of financial institutions to various markets. As new products and increased public information broaden financial markets, customers of financial institutions find it easier to insure their financial risk directly, thereby sidestepping the financial intermediary. However, the number of companies with sophisticated internal resources to deal in financial markets remains relatively small.

Fair value reporting may reveal greater economic opportunities than those in the external marketplace. Financial statement preparers and users should consider the cost of *not* closely monitoring the fair value of economic decisions. When institutions enter into transactions solely to manage financial reporting results, economic benefits may not offset transaction costs. Strategies that focus on accounting exposures rather than economic exposures may reduce the long–term value of an enterprise or, as in the savings and loan crisis, lead to failure.

Currently, the market rewards predictability in an inherently volatile world. Many management and employee incentives subscribe to this philosophy without regard to the cost of smoothing an inherently volatile yet profitable position. Consistent and comparable fair value information should provide a more realistic profile of future economic risks. The transaction costs and future exposures of risk management strategies should be easier to identify. Furthermore, they should result in more accurate measurements of economic performance. This should lead to more effective incentive systems and better business decisions.

As exhibited by the results of the follow–up study, the market will gradually assimilate and modify fair value information presented by institutions. The greater the effort that preparers and users put into the valuation process, the faster the quality of information will improve and the sooner the market will realize the benefits. Perhaps this is the only way to forestall excessive regulation.

If the market fails to demand and preparers fail to produce useful fair value information, then regulators will. Regulators will remain and prevail because they, too, are users of financial statements. Regulators such as the SEC will intervene if they perceive that the users of the market are not on an even playing field or that market participants are disregarding the rules. Regulative processes counter the force of competitive advantage that financial institutions seek to maintain. Their views on what constitutes essential information help maintain the integrity of the market.

Regulators of financial institutions, such as the OCC or OTS, exist to protect depositors' funds and to maintain trust in the monetary system. They have less direct interest in the usefulness of public financial statements since they command information from management. Their views should be critically analyzed and weighed against the cost of increased financial reporting standards.

One should expect regulatory reporting to build on public reporting while being more stringent, but this has not always been the case. Regulators must realize that disclosing fair value information is less important than knowing what economic exposures a financial institution has and how it manages them.

In the interim, standard setters should carefully consider their own deliberations and studies such as those cited above. A somewhat inexplicable gap is evident between what nonregulator users of financial statements want and what recent pronouncements require. Regulators appear to exert undue influence over the standard–setting process. SFAS 107 was an appropriate step down a new path that will eventually prove the usefulness of fair value information and initiate consistent, reliable practices. SFAS 115 may be the result of a regulatory–driven second step with more severe consequences.

The market has historically communicated its needs. Standard setters will benefit by listening to the market rather than leading it into uncharted territory. In the meantime, financial institutions must assume a leadership role in developing confidence in fair value information and in shaping its inevitable place in financial reporting.

References

Estimating Fair Values for Financial Institutions—Disclosure and Beyond, prepared for the Association of Reserve City Bankers by KPMG Peat Marwick, 1992.

Fair Value of Financial Instruments—An Insurance Industry Survey: The Views of Preparers and Users of Insurance Company Financial Statements and Fair Value Disclosure Implementation: Plans for 1992, KPMG Peat Marwick, November 1992.

Fair Value of Financial Instruments—Disclosure and Reaction, KPMG Peat Marwick, September 1993.

Notes

[1] Ronald L. Olson and Kurt Schneckenburger, "New Regulation Would Include Interest Rate Risk in Measures of Capital Adequacy." *Bank Accounting and Finance*, Spring 1993.

[2] George H. Hempel and Donald G. Simonson, "The Case for Comprehensive Market Value Reporting." *Bank Accounting and Finance*, Spring 1992.

Risk Measurement

William H. Beaver, Professor, Graduate School of Business,
Stanford University

Mark A. Wolfson, Professor, Graduate School of Business,
Stanford University

Introduction

Measuring risk is an essential part of managing it. To the extent that
proxies for risk measure the economic exposure with error, managing
the measured as opposed to economic risk exposure can lead to
transactional and risk allocation inefficiencies. We address methods of
measuring risk exposures and their consequences and ways of
communicating such information.

We refer to the measured risk exposure as the "accounting risk
exposure." We contrast this with the economic risk exposure, which is
the underlying risk associated with a given asset and liability position
where market values are well defined. The accounting risk exposure
coincides with the economic exposure in the case of perfect and
complete markets where (1) market values fully reflect the economic
value of claims; (2) market value accounting is used to measure
positions at any point in time; and (3) "risk loadings" are reported for
all asset and liability positions. Risk loading refers to the sensitivity of
asset and liability values to changes in the value of "primitive
securities." Primitive securities have a payoff structure providing one
unit of wealth (a dollar, say) if certain events occur but nothing
otherwise. Examples include a security that pays off if and only if
aggregate GNP over the next year increases at a nominal rate of 5%.
Another is a security that pays off if and only if the yield to maturity
on 5–year bonds three months from today is equal to 4%.

There are two major problems with risk measurement. One is that the present accounting system is based on historical costs. As a result, changes in the economic value of positions are not reflected in the reported value of the positions. This, in turn, leads to differences between the measured accounting exposure and the economic exposure.

The second problem relates to the "dimensionality" of risk exposure. A market value represents the single price at which buyers and sellers agree to exchange complicated bundles of uncertain future cashflows. Depending on a variety of factors that can take on one of many different values, the number of possible future cashflow outcomes can be infinite. Market prices are a function of the supply and demand for these cashflow bundles. In managing risk, the challenge is to buy and sell bundles of future cashflows that maximize the value of the overall portfolio while recognizing that the present value of future cashflows may differ depending upon the economy (e.g., recession versus expansion). It is easy to see that risk exposure cannot be represented nearly as succinctly as can market value.

Even if a full market value accounting system were employed, the income statement would only capture *ex post* changes in values of assets and liabilities and not the *ex ante* risk exposure. If income were measured with sufficient frequency and if risk exposures were unchanging, then *ex post* measures of risk exposure effects would permit good estimates of *ex ante* exposure. But income statements are not, and as a practical matter, *cannot* be constructed with sufficient frequency to disclose the underlying risk exposures. Besides, risk exposures can change dramatically as firms purchase and sell assets. In fact, risk exposures can change dramatically *even* if the firm engages in *no* transactions. In many cases, risk exposure changes where there are no transactions. This occurs where a *dynamic* trading strategy is required to maintain a constant exposure. Economic activities of others, along with naturally occurring events, can dramatically alter the non–transacting firm's risk exposure.

Supplemental disclosures of risk exposure can inform investors. For example, financial institutions disclose the maturity structure of their financial instruments along with an indication of whether the interest rate is fixed or floating. Although helpful, this information does not fully reveal the *ex ante* risk exposure associated with these instruments. For example, default risk and numerous other factors that affect future market values remain undisclosed. Other informative disclosures with respect to risk exposure include geographic segment reporting, significant customer reporting, and line–of–business reporting. SFAS 105 ("Disclosure of Information about Financial Instruments with Off–Balance–Sheet Risk and Financial Instruments with Concentration of Credit Risk") and SFAS 107 ("Disclosure about Fair Values of Financial Instruments") significantly expand the financial disclosures that help gauge risk exposures.

Regulations require thrifts to estimate the sensitivity of assets, obligations, revenues and expenses to a hypothetical range of basis–point changes along the yield curve. This regulation, however, is for internal purposes only, and disclosure is not required. In addition, balance sheets typically order assets by maturity ("closeness to cash"). It may be worth considering ordering assets by risk categories. But this may not address the *ex ante* exposure very well.

The above observations reflect the fact that current accounting rules are primarily valuation oriented. With modest exception, they do not convey information on the sensitivities of net asset values to changes in the underlying state variables. Such information could help investors better position themselves with respect to portfolio–level economic exposures.[1] Such information could also enhance the information efficiency of stock prices. Prices could more promptly reflect the valuation consequences of state–variable realizations on a firm's underlying assets and liabilities.

One cannot, of course, indiscriminately call for more disclosure. The above arguments address the potential benefits of additional exposure; but after all, disclosure is costly. There are both direct and indirect costs of measuring and verifying additional information (mandated disclosure of proprietary information reduces the incentives to produce and exploit it). This latter issue is familiar in the context of selecting disclosure rules designed to facilitate valuation as opposed to estimating risk exposure.

Strategies for Risk Management

This chapter assumes that business entities have a demand for risk management services. Empirically, this may seem self–evident given the amount of resources devoted to risk management. However, under a certain set of conditions, there would be zero demand. If the goal is to maximize shareholder wealth, and markets are perfect and complete, then shareholders can engage in risk management as effectively as firms themselves. Indeed, shareholders tend to be much better informed about the portfolio holdings of firms than firms are about the portfolio holdings of their shareholders. Shareholders do not share their personal financial statements with the firms in which they invest. As a consequence, firms can, and often do, unknowingly cancel hedges constructed by their shareholders on private account.

Even if the goal of management is to maximize total firm value (e.g., the value of securities held by both shareholders and creditors), the same point applies. In fact, for any general set of security holders, regardless of the particular form of the security held, it is impossible to know the effects of the firm's risk management activity on the portfolio of assets held by the security holders. In such a setting, management can focus exclusively on its "core competency" without being "distracted" by considerations such as risk management.

However, the idealized world of perfect and complete markets does not accurately describe the world—although markets for certain securities may approach these conditions. Factors such as asymmetries in information among market participants, tax laws with asymmetric treatment of gains and losses, and the importance of bankruptcy and restructuring costs induce risk–averse behavior.

In incentive compensation contracting, managers are often compensated based on the firm's performance (e.g., accounting profitability or stock prices). But managers cannot influence all elements of performance. Because managers tend to be more risk averse than the firm's shareholders, they require compensation for risks to which their incentive contract exposes them. Of course, if managers can hedge their risks costlessly on their personal account, they cannot demand a risk premium. But if it is less costly to hedge the risks within the firm due to market imperfections (e.g., economies of scale in contracting and monitoring positions), then shareholders prefer that hedging be undertaken within the firm.

"Traditional" Forms of Risk Management

The major portion of this chapter is devoted to accounting for transactions that arise from modern forms of risk management (e.g., those that involve the purchase or issuance of options, future contracts, and other forms of derivative securities). However, risk management has been practiced for many years in many forms, including: (1) management of the capital structure of the firm with attendant concerns over the optimal debt–to–equity ratio, (2) internal

---

diversification, such as geographical diversification or product–line diversification, (3) investment in less risky assets, (4) profit–sharing with employees (a form of risk sharing) via incentive compensation plans, and (5) public offerings (i.e., risk sharing via IPOs or secondary offerings). We do not mean to suggest that risk management has solely driven these transactions. Rather, we emphasize that each transaction has risk–shifting consequences for the firm's investors.

Derivative securities have dramatically expanded opportunities for risk management. They have also lowered the cost of reducing exposure to many risks. This has had several important implications for management and shareholders. In a sense, the markets became "more perfect and complete." As new securities were added, management could focus on core competencies. This allowed management to pursue earnings enhancement based on comparative advantage rather than on events beyond their control or expertise. However, this does not necessarily mean that overall investment risk has decreased as a result of these enhanced opportunities for risk management. Quite the opposite may be true.

At a simple level, any instrument used to hedge an already exposed position can also be used to *magnify* risk exposure. In economic settings where management has incentives to increase risk (e.g., as alleged in the thrift industry in the 1980s), these additional securities make it easier and less costly to increase risk exposure. However, somewhat more subtly, as risk can be shared more easily and at lower institutional costs, the market's appetite for risk grows. In equilibrium, more aggregate risk may be undertaken. Of course, in financial sectors, these instruments represent ways of sharing risk and from a societal perspective are a "zero–sum" game (holding constant the effects on the real sector). Significantly, expansion of these markets enhances society's ability to undertake risks in real terms because derivatives offer greater risk-sharing efficiency.

Accounting Methods to Measure Risk

The increase in the strategies available for risk management has been accompanied by increased interest in measurement. This development follows from the simple notion that something can be better managed as it is better measured. A navigator requires tools and instruments to indicate his position, direction, and speed. A similar analogy applies to financial risk management.

Much attention has been focused on market value accounting (also known as mark–to–market or fair value accounting) as a "solution" to risk measurement. The debate on market value accounting is long standing, and at least two recent forces have renewed it.

First, the thrift (and to a lesser extent the bank) "debacles" of the 1980s have led many observers to conclude that traditional, historical cost methods either failed to measure the risks being taken or to motivate regulators and others to act appropriately.

Second, the explosive development of derivative securities markets now makes assets, obligations, and positions easier to price. Consequently, market value accounting costs less and is more reliable. As we shall see, under idealized settings, comprehensive market value accounting (including off–balance–sheet items and intangible assets) dominates historical cost accounting as a measurement style and eliminates the demand for "hedge accounting." However, these idealized conditions do not exist, so market value accounting poses genuine deficiencies. This suggests that measurement alternatives such as hedge accounting in a historical cost system *can* be cost effective.

This chapter highlights the major issues involved in the choice of a risk measurement system so that both preparers and users may be better positioned to assess the usefulness of accounting reports.

Interest Rate Risk

Consider a firm that holds a (default–free) loan asset which pays a fixed coupon rate for a finite duration financed entirely with a variable–coupon–rate liability maturing on the same date. The variable–rate liability pays the instantaneous (short–term) rate of interest and adjusts constantly to changes in interest rates over time. A critical but realistic assumption is that interest rates move unexpectedly , i.e., that interest rate risk exists.

For simplicity, we assume that the net equity of the firm undertaking these positions is zero at the outset. By construction, the market value of the asset is interest rate sensitive in that it changes with interest rates over the life of the loan. Because of the instantaneous adjustment of the liability's income stream to interest rates, it has a constant market value over its life.

This pattern is familiar. The net cashflows are zero at inception and zero at the principal repayment date ("maturity"). In the interim, net cashflows are generated by the net position and equal the difference between the

fixed interest rate (assumed to be a cash inflow) and the var
determined by interim interest rate conditions (assumed to
outflow). The periodic flows occur at any number of predetermine
in time, perhaps even continuously. In any event, this position is equivalent
to entering into an interest rate swap agreement with a notional amount
equal to the "principal" in the above example. The interest rate swap
agreement produces net cashflows equal to the difference in the interest
rates under the fixed and floating rate assumptions.

Under any of these economically equivalent positions, the net cashflows
and the interim market values are affected by interim, unexpected
movements in interest rates. In particular, when interest rates rise
unexpectedly, the net cashflows are lower than expected (conceivably,
negative). The value of the fixed–rate asset declines while the economic
value of the liability position remains unchanged. The value of the net
position is negative. The converse will hold for unexpected declines in
the interest rates.

Accounting for Interest Rate Risk

Building on the above example, we assume that both positions are pure
discount bonds with no intermediate cashflows.[2] The terminal amounts
are equal to the accumulated fixed interest payments plus the principal
amount (known with certainty) and an uncertain accumulated amount
equal to the variable interest rate plus principal. For simplicity, we
assume that the term structure of interest rates is flat and contains no
liquidity premiums.

In perfect and complete markets, market values of both claims as well
as interest rate swaps are well defined at all times. Unexpected
movements in interest rates, and hence interest rate risk effects, are
reflected in the market values of the asset, liability, and interest rate
swap. Moreover, the absence of arbitrage profit opportunities ensures
the equivalence of market values of assets, liabilities and interest rate
swap contracts throughout time. The effects of this risk can be measured
ex post via mark–to–market accounting. Moreover, risk can be measured
ex ante by calibrating the sensitivity of asset and liability positions to
changes in the market value of "primitive" securities, as defined earlier.

In this setting, measurement of risk is relatively straightforward and
illustrates the "economic" exposure of the various positions. Of course,
generally accepted accounting principles may require or permit various

treatments. For example, in the case of certain investment securities, SFAS 115 ("Accounting for Certain Investments in Debt and Equity Securities," June 1993) requires one of three treatments: market value accounting for both balance sheet and income statement purposes if the security is held for trading purposes (intended to be traded before maturity); historical cost accounting for both balance sheet and income statement purposes (intended to be held to maturity); and market value on the balance sheet but historical cost on the income statement (intended to be neither held nor traded before maturity). Moreover, SFAS 115 applies to assets but not liabilities. Hence, economically identical positions (in the simple setting) can lead to divergent accounting treatments and different measures of interest rate risk effects.

First, we assume historical cost accounting is accorded to both the asset and the liability in the above illustration. The book values of both the asset and the liability remain fixed over time, and hence the net equity position (of zero) remains insensitive to changes in interest rates. Measured by the accounting system, there is zero exposure to interest rate risk as long as the positions are not liquidated. Considerable disparity arises between the economic exposure and the accounting exposure. While historical cost and market value can depart from one another for the asset position, historical cost and market value are identical for the liability position. In effect, the accounting treatment mixes historical cost and market value accounting. As a result, the net equity position is also a hybrid of these two measurement schemes and leads to an absence of accounting exposure, which differs from the economic exposure.

Hedging Activity

The above example illustrates net economic exposure to interest rate risk. This can be neutralized or "hedged" in a variety of ways. For example, the floating–rate liability can be retired and replaced with a fixed–rate liability that mirrors the exposure of the asset. In this particular case, historical cost accounting errs symmetrically on both the asset and the liability sides such that the net equity position has an accounting exposure equal to the economic exposure — zero. In this special case, "two wrongs make a right." This philosophy is implicitly embedded in various forms of "hedge accounting" and hence is often proposed in a broad class of circumstances that includes this special case.

Before further exploring hedge accounting, however, we note that even in cases where the economic hedges perfectly eliminate risk exposure, the accounting measurement rarely reflects this result. In the above example, an interest rate swap contract in which a fixed–rate interest stream is "sold" for a properly specified variable interest rate stream produces a portfolio position with no economic exposure to interest rate risk. Yet the accounting exposure depends upon the accounting treatment accorded the interest rate swap. If historical cost accounting is used for the asset and the liability but market value accounting is used for the interest rate swap, then the accounting system measures an interest rate exposure although no economic exposure exists.

Thus far, a simple illustration has shown how the accounting system overlooks exposure when there is a positive economic exposure and registers exposure when there is no economic exposure. This occurs for two reasons that generalize beyond the case of measuring risk exposure: (1) Historical cost accounting shows different accounting book values for items that have equal economic value, and it shows equal accounting value for items that have different economic value; (2) Any hybrid system of historical cost and market value accounting tends to "add apples and oranges" and produce anomalous properties and results.

"Hedge" accounting permits the deferral of gains or losses on certain positions, even after they are realized, to mitigate the anomalies of (1) historical cost treatment of risky assets and liabilities and (2) the reporting of some items at historical cost and others at market value. We suggest that if historical cost accounting could be replaced with "error–free," comprehensive market value accounting, then the demand for hedge accounting would disappear.

Hedge Accounting

Under generally accepted accounting principles in the U.S., two criteria must be met in order to defer gains or losses on a transaction: identifiability and correlation.[3] The identifiability criterion requires that the transaction on which the gain is being deferred represent a hedge against a clearly identified set of assets and liabilities. "Generic" hedges (e.g., hedges against firm–wide portfolios of assets and liabilities) fail to meet the identifiability criterion. Once the position is identified for which the hedge is being constructed, a second criterion must be met. The gains and losses on the hedging instrument must correlate "highly" with changes in the economic value of the unhedged (prehedged) items.

To see how hedge accounting works in the simplest of cases, we reconsider the above illustration. We assume that the fixed–rate asset/ floating–rate liability is the position to be hedged. As was shown, these positions expose one equity owner to interest rate risk. Considering the interest rate swap contract discussed above, we assume that the identifiability criterion has been met and that the swap is entered into with the same notional amount as the principal amounts of the asset and the liability. The contract specifies that an amount equal to the interest on the fixed–rate loan is exchanged for the receipt of the interest on the floating–rate liability. If we assume no default risk on the contractually specified swap payments, the swap contract clearly meets the correlation criterion. In fact, the changes in the market value of the (prehedge) net equity position and the gains and losses on the swap are not only perfectly correlated but also equal and offsetting such that there is no (unexpected) change in the net equity position (posthedge). Indeed, in this simple illustration, the net equity position (posthedge) is zero in all cases. This constitutes a perfect economic hedge and meets the accounting criteria as well.

In this setting, hedge accounting specifies that any gains or losses on the interest rate swap be deferred. An unexpected increase in interest rates lowers the market value of the asset and (prehedge) equity. However, it also produces a fully offsetting gain on the market value of the cashflows from the interest rate swap contract. Under hedge accounting, the deferred gain on the swap contract equals the unrecognized loss on the fixed–rate loan asset. The result is book value of net assets equal to the market value of net assets.[4]

Under market value accounting, the gain on the swap contract is recognized as is the loss on the asset. Net income is zero, the same as under historical cost with hedge accounting treatment accorded the swap contract. If, on the other hand, hedge accounting is not employed for the swap contract (either because the swap contract was not deemed to constitute an identifiable hedge or because the correlation test was not deemed to be met for some reason), then the gain on the swap position is recorded; and the book value of assets overstates the market value by the amount of the unrecognized loss on the loan. The accounting net income (and net equity) equals the amount of the gain on the swap, which overstates the economic net income and net equity value of zero.

The above illustration represents "ideal" conditions with respect to hedge accounting. However, it fails to answer two important questions. First, if the result of hedge accounting is to duplicate the properties of market value accounting, why not simply move to market value accounting and eliminate the criteria of specialized hedge accounting? We address this question in a later portion of this chapter. Second, what are the properties of hedge accounting in settings other than the ideal? We address this immediately below.

To begin, we focus on the criterion of correlation. In its strictest form, it measures the (linear) dependence between two variables — in this case, the returns from the prehedge position and from the hedging instrument. The most widely used measure of correlation is the correlation coefficient. We use it to illustrate our points although other measures of correlation lead to the same conclusions.

The correlation coefficient ranges from -1 to $+1$. At the extreme values, the two returns have perfect negative and positive correlation, respectively. A correlation coefficient of zero results when two returns are (linearly) independent. It is important to note that the correlation coefficient is scale free. In other words, it ranges between $+1$ and -1 regardless of the dollar magnitude of the positions taken. As a result, a correlation coefficient of .9, which more than meets the correlation test, tells us nothing about the variance of change in the market value of the net position. We do know that R^2 is .81 (or 81%), which implies that 81% of the variation in the return on the unhedged position can be explained by the variation in the hedging instrument. However, because R^2 is scale free, it tells us nothing about the dollar magnitude of the 19% of the variation that is uncorrelated and that constitutes the remaining risk after the "hedge" is effected. In fact, the residual risk could be quite high (indeed, infinite as in the case of zero net equity) as a percentage of net equity.

For example, consider a variation on the perfect hedge we employed earlier. Instead of purchasing an interest rate swap, the notional amount of which equals the principal of the asset being hedged, suppose the swap contract specifies a different notional amount. Regardless of the notional amount of the swap, the correlation between the two returns not only meets a test of high correlation but also one of perfect correlation. This result follows from the nature of the correlation coefficient as a linear regression of one variable on the other. For purposes of illustration, assume that the return from the net (prehedge) position is the dependent variable and the return from the interest rate swap is the explanatory variable. If equal notional amounts are purchased, the correlation is perfect and the implied slope coefficient is 1 (which is a coefficient of elasticity of changes in the unhedged position to changes in the hedging instrument). As the notional amount of the swap contract is increased (decreased), the correlation with the unhedged position remains perfect; but the slope coefficient (or elasticity of market value change) becomes less than (greater than) one. There could be enormous — indeed, unlimited — variance in the post–hedge market value change in the overall positions, yet the correlation test would be well met.

This, of course, is a blatant case, and one may argue that management and auditors know enough to look beyond the correlation test. Without addressing whether the blatant case would be recognized as an abuse of the substance (but not the form) of hedge accounting, it is easy to imagine cases which appear less extreme and are equally fraught with accounting mischief.

For example, the loan may pose not only interest rate risk but also default risk. Because of the additional default risk, the loan's price includes a "basis point spread" on the fixed rate above that of default–free, fixed–rate loans with the same maturity. This can be thought of as basis point risk because the fixed contractual risk premium changes over the life of the loan and may not always cover the underlying default risk. As a result, the market value of the loan varies for default risk–related reasons in addition to interest rate–related movements in market value.[5]

Yet from the perspective of a correlation criterion, the bulk of the variation in the market value of the loan (for example, 81% of the valuation) may be due to interest rate risk. If the correlation coefficient is .9, the correlation test is met. Yet the remaining 19% of the variation in the asset value may be an enormous percentage of the net equity position even if the scale of positions is the same. For example, in the context of our simple illustration, any remaining residual variation in the "posthedge" position represents an infinitely large risk position relative to the net equity position (which is zero because the firm is fully leveraged at the outset).

While a fully leveraged position may seem extreme, highly levered positions are not. Consider a financial institution where net equity represents 5% of the capital structure and where debt, broadly defined, represents the remaining 95% of total claims to assets. For this institution, 19% residual variation in the "posthedge" asset position represents an enormous risk position relative to the modest equity base. This position has the capacity to wipe out equity many times over. In this situation, the leverage ratio is 20 x (that is, 1.00 to .05); and a 1% movement in the value of the "hedged" position (expressed as a percentage of the asset's value) represents a 20% movement in equity value.

To highlight further the difficulty of measuring risks as well as inferring risk positions under current risk measurement rules, consider the possibilities when the dimensionality of the positions is increased, i.e., the accounting for *bundles* of claims. More specifically, consider a situation in which a company seeks economic exposure to a particular risk and accounting deferral of the gains and losses on this position. The desired economic exposure could be achieved by purchasing and holding asset A. Suppose, however, that if the asset were held in isolation, market value accounting would be required with the implied volatility or risk appearing as gains and losses on the income statement as the value of the asset changed. An alternative strategy is for the company to purchase a bundle of assets (perhaps a mutual fund) that includes asset A. At the same time, the firm could adopt a short position in another portfolio of assets that is identical to the first portfolio except that it does not include asset A. Suppose asset A comprises only a small fraction of the first bundle. Then the returns on the two bundles are very highly correlated because of the assets they hold in common. Such a position easily passes a correlation test. Yet the net position represents a pure "long" position in the target asset, asset A. Despite this, different accounting treatment could be accorded the highly correlated long and short positions relative to the equivalent economic positions of holding asset A directly. Under hedge accounting, the gains and losses are deferred and reflect no volatility in the interim income numbers. But if asset A is held in isolation, the gains and losses are recognized as the asset's value changes.

Identifiability

Now we turn to the second condition required for hedge accounting treatment—identifiability. Similar issues arise because of the failure to consider the proper scope of the set of claims that are eligible for hedge accounting. Requiring identifiability of the claim being hedged can drive a wedge between the accounting exposure and the economic exposure. If the accounting for nonidentifiable hedges is historical cost or a mixture of historical cost and market value accounting, then the accounting exposure could be greater or less than that implied by treating all claims as "identifiable."

For example, consider a firm that holds both financial assets and nonfinancial assets. Suppose further that the returns from these two classes of assets are perfect hedges for one another with respect to some defined risk. Current accounting rules generally show volatility in returns because of the asymmetric treatment of financial and nonfinancial assets (e.g., market value for the former and historical cost for the latter). Here, the accounting exposure overstates the economic exposure.

Suppose further that transactions have been undertaken to hedge the financial position. The accounting exposure is zero, and the economic exposure has in fact increased because the firm was perfectly hedged before this new hedge position.

Although the problem is large for recorded assets, it is aggravated for firms with unrecorded assets and liabilities. These off–balance–sheet items may either increase or decrease the overall risk of net assets, yet they often go unrecorded. The case is clearest when implicit future positions are unrecorded. For example, consider a domestic microchip manufacturer whose customer and supplier bases are also exclusively domestic. Despite the domestic concentration, such a firm may bear significant currency risk. In the chip market, the prices may be heavily influenced by competitors who are predominantly Japanese manufacturers. The effective dollar–denominated price at which they offer the product may well be a function of the exchange rate between dollars and yen.

The U.S. firm may have no transactions denominated in a foreign currency and no subsidiaries whose financial statements must be translated into dollars. Even then, if the yen increases unexpectedly in value vis-à-vis the dollar, the equilibrium dollar selling price may fall along with the firm's revenues. In some sense, this is an extension of the earlier example of financial and nonfinancial assets. The firm has an off–balance–sheet asset that reflects its incumbency in the industry and its ability to sell products at prices different from costs. Of course, such "assets" may carry negative value. More to the point, such assets may have a significant exposure to changes in the dollar–yen exchange rate. This exposure is only implicitly recorded as the revenue and expense consequences of exchange rate changes are realized.

Note that this firm could purchase a futures contract to hedge the yen–dollar exchange rate risk exposure. Here an unexpected increase in the value of the yen would produce a short–term accounting gain because the prevailing hedge accounting rules do not treat the intangible asset as an identifiable position against which the futures contract is a hedge.[6]

In fact, the principle is broader in that unexpected movements in exchange rates may also affect assets not currently recorded but likely to be booked in the future. In other words, the firm has intangible assets that are exposed to foreign currency movements. These assets may be thought of as the "franchise value" of the firm or its intangible investment in a market network. Economic hedges of these intangible assets are not likely to be treated as identifiable hedge positions since the current financial statements do not record them.

A similar issue arises in the case of an airline company and its exposure to energy price risk. The effect on current operations is directly reflected in increased short–term fuel costs. However, in the longer run, higher fuel costs mean higher ticket prices, which may lessen airline travel and reduce economic value for the firm. In other words, the net–cash–flow–generating ability of the current fleet may be adversely affected in ways not reflected in the current financial statements. Again, the airline could undertake long positions in energy commodities through futures contracts. Yet as in the microchip manufacturer illustration, this hedge is unlikely to meet the identifiability test. Hence, if the firm does not execute the hedge, the accounting exposure understates the economic exposure. If it does hedge the economic exposure, it can easily increase its accounting exposure.

Costs and Benefits of Market Value Accounting

Accounting standard–setters have long faced a curious paradox. Market value accounting possesses many of its attractive properties under conditions of perfect and complete markets. When these market conditions are relaxed, the desirability of market value accounting is no longer self–evident even if such information is costless (Beaver, Datar, and Wolfson 1992).

In perfect and complete markets, the market price captures the relevant attributes of an asset or liability, such as the time value of money and risk. But the market for many firm assets is incomplete. For example, a market for the results of research and development may be incomplete because revealing these results may destroy a project's value (i.e., a potential buyer no longer pays for the information). Similarly, a depository institution may possess information about a loan portfolio's default risk that the market does not possess. Such information asymmetry can result in the absence of a market for such assets. Such market incompleteness presents obvious difficulties for market valuation (Berger, Kuester, and O'Brien 1989).

Information asymmetries between managers and outsiders create a major difficulty in estimating market prices. This informational deficiency differs depending on the characteristics of the assets and liabilities that significantly influence changes in value. To the extent that interest rate risk is a factor and default–free interest rates of varying maturities are publicly available, for example, the computations of discounted cashflows at current interest rates may seem relatively straightforward. But even in this case, assessing prepayment risk, determining the effect of caps, floors, and collars on adjustable rate loans, and calculating the tax effects associated with the unrealized gains and losses are not straightforward operations.

For example, the present value of the tax consequences of changes in the market value of interest–bearing securities depends on (1) the time when the gains and losses are recognized for tax purposes (which is often well within the discretion of the institution's management), (2) the statutory tax rate that applies at that time, (3) the likelihood that the institution will face tax loss or tax credit carryforwards, and (4) the likelihood that the institution employs special bad–debt deductions that are linked to taxable income or are subject to the alternative minimum tax, among other factors. As for discretion in the timing of gains and losses from the sale of marketable securities, Scholes, Wilson, and Wolfson (1990) document that banks systematically forego tax benefits when loan loss provisions are higher than usual and when regulatory capital is relatively low.

Beyond the difficulties of measuring the market value of default–free assets, loans with default risk are a major asset category. Relative to regulators, auditors, and especially to investors and taxpayers, the institution's management is likely to have vastly superior knowledge of default risk and its effect on asset values.

Some proponents of market value accounting are motivated by the concern that managers have incentives to withhold relevant information with respect to important asset characteristics, such as default risk. But it is not clear that market value accounting will improve the quality of the information in this regard. In other words, if there is an incentive not to disclose certain information under the existing system, that same disincentive exists under the proposed. Thus requiring "market value" accounting may represent more of a change in form than in substance.

The extent of disclosure of *ex ante* risk positions versus *ex post* consequences compounds the difficulties in verifying representations of underlying exposures. This is especially so if one integrates the exposure of the firm's intangible assets and liabilities with various risks.

Interestingly, the Freddie Mac use of market value accounting relies on the already–reported allowance for loan loss accounts (under the current historical cost system) to reflect default risk. Most advocates of market value accounting adopt a similar recommendation with respect to default risk (Hempel and Simonson 1992). Moreover, there are a variety of ways to communicate default risk information, including the currently required schedules on slow, delinquent, nonaccrual, and restructured loans. Berger, Kuester, and O'Brien (1989) recommend the use of such data to supplement the allowance for loan losses, and their recommendation is supported elsewhere. Supplemental disclosures with respect to default risk and interest rate risk explain the common share prices of banks (Beaver, Eger, Ryan, and Wolfson 1989). In a similar context, Barth, Beaver, and Stinson (1991) find that supplemental disclosures with respect to default risk are significantly correlated with common share prices of thrifts but that interest rate sensitivity data are not.

Requiring discounted cashflow computations to estimate market values of nontraded loans does not necessarily enhance the available information. In fact, requiring estimated market values as a replacement for more easily audited historical cost and other supplemental information may make it more difficult for outside parties to monitor a financial institution's performance.

The arguments in favor of market value accounting have largely focused on the shortcomings of historical cost accounting. For instance, White (1988) argues that under historical cost accounting, identical financial assets may be carried on the books at different values (depending on when they were acquired) while different financial assets with different market values may have identical accounting values. A related issue is the distortionary effect of historical cost accounting on managers' incentives to undertake transactions for accounting benefits even though these transactions may jeopardize the firm's economic worth. An example of such behavior is management's incentive to sell assets that have appreciated in value and to hold assets that have declined.

As a counterpoint to the criticism that historical cost accounting encourages manipulation of income and capital through judicious choice of asset and liability transactions, we note that market value accounting is hardly immune from such distortions. For example, suppose an institution builds a portfolio of loans of varying quality and that management has vastly superior knowledge, relative to outside parties, of the default risk of the individual loans in the portfolio.

Suppose further that management shares its private information with a buyer on a few of its most valuable (that is, highest risk–adjusted yield) loans and sells these loans at premium prices. An opportunistic management may use such nonrepresentative transaction prices as a surrogate for the market values of the remaining lower–quality loans. And since only management knows that the retained loans are not equal in value to those that were sold, its capacity to distort income and capital under market value accounting may well exceed its ability to do so on an historical cost basis.

From the outside party's viewpoint, market value accounting is intended to provide a better picture of the economic net worth of the reporting entity and consequently of the *ex post* effects of the risk exposures. In this context, the benefits of market value accounting can be perceived from either a valuation or an information perspective. As argued earlier, a valuation argument has obvious appeal in a world of perfect and complete markets. Since the market for assets and liabilities is largely imperfect and incomplete, however, we adopt an informational perspective in evaluating the benefits of market value accounting.

Presumably, one benefit of market value accounting is the information it provides about various types of risk, such as default risk and interest rate risk. But as discussed earlier, this information may already be available in the form of supplemental disclosures on fixed and variable interest income, e.g., information regarding nonaccruing loans. Thus, a case for market value accounting cannot be made based only on the additional information it provides over historical cost accounting. At a minimum, the case for market value accounting must be made in terms of the information advantages over supplemental disclosures, such as those pertaining to interest rate and default risk. In fact, information about default and interest rate risk is probably available from other sources as well. Where markets exist for the individual assets, outside parties use market prices to infer the economic status of individual firms.

This suggests that the greatest potential value of market value accounting comes from the information it provides about assets whose direct market values are not easily determined, e.g., nonstandardized loans without securitized analogs (consumer and commercial loans), direct equity positions in real estate, and intangible assets such as franchise value. However, at least three factors counteract this benefit of market value accounting.

First, as discussed earlier, the firm lacks proper incentives to disclose private information such as that relating to default risks of assets. How will market value accounting change those basic incentives? If incentives for disclosure are unaltered, it is unclear what market value accounting will achieve. Firms may disclose "market values" that do not fully reflect what they know about default risks and other factors relating to the valuation of assets and liabilities. An assessment of the informational benefits of market value accounting must simultaneously consider the firm's incentives to disclose such information.

Second, measurement problems abound in determining market values of certain assets (and liabilities) such as nonstandardized loans, real estate, and goodwill. Determining market values of nonsecuritized loans requires an evaluation of creditworthiness, maturity, and the likelihood of prepayment, among other considerations. Even with no intention to mislead or obfuscate on the firm's part, the market values for these assets are likely to be measured with significant error.

Many market value accounting proposals understate the problems noted here. They argue that the vast majority of assets held by financial institutions, for example, have easily determinable market values. Even if this were true (which we doubt), it fails to recognize that difficulties in valuing a small fraction of total assets can translate into huge problems relative to the market value of equity due to the high leverage of many financial services firms. Valuation difficulty relative to the equity base is the relevant issue.

Finally, difficulty in measuring the market values of certain assets creates its own distortionary incentives. Financial institution managers may favor investments in assets whose market values are difficult to measure. For example, instead of holding mortgage–backed securities, financial institutions may prefer to retain the mortgages they have originated themselves and to contractually arrange for managers to have an informational advantage over outside parties. More generally, the market value accounting system may encourage financial institutions to increase their concentration in assets that have equity–like features. As a result, institutions can manipulate reported values by virtue of their superior information and the market's incompleteness. Such a strategy reduces the informational and evaluative value of market value accounting.

A potential benefit of market value accounting is its ability to evaluate the economic risk of a financial institution relative to its overall portfolio rather than to individual assets and liabilities. Market value accounting, in principle, captures covariances in returns among assets by reflecting increases and decreases in asset values on a more timely basis than does historical cost accounting. This information may lead to better minimum risk–based capital standards and risk–based deposit insurance premia.[7]

The two methods also differ in their ability to communicate information clearly. Market value accounting is probably the easiest form of communication for owners to understand because it claims to report the economic values of assets and liabilities. Historical cost accounting applies various accounting principles that outside parties may find complex. In addition, owners may find historical cost–based income statements and balance sheets more difficult to interpret.

Moving to market value accounting involves various costs. The most obvious and direct cost is the out–of–pocket expense of data gathering, computation, summarization, and analysis. Market values of assets are not readily available. Often, asset cashflows and discount rates must be estimated. The computation of market values is a significant task. Besides the direct costs, market value accounting is fraught with measurement errors. As discussed earlier, measurement errors reduce the value of information. Difficulties in measurement also distort managerial incentives by encouraging investment in assets whose market values are more difficult for regulators and third parties to determine than for management.

Conclusion

Among the greatest limitations of current financial statements is their failure to inform users of *ex ante* risk exposures. Even a measurement–error–free market value accounting system would not make a significant dent in solving this problem. On the other hand, a substantial increase in supplementary disclosure *could*, in principle, provide the desired information. To the extent that management is privately informed about such exposures and that such information is difficult to credibly convey to an auditor, the reporting of such exposures could pose significant reliability problems.

Although not a perfect substitute for the reporting of *ex ante* risk exposures, income statements report on the *ex post* consequences of risk positions. Here we have explored desirable and undesirable features of hedge accounting as well as market value accounting. As with the reporting of *ex ante* exposures, a major impediment of market value accounting is the superior information that managers have about asset values and the difficulties in providing incentives for them to truthfully share this information.

Selected Bibliography

Barth, M, W. Beaver, and C. Stinson. "Supplemental Data and the Structure of Thrift Share Prices. " *Accounting Review* 66 (January 1991): 56–66.

Beaver, W., S. Datar and M. Wolfson. "The Role of Market Value Accounting in the Regulation of Insured Depository Institutions." In *The Reform of Deposit Insurance: Disciplining the Government and Protecting Taxpayers*. New York: Harper Collins Publishing, 1992.

Beaver, W., C. Eger, S. Ryan, and M. Wolfson. "Financial Reporting and the Structure of Bank Share Prices." *Journal of Accounting Research* 27, 2 (Autumn 1989): 157–178.

Beaver, W., P. Kettler, and M. Scholes. "The Association Between Market Determined and Accounting Determined Risk Measures." *Accounting Review*: 45, 4 (October 1970): 654–682.

Berger, A., K. Kuester, and J. O'Brien. "Some Red Flags Concerning Market Value Accounting." Working Paper, Board of Governors of the Federal Reserve System, Washington, D. C.: (August 1989).

Jacklin, C. "Bank Capital Requirements and Incentives for Lending." *Risk Management: Problems and Solutions*, New York: McGraw–Hill, 1994.

Financial Standards Accounting Board. *A Report on Deliberations, Including Tentative Conclusions on Certain Issues, Related to Accounting for Hedging and Other Risk-adjusting Activities*. Norwalk, CT: 1993.

Hempel, G. H., and D. G. Simonson. "The Case for Comprehensive Market Value Reporting." *Bank Accounting and Finance* (Spring 1992).

Stewart, J., The Challenges of Hedge Accounting." *Journal of Accountancy* (November 1989): 48–60.

White, L. "Market Value Accounting: An Important Part of the Reform of the Deposit Insurance System." Association of Reserve City Bankers, *Capital Issues in Banking*, Washington, D. C. (1988): 226–242.

Notes

[1] This is consistent with the motivation for the work of Beaver, Kettler and Scholes (1970), which used accounting disclosures to enhance estimates of the sensitivity of firms' net asset values to changes in the market value of aggregate net worth.

[2] This is equivalent to an interest rate swap where payments are made only upon termination of the contract.

[3] Issues of hedge accounting are discussed in Stewart (1989) and FASB (1993).

[4] An asset account, swap contract receivable, is recorded (debited) as an asset, and a

deferred gain is recorded (credited) for the amount earned from "selling" the swap. Here, in substance, the deferred income account (with a credit balance) is a contra–asset account.

[5] Note that there may arise a second source of default risk, namely, that on the promised payments as specified in the swap contract. Counter–party risk is often of paramount importance in derivative contracts.

[6] The exchange rate change might affect sales and profit margins. For one–time effects, a futures contract accurately hedges against the changing exchange rate. If the effects on sales and margins are more permanent, however, the margin effect is recognized over time while the futures contract effect is recognized all at once. The result could be far greater volatility of reported earnings despite the perfect economic hedge.

[7] Having been introduced recently in banking, life insurance, and, most recently, property and casualty insurance, risk–based capital rules are in relatively early stages of development in the financial services industry. The objective appears to be to standardize assets in terms of *ex ante* market value risk exposure.

Of course, as discussed earlier, risk is multidimensional. Risk–based capital rules fail to consider a variety of risk factors, and they distort managerial incentives with respect to balance sheet composition (Jacklin 1994). They also fail to consider covariance among institutions' assets and liabilities. As with the market value accounting controversy, a potential alternative to risk-based capital rules is greater disclosure along with greater market freedom in scrutinizing and disciplining financial institutions.

Operating Risk in Financial Services

Joel P. Friedman, Managing Partner,
  Andersen Consulting
Frank Terzuoli, Manager, Financial Services,
  Andersen Consulting

Introduction

This chapter describes the scope and major sources of operational risk particularly as it pertains to securities transactions in financial services. The chapter examines the complexity of managing such risk as a result of recent developments in financial markets, e.g., derivative securities. It also outlines an approach as to how firms can manage many of these risks.

Operating Risk

For a financial services firm, operating risk is the chance that inadequate controls, human errors, or system failures will create unexpected losses from a financial transaction. For securities transactions, operating risk thus exists from the time a firm first executes a contract or commitment through the time of the final settlement. As distinguished from other major forms of risk, operating risk results from problems unrelated to a party's inability to fulfill a financial obligation (credit risk) or from movements in prices or trading volumes (market and liquidity risks). In addition, unlike most other forms of financial risk where there is an opportunity for gain or loss (e.g., market risk), operating risk is a one-sided risk since it provides opportunities for loss only.

Recent Changes in Financial Markets

Among the major trends affecting financial institutions during the past decade, three stand out with respect to their influence on the nature of operational risk: globalization, the increased volatility of financial markets, and the emergence of sophisticated new financial products in response to those trends. As described below, this new reality has complicated the handling of financial transactions and lengthened the transaction processing chain. This effect in turn multiplies the operational risks facing financial firms that invest and deal in these new products.

One of the most significant trends in the financial services industry is an increase in the international flow of capital. Transactions which were once confined to a single country now increasingly involve participants from around the world. Innovation in information technology has provided global investors with more rapid and comprehensive data on foreign financial markets and instruments, allowing them to better evaluate the risks and returns of foreign investing. In addition, growth in investor sophistication and the desire by corporate treasurers to find the lowest–cost funding sources have increased the flow of capital across borders. At the same time, innovative ways of structuring transactions to redistribute interest rate and currency risks among parties have linked the financial markets of the major industrial countries. As an illustration of this growth, from 1980 to 1990, the volume of foreign transactions in securities of U. S. firms grew nearly fivefold—from $75 billion to $361 billion. Likewise, U. S. transactions in securities of foreign firms during the period exploded from $179 billion to $253 billion.[1]

From an operational perspective, the internationalization of financial markets has created an environment in which firms have begun to operate 24 hours a day around the world. A new practice is that of "passing the book." Control of trading is passed between traders around the globe as one exchange closes and another opens. This enables 24–hour trading of a financial instrument. For example, a firm trading in New York can trade during U. S. hours and from London during U. K. hours by passing an electronic position book from one country to the other.

In addition to becoming more global, markets have also become increasingly more volatile. During the 1970s, a rapid rise in inflation, oil price shocks and a breakdown of the Bretton–Woods fixed exchange rate mechanism were major factors leading to increased swings in interest rates, commodity prices and foreign exchange rates. The heightened volatility of these markets has prompted corporations and financial institutions to seek new ways of managing risks to their earnings streams. At the same time, advances in financial theory and computer technology have provided financial institutions with powerful tools for designing new products capable of tailoring risk to meet this emerging demand.

Much of the innovation that has occurred in these new risk management products involves the use of financial derivatives. This general term refers to financial contracts such as swaps, options, futures and forward contracts in which the product's value is based, or "derived," from the value of the underlying asset, market index, or interest or currency rate. These products also constitute fundamental building blocks which allow product designers to replicate or modify the behavioral characteristics of traditional financial products, both debt and equity, or to create new products with risk and cashflow profiles unavailable through existing products.

A simple example of a financial derivative is a "plain vanilla" interest rate swap. In a swap transaction, two parties agree to exchange interest payments on a fixed amount of principal (the "notional amount"). One party pays a floating rate tied to an index, such as the Treasury bill rate or the London Interbank Offered Rate (LIBOR), in exchange for a fixed rate of interest from the other party. The cashflow exchanges take place on specific dates (e.g., quarterly or semiannually) over a specified period. This transaction can be mutually beneficial if, for example, the party paying the fixed rate of interest has assets which generate a fixed flow of income but are funded by liabilities which are more sensitive to interest rates. The swap effectively locks in a spread of the asset revenue over the liability costs and removes the risk of interest rates affecting the institution's net income. Likewise, the party receiving the floating rate may have the reverse asset/liability structure and thus will seek a floating rate payment to fund a floating rate asset. This example illustrates the ability of a swap product to alter the characteristics of existing assets and liabilities in a single transaction. Such a modification would have otherwise been extremely difficult, if not impossible, to do. It would require restructuring the existing balance sheet asset and liability mixes of the parties.

The demand for these new products has opened up new opportunities for financial firms to not only manage the inherent risks they face as financial intermediaries but also to earn fee income from the sale of these new risk management products. These opportunities have arrived at a time when financial institutions, particularly commercial banks, encounter stiff competition from nonbank competitors for traditional banking services. Mutual funds, for example, pose a major competitive threat to depository institutions by providing easy access to money market funds, which rival banks' traditional deposit products for convenience and liquidity. In addition, the increasing ability of corporations to tap investor funds directly through commercial paper, bond and note markets or through commercial and consumer finance companies has eroded some of the traditional markets for bank financing. As a consequence, banks have responded to the encroachment by seeking opportunities to earn trading and fee revenues from financial risk management services. Indeed, many have created "financial engineering" departments to develop derivatives–based risk management solutions tailored to the needs of the evolving market. The result of this movement of financial institutions into new areas of risk management has been a fivefold increase (from approximately $2 trillion to approximately $10 trillion) in the notional amount of financial derivatives outstanding worldwide from 1986 to 1991.[2]

Operational Risk Implications of New Markets and Products

As would be expected, the collective impact of changes in the financial markets and the increased complexity of new products such as financial derivatives have raised questions among industry analysts, regulators and financial institutions about the ability of the operating infrastructure of financial institutions to support this new environment. The increased length and complexity of the transaction processing flows of derivative instruments demand an operational apparatus substantially different from that supporting traditional financial products such as loans and deposits. For example, derivative transactions typically require complex valuation and pricing analysis and can often involve combinations of multiple instruments, each with different clearing, settlement and accounting procedures. In addition, as derivatives transactions are processed, transaction data usually flows through several different functional units of an organization. This is also true of loans. Derivatives are unique in their sensitivity in value to market conditions and thus their great volatility. This time–horizon difference substantially affects the management of derivatives as compared to traditional loans. Transactions are initiated in a "front office" or dealing room responsible for the design, valuation and pricing of each transaction. Prior to execution, the credit unit of the institution must review the transaction and approve the creditworthiness of the transaction counterparties. Once agreed to, transactions flow to the "back office" where account posting, settlement and reporting are performed.

In many institutions, advances in operational capabilities have not occurred as rapidly as advances in product sophistication. This increases the firm's exposure to operational risks. These risks can be separated into several categories.

Technology Risks

Perhaps the most obvious source of operational risk is a *software* or *hardware failure* leading to information losses or delay in processing transactions. Institutions participating in today's financial markets are constantly seeking new ways of leveraging technology to gain a comparative advantage in product innovation. Technology has thus become indispensable in key areas of today's financial markets. These include:

- Product design and valuation: Computers have become indispensable to the "front–office" design and pricing of derivative products. Understanding the complex financial relationships which drive the pricing behavior of derivative instruments demands sophisticated mathematical models, the analysis of large quantities of historical data and an ability to dynamically alter assumptions and forecasts under "what–if" scenarios. In addition, software modules must track positions and provide ongoing management information on position exposures and profit and loss. These processes can only realistically be done with powerful computers that access large databases containing current position and market price information.

- Transaction posting and reporting: Computers can also accommodate the general ledger accounting and reporting of financial derivatives, including the capability to measure instruments on a mark–to–market as well as an accrual basis. In addition, the regulatory reporting for financial derivatives is extensive. It includes complete financial disclosures under FASB, OCC, Federal Reserve and International Securities Dealers Association (ISDA) standards. Increasing the frequency of posting and reporting requirements is becoming more evident. This places even greater demands on systems to provide necessary information in a timely manner.

- Settlement: Technology also plays an important role in transaction settlement. Settlement modules offer flexibility in accommodating all types of rates —prime, T-Bill, commercial paper, LIBOR, simple, compound, etc.—and in processing what are often arcane reset dates. Many institutions are striving to shorten the time to process entire transactions— from order to settlement—by converting batch processing systems to real time.

Given the heavy reliance firms place on technology for designing, processing and settling of transactions, it is not surprising that systems failures can lead to large losses. These failures can occur in a variety of ways:

- Hardware failures: The failure of computer hardware is a well understood and not uncommon occurrence. Typical sources of hardware failure are disk drives, communications networks, or computer processors. According to one survey, securities firms in the United States each typically suffer 6.9 on–line system failures per year, which collectively resulted in $3.4 billion in productivity losses in 1992.[3] Moreover, hardware does not necessarily have to fail to be unusable. For example, recent events such as the major flooding in downtown Chicago and the bombing of the World Trade Center illustrate instances where firms were forced to abandon their offices and thus their computer systems even though the systems were operational. The failure of some firms to arrange offsite disaster recovery support systems for such events is equivalent to a major hardware failure.

- Software failure: Software failures include programming "bugs" which cause programs to crash or, still worse, to produce invalid or specious information. Less direct software failures occur when applications are not capable of processing a transaction in the original form. Innovations in hardware and software systems may lag the product innovations they are designed to support. In these circumstances, the temptation to develop stopgap solutions is strong. For example, some firms lacking the systems capability to handle interest rate swaps enter the transaction into their system as a series of forward rate agreements. Such substitution carries obvious risk: the entry may not be valid and could misstate the firm's capital at risk.

Systems also can fail simply as a result of their inability to deliver accurate information within relevant decision–making timeframes. Effectively competing in today's financial markets requires that information be collected globally, processed swiftly, and incorporated immediately into decision–making. However, the need to span large distances and to reconcile the disparate systems architectures of most financial firms impedes the timeliness of the information. Often hardware and software solutions are developed departmentally without centralization into an institution's overall information technology strategy. Front and back offices lack integration and common databases. The fragmented nature of these systems can result in misstatements of risk as well as system inflexibility and inefficiency.

Human risks

Another major source of operational risk involves the inherent capability of humans to err—either intentionally or unintentionally. The increased complexity of new financial products such as derivative securities and the associated lengthening of the processing flow of many transactions have increased this risk. They have also created the need for the development and management of new human resource skills.

- Transaction execution: Rapid growth in the development, sales and trading of derivative products has spawned a new generation of "rocket scientists." These individuals, armed with powerful computers, now occupy the front offices of many financial institutions and risk the capital of the bank each day with complex positions in exotic products. The sophistication with which these individuals trade and the complexity of their positions are rarely understood by senior management and directors. As a consequence, the potential that these individuals could make serious errors of judgment on expected market conditions, valuation, or data input or interpretation exposes the firm to considerable losses.

A well–known illustration of this risk occurred in 1987, when a trader from Merrill Lynch lost $377 million in just a few days. At the time, this was the largest loss in the history of Wall Street. It resulted from a trader's taking an exposed position in derivative instruments known as "stripped" mortgage–backed securities. These products are highly sensitive to interest rates and can be very volatile if not hedged properly. The trader left himself unhedged. When interest rates moved in an unfavorable direction, Merrill suffered substantial losses. More recently, in 1993, traders in the Treasury department at Japan's largest oil company, Showa Shell Sekiyu, lost $1.1. billion (equal to 82% of its shareholders' equity) as a result of unauthorized speculation in currency futures contracts. These two examples show how human errors generate significant and avoidable losses. In both instances, senior management was apparently unaware of the risks its firm was exposed to as a result of a few employees' actions.

Organizational failures to monitor and control day–to–day activities can also result in substantial risk from fraud, embezzlement or theft. Derivatives–based fraud has taken the forms of unauthorized trading, unrecorded transactions, off–market trades and fictitious counterparties. Because dealing rooms can commit billions of dollars in seconds, such risk is difficult to control. Further, employee collusion can derail even the most sophisticated control systems.

- Transaction processing: Potential for human error pervades the entire transaction processing flow. As transactions move from front office to back office and across disparate computer systems, data are often rekeyed up to five or six times. Many firms lack full front– and back–office systems integration. Thus data are often entered into front–office systems, accounting systems, settlement systems, and decision–support or analysis systems. The multiple entry of data into different systems increases the likelihood of human error and requires constant reconciliation. Any one or combination of simple data entry errors contains potentially serious consequences. The result could be misstatement of a financial or risk position or the failure of a transaction to clear and settle properly.

Operational risk associated with human errors is often rooted in the tendency of firms to organize responsibilities around functions rather than processes. The treasurer may only be responsible for buying and selling securities. A separate financial unit may be responsible for match–funding these securities to eliminate interest rate risk. Thus, no single unit assumes responsibility for the entire security management process. As a result, transaction flow often spans different departmental, divisional and organizational responsibility boundaries with no clear ownership. Certain tasks thus are either poorly controlled or coordinated and often "fall" through the organizational "cracks."

Valuation ("Model") Risks

Another form of operating risk rapidly becoming important in today's financial markets is valuation or "model" risk. Because of their complexity, the values of most derivative instruments can be calculated only with mathematical models. While these models are indispensable in managing and measuring derivatives positions, often the algorithms

---

are well beyond the sophistication level of the internal audit departments and outside regulators. Moreover, the software is frequently untested. Thus, many institutions rely on the assurance of their product development staff that models perform accurately under most market conditions. As would be expected, the absence of an independent "audit" of these models exposes the firm to large risks. Such an event occurred in 1987. A flaw in a computer model used to hedge interest rate caps led to a $33 million loss for Chemical Bank.

A similar risk is posed by models which, while theoretically sound, are not robust enough to handle deviations from the model's underlying assumptions. Generally, the accuracy of these models depends on an assumption of smoothly functioning markets operating under conditions of "normal" volatility with small, continuous price adjustments. However, in periods of market turmoil or unusual volatility, these assumptions may not hold. A recent example is the breakdown of the European Community's Exchange Rate Mechanism, a system for fixing exchange rates, in September of 1992. Commonly used currency hedging models based on assumptions of stable interest rates and small currency price adjustments proved to be inappropriate when prices fluctuated dramatically and interest rates soared in the turbulent days before the French referendum on the Maastricht treaty. Several firms which based their hedging positions on these models lost money when hedges slipped under the extreme market conditions.

Clearing and Settlement Risk

Breakdowns associated with clearing and settling transactions are another potential source of operational risk. Clearing a transaction involves confirming the type and quantity of the instrument, the transaction date and price, and the parties involved. Settlement involves the transfer of value from one party to another. The modern globalization of securities markets has highlighted the risks involved in clearing and settling cross–border transactions. These risks can pose significant problems to institutions. For example, they could lead to liquidity problems for firms that pay out funds in one transaction based on anticipated funds from another transaction which fails to settle. One international study identified five critical deficiencies in the clearing and settlement systems:[4]

1. Absence of compatible trade confirmation and matching systems for both domestic and international trades: Trade comparisons involve matching the terms of a trade to ensure accuracy. A failure of a trade to be rapidly confirmed and matched exposes parties to default.

2. Unequal settlement across countries: Unequal settlement periods present risks to firms since payments and counterpayments are settled at different times in different countries. The party making the first payment is exposed to default by the party making the later payment. This temporal difference, in which payment has been made in one time zone but not received in another time zone, is often called "Herstatt" risk, in reference to the 1974 failure of a German bank, Bankhaus Herstatt. In this case, U. S. banks paid out dollars in the morning but did not receive German marks through the German payment system when German banking authorities closed at 10:30 a. m. New York time. Since the U. S. payments were irreversible under the international payment system rules in place at the time, Herstatt received the dollars through its U. S. correspondent but did not pay out the marks.

3. Absence of formal delivery versus payment mechanisms in some markets: Delivery versus payment is a two–sided payment system. It simultaneously debits and credits appropriate cash and security accounts of parties to a transaction to eliminate a discrepancy between the timing of payments and receipts on settlement date.

4. Absence of standardized trade guarantees. A trade guarantee ensures the trades which have successfully been matched will be settled even in the event of a counterparty default. To assure this guarantee, each member of a settlement system assumes the default risks of the system.

5. Limited availability of book–entry processing. Book entry refers to the payment and ownership transfer of securities through credits and debits to computerized accounts on the books of a centralized depository. This eliminates the need to transfer paper between counterparties on a trade–by–trade basis, which can be quite cumbersome and time consuming, particularly when it involves worldwide delivery.

Legal Risk

Legal risk is the risk of loss a firm faces because a contract cannot be enforced. Because derivatives are relatively new and untested, legal risk is a significant operating risk in derivatives markets. Two of the key legal risks raised by derivatives are as follows:

• Counterparty insolvency: One source of concern in derivatives markets relates to the legal enforceability of "netting" provisions. Netting occurs when two parties entering into mutual multiple contracts use a master agreement to protect themselves from counterparty credit risk. These agreements specify that in the event of default by one party, all the transactions covered in the master agreement will be netted against each other and the party owing the difference will make one payment. Although netting contracts are generally valid in the U. S., their legal enforceability outside the U. S. is questionable.

- Capacity to transact: There is uncertainty about the legal capacity of certain municipalities and associations to engage in derivative contracts. For example, in the 1980s, the London Borough of Hammersmith and Fulham entered into interest rate swaps on which it suffered large losses and subsequently defaulted. In 1991, the British House of Lords ruled that the borough lacked the legal authority to enter into the swaps and invalidated the contracts.

Regulatory Risk

Regulatory risk has recently gained importance because derivative markets are relatively new and several aspects of their regulatory treatment are still evolving. Regulators have recently forced banks to expand their reporting of derivative positions. In addition, the treatment of netting schemes and derivatives positions in the calculation of bank capital will likely change as derivative markets continue to develop. (Some of the current proposed capital guidelines are exceedingly complex and require a significant investment in systems to monitor and measure, much less ensure, such compliance.) Standards for hedge accounting, a major purpose of derivatives, may also be refined in the future. Such changes in the regulatory treatment of derivatives can affect the reported financial condition and earnings performance of banks as well as their required capital levels. They are bound to react to political pressures as regulators pursue further disclosure of banks' off–balance–sheet activities.

Operating Risks—Summary

Most of the operating risks created by derivative instruments are not new risks to financial institutions. These institutions faced human and systems risks, for example, long before financial derivatives existed. What is significant about these instruments, however, is the degree to which they have exacerbated operating risk exposure. Moreover, these instruments have introduced new forms of operating risk, such as "model risk," which financial firms have not previously encountered and as of yet have no effective, efficient way to manage.

Because the operating risks faced by institutions participating in derivatives markets are not the same as those in traditional markets, existing risk management techniques will probably not be effective. As a result, firms need to develop a new approach to the management of their derivatives risk which recognizes the complexity of these instruments and the additional operating risk exposure this complexity creates.

An Approach to Managing Operational Risk

The Concept of Business Integration

For successful management of operating risk in financial services, firms must concurrently align the multiple components of their operations in support of their key business objectives. As described above, many sources of operational risk and instances of operational failure derive from a business design which fails to provide the appropriate operational infrastructure to support new financial products and services. Examples include the development of incompatible information systems across organizational units, absence of strong internal controls to handle unauthorized activities by traders or other employees engaged in risking the firm's capital, and a poor understanding and management of increasingly complex transaction flows.

Business integration is a concept which recognizes the need to develop complementary strategies for a firm's key business elements in support of a clearly defined vision. This concept provides a strategic framework which aligns key business design elements—people, business processes, and information technology—under a cohesive strategy. Successful implementation of this concept will help to eliminate the "gap" between the strategic goals supporting operational activities. Ultimately, it will lead to better management of operating risk.

Business Integration Components

Strategy

Successful management of operating risk arising from new financial products begins with a clear and compelling vision of the firm's key business objectives. These objectives must articulate the firm's vision of the future financial marketplace and the anticipated competitive positioning of the firm therein. In addition, these objectives serve as the focal point for how the firm offers its products and services and how it designs its business system. Structuring its supporting operations based on these objectives, the firm can well understand—and thus successfully manage—operating risk.

For example, firms which envision a marketplace characterized by opportunities to earn fee income by offering innovative risk management services might seek to broker financial derivatives products among their customers or to establish themselves as marketmakers in derivatives. Alternatively, firms might view derivatives as indispensable tools in achieving their asset and liability objectives. Such firms would establish themselves as end users of derivatives.

The decision by firms to incorporate financial derivatives into products and services as a means to attain business objectives implies that the firm's operating infrastructure components are sufficiently developed to support these products. This means adopting a business integration framework which focuses on implementing the core people, technology and business process strategies which comprise the operational infrastructure.

People

Because a significant source of operating risk from derivatives is human error, "people" strategy must address important human resources issues such as organizational structure, critical skills development, and control procedures. Firms must adopt an organization–wide view of responsibilities from top to bottom and information channels from bottom to top.

- Organizational structure: Individual departments as well as jobs need to align with the organization's strategic objectives. For example, firms engaging in the active trading or investment of financial derivatives need to redefine front– and back–office roles. Under the traditional model, the front office develops, values and prices products and positions; and the back office handles accounting and settlement. This model is not sufficient in a world of complex derivative products. Regulators expect firms to provide independent controls of the measurement of the market and credit and legal risk positions of their front–office dealers. These tasks exceed the capabilities of traditionally low–skilled, back–office workers. In addition, the multiproduct deals constructed in the front office often require specialized accounting treatment and multiple product settlements, usually unfamiliar processes to back offices accustomed to concentrating on single instruments.

In addressing their organizational designs, firms must appreciate the critical importance of timely and accurate information for managing derivatives. Recently, regulators have intensely scrutinized derivatives precisely because they did not perceive senior management's difficulty in fully understanding instruments such as derivative securities. Consequently, executives do not fully grasp their exposure to risks created by these products. In other instances, the reporting structure impedes effective risk management. For example, structures in which risk information is generated by dealers themselves or by individuals not sufficiently skilled to effectively rebut a dealer's valuation produce unreliable information as to the firm's true exposure.

Firms must build communications channels which break down traditional organizational boundaries and streamline the flow of information about their products to the right decision makers, in the right time frame, and in the right format to facilitate understanding. Senior management at J. P. Morgan, for example, receives a one–page summary of the bank's risk positions each business day. Using bar charts and straightforward language, this useful tool gives numbers on actual position and asset value at risk. It also provides the timeframe and rationale for each of Morgan's major market positions.

- Skills alignment: In developing a people strategy to support the delivery of financial derivative products, firms must inventory their current skills capabilities and identify the critical gaps between existing and required capabilities. The skill inventory must include an assessment as to whether senior management, front–office and–back office personnel have sufficient understanding of derivative products to effectively perform the product delivery process. This includes making sure product authorizations are consistent with resource capabilities.

- Controls: Firms must also strike the appropriate balance between empowering employees to perform their jobs in an unhampered environment and implementing controls on their behavior to minimize human error. Enforcement of a minimum set of controls over employee activities mitigates much of the operating risk firms face in derivative transactions. For dealers or traders authorized to invest the firm's capital in derivative positions, firms must establish and enforce maximum exposure limits by individual, product, counterparty and market. These controls must also have a time dimension to insure that frequent monitoring of a trader's position, for example, protects one institution from intraday limit overexposure. Additional controls are listed below and represent many practices of firms with substantial involvement in derivative markets:

Repeated trade terms to counterparties;

Recorded telephone lines;

Enforced timely completion of trade tickets;

Enforced independent callback of trade terms, positions, etc.;

Maintenance of an unconfirmed deal log for ongoing monitoring of pending confirmations;

Enforced dual input of sight verification of trade data;

Prenumbered transaction tickets for accountability;

Enforced reconciliation of trade transactions to broker statements, physical securities, contracts, etc.;

Investigation of all failed transactions;

Enforced timely reconciliation of accounts and clearance of suspense items;

Segregation of duties between transaction execution and settlement; and

Implementation of separate receipt of broker statements.

The "Middle" Office

As part of a people strategy to meet the new operational demands of derivative securities, firms should consider creating a "middle" office. This is a support function which bridges the gap between front– and back–office capabilities and which ensures accurate product processing flow and dealer position descriptions. Their responsibilities include valuation of positions, risk reporting, profit and loss reporting, and model verification. In contrast to traditional back offices, the middle office is aligned to support a whole business rather than a single product. This orientation allows middle–office employees to support multiple product deals and ultimately increases the business unit's efficiency. In addition, these offices are staffed with skills in both accounting and trading. Employees report to risk management executives—not to front–office personnel.

The middle–office concept has been implemented at many of the largest derivatives dealers in the U. S., including Chase Manhattan Bank, Merrill Lynch, Goldman Sachs, Nomura Securities, Sumitomo Bank, and J. P. Morgan. Sometimes it is included as part of an overall Risk

Management Unit (RMU) which oversees all aspects of an institution's risk–taking activities (market risk, credit risk, liquidity risk, operational risk, etc.) to optimally manage the balance sheet.

Process

The second component of the Business Integration framework is concerned with reengineering business processes to ensure that they conform to the overall business objectives. From an operating risk standpoint, business process reengineering involves a fundamental review of the entire transaction process—from initial product development to final payment settlement—altering the work flow and ultimately improving operational performance and reducing process risk. As noted earlier, a key source of operating risk today is the failure of firms to develop measures which address the growing length and complexity of derivative transaction processes. Examples include the multiple rekeying of data, inconsistent pricing models among departments, and multiple reconciliation reports.

The fundamental goals of business process reengineering are to eliminate redundant or non–value–added activities, simplify the processing of key transactions, consolidate departments and geographic locations, and automate major functions to improve productivity and quality. As with a people strategy, process reengineering must be conducted organization–wide and with a cross–functional perspective.

The lag with which many firms today have upgraded their capability to handle the complex processing flows of derivative transactions suggests a critical need for process reengineering to reduce their operating risk. Illustrative of some of the key steps firms should consider are:

1. Elimination of redundant or nonvalue–added activities
    - Adoption of once–only data entry procedures per transaction
2. Simplification of processes
    - Development of standardized products which simplify work flows and enhance automation
    - Development of sufficiently parameterized systems to allow complex products to be built and processed without customizing

3. Consolidation of departments
   - Creation of a "middle" office to handle front– and back–office procedures
4. Automation of functions
   - Integration of front– and back–office systems to eliminate the passing of paper transactions
5. Implementation of electronic imaging to electronically store and retrieve derivative documentation
6. Automation of position and reference data (prices, volumes, etc.) feeds into front office systems

Technology

The final component of the Business Integration model concerns the integration of technology into the operations strategy in support of the firm's business vision. In markets where the ability to compete depends heavily on harnessing the appropriate technology—such as derivative markets—development of and adherence to a coherent technology strategy is a critical survival factor. Moreover, proper deployment of technology can significantly reduce the operating risk of processing derivative transactions.

Much of today's technology to support derivative departments was developed to handle the low–volume, "plain–vanilla" needs of an earlier age. As discussed earlier, recent trends in financial markets have created a different environment in which these solutions do not sufficiently support the development and delivery of complex new products. These trends include:

- Globalization of markets: Derivatives players today need to track, hedge and pass their international derivatives positions around the clock and around the world. Thus, the traditional overnight batch processing of transactions performed on mainframes will not adequately meet the emerging demands of the marketplace for the instantaneous creation, updating and transmission of "electronic books."

- Complexity of products: The increasing complexity of customized derivative transactions requires advanced analytical software and powerful hardware to support their creation, valuation and hedging. Many deals are complicated, multitiered transactions with cashflows tied to more than one currency and interest rate. In addition, because the value of most derivative instruments is extremely sensitive to changes in market conditions, maintenance of a fully hedged position requires that firms have the capability to measure and alter their positions dynamically. Yet many institutions are equipped with systems that cannot provide necessary position updates. Moreover, regulators have cast a nervous eye on the growing volumes and complexity of the derivatives markets and increasingly demand improved risk management practices—including better information reporting and measurement systems. This situation is exacerbated by major financial institutions' dependence on third–party software with all of the attendant reliability, training, and systems integration concerns.

Information technology has not kept pace with financial market innovations. As a result, financial services firms face increased operational risk. This demonstrates the need for a coherent technology strategy to support strategic business objectives. Some steps firms should consider in their technology strategy include:

- Front–and back–office systems integration: Firms need to approach the derivatives business with a technology strategy common to both front and back offices. All analysis, valuations, reports, and calculations for both offices must be based on the same data. This means a common database accessed by all office staff.

- Integration across products: Since most derivative products are related, derivative systems must provide for cross–product integration. This allows firms to evaluate aggregate exposure across derivative products and exploit the benefits of overall position netting. To the extent that firms maintain additional product relationships with their customers, derivative product technology strategies must also address the costs and benefits of integrating with loan, deposit, trust and capital market systems. A fully integrated system provides firms with extensive customer profitability and risk exposure information. It also opens opportunities for competitive marketing advantages.

- Creation of a platform for change: The technology strategy must focus on the development of hardware and software platforms that allow for transitions to open systems and distributed processing. Long–term migration paths must address some of these key trends in the technology industry toward distributed processing, client–server architectures and open systems.

- Real–time systems support: The emerging need to operate a derivatives operation around the clock and to have intraday updates of risk exposure suggests that firms incorporate real–time processing architecture in their technology planning. Basing a technology strategy on batch processing is likely to leave firms at a comparative disadvantage in the coming years.

- Backup and disaster recovery support: Backup and disaster recovery planning are critical components of a derivatives technology strategy. The need to constantly monitor positions requires that firms have plans and systems in place to recover quickly from disasters or major equipment failures.

Conclusion

This chapter has highlighted many of the operational risks that firms face as a result of innovations in financial markets and products. For many firms, the advent of new financial instruments such as derivatives has brought new opportunities for managing financial risk and for profiting from trading and brokering. However, these new instruments are also fraught with many risks—including increased operating risks from running a derivatives department and processing its transactions. The fundamental source of this risk is the failure of firms to adopt operational strategies which are consistent with their business strategies in entering these new markets. An approach to managing these risks should thus involve a framework that recognizes the importance of aligning the business–supporting strategies of people, processes and technology with the overall business objectives of the firm. Without such a comprehensive, coherent framework, firms risk suboptimal earnings and excessive risk.

Notes

[1] Scarlata, Jodi, "Institutional Developments in the Globalization of Securities and Futures Markets," Federal Reserve Bank of St. Louis, *Economic Review*, January/February 1992.

[2] Remolona, Eli M., "The Recent Growth of Financial Derivative Markets," Federal Reserve Bank of New York, *Quarterly Review*, Winter 1992–93.

[3] "The Impact of Online Computer Systems Downtime on the Securities Industry," Stratus Computer, Inc. Survey, 1992.

[4] Group of Thirty, *Clearance and Settlement Systems in the World's Securities Markets* (New York and London), March 1989.

Risk Management and New Financial Products

Eff W. Martin, Partner, Goldman, Sachs & Co.
Jan B. Brzeski, Corporate Finance, Goldman, Sachs & Co.

Introduction

New products play a central role in the ongoing success of a financial services firm. Financial innovation and new product offerings have introduced both new revenue and profit opportunities as well as new risks. Some of these risks have historically attended the normal operations of businesses, but entirely new risks or levels of risk have also arisen. Developing new products and managing the associated risks have become central management functions at investment banks and other financial institutions.

This chapter addresses the importance of financial innovation, some of the important drivers and examples of new financial products, the risks associated with new financial products, and the practices financial services firms can use to address them. Among these risks, market or trading risk, credit risk, liquidity risk and intangible risk are examined individually. The discussion is practical rather than theoretical, based largely on current experience in the financial services industry.

The Importance of Financial Innovation

The greatest risk associated with financial innovation is that of failing to innovate. Stephen Friedman, Senior Partner of Goldman, Sachs, has observed that great enterprises are often created by the conception and execution of "big ideas." Frequently corporations and firms rely on past innovations for sustained periods without generating the next important driver of growth. The financial press is replete with examples of major companies whose failure to produce a continuing stream of "big ideas" eroded their leadership and even threatened their survival.

Financial services firms are frequently more susceptible to this danger than industrial corporations whose products and services may have longer lives. A firm does not have to be first in the market with new financial products, but it may need to be a "fast second" to avoid being shut out of the market. Pioneering products can often be improved, thereby reducing the risks of the second wave of new products. The reality is nonetheless clear: Innovation is critical to survival.

The necessity of innovation is inherent in any financial services firm seeking to offer solutions to changing client demands. New products have recently addressed such fundamental needs as investors' requirements for (1) yield in a low–interest–rate environment, (2) stability amid volatile interest rates and currency values, and (3) cross–border financial products and services in the midst of globalization of market opportunities.

These changes are so basic that an inability to address them adversely affects relationships between financial services firms and their clients.

Innovation and new product development are not merely defensive necessities. They provide important opportunities to gain new clients and increase market share. In most aspects of financial services, there is a historical relationship between clients and financial firms. Clients execute most conventional transactions with their relationship firms as long as those firms provide satisfactory products and services at competitive prices. Absent extraordinary circumstances, firms cannot easily overturn existing relationships to gain new clients on the basis of marginally better performance.

Given the importance of access to innovative ideas, clients usually distinguish between new and conventional products or services. While rewarding relationship bankers with conventional transactions, issuers and investors frequently pursue innovative ideas with their originators. New relationships can sometimes be formed only by offering new products and services which clients need and which they feel justified in pursuing outside existing relationships. The financial return on these products is magnified if the initial transactions lead to follow–on business and a permanent relationship. An example of this benefit of product innovation at Goldman, Sachs is Monthly Income Preferred Stock (MIPS). MIPS is a new security which receives equity treatment from the rating agencies while affording the issuer tax–deductible dividend payments, thereby fusing two of the primary advantages of equity and debt into a single instrument. MIPS has provided a mechanism to achieve an increased presence in the perpetual preferred market as well as a number of new client relationships.

Goldman, Sachs manages its business to promote creativity. Structurally, it has set aside resources and dedicated individuals to new product groups in various areas. More fundamentally, however, innovation begins with an affirmation of its importance in the Firm's culture. Much internal communication and training is directed toward recognizing and rewarding innovation. Managers do not unduly criticize or penalize failure because this practice would discourage future efforts.

Product Innovation — Drivers and Examples

The introduction of new financial products and services by financial services firms has accelerated in recent years. Driven by competitive pressures and the need to develop new, higher–margin business, financial services firms have devoted substantial resources to new product generation. As is increasingly the case in many industrial and manufacturing companies, new products now account for significant revenues. In addition, the higher value–added associated with many new products frequently affords higher fees and therefore results in disproportionate contributions to profits.

The growth of financial derivative products demonstrates the importance of new products. Derivative products in the investment banking agency and proprietary trading businesses in the late 1980s and early 1990s replaced the merger and acquisition and leveraged buyout boom that fueled previous growth and profitability. Figure 1 illustrates the growth of both exchange–traded derivative instruments (including interest rate, currency and stock market index futures and options) and over–the–counter instruments (including interest rate and currency swaps and other derivative instruments such as caps, collars, floors and swaptions).

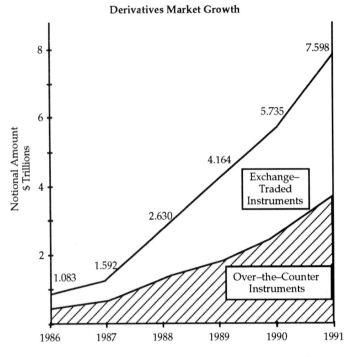

Figure 1

Derivatives Market Growth

New product innovation has historically been driven by changes in tax laws, accounting conventions and other regulatory considerations as well as by fundamental economic and capital market conditions. Today, advances in telecommunications and information technology also drive innovation. The ability to perform large numbers of calculations in real time allows for customization to a degree not previously possible. Another driver of innovation has been the increasingly complex needs of companies as they have widened their global reach. Improved global networking and information sharing have enhanced collaborative innovation and extended the new product vista into many currency–related areas and cross–border transactions. Improved computer technology and increased comfort with financial modeling and data analysis techniques also help manage the risk associated with these new products.

Many recently developed financial products are themselves producing further innovation. A financial services firm incurs a variety of risks when introducing new products. The feasibility of new products relates to a firm's ability to hedge the risk of the new activity. Many of the recent derivative product innovations have provided mechanisms which firms can use themselves to hedge their trading in futures, options or swaps. In addition, new products that provide liquidity in individual investments or for the firm as a whole allow further innovation and risk assumption.

New products in a financial services firm take a variety of forms and include a wide range of issuer and investor constituencies and markets. New products may be directed to investing clients; trading partners; corporate, municipal or sovereign issuers; or a combination of these parties.

New products offered to investing clients typically consist of new packages of securities or instruments which allow investors to participate directly in or hedge against economic events. The products may cover an entirely new event or segregate existing events into discrete components. Recent examples include Nikkei put warrants, which allow participants to express a view on the future direction of the Japanese stock market; longer–dated oil and natural gas price options, which allow companies and investors to manage energy price exposures for longer periods than before; and fixed–income investments, which segregate principal, interest and currency features.

New products offered to issuers may also give the financial services firm an opportunity to take the other side of a transaction. An issuer may desire to manage risk or extract value from a financial position due to the nature of his underlying business or outlook. Financial firms may trade directly with an issuer and thus remove the market risk of the issuer's exposure to the investment position. For example, a corporation may sell equity put or call options to a financial services firm which retains the option on its own books. The financial services firm can reduce market risk by using dynamic hedging techniques while trading the company's underlying common stock. Through this approach, the financial services firm can establish a neutral position with regard to the direction of movement of the company's stock. In addition to managing risk, this practice avoids placing the interests of the financial services firm and its client in opposition.

New products may also encompass new services as well as new financial instruments. At the inception of the leveraged buyout and raid mania of the early 1980s, Goldman, Sachs began offering an anti–raid service which defended corporations from hostile overtures. Although this activity was a service rather than a financial instrument, it was an effective new product which developed a business and met client needs. While new services typically involve less direct financial risk, they do entail other types of risk which are discussed below.

Risk Management

New products and services generate both tangible and intangible risks. At most financial services firms, risk management is a top priority and demands attention at the highest level.

Risk management does not mean risk avoidance. In many cases, senior managers encourage operating units to assume greater market or trading risks when the risk/reward ratios are favorable. Risk is associated with profit. A financial services firm should not avoid all risks; rather, it should identify and quantify risks correctly and prepare accordingly.

In addressing overall risk, a financial services firm may analyze a number of different types of risk, including market or trading risk, credit risk, liquidity risk, and other forms of intangible risk. The latter category encompasses a broad range of risks ranging from legal, compliance and control issues to the protection and enhancement of public image and reputation.

These risks must be considered at the level of individual financial positions as well as that of the entire firm. Individual risks must be analyzed as part of overall exposures to given credits or markets. In large institutions with many different trading areas, monitoring cumulative exposures is a significant challenge. An overall exposure may result from completely unrelated instruments or positions assumed by various operating units. Recognizing the correlations and instituting appropriate reporting techniques require constant attention and systemic controls.

Risk management reporting systems have undergone important changes to reflect these issues. For example, some systems are constructed to measure risk by reflecting positions of individual trading desks. The risks are then aggregated into a total risk position for the firm. A second step involves netting various positions among trading desks to eliminate reporting risks which are hedged within the firm's overall portfolio. Specifically, if one trading desk is "long" 10-year Treasuries while another area is "short" the same amount (that is, has borrowed and sold 10-year Treasuries which it does not own), the firm has no net exposures from these two positions. However, without the tracking systems to find and net these positions across diverse areas, the risk would be overstated and the firm might execute two unnecessary offsetting transactions.

Much attention is now focused on identifying correlations between assets or liabilities that do not directly offset each other. Determining these relationships, programming them into a risk management system and monitoring their validity requires substantial effort. A model may involve thousands of different assets and liabilities. Reporting systems which provide more sophisticated information on a firm's risk repay their investment by providing substantial competitive advantage.

One of the most sophisticated risk management tools utilized at Goldman, Sachs originated from the Global Asset Allocation Model developed by Fischer Black and Bob Litterman. This model was originally employed for our investing clients and was later adapted to our own risk management purposes. The model is used to suggest optimal asset allocation and to measure risk for a portfolio containing many different asset types denominated in different currencies; including equities, fixed–income securities, commodities and derivatives such as swaps. Central to the model is a covariance matrix of correlations among volatilities of different asset classes. Currently, over 500 asset classes are included, and that number is constantly increasing.

The Black–Litterman framework offers significant advantages over earlier asset allocation models. Because it was designed for many asset classes and currencies, the model is better suited for global asset allocation than earlier models which focused on only a few asset classes or a single currency. The model also uses daily return data instead of the monthly data in most other asset allocation models, and therefore it provides a more timely measure of market risk. Another innovative feature of the model is its ability to recommend "best next trades." This feature prioritizes the trades a client might execute to reach optimal portfolio allocation. Another of the outputs of the model is a "risk landscape" within a specific portfolio's country and product matrix. An example of such a risk landscape is shown in Figure 2.

The Black–Litterman model determines the distribution of outcomes for various asset classes. Volatility can be used as a first approximation to generate real–time information. However, normal distributions provide misleading results since markets typically have "fat tails": the probability of extreme outcomes is greater than that expected in a normal distribution. We often analyze "worst–case" results at the four–standard–deviations level, but examples of ten–standard–deviation moves sometimes occur. The firm analyzes tail risk using a variety of historical and prospective scenario analyses; but by definition, tails involve substantial uncertainty.

To control trading–related risks, all traders report to senior professionals in the trading area. In addition, many trading risks and positions are reviewed individually and globally by managers outside the trading function. Finally, to ensure that senior management has the clearest possible

---

view of the risk position at Goldman, Sachs, risk control functions generally report directly to the Management Committee. This procedure provides top–level information flow and unifies the risk management function.

Market Risk

Market or trading risk involves both directional risk and volatility risk. Directional risk refers to the risk of adverse movements in the price of equity or fixed–income securities, commodities, foreign exchange or other assets. A financial institution risks loss (1) when prices decline and it has long positions due to agency–related or principal trading or (2) when prices rise and the institution has short positions. Volatility risk relates to the difference between actual and expected volatility in asset prices. Such a divergence results in gains or losses depending on the degree of underestimation or overestimation of volatility.

The assumption of both directional and volatility market risk is a primary business for many financial services firms. Such risks are therefore monitored carefully. At Goldman, Sachs, senior managers with direct accountability run every trading activity. In addition, a committee of senior trading partners and members of the Firm's Management Committee monitors trading risk. Goldman, Sachs also monitors risk in each trading or investment activity with a quantitative "risk of loss" metric. Risk of loss is an estimate of certain loss scenarios, including worst–case losses based on historical market movements and other technical analyses. Historical market movement models used in other trading areas measure past price changes for several standard deviations and apply those changes to the current portfolio. The probability of various gains or losses based on price movements can then be determined. Risk of loss is calculated daily by risk control managers as well as the individual trading areas. This calculation incorporates all products.

As mentioned above, trading groups may utilize several approaches to evaluate risks and rewards associated with new products or with particular transactions. One approach evaluates risks algebraically; it seeks formal solutions based on expected cashflows. A second approach involves scenario analysis, which evaluates costs and returns under a variety of market outcomes. These outcomes can then be analyzed individually or together to yield an average expected outcome. Finally, Monte Carlo simulation techniques provide a more rigorous approach. These simulations are particularly effective in analyzing the risks associated with derivatives.

For example, a financial services firm may wish to evaluate two different strategies for accumulating a particular stock either as a principal or an agent for a client. One strategy involves purchasing stock at regular intervals until the desired amount has been bought. The other strategy involves purchasing stock at regular intervals and selling puts on it to a third party, giving that party the right to sell additional stock to the financial services firm at a predefined price. Monte Carlo simulation techniques generate a probability distribution, such as that in Figure 2, which represents the range of outcomes under each strategy.

Figure 2

Probability Distribution for Share Repurchase Strategy

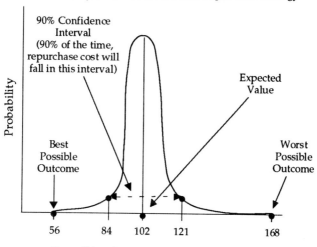

Cost of Purchasing Fixed Number of Shares
(Arbitrary Units)

Figure 2 illustrates the expected cost of accumulating the shares under one strategy. This is the most likely cost given inputs such as the initial price of the stock, the stock's volatility, the dividend rate, the interest rate, and the expected trend–line growth rate of the stock price. It also illustrates the best (lowest–cost) and worst (highest–cost) possible outcomes of the strategy. The curve can be defined further by its 99%, 95% and 90% confidence intervals. The 90% confidence interval illustrates the range of possible costs which will result 90% of the time. The cost will be above or below this range 10% of the time. Geometrically, 90% of the area under the curve falls above the horizontal line, corresponding to the 90% confidence interval; and 10% of the area falls below this line. The curve for this strategy can then be compared to others to assess the relative risks and rewards. In this example, using puts in connection with a share accumulation may yield a lower expected overall cost, more attractive confidence intervals, superior best– and worst–case outcomes, or a combination of these advantages.

Because computer–based Monte Carlo simulations can effectively assess a large number of trading strategies and their risks, they are used in modeling many new financial products. Monte Carlo simulations follow a three–part process: defining a valuing tool, determining a strategy, and testing the strategy to generate a probability distribution similar to the one shown. In the first step, a value function is defined based on inputs such as the market price and volatility of underlying securities. In the second step, the strategy is selected. The final step involves running a computer program which repeatedly applies the strategy to a large number of random walks over many periods. Each random walk provides one value data point, and the sum of these data points generates a probability distribution such as that in Figure 3.

Monte Carlo analyses quantify market risk. In addition to the types of risk already described, two types of risk are implicit in all analyses used by financial services firms, including Monte Carlo simulations: model risk and input risk. Model risk refers to the likelihood that models used to evaluate certain important variables such as interest or foreign exchange rates prove unreliable. There is no assurance that a model will correctly predict a new financial instrument's performance until it is tested in the market. Input risk relates to the inherent stochasticity of variables which are typically inputs into financial models, such as inflation or future volatility. In practice, model risk is usually limited because pricing offered by other market participants provides a check on model outputs. However, this counterbalance is not available to the first firms to bring new products into the market. Thus input risk remains a significant and largely uncontrollable concern for financial services firms.

Credit Risk

Credit risk relates to the possibility that a debtor defaults on its loan or is unable to repay its obligation in a timely manner. Some financial institutions consider the assumption of credit risk as a primary business, but many investment banks and trading firms do not. Even if a firm regards its primary business as assuming market risk, increasingly complex transactions and direct customer interactions have made credit risk increasingly necessary. The explosive growth of the swap and other derivative markets has contributed significantly to this trend.

At most financial services firms, a credit department evaluates the clients and counterparties to whom the firm will have risk exposure. Typically these groups rely on classic business analysis techniques. Given the enormous number of corporations and institutions involved in worldwide investment banking activities and trading markets, credit departments also rely heavily on public rating services such as Moody's Investor Services and Standard & Poors Corporation.

At Goldman, Sachs, the Credit Department establishes limits independent of producing areas based on both public and internal credit analyses. It assures that credit exposure complies with the Firm's credit limits. A global computer network reports credit exposure by product, counterparty and country for all trading and hedging activities. Underwriting and other substantial commitments must be approved by the Firm's Commitments Committee and the Management Committee.

One of the challenges in managing credit risk revolves around the constantly changing exposures which occur as the liabilities in swaps or other transactions increase due to underlying interest rate, currency or other market movements. A transaction may initially fall within the Firm's credit limits. However, as economic conditions change, the liability of the client may exceed these limits.

Scenario modeling techniques analyze the degree of credit risk created by these currency and interest rate swap transactions. By applying historical default rates for the various rating categories, using the default rates implicit in rate spreads, and projecting certain "depression scenarios," potential losses due to credit exposures can be estimated.

Marking transactions to market with corresponding collateral commitments has become increasingly popular for managing credit risk. In this process, the financial services firm and its client agree to monitor exposures under the transaction and routinely mark them to the market. When the exposures exceed certain limits, collateral may be posted to keep the exposure to predetermined levels, or the transaction may be terminated after reaching maximum exposure.

One significant aspect of new product innovation has been the extension of transaction terms. For example, interest rate and currency swaps are now typically available for up to 10 years. This extended length creates additional credit risk. One approach to managing the inherent uncertainty over these extended periods is to agree on certain event protections. For example, a ratings downgrade might trigger either the posting of additional collateral or the termination of a contract. Since these obligations restrict future flexibility and are often resisted by clients, they occur more frequently with lower–rated entities which do not have the same safety as stronger companies.

Since many new products involve mutual commitments and exposures between financial service firms and their clients, most mark–to–market commitments or event triggers are symmetric; they apply to both parties. However, these provisions are not universally applied when parties have a significant disparity in creditworthiness.

Liquidity Risk

Liquidity risk involves the ability to meet financial obligations, both globally and in the context of particular transactions. At the global level, financial services firms follow a number of policies relating to both asset management and funding to maintain liquidity during prolonged periods of stress. This involves carefully building upon the firm's equity base and sometimes using long– rather than short–term debt. All new financial products which involve capital commitments are carefully analyzed to assess their individual liquidity ramifications and their impact on overall liquidity. An important component of this analysis involves the firm's ability to hedge the instrument through direct offsets or through trades in underlying debt or equity markets. At one end of the spectrum, highly leveraged bridge loans offered very little liquidity to creditors when the credits deteriorated. With few buyers for these loans, there was little opportunity to hedge the exposures. On the other hand, equity derivative options executed in liquid stocks can be hedged using the underlying liquidity in the stock market. As a result, there is no real need to capture liquidity in the option itself.

As noted above, one example of a new financial product with liquidity risk ramifications involves equity put and call warrants. Such warrants can be bought or sold by an issuer with a financial services firm acting as counterparty. This arrangement gives the owner of the warrant the right to buy or sell shares of the stock at a predetermined price over some period. Such transactions offer the ability to capture value from a directional view or from the issuer's stock price. Furthermore, they give the financial services firm the opportunity to profit from the stock's volatility. When a financial services firm buys equity calls from an issuer, it must set aside scarce regulatory capital representing a portion of the value of the warrants. Upon entering into such a transaction, the firm typically requires the issuer to register shares sufficient to fulfill the exercise of the call warrants. This measure limits the firm's liquidity risk by assuring that the call warrants can be converted to shares in a timely manner. This practice has the additional benefit of conserving the firm's regulatory capital since a lesser proportion of capital is required when the shares underlying a call have been registered with the SEC.

Goldman, Sachs has developed sophisticated computer systems to evaluate the expected cash and regulatory capital usage associated with new products and strategies. Pricing of longer-dated principal transactions such as forwards, swaps and options is frequently influenced by return on capital requirements. On a macro level, the Firm places a high priority on maintaining liquidity. It has developed contingency plans to manage such risk.

Other Risks

Many other risks are associated with the creation of new financial products. These risks begin with the opportunity costs of pursuing uncertain development activities. They also include the risk of depending on too few new products, reputational risks associated with the perception of the new products, future responsibility risks if the product does not produce desirable results, and legal and regulatory risks.

Opportunity Costs. New product development often requires the commitment of significant resources and the incurrence of substantial legal and accounting fees. Those involved in new product innovation are often among the most gifted and creative individuals in the firm. As in more conventional research and development activities in industrial corporations, the cost for these resources is substantial. In addition, risk continues as the marketing process demands further time and energy prior to launching the new product. If new products are not accepted by the market or if they fail to solve key legal, accounting, tax, regulatory or economic problems, the firm has already incurred these direct costs. Perhaps more importantly, it has also suffered the opportunity cost of not employing its new product development and marketing resources in more productive efforts.

Product Concentration Risk. A useful model for a financial services firm engaging in product innovation is that of the venture capitalist. New financial products, like seed venture investments, have a high variance of returns. As shown in Figure 3, an investor in venture–capital–type investments depends on the extraordinary returns of a few investments to outweigh the minimal and often negative returns of a majority of the investments. As a result, venture investors take a portfolio approach. They ensure that the number of investments is large enough to include a few winners. A firm would expose itself to extreme product concentration risk if it developed only one or two new financial products. Odds are that with only two products, neither would deliver the return necessary to justify the high risk of a new venture–capital–type investment. One of the many reasons small firms have more difficulty pioneering new financial products is their inability to diversify their new product investments. A larger firm can mitigate this risk with a steady flow of new products, some of which will deliver extraordinary returns.

Figure 3

Returns on a portfolio of Venture Capital–Type Investments

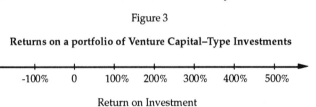

Return on Investment

Reputation Risk. The impact of a new product on a firm's reputation is the most difficult element to assess, but it carries the most damaging potential consequences. Financial innovation and new products can create negative perceptions in a variety of ways. Financial innovations have adverse effects for the system as a whole by introducing excessive leverage or creating additional volatility. For example, program trading has been criticized for causing volatile stock prices.

Since many new products address legal, tax or regulatory issues, their developers must ensure that the new products are not inappropriately aggressive. The classic distinction between tax avoidance and tax evasion illustrates this issue. Financial products which cross the line are ethically inappropriate and may tarnish credibility.

Financial institutions rely upon their reputation for high standards and integrity to a greater degree than most businesses. The impact of a damaged image will be felt across a broad range of the firm's businesses over a protracted period. For this reason, the "Caesar's wife" test is usually applied to issues involving reputational risk. Caesar's wife was not only held accountable for acting in a morally correct fashion; she was also expected to avoid behavior which could subject her to gossip and suspicion. Credit and market risks typically have limits, but the "above suspicion" standard is necessary in ethical or reputational areas.

Risk Management and New Financial Products

More subtle forms of reputational risk must be managed as well. Certain clients may view new product ideas as "financial gadgetry." Innovations which do not directly address client needs may be viewed as self serving. They cast the financial institution in an unfavorable light. This risk can only be managed by careful targeting and judicious marketing. Balancing this risk, however, is the firm's risk of reputation erosion due to a failure to innovate. A reputation for excellence can only be maintained with a continuous flow of new financial products which serve clients' needs.

Future Responsibility Risk. Any new, untested product carries the potential to surprise issuers or investors. If the security does not perform as expected by either side, the disappointed party may believe that the financial services firm did not correctly anticipate or explain these impacts. This situation can easily occur with the many new, highly leveraged financial products. During periods of market discontinuities, structured trades involving currency or interest rate relationships have caused substantial unexpected losses. Serious customer disappointments create risk for the financial institutions involved. Unexpected losses may even subject them to claims that the financial services firm inappropriately sold or sponsored the new product and should bear the financial losses. Clients may claim that they did not understand and are not responsible for highly complex and sophisticated transactions. In some cases, parties have even alleged that the individuals or government bodies entering into transaction did not have authorization to do so and that this factor invalidated certain trades.

These situations are extremely unfortunate. They invariably cost a financial services firm time, money and goodwill. Managing this risk involves a variety of activities beginning with careful selection of the parties to whom new products will be offered. Ensuring the suitability of the product for either the issuer or investor provides the most important form of protection. Dealing with sophisticated corporations and institutions rather than individual investors or political entities in the early stages of a product offering is a typical and routine safeguard.

Correctly documenting the product and any contractual obligations also minimizes new product risk. This task is often complicated by the difficulty of documenting all potential outcomes, especially unforeseen ones. However, careful attention to legal materials can help establish the original intent of a transaction and reduce future controversies.

Disclosure of primary risks of a transaction to both investing and issuing clients, to the extent that it informs them and establishes consent, remains an important aspect of risk management.

Legal Risks. Numerous legal issues are involved in new product introductions. One example of legal risk arises from the complexity involved in global execution of new product transactions. In many cases, financial services firms and their clients enter into a multitude of transactions, many of which may offset each other to some extent. The legal ability of the financial services firm to "net" these transactions in the event of a credit problem helps determine the amount of risk which the firm may undertake. Additional issues may arise if the transactions are consummated through various subsidiaries in different localities governed by different laws. Managing these risks requires careful analysis of the enforceability of contracts and the ability to net exposures incurred in different legal jurisdictions.

Conclusion

Financial services firms face increasing requirements to develop new products that meet client needs. These products protect market position and offer enhanced profit opportunities. At the same time, many of these products involve greater levels of both implicit and explicit risk than the older products which they complement or replace. Financial services firms have responded by developing more powerful quantitative techniques and more comprehensive reporting systems. Despite these improvements, effective risk management ultimately depends on the effort devoted to the task and the quality of management judgments. Even if risk could be measured perfectly, which it cannot, management would still need to determine the amount and types of risk it desires to bear.

Bank Capital Requirements and Incentives for Lending

Charles J. Jacklin, Professor, Graduate School of
Business, Stanford University

Introduction

This paper provides insights on the recent "credit crunch." First, we document the dramatic changes affecting the banking environment over the past ten years to provide a context for understanding the credit crunch. Second, we analyze how the new bank capital requirements have affected banks' incentives for different types of lending based on a review of corporate capital structure theory. We argue that the new bank capital requirements in conjunction with other regulatory and legislative changes have made investing in securities relatively more attractive to banks than many more traditional types of lending. This is particularly true for banks that are accumulating higher levels of capital to meet the new guidelines. Banks without adequate capital buffers may ration or limit forms of lending that require the highest amounts of capital, and they will require greater interest spreads for such lending to cover their increased costs. Thus, the credit crunch may reflect both the capital shortfalls and a permanent shift in the price of certain types of lending.

Background

Over the past three years, bank borrowers have repeatedly complained of a credit crunch. This period coincides with the implementation of new risk–based capital standards in banking, so many have questioned whether there is a connection between the perceived lack of credit and the new capital standards. Much of the debate has focused on whether the slow growth in bank lending is due to reduced demand or the new bank capital requirements.

Sorting out demand versus supply effects is difficult because there is an identification problem. Lack of bank credit can lead to sluggish economic activity and vice versa. Moreover, isolating the roles of bank capital and bank capital requirements is even more difficult. Consider a regional downturn that leads to loan losses and reductions in bank capital. Lower levels of bank capital combined with capital requirements may limit banks' ability to extend credit. If credit is not available, then economic activity may be slow. Of course, other sources of credit may arise; but as Bernanke (1983) points out in the context of the Great Depression, if the primary, most efficient allocators of credit have been displaced, then such adjustments may be quite costly.

Several researchers have examined the possibility of a connection between the capital standards and the credit crunch. Peek and Rosengren (1992) examine bank behavior in New England and conclude that "bank behavior was altered by the loss of capital." However, they do not attribute the credit crunch to a lack of bank capital. "Using currently available sources, the link between a capital crunch and a credit crunch cannot be tested definitively." Bernanke and Lown (1991) state that "demand factors, including the weakened state of borrowers' balance sheets, caused much of the slowdown" in lending. Nonetheless, they conclude that shortfalls in capital have limited banks' ability to make loans, particularly in the most affected regions. However, they note that their "estimates of the effect of falling bank capital on lending are statistically significant but small." Hancock and Wilcox (1992) estimate the effect of real and financial factors on bank credit flows during 1990. They find that "the majority of the decline in bank credit flows, especially to sectors like commercial real estate, can be traced to conditions in those sectors." Evidence indicates that capital shortfalls affected lending decisions and significantly restrained credit flows and that capital shortfall accounted for an aggregate decrease in lending of over $20 billion in 1990.

Risk–Based Capital Requirements

In July 1988, the central bankers of 12 major industrialized countries reached an agreement to adopt uniform risk–based capital standards (the Basel Accord), to be implemented in two steps: the first effective December 31, 1990; and the second and final step, December 31, 1992. Although the international agreement applies only to internationally active banks, the U.S. banking regulators applied the standards to all federally regulated or insured banks and thrifts. The new capital standards differ from those previously in place in three principal ways: (1) they are risk–based in that different amounts of capital are required to be held against types of assets; (2) they define capital more restrictively;[1] and (3) they incorporate off–balance–sheet items.

In discussing the new capital requirements, we begin by considering the nature of capital. Capital takes many forms. Often, it refers to owners' equity or the owners' financial stake in the company. If one thinks of capital as a buffer that protects debtholders, then one might include preferred stock in this definition. Preferred stockholders do not hold an indenture, and failure to pay preferred dividends does not constitute a default. Moreover, in banking, the buffer provided by capital is often viewed as protection for depositors and the deposit insurer. If this is the case, then subordinated debt instruments may also be considered as capital. In this regard, the newly instituted bank capital requirements define two types of capital—Tier 1 (core) capital and Tier 2 (supplementary) capital. Tier 1 capital could be viewed as a buffer for all debtholders. It approximates tangible equity capital. Tier 2 capital could be viewed as an additional buffer protecting depositors and the deposit insurer. The two types of capital are as follows:

- Core capital is defined as common stock plus surplus, retained earnings, noncumulative perpetual preferred stock and minority interest in the equity accounts of consolidated subsidiaries less goodwill.
- Supplemental capital includes subordinated debt and intermediate–term preferred stock only up to an amount equal to 50% of Tier 1 capital. Allowance for loan losses up to 1.25% of total risk–based assets can be counted as supplemental capital. However, *specific reserves* for loan losses and all *allocated transfer risks* are excluded.[1]

The new risk–based capital standards establish *minimum* levels of capital to be maintained as a percentage of weighted risk assets, which will be defined below. Stated capital standards are bare minimum levels of capital, and bank regulators generally expect banks to operate well above these levels.

Prior to the new risk–based capital standards, capital requirements were specific as a percentage of total bank assets regardless of their composition. Moreover, any risks that did not appear on the balance sheet did not affect a bank's capital requirement. But the new *minimum* standards tie capital requirements to the composition of the bank's asset portfolio and its off–balance–sheet risks for the first time. Capital requirements are stated as a percentage of *weighted risk assets*—not total assets. A bank's weighted risk assets are a weighted average of its assets and *credit–equivalent amounts* of its off–balance–sheet credit risks. For risk–weighting purposes, assets and credit–equivalent amounts of off–balance–sheet risks are classified into four categories intended to reflect the credit risk of the items.

By applying different weights to different types of assets, the capital requirements reflect risk since the weighting scheme effectively varies the amount of capital to be held against different types of assets. However, although banks face a variety of risks (e.g., credit risk, interest rate risk, foreign currency risk), the new capital requirements are tied only to credit risk. Furthermore, the asset risk categories that determine a bank's required capital level are broadly defined. For example, commercial and industrial loans fall into the highest risk category regardless of the borrower's financial soundness. Also, long–term bonds issued by the United Kingdom fall into the lowest risk category for U.S. banks because they are presumed to have no default risk even though the bank faces both interest rate risk and foreign currency risk in holding such bonds. On the other hand, a short–term commercial loan to the most financially sound U.S. corporation still falls in the highest risk category and requires substantial capital position. We should not overstate the lack of sensitivity of capital requirements to risks other than credit risks. The capital standards only reflect minimum capital levels. Federal banking agencies are also concerned with all of the risks faced by banks and may require that banks exceed the minimum capital level if a risk is significant.

There are four risk weighting categories, the principal items of which are as follows:

0% Weight Category
    Cash
    Government securities
20% Weight Category
    U.S. government agency guaranteed securities
    Balances at domestic banks
    General obligation of U.S. states and municipalities
50% Weighted Category
    Mortgages (1–4 family residences) first lien
    Revenue bonds of U.S. states and municipalities
    Credit–equivalent amounts of interest rate and foreign exchange–rate–related contracts
100% Weighted
    All other loans

Off–balance–sheet credit risks, such as loan commitments, loan guarantees, futures and swap contracts, are also included in weighted risk assets. Computing their contribution to weighted risk assets involves two steps. First, a *credit–equivalent amount* of off–balance–sheet items is computed on a set of credit conversion factors based on the nature of the bank's commitment. Then, the credit–equivalent amount is weighted (using the above weighting scheme) and included in the weighted risk asset computation *as if* it were an asset. For example, the credit–equivalent amount for a standby letter of credit (SLC) backing a municipal bond is 100% of its face value. The risk weighting for a credit–equivalent amount is 50%. So, the bank would count 100% x 50% = 50% of the face value of the SLC in computing its total weighted risk assets.

The credit conversion factors used to compute the credit–equivalent amount of a particular off–balance–sheet item are based on the nature of the credit risk to which the bank is exposed. For example, items that are direct credit substitutes or items that subject the bank to direct credit risk have a 100% conversion factor. Items that represent transaction–related contingencies have a 50% conversion factor, and items that relate to short–term, trade–related contingencies have a 20% conversion factor. In addition, interest rate and foreign exchange contracts are converted into credit–equivalent amounts. The computation of these credit–equivalent amounts includes both the current marked–to–market value of such contracts (if positive) plus a potential future exposure based on the notional amount of the contract.

The new minimum capital requirements were introduced in two steps, the first of which was effective December 31, 1990. The standards were fully implemented as of December 31, 1992.

Implementation Schedule

7.25% of total weighted risk assets as of December 31, 1990, half of which must be core capital.[2]

8.00% of total weighted risk assets as of December 31, 1992, half of which must be core capital.

Under the new capital requirements, banks must simultaneously meet three minimum capital requirements. Two of them are the capital requirements associated with the Basel Accord and are computed as a percentage of weighted risk assets. As of December 31, 1992, these two requirements were:

$$Total\ capital\ ratio = .08 = \frac{total\ capital}{weighted\ risk\ assets}$$

$$Core\ capital\ ratio = .04 = \frac{core\ capital}{weighted\ risk\ assets}$$

The third capital requirement was introduced by U.S. banking regulators in addition to the two capital ratios defined above. This is the leverage ratio, which is defined as:

$$Leverage\ ratio = \frac{core\ capital}{average\ total\ assets}$$

The minimum leverage ratio has been set to 3%.

The sections that follow present a comprehensive, though informal, analysis of banks' incentives to lend given recent changes in the banking environment (including risk–based capital standards). If one accepts the premise that capital is costly to hold on a risk–adjusted basis, there are straightforward ways of analyzing these incentives. For example, in a model where banks are treated as risk adverse and the expected return and risk characteristics of the pool of assets from which banks invest are held constant (as capital requirements vary, not across classes of assets), Furfine (1992) shows that capital constraints which apply different weights to different types of assets will lead banks to invest more in the lower–weighted and less in the higher–weighted assets.

Figure 1 depicts recent growth rates in aggregate bank assets segregated by four categories of assets that receive different risk weightings under the new capital standards: government securities (0% or 20% weight), real estate loans (50% or 100% weight), commercial and industrial loans (100% weight) and loans to individuals (100% weight). These growth rates are consistent with Furfine's portfolio analysis. Interestingly, the decline in growth in lending to the 100% asset categories began before the 1990–91 recession and continued after it. Since the initial phase of the new capital requirements began at the end of 1990, many banks may have changed their asset portfolio mix in 1990 to lower their weighted risk assets and thus meet the year–end capital requirements.

In the next section, we describe a variety of other considerations that influence a bank's investment decisions. We explore the reasons capital may be costly to hold on a risk–adjusted basis and consider the possibility that the relative asset prices may change as capital requirements change.

Figure 1

Annualized Growth Rates in Assets at Commercial Banks in the United States

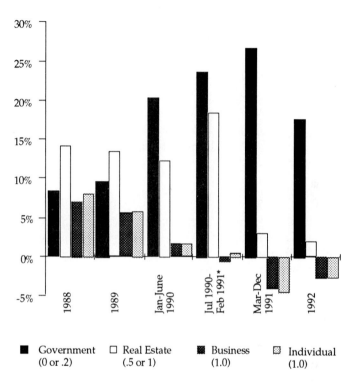

* NBER Recession Dates

Other Recent Changes in the Banking Environment

Comparing bank lending activity during the 1990–91 recession with that of previous recessions may be problematic given the changes in the banking environment between that and earlier recessions. These changes are important in understanding the impact of the new risk–based capital requirements due to interactions among the banking environment, capital standards and banks' incentives to lend. We focus on changes occurring since the two recessions of the early 1980s to emphasize how bank lending decisions differ from the recent recession and from current practice. Some of the significant changes in the banking environment since the early 1980s are:

- The introduction of risk–based capital requirements (discussed in the previous section),
- The elimination of deposit interest ceilings,
- Changes in corporate and individual tax rates,
- Changes in taxation of loan loss provisions,
- The increased use of market value accounting principles,
- Increases in deposit insurance premiums, and
- Changes in procedure mandated by the Federal Deposit Insurance Corporation Improvement Act of 1991 (FDICIA), such as prompt corrective action and early closure.

Elimination of Deposit Interest Ceilings

The Depository Institutions Deregulation and Monetary Control Act of 1980 phased out deposit interest rate ceilings over a six–year period. With the elimination of deposit interest rate ceilings, banks could compete for funds in any interest rate environment. To the extent that banks were constrained in their ability to raise funds in past recessions, their lending decisions would have been influenced by rate ceilings. Thus, any comparison of bank lending behavior across recessions must account for the influence of such ceilings in previous recessions.

Changes in Corporate and Individual Tax Rates

The Economic Recovery Act of 1981 and the Tax Reform Act of 1986 dramatically changed the tax code. As discussed below in the section on capital structure, these changes greatly increased the preference for debt over equity financing. In doing so, they increased the cost of equity financing relative to the cost of debt financing and thus bear directly on bank capital requirements.

The tax changes also have bearing on the evaluation of a borrower's financial condition. The tax preference for debt that was introduced in the 1980s led most corporations to increase their leverage. Consistent with this, Bernanke and Lown (1991) found that corporate borrowers had increased debt. Holding everything else constant, increased levels of debt may indicate that borrowers are less creditworthy. However, everything else has not been held constant. *Given the tax changes* in the 1980s, higher debt may make perfect sense regardless of creditworthiness. According to Ross, Westerfield and Jaffe (1992), although many corporations issued additional debt and repurchased their own shares throughout the 1980s, the ratio of the market value of debt to the market value of equity did not change significantly.

Changes in Taxation of Loan Loss Provisions[3]

Banks record expenses (provisions for loan losses) to reflect expected losses on their loan portfolios. These provisions reduce current income (and thus reduce increases in owners' equity) and accumulate as a loan loss reserve on the balance sheet. Subsequently, when a bank experiences an actual loss, the bank charges off the loan (or a fraction of it) against the loan loss reserve.

The tax treatment of provisions for loan losses has changed considerably. Prior to 1965, banks were allowed to deduct all provisions taken for loan losses for tax purposes. Thus banks had substantial incentives to reduce current income by maintaining large reserves for loan losses. In 1969, the Internal Revenue Service (IRS) limited loan loss reserve to an amount reflecting actual experience or 2.4% of total loans (an amount significantly above actual experience for most banks). Since then, the allowable percentage loan loss reserve was reduced several times until the Tax Reform Act of 1986 (TRA 86) eliminated it entirely. With the implementation of TRA 86, large banks[4] could deduct only actual loan losses. All other banks could deduct provisions for loan losses which maintained a loan loss reserve consistent with the banks' experience over the proceeding five years.

The generous treatment of loan loss provisions that existed until recently provided a tax incentive for banks to lend (as opposed to invest in securities) since an increase in total loans also increased the immediate deduction that could be taken against income. The current tax treatment of loan losses by banks does exactly the opposite. By allowing banks only to deduct realized losses, the tax cost effectively requires banks to report higher income (and pay higher taxes) than would be required by the bank regulators or by Generally Accepted Accounting Principles (GAAP).

The conflict between tax treatment and regulatory treatment is even more severe when interest accrual and capital requirements are also considered. Accounting principles and bank regulators require banks to make *specific provisions for* losses against loans that fail to meet certain criteria. These provisions reduce current income and increase loan loss reserves. Unlike *general reserves for loan losses*, specific reserves do not count as supplemental capital. Banks also stop accruing interest for accounting and regulatory purposes on such loans. However, for tax purposes, banks must continue to accrue interest (and pay taxes on the interest) until the loan is charged off. Even if a loan is partially charged off as uncollectable, banks must accrue interest on the remaining portion of the loan. *Thus, banks must pay taxes on accrued interest, which does not accrue as capital for regulatory purposes, on loans that have been discounted for capital purposes.*

These conflicts between tax and regulatory treatments create disincentives for banks to lend to all but the most creditworthy borrowers even if the expected profit would more than compensate for the risk (ignoring the tax and regulatory issues). Moreover, they create an incentive for banks to sell nonperforming loans even if the economic value of the loan (ignoring the tax and regulatory conflicts) is highest when the bank continues to hold the loan due perhaps to information costs.

Banks that are capital constrained may mitigate their problem by raising additional capital. However, this may be much more difficult than it appears. First, problems related to asymmetry of information associated with equity issues may be severe for a bank in poor financial condition (see Myers and Majluf 1984). In addition, banks may have to sacrifice "tax assets" in order to issue new equity. Section 382 of the Internal Revenue Code limits net operating loss carryforwards whenever there is a cumulative change over a three–year period of more than 50% in ownership by parties holding more than 5% of the equity (where all shareholders holding less than 5% ownership are considered a single 5% owner). This constraint can come into play more easily than might be anticipated, particularly if the bank has recently issued equity or if there has been turnover in the holdings of large shareholders. Thus, banks that attempt to raise capital may suffer tax costs. Moreover, any new issue of shares that triggers the loss of tax assets results in the total value of the banks' assets rising by less than the amount raised in the issue.

Increased Use of Market Value Accounting Principles

In recent years, there has been an increased emphasis on the use of market value accounting for financial institutions. In particular, the Securities and Exchange Commission has advocated the use of market value accounting and has "encouraged" the Financial Accounting

Standards Board (FASB) to incorporate such standards. Moreover, FDICIA of 1991 requires footnote disclosure of the "fair value" of all balance sheet items. Market value accounting may well have led to an increase in specific provisioning for loan losses when loans are nonperforming or when the loan collateral has diminished in value, even if the loan is currently performing. The increased use of market value accounting principles has two effects on bank incentives for lending.

First, in considering capital requirements, it is important to recognize that the more accurately assets, liabilities and thus capital are measured, the more stringent capital requirements become. If there is (or was) flexibility in the accounting standards, then banks faced with capital constraints can use the flexibility in the accounting standards to minimize the cost of the constraint.[5] Second, investing in assets with values that are more difficult to establish, such as commercial loans, becomes more costly since the accounting cost of holding such assets increases as banks are required to continually assess market values. Moreover, given the conservatism principle of accounting, it is unlikely that banks will ever recognize an increase in the value of commercial loans precisely because they are difficult to value. Thus market value accounting will most likely mark loans down—never up. This unfavorable option makes lending less attractive than investing in securities.

Increases in Deposit Insurance Premiums

Annual deposit insurance premiums have increased from 8.33 cents per $100 prior to 1989, to 12 cents per $100 in 1989, to 23 cents per $100 in 1991. As of January 1, 1993, the FDIC introduced a limited form of risk–based deposit insurance premiums with premiums ranging from 23 cents to 31 cents per $100; the estimated average premium was 25.9 cents per $100. Previously, all banks paid the same insurance premium per dollar of deposit regardless of cost. The increase in insurance premiums increases the funding costs of banks. For a bank to maintain its profitability, these costs must be passed either to depositors in the form of lower deposit interest or to borrowers in the form of higher loan rates. Since banks are likely to be inframarginal in the securities markets, it is unlikely that costs will be passed on to issuers of securities in the form of lower prices. It should be noted that deposit insurance premiums are paid on all domestic deposits even though only the first $100,000 of deposit balances are insured. Banks that rely heavily on large deposits may feel the burden of the higher deposit insurance premiums disproportionately since FDICIA of 1991 makes it much less likely that large uninsured depositors would be covered in the event of a bank failure. Thus, these banks pay higher insurance premiums but receive less overall insurance coverage (considering both explicit and implicit coverage). While risk–based insurance premiums could, in theory, offer some relief to well–capitalized banks, FDICIA prohibits insurance premiums of less than 23 cents per $100 for any bank until the Bank Insurance Fund exceeds 1.25 percent of total deposits. Estimates indicate that it may be 15 years before the insurance fund reaches this level. Therefore, well–capitalized banks are likely to continue paying more for effectively less insurance coverage for the foreseeable future.

Changes in Procedure Mandated by FDICIA of 1991

FDICIA of 1991 increased the cost of violating the bank capital requirements by instituting a capital–based supervision mechanism that forces regulators to impose sanctions on banks which do not meet the risk–based capital requirements. The law requires the bank regulators to establish five capital categories: well capitalized, adequately capitalized, undercapitalized, significantly undercapitalized, and critically undercapitalized, defined as follows:

Well Capitalized:	Total capital/weighted risk assets:	10% or greater; and
	Tier 1 capital/weighted risk assets:	6% or greater; and
	Tier 1 capital/average total assets:	5% or greater
Adequately Capitalized:	Total capital/weighted risk assets:	8% or greater; and
	Tier 1 capital/weighted risk assets:	4% or greater; and
	Tier 1 capital/average total assets:	4% or greater[6]
Under-capitalized:	Total capital/weighted risk assets:	less than 8%; or
	Tier 1 capital/weighted risk assets:	less than 4% or;
	Tier 1 capital/average total assets:	less than 4%[7]
Significantly Under-capitalized:	Total capital/weighted risk assets:	less than 6%; or
	Tier 1 capital/weighted risk assets:	less than 3% or;
	Tier 1 capital/average total assets:	less than 3%
Critically Under-capitalized:	Tier 1 capital/average total assets:	less than 2%

The new law does not affect well–capitalized institutions. Adequately capitalized institutions can only accept brokered deposits if they receive a waiver from the FDIC. In addition, they must apply to the FDIC for insurance coverage of pass–through instruments.[8]

Undercapitalized institutions must (1) file an acceptable capital restoration plan; (2) obtain prior approval for acquisitions, branching, and new lines of business; and (3) refuse brokered deposits. Pension deposits in such institutions do not receive pass–through insurance coverage. In addition, bank regulators may restrict asset growth and apply other regulatory sanctions including restricting dividends, removing management, or limiting risky activities.

In addition to the limitations on undercapitalized institutions, significantly undercapitalized institutions may also face mandatory recapitalization through the sale of voting shares, acquisition by a bank holding company, restrictions on interest rates paid on deposits, restrictions on transactions with affiliates, forced divestiture of nonbank subsidiaries, restrictions on executive compensation, and other sanctions. Banks that become critically undercapitalized will have a conservator or receiver appointed within 90 days. Moreover, a variety of severe limitations to maintain assets within the bank are also imposed.

Capital Structure and Capital Requirements

Capital requirements constrain decision making to the extent that meeting the requirements is costly. In analyzing the nature of the costs associated with bank capital requirements, we review corporate capital structure theory. After discussing the factors that are important in corporate capital structure decisions, we examine bank capital structure and bank capital requirements within the context of corporate structure theory.

Modigliani and Miller (1958, 1963) first examined the implication of corporate taxes on the cost of capital and corporate capital structure. They concluded that debt financing was tax preferred to equity financing and that the degree of leverage in corporate capital structures would be limited either by nontax costs of debt (or nontax benefits of equity) or by potential uncertainty as to the ability to use the tax shields generated by debt financing. However, contrary to Modigliani and Miller's prediction, many firms were fully utilizing their debt tax shields and the nontax costs of debt were not obvious. Thus it was difficult to reconcile Modigliani and Miller's finding with corporate capital structure decisions.

In his 1976 presidential address to the American Finance Association, Miller rectified this situation by presenting a simple equilibrium model of capital structure in which he showed that when both corporate and personal taxes are considered, capital structure may be irrelevant for individual firms (Miller 1977). He noted that while interest on debt was deductible at the corporate level, interest income was taxed more heavily than income from equity at the personal level. (The advantage of equity income at the personal level was due to taxpayers' ability to defer capital gains and to partially exclude capital gains income.) Given progressive personal income taxes, Miller argued that, in equilibrium, the amount of the debt in the economy would be large enough that the tax disadvantage of interest income to the marginal debtholder would exactly offset the tax advantage of debt at the corporate level. Thus, in equilibrium, the explicit tax advantage of corporate debt would be offset by the implicit tax paid through higher interest payments to marginal debtholders due to the disadvantage of interest income (relative to equity income) for personal taxpayers. Consequently, while there would be an equilibrium level of debt in the overall economy, individual firms would not have an optimal capital structure (considering only taxes).

Following Miller's work, a number of authors developed models in which individual firms had optimal capital structures despite both personal and corporate taxes. These models were driven by (1) uncertainty as to firms' ability to use their debt tax shields, (2) other forms of tax shields (such as depreciation, research and development expense deductions or investment tax credits), or (3) nontax costs of debt. In *Taxes and Business Strategy* and several related research papers, Scholes and Wolfson (1992) take the issue of corporate capital structure a step further. They argue for consideration of a larger menu of capital structure components than debt and equity and greater attention to the nontax costs and benefits associated with these components. They summarize, "The capital structure problem is but a small piece of a larger tax planning problem, which itself is a problem of the optimal design of organizations."

While the research following Miller justifies qualifying his findings, a much more important change has taken place recently that makes Miller's prediction of capital structure irrelevance moot. The tax code has changed dramatically. The Economic Recovery Tax Act of 1981 and the Tax Reform Acts of 1986 would make it less likely that Miller's equilibrium could hold without considering the loss of tax shields and nontax costs of debt. Most importantly, the maximum marginal tax rate on individuals is now lower than the (maximum) corporate tax rate. Thus, tax costs at the personal level could not offset the tax benefits of debt at the corporate level. In fact, Scholes and Wolfson argue that with the passage of the Tax Reform Act of 1986, the corporate form of organization is at a severe tax disadvantage relative to the partnership form, a disadvantage that corporations can only partially offset by holding high degrees of leverage.

Rather than describe the relevant changes in the tax code in detail, we will summarize the key changes and their implications for Miller's capital structure equilibrium. Both tax acts phased in changes to individual and corporate tax rates. Our analysis only treats the ultimate target rates. Table 1 compares maximum marginal personal and corporate and capital gains tax rates before and after the 1981, 1986 and 1990 tax acts.

Table 1

Maximum Federal Tax Rates for Different Types of Income

Marginal Tax Rates	Prior to 1981 Act	1981 Act Implemented	1986 Act Implemented	1990 Act Implemented
Ordinary Personal Income (highest income bracket)	70%	50%	28%*	31%
Personal Capital Gains	28%	20%	28%*	28%
Corporate	48%	46%	34%	34%

* Note: With the implementation of the 1986 Act, there was income range over which the marginal rate was 33%.

To see how these tax changes affect Miller's equilibrium, consider the individual investor's amount per dollar of corporate operating income assuming (1) the income is received as interest on debt or (2) the interest is received as return on equity. Let t_C, t_D and t_E be the effective marginal tax rates on corporate income, on interest income to individuals, and on equity income to individuals, respectively. Since interest payments are tax deductible at the corporate level, for each dollar of operating income paid out as interest, the debtholder retains a fraction $(1-t_p)$. However, for each dollar of operating income paid out in equity returns, the equityholder retains a fraction $(1-t_E)(1-t_C)$ since the income is taxed at both the corporate and personal levels. It is quite reasonable to use the corporate rate for t_C and the personal rate on ordinary income for t_D.

However, the appropriate rate on equity returns is more complicated. Equity returns can be received as dividends, in which case they are taxed as ordinary income. Or, they can be received as capital gains, which can be deferred and in some circumstances partially excluded from taxation or taxed lower than ordinary income. Rather than approximate the tax rate on equity income, we will instead solve for the rate which would lead to indifference between debt and equity for tax purposes. That is, there will be no difference in total taxation between debt and equity if the tax rate on equity income is equal to t_E^* where t_E^* solves the following:

$$(1-t_D) = (1-t_E^*)(1-t_C), \text{ or}$$

$$t_E^* = 1 - \frac{(1-t_D)}{(1-t_C)}.$$

If the tax on equity returns exceeds t_E^*, then debt financing will be tax preferred to equity financing. Otherwise, Miller's equilibrium is likely to hold, in which case neither debt nor equity is tax preferred. Table 2 presents the values of t_E^* for the three tax regimes discussed above.

These are the effective marginal tax rates on equity income that imply indifference between debt and equity financing (for tax reasons) if corporate and ordinary personal tax rates in Table 1 are considered to be the effective marginal rates:

	Prior to 1981 Act	1981 Act Implemented	1986 Act Implemented	1990 Act Implemented
t_E^*	42.3%	7.4%	-9.1%	-4.5%

In the aftermath of the 1986 Act, debt has clearly been tax preferred to equity. Given typical dividend levels (tax at the ordinary income rate) and typical holding periods for equities, it is also likely that the effective tax rate on equity returns exceeded 7.4% and debt became tax preferred with the 1981 Act. Debt became even more preferred with the 1986 Act. The 1990 tax changes reduced, but did not eliminate, tax preference for debt over equity.

Although Miller's results should not hold given tax code changes that are inconsistent with the assumptions required for equilibrium, the dramatic increases throughout the 1980s in corporate borrowing and equity repurchases follow his logic. Tax preferences for debt promote the issuance of debt. Consistent with Miller's model, one could argue that debt in the economy expanded until it was offset by the potential inability to use the resulting tax shields and by the nontax costs of debt. In this setting, we would expect a firm to have an optimal capital structure where it increases its leverage until the marginal benefits of additional leverage equal its marginal cost. Typically, we think of the marginal benefit of debt as decreasing with the leverage because the tax shields generated by the interest payments on the debt are not fully utilized under high leverage. Moreover, nontax costs of debt, such as deadweight bankruptcy costs and agency costs of debt, are likely to increase with the degree of leverage.

From a capital budgeting perspective, investment and financing decisions are interdependent. In evaluating potential capital expenditures and investments, corporate managers must not only evaluate an investment on its own merits, but also they must consider its impact on the firm's debt capacity. Two proposals that appear comparable before financing and tax considerations may end up ranked after considering these factors. For example, the nature of the taxable income generated from a project may increase the firm's ability to utilize its debt tax shields. The nature of the project's cashflows could increase the firm's overall debt capacity. A project may also have specific tax benefits, such as investment tax credits or foreign tax credits. On the other hand, particular projects may carry tax and financing costs. For example, projects that are not easily monitored by debtholders may reduce debt capacity since they increase agency costs associated with debt. Moreover, projects that require investment in illiquid assets may increase deadweight costs of bankruptcy and thus reduce debt capacity.

For a variety of reasons, banks find high degrees of leverage to be advantageous, so capital requirements are costly to them. Banks (and other depository institutions) are the most highly levered companies in the U.S. While they have been highly levered for decades, they have been increasing debt financing (at least prior to the new risk–based capital standards). The context of corporate capital structure theory provides several reasons for this.

First, a primary source of bank funds is transactions deposits. For many years, banks were prohibited from paying interest on these deposits. Under competition for deposits, banks compensated depositors by offering services. Although banks could deduct these services, depositors did not recognize them for tax purposes. Thus, to the extent banks provided services in exchange for deposits, they could issue tax–exempt debt. Following Miller's analysis, we would never expect the marginal tax cost of debt at the personal level to offset the tax benefits of debt at the corporate level if interest on the debt were paid through services. Thus, regardless of the tax regimes described above, we would expect banking institutions relying heavily on transactions deposits to be highly levered. (Of course, it is not clear whether depositors or bank shareholders are the ultimate beneficiaries since competition for deposits gave depositors the lion's share of the tax benefit. However, we would expect low–cost banking service providers and banks with local market power to retain some benefit.) Interestingly, even after the removal of deposit interest restrictions, a substantial portion of the return on transactions deposits comes in the form of services. This contradicts Black (1975) and Fama (1980)—neither of whom considered the tax implications—that absent deposit interest ceilings, banks would provide services strictly on a fee basis.

Federal deposit insurance also contributes to the highly levered status of banks. This subject immediately suggests the moral hazard and risk–taking incentive inherent in deposit insurance whose premiums do not reflect the banks' risk. Such incentives do exist, particularly for poorly capitalized banks, and one way to increase risk is to increase leverage. Of course, insured depositors need not demand additional returns as compensation for risk since they bear none.

When banks pay explicit interest on deposits or debt, they act just like other corporations. Thus we would expect that the tax changes in 1981 and 1986 made debt tax preferred for banks. For reasons discussed below, we are apt to find desirable levels of leverage that would be extreme for other types of corporations.

Deposit insurance, particularly when coupled with bank regulation and supervision, goes beyond increasing leverage in the capital structure: it increases risk. Deposit insurance and bank regulation and supervision influence the capital structure of risk–averse institutions because (1) bank supervision reduces the agency costs of debt and (2) many of the deadweight costs of bankruptcy are borne by the deposit insurer rather than stakeholders. Consequently, banks maintain highly levered capital structures due to the tax benefits and the relatively small nontax costs.

With regard to capital structure and decisions about appropriate leverage, the ability to use the tax shields generated by the debt is a key factor. Historically, banks have had great latitude in managing their taxable income. They did this through loan loss provisions and municipal bond arbitrage.[9] Moreover, banks also had separate net operating loss (NOL) carryforward and carryback periods (10 years back and 5 years forward). Their ability to manage taxable income and use tax loss carrybacks and carryforwards should result in higher degrees of leverage due to less uncertainty as to the ability to use tax shields. As discussed above, recent changes in the tax law eliminated all the advantageous treatment of loan loss provisions. In fact, many banks were required to recapture loan loss reserves as income. Banks also adopted the same loss carryforward/carryback periods as other corporations. However, as an interim measure, large banks[10] continue to use the 10–year carryback/5–year carryforward NOL provisions for their loan losses.[11] Thus, banks with income over the past ten years may use tax shields generated by debt with reasonable certainty and should maintain high degrees of leverage.

Incentives for Bank Lending

In the last section, we argued that banks, left unconstrained, would maintain high degrees of leverage. Thus, capital requirements would be costly for banks and would therefore influence their investment behavior, particularly since different types of assets have different implications for the capital requirements. This section elaborates on the incentives created by the new capital requirements as well as the other recent changes in banking. We begin by discussing how incorporating off–balance–sheet items into the capital requirements affects the *relative* attractiveness of different investments.

Including off–balance–sheet items in the computation of weighted risk affects provision of credit in the economy, as well as incentives for bank lending, in many ways. First, commercial paper markets represent an alternative source of borrowed funds for many companies. However, many companies need a letter of credit (often from a bank) for their commercial paper to be accepted in the marketplace. Thus, the inclusion of letters of credit in the computation–weighted risk assets may also affect the issuance of commercial paper. Studying how the new capital requirements affected the credit availability during the recent recession, Bernanke and Lown (1990) cite slow growth in new commercial paper issuance as evidence of a lack of demand for credit. However, since banks were now required to hold capital against letters of credit for the first time, the new capital requirements may have affected the commercial paper market.

The inclusion of off–balance–sheet items into bank capital requirements may also influence banks' incentives to lend. Many off–balance–sheet items relate to commercial lending arrangements. For example, unused lines of credit with original maturities exceeding one year are converted into credit equivalents at a rate of 50%. Under the new capital requirements, banks with long–term customer relationships must maintain capital against potential future lending. Thus, the cost of the capital requirement not only includes the direct cost of holding capital against loans outstanding but also the indirect cost of holding capital as part of the lending arrangements before the actual amounts are borrowed. Not surprisingly, a new arrangement referred to as a 364–day lending facility has arisen. No capital is required to be held against credit lines that mature within one year.

The risk weighting of on–balance–sheet items further affects banks' lending incentives. For example, it may be more cost effective from a capital perspective to hold mortgages indirectly rather than directly. Creating and holding synthetic mortgages require less capital. This is done by holding U.S. Treasury securities directly and then swapping interest flows with the holder of a mortgage pool or mortgage–backed security. The bank gets interest flows identical (less any intermediary fees) to those from a mortgage pool but at a lower capital cost.

We continue our analysis by focusing on how the new capital requirements and other changes in the banking environment have affected banks' incentives to lend. How could purchasing securities (presumably a zero–net–present–value activity) ever be more attractive than loan origination?

Earlier, we argued that for a number of reasons, banks find capital a relatively costly method of finance. Since banks are required to hold more capital against business loans than many other types of lending, business lending is relatively unattractive to banks (holding loan rates constant). While banks earn a risk premium for bearing the credit risks associated with business lending, they can also earn a premium for bearing interest rate risk if they instead hold fixed–rate government securities, government–guaranteed mortgages pools, or mortgage–backed securities without hedging their interest rate risk exposure. Since the capital requirements only reflect credit risks, banks most likely prefer to earn risk premiums associated with interest rate risk.

The analysis just presented runs counter to the notion that banks create value by loan origination and the provision of services. After all, why would we ever expect to see an intermediary borrowing money to invest in securities when individuals could take such positions themselves, particularly given the double taxation of equity returns. There are several possible answers to this puzzle.

First, recall that banks accept transaction deposits and pay interest at least in part through services that are not considered taxable income. Thus, banks might make such investments because they have low–cost transaction deposits available; but given the costs associated with business lending and the interest rates borrowers will accept, securities investments are more attractive than lending. To see that such a bank could be viable, consider an individual who is choosing between two alternative investment strategies: (1) to borrow money to invest in government securities, and (2) to buy shares of a bank that accepts transactions deposits (paid for totally in services) and buys government securities. If the investor borrows and invests directly, he will pay personal income tax on the difference between the interest income on the bond and the interest expense on the borrowing. In addition, the rate at which he borrows reflects the fact that the interest he pays is taxable income to the lender. If the investor buys the bank shares, the bank will pay corporate taxes on the difference between the interest on the securities and the cost of providing the depositor services. In addition, the investor will pay personal tax on the equity returns. At first glance, it appears that this bank would not be viable; since corporate tax rates are higher than personal tax rates, corporate taxation alone will ruin the bank. However, recall that the bank pays for its deposits in the form of services that are not taxable to the recipient. Thus, the effective rate of interest may very well be less for the bank than for the direct investor. If this is the case, and equity returns are sufficiently deferred, then the bank may indeed be viable.

A second answer to the puzzle can be seen by considering a different twist on this same theme. Consider a bank that has had substantial losses in recent years and has a large amount of NOL carryforwards (as many banks currently do). Such a bank cannot effectively sell these NOLs because of IRC Section 382 restrictions discussed above. Moreover, if it has so many NOLs that it cannot use them before they expire, then on the margin the bank is essentially a tax–exempt corporation. In this case, our story of borrowing money to buy securities makes perfect sense, even if the bank has to borrow money by paying interest that is fully taxable to depositors. Since government securities have a zero–risk weighting, the bank can increase its scale and use its NOL carryforwards with higher probability by investing in securities rather than by lending.

In addition to differences due to the direct cost of holding capital, the following recent developments also make securities holding more attractive than lending:

- The increased use of market value accounting principles. These increase the relative cost of business lending due to the direct cost of continually estimating market values for illiquid loans and the likelihood that such loans will be marked down—but never up.

- The elimination of the tax deductibility of loan loss provisions. This increases the relative tax cost of loans relative to security holdings. (This change occurred in 1986. It is mentioned here in reference to comparisons that researchers may wish to make to the 1990–1991 recession and previous recessions.)

- The disparity between the tax and the regulatory treatment of nonperforming loans. Banks are effectively penalized for capital purposes, but they receive no corresponding tax benefit.

Conclusion

We have described recent changes that affect banks' incentives to lend. We have also analyzed the impact of the new risk–based capital standards on incentives to lend and concluded that the standards will make certain types of activities, in particular business lending, less attractive. We are expanding our analysis in two directions. First, we have begun to formally model the constrained optimization problem that risk–based capital requirements pose to banks. This effort should provide greater insight into the impact of the new capital requirements on bank behavior. Second, we are incorporating demand factors into an empirical analysis of bank portfolio composition to estimate how much of the "credit crunch" can be attributed to lack of credit demand as opposed to the risk–based capital requirements.

References

Bernanke, B. S. "Nonmonetary Effects of the Financial Crisis in the Propagation of the Great Depression." *American Economic Review* 73, 3: (1983): 257–276.

Bernanke, B. S. and C. S. Lown. "The Credit Crunch," *Brookings Papers on Economic Activity* (1991): 205–247.

Black, F. "Bank Fund Management in an Efficient Market," *Journal of Financial Economics* 2, 4 (1975): 323–340.

Furfine, C. "Risk–Based Capital and the Effectiveness of Monetary Policy," Stanford University Mimeograph (1992).

Hancock, D. and J. A. Wilcox. "Capital Crunch or Just Another Recession." Washington D. C.: Board of Governors of the Federal Reserve System Mimeograph (1992).

Miller, M. "Debt and Taxes." *Journal of Finance* 32, 2 (1977): 261–275.

Modigliani, F. and M. Miller. "The Cost of Capital, Corporation Finance and the Theory of Investments," *American Economic Review* (June 1958): 261–297.

Myers, S. and N. Majluf. "Corporate Financing and Investment Decisions When Firms Have Information That Investors Do Not." *Journal of Financial Economics*, 13 (1984): 187–221.

Peek, J. and E. Rosengren. "The Capital Crunch: Neither a Borrower Nor a Lender Be." Washington D. C.: Federal Reserve Bank Mimeograph (1992).

Ross, S., R. Westerfield, and J. Jaffe. *Corporate Finance*, Third Edition, Homewood, IL: Irwin, 1992.

Scholes, M. S. and M. A. Wolfson. *Taxes and Business Strategy: A Planning Approach.* Englewood Cliffs, NJ: Prentice Hall, 1992.

Notes

[1] The old capital standards recognized two types of capital (primary and total). The international risk–based capital standards recognize two types of capital (core or tier 1 and supplementary or tier 2).

[2] General reserves for loan losses are counted as capital since they represent reserves against anticipated, but as yet unidentified, losses. This is consistent with the notion that capital represents a buffer to absorb future losses. Specific provisions are taken against loans that are identifiably at risk and thus do not represent a buffer. Allocated transfer risks are reserves against international loans that have protracted problems.

[3] During the interim period, supplemental capital could be used to fulfill 0.4% of the total 3.625% core capital requirement.

[4] The following discussion relies in part on the Board of Governors of Federal Reserve System (1989).

[5] Large banks are defined as those with gross assets in excess of $500 million or members of parent–subsidiary groups with total assets in excess of $500 million.

[6] One way banks and thrifts used such flexibility to increase measured capital was by holding depreciated securities in their investment portfolio at historical cost while selling appreciated securities to realize their full market value. There are a number of variants on this theme alone. Recent accounting and regulatory changes have greatly reduced the viability of such maneuvers.

[7] Banks receiving a composite CAMEL rating of 1 (the highest rating) in their most recent examination may have a leverage rating of 3% or greater and still be considered adequately capitalized.

[8] Banks receiving a composite CAMEL rating of 1 (the highest rating) in their most recent examination have a leverage rating of less than 3% to be considered undercapitalized.

[9] A bank certificate of deposit (CD) for an amount over $100,000 purchased by a pension plan is fully insured despite exceeding the $100,000 limit on insured deposits because insurance coverage passes through to the pension plan beneficiaries.

[10] Unlike individuals or other corporations, banks had been able to deduct interest on funds used to finance the purchase of municipal bonds. This allowed them to engage in a form of tax arbitrage if the differential between taxable bond yields and municipal bond yields did not reflect their marginal tax rate. This special status of banks no longer exists.

[11] These are the same banks that are no longer allowed to deduct loan loss provisions. See preceding section on tax treatment of loan loss provisions.

[12] There is a catch, however. Banks must use all nonloan–loss NOLs before applying loan–loss NOLs to current income, even though the nonloan–loss NOLs would expire in 15 years rather than in 5 years. A number of banks that suffered severe loan losses are likely to lose their NOL "tax assets" due to these provisions.

Comparative Risk Management Practices: Japan Versus the U.S.

Yasunori Nagai, Joint General Manager and Senior Economist, International Finance Research Department, Industrial Bank of Japan, Ltd.

Introduction

This chapter compares risk management practices of Japanese financial institutions to those of comparable U.S. institutions. Rather than highlighting differences or similarities between the two, the chapter will describe current risk management practices and their evolution in Japanese financial institutions. U.S. institutions' risk management practices are cited to better describe the Japanese cases. Japanese securities firms and other institutions are increasingly introducing risk management as a management tool, and banks face a new phase of risk management due to new securities regulations. However, the discussion will focus on major banks since deregulation has significantly affected this industry.

Japanese banks take risk management seriously as a management tool; risk management systems have been introduced in most major banks. Many factors led to the development of risk management systems including: (1) current and new Bank International Settlements (BIS) rules under consideration, (2) the EC capital adequacy rule, (3) the collapse of the bubble economy in Japan, and (4) the emphasis on credit risk management. In essence, growing attention to risk management results from the underlying trend to deregulation and associated changes in customer behavior.

Corporate Finance and Risk Management in Japan

This section describes financial practices and trends at Japanese corporations and profiles their clientele. As all financial institutions, Japanese banks respond to external events such as fluctuations in interest and exchange rates and competitive behavior of market players. Yet Japan has a different regulatory environment, and Japanese customers are also different. External environment changes and changes in customer behavior interact with each other. We begin with the premise that Japanese customers dictate the fate of their banks.

Traditionally, Japanese corporations have been conservative players, relying on bank loans as their main source of finance. However, the situation has changed dramatically over the last five years, especially for large corporations. The persistent bull market in Tokyo has enabled many corporations to issue equity warrants in the Euro market at a minimal cost, thereby bypassing the banking system. Foreign equity warrants (i.e., equity warrants issued overseas) accounted for 13% of all capital market financing in 1985; this figure increased to 29% in 1989. Some features of disintermediation in Japan are noteworthy. First, unlike the U.S., disintermediation on the borrowing side did not occur from traditional debt financing. Rather, it occurred through equity warrants, which at one time provided extremely cheap quasi-debt financing. Second, the commercial paper market in Japan is still developing; currently, commercial paper has a minor role in external financing.

Of course, financing through means other than bank loans has increased. But recent bypassing of the banks in favor of equity warrants differs from what is traditionally known as disintermediation. The question raised here is twofold. First, are corporate treasurers willing to bear more risk by using equity-related instruments in financing? Second, will the corporations return to banks for financing or will disintermediation processes prevail in the near future?

The first question requires an understanding of Japanese corporations' philosophy of financing and risk management. This is not an easy task. We will consider the characteristics of treasury management, particularly capitalization, at the top 100 Japanese corporations. These corporations have considerable exposure to foreign markets, both in terms of business and financing. They are sufficiently sophisticated to employ advanced financing techniques. Risk management at these corporations includes the control of diverse risks related to product obsolescence, the environment, and inventory, among others. The following comments focus on risks related to finance and treasury management.

These large corporations have a single division dedicated to finance and treasury management aside from accounting. Corporations with a strong cashflow have more bargaining power with financial institutions. They also practice *zaitech*. A typical *zaitech* operation involves the investment of low-cost funds acquired through the issuance of equity warrants into bank CDs or fixed-income securities. Another example is the investment of funds acquired through the issuance of domestic CPs into bank CDs. The former was possible, of course, due to the persistent bull stock market; and the latter was possible due to strong bargaining power resulting from reduced reliance on bank funds. In any case, both examples contradict the norm of finance and result from the excess liquidity created by a persistent bull market. Unfortunately, some corporations were hurt by their equity investment, making corporate treasurers' attitudes extremely defensive toward unconventional financing or risk management. Corporate treasurers have been and will continue to be conservative. They have used equity-related instruments and foreign-denominated instruments because of their relative cost advantage over other instruments. In most overseas financing, corporate treasurers of large corporations only accept proposals that are fully hedged. It was the relatively smaller corporations that were hurt from unhedged foreign currency issues. Therefore, even in the case of equity warrants, many treasurers opted for this cheaper financing alternative despite risks such as the dilution of equity. Now they must refinance huge amounts of debt either from the capital market or from banks.

At the same time, however, the corporate treasury has changed its status from a passive to an active profit center. With the crash of the bubble economy, despite signs of the reevaluation of traditional relationship banking, the fundamental trend is clear. More corporations have become cost conscious and will control their assets and liabilities in a more efficient and conservative manner. The implications for the financial intermediaries are complex. Some will opt for a risk advisory and some will opt for risk intermediation.

The second question, as to the possibility of reintermediation, has no definite answer. Although the forthcoming need to refinance equity warrants is huge, the demand for bank loans in general is not high due to the sluggish Japanese economy. Reintermediation may occur in the short run due to the need to refinance equity warrants. Since banks are still constrained by the BIS requirements to increase loans, the trend toward disintermediation appears inevitable. In the long run, however, financing instruments will be chosen as a function of cost.

The historical growth of loans in Japan (Table 1) shows a decline. Slow growth is expected in both the corporate and consumer sectors. It is often asserted that Japanese banks will focus more on consumer business to complement the decline in corporate business, but even

---

the consumer business appears to be a battlefield. In contrast with the slow loan growth of the private sector lenders, public sector lenders are enjoying relatively high growth. The past will not simply repeat itself, but clearly Japanese banks cannot survive by merely increasing their balance sheets, let alone their BIS requirements.

Table 1

Loan Growth in Japan

Year-to-Year Growth in %		Average FY 1980-86	Average FY 1987-89	Average FY 1990-91	FY 1992
Corporation	Total Loan	8.3	10.2	6.8	2.2
	From Private Sector	9.0	10.4	6.0	1.2
	From Public Sector	4.0	8.6	12.2	8.9
Household	Total Loan	9.3	14.4	5.7	4.2
	From Private Sector	8.9	15.8	5.1	2.2
	From Public Sector	10.8	9.2	8.5	11.9
Total	Total Loan	8.6	11.6	6.4	2.9
	From Private Sector	9.0	12.2	5.7	1.5
	From Public Sector	6.6	8.8	10.5	10.2

(Source: Bank of Japan)

This does not imply that the banking business will deteriorate one-sidedly. Corporations are expected to put more emphasis on risk management, thereby increasing the need for off-balance–sheet instruments such as derivatives. Moreover, banks will eventually be permitted to engage in the securities business. However, the use of new financial technologies such as derivatives and asset securitization is steadily gaining popularity among corporate treasurers. Several factors such as accounting and taxation treatment will complicate the introduction of these new financial technologies. In the meantime, banks must cultivate large corporations' use of new financial technologies; but at the same time, they must rely heavily on the interest income as the major revenue source. This implies increases in middle market loans and consumer loans. Hence, the key task of risk management at Japanese banks becomes one of managing market risk and credit risk in tandem.

The deregulation of deposit interest rates in Japan started in 1985, when the U.S. had completed such deregulation. Since then, Japanese financial institutions have followed the American experience in a fairly short time frame. As of June 21, 1993, the interest rate ceiling on all time deposits had been lifted, putting Japan in the final stage of interest rate deregulation.

The ratio of deposits with deregulated interest rates to total deposits at Japanese banks has increased threefold since 1987. Japanese banks' profitability (the percentage of net interest income to the total average balance sheet) has declined since 1979. Moreover, the increase in the cost of retail deposits has fueled the downward pressure. Regional banks were affected by the rapid pace of deregulation primarily because they had a higher share of regulated retail deposits in their funding base. To cope with the declining margin, most banks have increased loans to small and medium corporations. Compared to U.S. banks, a major part of the Japanese banks' assets consist of C & I (Commercial and Industrial) loans. The percentage of C & I loans at all Japanese banks was 83% as of March 1993. For U.S. banks, C & I loans accounted for only 17%. Of this 83%, almost 60% were loans to the middle market. Thus, Japanese banks have tried to maintain their profit margin by increasing the share of middle market loans in their portfolio.

In summary, interest rate deregulation has reached its final stage in Japan, thereby increasing the volatility of the funding base and the need for liability management. Moreover, portfolios are predominantly composed of C & I loans, which make banks vulnerable to further disintermediation. The heavy dependence on loans as a source of revenue represents a challenge to asset management.

General Risk Management Practices in Financial Institutions

The earliest form of risk management at Japanese banks started with the establishment of a Credit Analysis Department or a Financial Analysis Department, whose mandate was to analyze a borrower's credit. The Industrial Bank of Japan, Ltd. (IBJ) illustrates the credit decision-making system at a Japanese bank. At IBJ, all credit-related business is forwarded to the Credit Department, where it is handled differently depending upon the nature and amount of the transaction. Routine transactions with established clients may not go through credit analysis every time, but credit will be reviewed periodically for fundamental changes. In addition to the Credit Department's analysis, the Industrial Research Department also follows industry trends. Such an analysis examines a specific company's credit fundamentals, but it also takes into account the need for a continual analysis of each industry segment for both specific credit analysis and overall loan portfolio control. The Business Coordination Department makes the final credit decision. The Business Coordination Department also oversees IBJ's loan portfolio. In addition to managerial assesssment of the client's credit history, a PC Credit Warning System based on financial ratios provides a technical supplement. Of course, there are variations in the credit control system among banks, but most resemble that at IBJ.

With the advent of BIS requirements and the increase in transaction volume and complexity, many banks have integrated their risk control system into their overall system. Basically, most banks include various aspects of their loan portfolio's profile. A popular approach is to introduce an internal credit rating system and to measure total portfolio risk in terms of a point-scoring system. This method is popular in the U.S. but has had implementation difficulties in Japan. First, the statistical data on default rates and recovery rates are not readily available. Therefore, each bank must devise its own methods. In the absence of widely available data, the degree of objectivity is difficult to measure. An internal analysis ensures consistency within each bank's universe. However, the differences among competing banks could be significant and problematic, especially if a bank intends to allocate capital according to an internal risk-point system. A competing bank could propose significantly lower rates due to a totally different credit evaluation. Without concrete evidence, clients would hardly accept the market pricing in the face of competition. Moreover, at this stage, it is difficult to allocate capital to each business segment using a risk-point system. Most of the banks are trying to introduce some kind of a capital allocation system using the risk-point system, but the full implementation of such a system is years away.

Large Japanese banks, especially major city banks, have been exposed to the credit risk control system adopted by U.S. banks through their domestic operations. It was natural to adopt such a system in their U.S. branch, which provides the necessary conditions for implementing a risk-based control system. Therefore, most of the internationally active banks have applied a risk-based control system to their foreign currency-denominated portfolio.

Partial implementation of such a system derives from the need to separate domestic and foreign portfolios. Of course, it is better to control foreign portfolios based on risk to allocate capital and other resources efficiently. But the implementation of the risk control system may distort the efficiency of resource allocation for the bank as a whole. Therefore, management must bridge the potential gap between the domestic and foreign control systems. Overall, credit control systems have favorably impacted credit risk control policy as a whole and have initiated sound methods for controlling domestic portfolio risk exposure.

In sum, most international Japanese banks have operated risk control systems similar to those of U.S. banks for some time, and they are either implementing or testing risk control systems for their domestic portfolios as well. However, in aggregate, such systems are not yet fully embedded into the total management strategy.

Since interest rate deregulation started in March 1985 with the introduction of the Money Market Certificate (MMC), interest rate risk has become an important factor in Japanese bank management. However, the deregulation of small deposits had an even more significant impact on bank funding and thus profit.

Deposits made up 67% of the Japanese city bank's average liability as of March 1991. At a typical city bank, the ratio of wholesale deposits to retail deposits is about 60:40. By 1989, when large-scale deposits were deregulated, most wholesale deposits and part of the retail deposits had been affected. Since 1989, we have witnessed an interest rate-sensitive shift of retail deposits among financial institutions. Institutions had clearly recognized the need to control interest rate risk early in the 1980s. But the massive shift of short-term deposits into longer-term deposits and debentures in anticipation of a further interest rate decline signaled the need for liability management.

Asset and Liability Management

Although the importance of Asset and Liability Management (ALM) has grown rapidly, the current state of ALM at most Japanese banks can be characterized as liability driven. This is not surprising considering that interest deregulation exposed Japanese banks to a volatile funding environment. As for asset management, the disintermediation on the borrowing side has significantly impacted Japanese banks. Loans account for a sizable portion of the balance sheet. In contrast, trading securities are minimal compared to U.S. counterparts. The Asset Liability Committee (ALCO) at a typical Japanese bank must consider its loan portfolio as fixed rather than variable, at least for the short term. Moreover, the disintermediation process experienced by large corporations has pressured the banks to increase their exposure to the middle market. Although disintermediation was underway, most banks increased their loans to small- and medium-sized corporations.

Similar to Credit Risk Management, ALM was introduced earlier in international than domestic operations. A typical ALM operation at an international Japanese bank would have started with the funding of

LIBOR-based Euro syndicate loans. ALM operations probably began with short funding in the cash market and added futures and swaps later. Many people attribute the development of ALM for international business to hedge instruments. Of course, the availability and depth the cash and futures markets and subsequent growth in derivatives have benefited the Japanese banks' international ALM. However, most of the Japanese banks' early international business consisted of Euro syndicate loans and, later, Euro FRNs. Both syndicate loans and FRNs are more transaction oriented. This development simplified asset management.

Treasury managers of domestic business observed international developments. When interest rate deregulation started in 1985, the exchange-traded bond future was the only hedge instrument, and it had just been devised. New methods of domestic liability management were extremely limited. Japanese banks waited until 1989 for the introduction of exchange-traded yen interest rate futures at the Tokyo International Financial Futures Exchange (TIFFE), which increased the breadth of hedge instruments.

The liberalization of currency swaps in 1984 was a milestone for the Japanese off-balance-sheet market. By using currency swaps in association with overseas issues, large corporations could bypass the banking system much more easily than ever before. Furthermore, the liberalization led to the creation of OTC interest rate swaps. The exact date and specific deal of the first yen interest rate swap differ among the sources, but several deals were executed in 1985. With a very limited number of hedge instruments and opportunities, deals were structured to match two counterparts.

Around 1985, several Japanese banks created a swap book along with a specialized swap team. U.S.-dollar interest rate swaps and cross-currency swaps were the two main products. Yen interest rate swaps started to increase in volume from 1989 onwards in line with exchange-traded interest futures at TIFFE. In 1989, the volume of yen interest rate swaps surpassed that of the yen/dollar currency swap. By 1992, the volume had grown to approximately $190 billion. The maturity profile of the interest rate swap executed in the Tokyo market is noteworthy. Table 2 reports transactions executed through domestic brokers. It shows that the volume of short-term interest rate swaps, including both yen/yen and dollar/dollar, has almost doubled. However, there is a marked difference. For the latter, most transactions are conducted in the short term. The former, however, is dominated by medium- to long-term swaps. The maturity of a short-term interest rate swap is up to 1 year. A medium- to long-term interest rate swap typically matures in 3 to 5 years, but a growing volume extends to 7 to 10 years. This suggests a need for banks to hedge against interest rate volatility in the medium to long term.

Table 2

Interest Rate Swap Transactions in the Tokyo Market
(in billions)

	Short Term			Medium to Long Term				Total
	¥/¥	$/$	Total	¥/¥	$/$	Others	Total	
1990	10.2	95.3	105.5	48.1	26.6	3.4	78.1	183.6
1991	20.8	120.0	142.4	49.6	14.4	2.8	67.0	209.4
(%)	(200)	(25.9)	(35.0)	(3.1)	(45.9)	(17.6)	(14.2)	(14.1)
1992	60.1	163.0	245.6	98.2	22.1	5.7	127.2	372.8
(%)	(360)	(52.6)	(200)	(200)	(63.5)	(210)	(210)	(200)

Parentheses denote quarterly change in percent.
(Source: *The Bank of Japan Monthly Bulletin*)

The yen/yen interest rate swap market is expected to grow further, which reflects increased demand not only from banks but also from corporations. In turn, banks must protect their portfolios from unwarranted interest rate movements; but corporations utilize swaps as a useful, cost-efficient risk management tool. As discussed earlier, banks are approaching sophisticated clients with a diminished appetite for straight bank loans by offering derivative products. In this context, clients accept swaps as the most palatable tool. For banks, off-balance sheet products help them do business while controlling asset growth.

The liquidation of loan assets at Japanese banks started with the sales of dollar-denominated loans around 1985. However, the motive for the liquidation of dollar-denominated loan assets was neither capital adequacy nor ALM. Rather, the loans were sold by international banks to regional banks and other financial institutions to increase profits, control exposure for the original borrowers, and cultivate relationships.

The liquidation of domestic loans started with the liberalization of home loans in 1988. Home loans to be liquidated were limited to fixed interest rate mortgages, which reflected banks' need to reduce the mismatch risk of the balance sheets. However, banks have increased floating–rate mortgage loans to reduce interest rate risk and have more actively pursued the liquidation of floating-rate mortgage loans. In 1990, loans to municipalities were liberalized. Finally, the liquidation of general loans was authorized in 1991, and restrictions have been relaxed since then.

The liquidation of loans has served more to fulfill BIS requirements than to support ALM operations. Some hurdles must be cleared before loan liquidations can contribute to ALM (e.g., the method of loan sales such as assignment versus the use of trust). However, the main obstacle appears to be the nature of the loan itself. Some large corporations have become accustomed to their loans being sold in the secondary market as long as they can enjoy low-cost financing through loan liquidation. On the other hand, typical Japanese corporations do not accept having their loans sold to banks with which they have no relationship.

The sales of loans at Japanese banks have been increasing. According to *American Banker*, U.S. banks reported $58.6 million in loans as of May 1993. Therefore, the liquidation of approximately $20 billion equivalent by Japanese banks is significant in relation to account restrictions and history. However, the turnover in loan participation shows a totally different picture. Although there are no comparable figures available, the turnover in the U.S. could well be more than 20 times the balance, but the turnover in Japan has been negligible. Therefore, more time is obviously needed to develop a secondary loan market, especially for distressed loans, for loan liquidations to serve as an effective tool for ALM operations. Otherwise, banks will be left with low-quality loans. The acceptance of loan liquidations by corporations is crucial in this regard.

So far we have seen that the Japanese banks lack some of the tools of ALM available to their U.S. counterparts. The following remarks describe how ALM operations are carried out in most Japanese banks. Naturally, this differs depending upon the institution. Broadly speaking, ALM is typically carried out through the Asset and Liability Management Committee (ALCO), consisting of senior operations executives and members of the board of directors responsible for the Business Coordination Division and/ or Treasury Division. ALCO serves to set limits on the bank's overall interest rate and foreign exchange, to make decisions about exposure and off-balance–sheet transactions, and to approve the introduction of new instruments.

At ALCO, senior executives present the results of various profit and loss simulations which are carried out for the next 3 to 12 months. The scenarios are based on economic fundamentals and use various statistical models.

ALCO meets regularly, usually monthly. In addition, a shadow ALCO consisting of executives in charge of operations convenes in the interim to discuss urgent topics. Daily market and portfolio risks are measured over a modified duration to examine the impact of interest rate movements in relation to the maximum allowable loss. For those transactions not suitable for measurement through duration (e.g., options), a measure such as delta is used to derive overall risk position. Thus Japanese banks are adopting methods similar to those of their U.S. counterparts.

As mentioned earlier, most city banks and an increasing number of regional banks have already introduced or are introducing some form of ALM and risk management. This compares dramatically with the situation of only two years ago, when the largest banks had no comprehensive risk management system. Assuming that "comprehensive" refers to a bank's ability to see the entire risk profile at the close of the business day, then almost all large banks in fact have quantitative risk management systems and operations managers know their risk position. However, just because risk figures are available each business day does not necessarily mean that the management is managing aggregate risk.

After 1990, interest deregulation created a more volatile environment. Moreover, BIS requirements necessitated effective balance sheet management. The motives for ALM systems have been defensive in nature. City banks have become more active in profit-seeking. From 1991 to 1992, Japanese banks have benefited from declining interest rates. It is difficult to quantify their aggressiveness; but in 1991, they took mismatched positions between loans and deposits. Figure 1 shows the ratio of deposits with 3-month maturity to total deposits and the ratio of fixed-rate loans to those with a maturity over 1 year. Banks located on the far side of the 45-degree line potentially have a greater mismatch or gap in their asset and liability structure. They benefit more than banks near the origin. At the same time, this figure does not reveal the actual risks taken since the mismatched positions may be hedged with swaps or futures. Yet the figure indicates (1) the potential need for ALM and (2) the degree to which some banks are more active than others in managing their interest rate risk exposure.

Although tools for liability management have become more available, Japanese banks still lack the means for effective asset management. Furthermore, ALM operations at Japanese banks are moving from defensive to offensive.

Figure 1

Fixed–Rate Loans Versus Short-Term Deposits

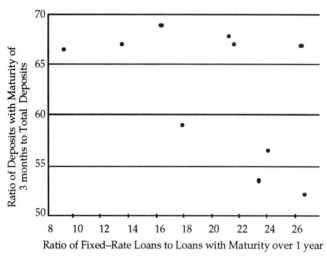

(Source: Federation of Japanese Banks and Annual Reports)

Obstacles ranging from philosophical to technical issues have already been mentioned. Starting with the former, the purpose of ALM must be reexamined. Are managers aware of the potential impact of the asset and liability structure on the bank's overall profit strategy? Are the ALM operations serving to maximize profit or merely to minimize interest rate risk? Operations managers strive for the best of both worlds, but their goals must be clear if the bank as a whole is to benefit from ALM. This philosophy will vary among banks depending upon their nature and clientele. Japanese bank executives must realize that ALM requires a clear goal or mandate. This philosophical problem derives not from ALM itself but from the more fundamental question of a long-term strategic focus.

Technical problems must be addressed. First, efficient asset management requires a change in the perception of loan sales and a change in the regulations regarding asset securitization. Second, the tools of effective liability management do not grow by themselves. For instance, leading banks would have to be more active in OTC product markets to add breadth to the market. Otherwise, banks could not execute hedge operations in a volatile environment. Thirdly and most importantly, ALM by itself is not top management's ultimate goal. ALM must work in conjunction with credit risk management to achieve results consistent with long-term strategies.

Structural Changes in Banking

Credit risk management and asset and liability management are two indispensable components of risk management. But the task of bridging the two to derive portfolio and liability management is challenging for Japanese banks. It would require regional banks to underwrite municipal bonds, even in an unfavorable environment. City banks might have to hold a customer's equities for strategic purposes rather than for short-term profit. Therefore, the portfolio approach of risk management would have to encompass these nonquantitative variables, some of which are the direct results of relationship banking. As more and more corporations tap capital markets directly, banks are forced to rethink the value of their relationships with clients. In order to serve clients and receive adequate returns on capital, banks must weigh not only the potential risk-weighted return but also the impact of transactions on ALM portfolios. This has become even more important with the BIS Capital Adequacy Requirement.

The BIS requirement limits the growth of assets if a bank's BIS capital adequacy ratio is above 8%. A BIS ratio of over 8% allows a bank to do business in an international market. Japanese banks' first reaction to the BIS requirements focused on asset growth in order to stay above the 8% ratio. For example, transactions with low customer orientation, such as Eurodollar deposits, were decreased. To meet the BIS requirement, banks could increase their capital base or decrease their assets. However, because loan sales were only marginally used in asset management, banks had to be more selective in extending credit. To compensate for the declining margins of loans made to large corporations, banks increased their loans to the middle-market corporations. The liquidation of the middle-market loans would have most effectively fulfilled the BIS requirements. However, the middle-market loan is the most difficult loan to liquidate. The Japanese banks realized that they needed higher returns on assets to justify the growth of their loan portfolios. In summary, the BIS requirements made Japanese banks more oriented to ROA.

Japanese banks are moving from ROA to ROE in measuring their performance. The BIS requirements intensified Japanese banks' focus on ROA but not ROE. This is not at all peculiar considering the share of loans on their balance sheets. Interest income from loans accounted for 62% of total revenue in 1991. In contrast, fee income occupied only 2%. Increasing fee income would contribute to fulfilling the BIS requirement and enhancing income stability.

Although banks may engage in the securities and trust businesses, they profit from them by making considerable investments of time and resources. In the meantime, they rely on fee increases for ATM or remittance services, among others. Fee income from investment banking products eventually increase, but growth is slower compared to that in the U.S. due to clients' reluctance to pay for such services.

The various factors related to risk management highlight the fundamental nature of banking. For most Japanese banks, their essential functions would continue to be credit risk intermediation and interest rate risk intermediation. Developments in deregulation and securitization would not diminish the importance of credit risk management. Rather, they would increase the need to integrate credit risk measurement and market risk management for strategic decision making. The majority of banks are now refining credit risk management and ALM systems to develop adequate RAROC (risk-adjusted return on capital) systems.

Conclusion

To date, Japanese banks have used risk control systems identical to those of U.S. banks. Japanese banks could, and should, follow the basic concepts underlying risk management. However, failures to adjust the U.S. model to Japanese business realities may be dangerous. International banks must follow the rules of the game as dictated by the BIS, EC or Federal Deposit Insurance Corporation Improvement Act (FDICIA). International regulatory frameworks will no doubt converge, making it difficult for Japanese banks to distance themselves based on customer differences.

Merely fulfilling the regulatory requirements *per se* is not the primary objective. If a bank's goal is to fulfill a certain requirement, be it a ROE target or the BIS ratio, it will conduct pure transaction banking. A bank may modify its client base as customer needs change, but a commercial bank cannot match a merchant bank for pure transaction banking. And even in merchant or investment banking, relationships do count. In conclusion, Japanese banks must modify the U.S. model to match the Japanese situation and communicate the cost and benefit of doing so to their clients.

Now that the proposal for revised BIS requirements has been released, a convergence of regulatory frameworks is emerging. Moreover, the international accounting standards are also moving toward the

International Accounting Standards (IAS) rules possibly endorsed by IOSCO. The implication is clear. Banks around the world will be more exposed to mark-to-market accounting, and the room to rely on hidden resources will diminish. Therefore, the challenge to Japanese banks is to establish a coherent framework for measuring and managing risk consistent with corporate goals and responsive to the developments in the market, the convergence of regulatory frameworks, changes in international accounting standards, and finally—and most importantly—changes in clients' business practices.

Yield Curve Risk Management for Government Bond Portfolios: An International Comparison

Kenneth J. Singleton, Professor, Graduate School of Business, Stanford University

Overview

This chapter explores the effectiveness of standard *factor–based* risk management in the German and Japanese government bond markets compared to those for the U. S. Treasury market.[1] Specifically, we characterize the nature of yield curve risk in the Japanese and German government bond markets empirically using a simple linear factor model of interest rate risk. Then we relate the implied optimal hedges against factor risk to standard duration–based hedging strategies. Though our focus is on government bond markets, the findings have implications for risk management of most interest–sensitive instruments, especially those that are priced relative to government bonds (e.g., corporate and mortgage bonds).

Introduction

Approaches to managing the interest rate risk of bond portfolios or debt financings are now well integrated into financial institutions' risk management systems. Typically, institutions achieve *first–order hedging* of interest rate *level* risk using the concept of duration and the hypothetical experiment of a parallel shift in the yield curve. Depending on the risk management problem, they may hedge against changes in the shapes of yield curves (e.g., *slope* risk) or higher–order effects of level changes (e.g., *convexity* risk). The motivation for these hedges is often experiential or based simply on convention, but it is rarely conceptual. For instance, most term structure theories do not imply linear price–yield relations or the single *parallel shift* risk factor presumed in duration–based hedging. Theory is also silent on the nature and relative importance of candidate sources of interest rate risk in multi–factor models; what works in practice depends on the probability distribution of yield curve changes.

Given the empirical foundation of practical interest rate risk management, it is natural to inquire whether immunization strategies widely applied in the U. S. markets work equally well in nondollar, fixed–income markets. One might presume that yield curve risk in nondollar markets is not the same as in the U. S. Treasury market for at least two reasons. First, fiscal financing and macroeconomic policies may differ across countries, affecting the economic forces that shape yield curves. For instance, the yield curves of the U. S. and Japan have recently been relatively steep while the yield curve in Germany has been inverted. These different shapes and the way they have changed over time reflect differences in the reactions of monetary authorities to changes in inflation, exchange rates, and so forth.

Second, many nondollar government bond markets are relatively illiquid, and institutional factors such as high financing costs and accounting practices help determine the relative pricing of bonds of different maturities. The presence of such institutional considerations influenced our selection of Japan and Germany in contrast to the U. S. In Japan, for example, the domestic legal and accounting framework leads some institutional investors to prefer current income over capital gains from Japanese government bond (JGB) positions. Similarly, domestic holders of German government bonds (GGB) are subject to withholding taxes on coupon income. Consequently, high–coupon bonds trade at lower prices than otherwise equivalent low–coupon bonds. Large differences in liquidity along the yield curve also characterize the GGB market. These frictions may influence how various sectors of the yield curve respond to economic events and, hence, the selection of risk management strategies.

We describe three conceptual approaches to yield curve risk management. The first presumes availability of a fully specified valuation model that characterizes the relation between bond prices and the underlying *risk factors* that determine the term structure. This model makes it possible to compute the portfolio weights for optimal "immunization" against any subset of these *risk factors*. The modeling

---

effort typically goes well beyond the limited objectives of risk management; so, in practice, risk management has typically focused (at least implicitly) on linearized versions of such valuation models. Specifically, changes in zero–coupon bond yields are expressed as linear functions of a small number of risk factors (Schaefer 1984), from which changes in coupon bond prices in response to small changes in the risk factors can be computed. The second approach determines optimal immunization weights for coupon bonds based on such linear representations of zero–coupon yield curves. This approach is likely to work well in countries where there are regularly scheduled new issues along the yield curve and active secondary trading for many maturities (e.g., the U. S. Treasury market). However, for some countries, institutional considerations such as those outlined above imply that there is not a unique discount function for valuing all government bonds. In such cases, a third approach, based on linear representations of the risk structure of bond–equivalent yields (BEYs) on coupon–paying bonds, may result in the most reliable strategies. Presenting all three of these approaches together highlights the tradeoffs faced when designing risk management strategy amid institutional frictions.

All three approaches to risk management require a characterization of the primary sources of interest rate risk or the *risk factors*. In light of our focus on Japan and Germany, we will illustrate the third approach to determining optimal portfolio weights. Specifically, we study the case of a portfolio manager who is long 2–year and 10–year bonds and short a 5–year bond and whose objective is to construct a portfolio—a *butterfly* position—that is sensitive to small changes in the risk factors. Toward this end, we estimate one– and two–factor models of yield changes for the U. S., Japan, and Germany. Simple general equilibrium models of the term structure of interest rates such as Cox, Ingersoll and Ross (CIR; 1985) and Duffie and Kan (1993) suggest the use of interest rates as the state variables or *risk factors*.[2] We associate the factors with interest rate *level* and *slope* risk and use the 10–year bond yield and the 2– to 10–year spread as the *level* and *slope* factors, respectively.

Longstaff and Schwartz (1992) develop a special case of the CIR model. Volatility of the short–term interest rate substitutes for the long–term rate in the CIR model and leads to a two–factor model of interest rate risk expressed in terms of the distribution of the short–term interest rate. Since short–rate volatility is often associated with changes in the slope of the yield curve, we also explore the relative contributions of *slope* and *volatility* to interest rate risk.

The empirical results show substantial variation in the nature of yield curve risk across countries, which appears to have natural interpretations in terms of the institutional and macroeconomic environments of the respective countries. Common across countries is the conclusion that *duration–based* hedging is typically not optimal given the structures of these yield curve risks. Further insights into the practical importance of these different representations of yield curve risk are provided by an examination of the out–of–sample performance of optimal one– and two–factor hedges for the illustrative butterfly portfolios.

Conceptual Approaches to Risk Management

In principle, risk management and valuation present different aspects of the same problem. Both require characterizing the sources of risk that affect bond prices, including the number, nature, and behavior as regards bond prices. However, since risk management is typically a *local* calculation—that is, it involves examining how small changes in risk factors affect bond prices—practical risk management is often simpler than valuation. This section links valuation (in the context of a fully specified model of the term structure) and *factor* hedging. We also discuss some assumptions that rationalize the popular simplified approaches to factor hedging. This framework aids in the empirical analysis of yields, presented subsequently.

Consider a portfolio of N bonds with the price and maturity of the nth bond denoted by $P^n(t)$ and m_n, respectively. Suppose K state variables or factors $f_1, f_2, ..., f_K$ are the sources of interest rate risk, where K is much smaller than N. These factors may or may not be easily measurable. The nth bond price is assumed to depend on the K factors according to the function

$$P_t^n = P^n(f_{1t}, f_{2t}, ..., f_{Kt}).$$ (1)

For hedging purposes, we are interested in how bond prices change in response to small changes in the factors:

$$\Delta P_t^n \approx \sum_{k=1}^{K} \frac{\partial P_t^n}{\partial f_{kt}} \Delta f_{kt} .$$ (2)

In words, the change in the nth bond price equals the sum of the sensitivities of the bond price with respect to the factors times the changes in the factors. In general, a change in one risk factor may induce changes in other factors (e.g., changes in the *level* of interest rates often induce changes in the slope of the yield curve), so there is no presumption that Δf_{jt} is independent of $\Delta f_{kt}, k \neq j$.

For a portfolio of the N bonds with portfolio weights ω (an $N \times 1$ vector), the change in the portfolio value implied by a change in the risk factors is

$$\omega' \Delta P_t \approx \omega' \sum_{k=1}^{K} \frac{\partial P_t}{\partial f_{kt}} \Delta f_{kt} , \qquad (3)$$

where P_t is the vector of N bond prices. Faced with the relation (3) between changes in economic factors and portfolio value, the best choice for the weights ω depends on the portfolio manager's objective. Since we focus on risk management, we assume that the goal is to minimize interest rate risk. The measure of interest rate risk we adopt is that of the variance of changes in portfolio value (i.e., the variance of the profits and losses on the portfolio). More precisely, we assume that the portfolio manager seeks the weights ω that solve

$$\min_{\omega} var\left[\omega' \Delta P\right] . \qquad (4)$$

Given the model (1) for bond prices, there is an equivalent way of expressing this optimum problem in terms of the factor sensitivities. Let D_f denote the $N \times K$ matrix of sensitivities of the N bonds to the K factors, where the nk^{th} element of D_f is

$$\frac{\partial P_t^n}{\partial f_{kt}} .$$

Also, let d_{fj} denote the jth column of D_f; that is, the $N \times 1$ vector of sensitivities of the N bond prices to the jth factor. Suppose that one is interested in designing a portfolio that is insensitive to small changes in the K factors. This is accomplished by finding the ω that solves

$$\min_{\omega}\left[\omega' D_f \, var(\Delta f) D_f' \omega\right] = \min_{\omega} var\left[\sum_{k=1}^{K} \omega' d_{fk} \Delta f_{kt}\right] . \qquad (5)$$

In general, the objective function (5) depends on the variances and covariances of the factor changes. However, in the special case where the changes in the factors are uncorrelated and normalized to have unit variances,[3] this expression simplifies to

$$\min_{\omega} \sum_{k=1}^{K} \left[\omega' \mathbf{d}_{fk} \right]^2 . \tag{6}$$

In either case, when $K < N$, constraints may have to be imposed on ω to obtain a unique hedge portfolio. Examples of such constraints are discussed below.

To implement this hedging strategy, one must know the form of the P^n as functions of the factors. One must also be able to compute the partial derivatives of these functions evaluated at the current values of the factors. In addition, the second moments (variances and covariances) of the Δf_{kt} must be estimable. *This usually requires that the factors be observable.*

Although this is an ambitious modeling effort, financial institutions have developed such complete models of the term structure of the U. S. Treasury market. These models can be (and sometimes are) used for portfolio risk management. The objectives of valuation and hedging are very different, however. Valuation typically requires a description of the evolution of interest rates over the entire range of possible future paths. Consequently, considerations of computational tractability often lead to relatively simple one– and two–factor models of the term structure for valuation purposes. In contrast, hedging is a dynamic process that focuses on *local* changes in interest rates and often involves more than just shifts in the level of rates. Hedging against a higher dimensional set of risks for small changes in the sources of these risks is feasible.

Interest rate risks brought about by small changes in the factors can be managed using a linearization of the present value relation for bond prices. Specifically, let B_t^τ and b_t^τ denote the price and yield, respectively, of a pure discount bond with τ years to maturity at date t. Then the price of the nth bond paying coupon c^n semi–annually is:

$$P_t^n = \sum_{s=1}^{m_n \times 2} c_s^n \times B_t^{.5 \times s} . \tag{7}$$

Since prices of coupon–paying bonds are linear combinations of prices of zero–coupon bonds, the risk management problem can be restated in terms of the zero–coupon bond prices. As a first–order approximation, the change in the price of each zero–coupon bond is linear in its yield change

$$\Delta B_i^{.5s} \approx \$D(.5s,0) \times \Delta b_i^{.5s} \ ,$$

where $\$D(\tau,c)$ denotes *dollar duration* for a bond with maturity τ and coupon c per year. Substituting this expression for $\Delta B_i^{.5s}$ in the time–differenced version of (7) gives

$$\Delta P_t^n = \sum_{s=1}^{m_n \times 2} c_s^n \times \Delta B_i^{.5s} = \sum_{s=1}^{m_n \times 2} c_s^n \times \$D(.5s,0) \times \Delta b_i^{.5s} \ . \tag{8}$$

Equation (8) by itself does not simplify the risk management problem because for a coupon bond with maturity m_n, the effects of interest rate changes on $m_n \times 2$ zero–coupon bond prices must be assessed. The key step in reducing the dimensionality of the risk management problem comes with the assumption that the changes in zero–coupon bond yields on the right–hand side of (8) can be expressed as linear combinations of changes in a small number of underlying risk factors.

For instance, if there are K sources of risk, $\mathbf{f}_t$, and $2N$ zero–coupon bond yields, $\mathbf{b}_t$, then we assume that

$$\Delta \mathbf{b}_t \approx \Lambda \Delta \mathbf{f}_t \ , \tag{9}$$

where Λ is a $2N \times K$ matrix of "factor sensitivities" of the zero–coupon bond yields to the risk factors. Combining (7)–(9) gives

$$\Delta P_t^n \approx \sum_{s=1}^{m_n \times 2} c_s^n \times \$D(.5s,0) \sum_{k=1}^{K} \lambda_{sk} \Delta f_{kt} \ , \tag{10}$$

where λ_{sk} is the sk^{th} element of Λ. This is the counterpart to equation (2). The linearity comes from the use of dollar duration to express price changes in terms of yield changes and the assumption that zero–coupon bond yield changes are linear functions of the state variables $\{f_1, f_2, ..., f_K\}$. Substituting (10) into (4) gives the following simplified objective function for risk management:

$$\min_{\omega} \mathrm{var} \left[\sum_{n=1}^{N} \omega_n \sum_{s=1}^{m_n \times 2} c_s^n \times \$D(.5s,0) \sum_{k=1}^{K} \lambda_{sk} \Delta f_{kt} \right].\qquad(11)$$

Implementation of this linearized risk management scheme requires estimates of the zero–coupon bond yield curve and the sensitivities of these yields to changes in the K risk factors. Estimates of zero coupon bond yields from data on U. S. Treasury coupon–paying bond yields are frequently correlated using spline functions.[4]

A subset of the zero–coupon bond yields has typically been chosen as the risk factors. This choice has been motivated in part by good empirical fit and in part by theoretical considerations. The CIR model, for instance, implies that the unobservable sources of uncertainty affecting investors' production and consumption decisions can be replaced by continuously compounded yields to maturity on K zero–coupon bonds for valuation purposes. Furthermore, the yield on a τ–year zero–coupon bond, $-\ln B_t^\tau / \tau$, can be expressed as a *linear* function of the continuously compounded yields to maturity on these K zero–coupon bonds. Thus, in the context of a two–factor CIR model, the level (e.g., b_t^{10}) and slope (e.g., $b_t^{10} - b_t^2$) of the zero–coupon bond yield curve serve as the factors in (9).

The variance of the short–term zero–coupon bond yield in the CIR model and in the extensions examined by Duffie and Kan (1993) is a linear function of yields on zero–coupon bonds. Longstaff and Schwartz (1992) exploit this fact to derive a two–factor CIR model in which the two factors are the short rate and its volatility, V. The volatility of interest rates is generally perceived to correlate with the slope of the yield curve, but this correlation changes over time with macroeconomic conditions and is far from unity. Therefore, two–factor models based on two yields versus a yield and volatility are not likely to be empirically equivalent. Indeed, in their analysis of interest rate risk for the U. S. Treasury yield curve, Litterman and Scheinkman (1988) find that volatility acts as *curvature* factor that follows third in importance (after level and slope) in explaining the variability of bond yields. The next section examines this relation for the case of Japan.

An alternative approach to estimating Λ is to treat the factors as unobservable variables and then use *factor analysis* to estimate Λ. With unobservable factors, the allocation of overall volatility of zero–coupon bond yields to changes in the factors is not unique. Normalizations must be imposed in estimation. This is not an issue if one is concerned about immunizing a portfolio against all K factors simultaneously; one achieves the same reduction in factor risk regardless of the normalizations imposed. But to interpret the factors in terms of such common notions as slope or level risk and design portfolios which are immunized against a subset of these factors, further calculations are typically required (Litterman and Scheinkman 1988).

Risk management strategies using factor sensitivities based on a complete model (2) or its linearized counterpart based on zeros (10) with a small number of factors K are widely used for the U. S. Treasury bond market. The success of these models results from the fact that a small number of factors explain over 90% of the temporal variation in U. S. Treasury bond yields. In addition, the regular issuance of on–the–run bonds at various maturities along the yield curve contributes to substantial liquidity in the market and the reliable estimation of zero–coupon bond yields for the coupon yield curve. The depth of this market also implies that yields typically do not "jump" in response to new information. So, over short intervals of time, the linear approximations underlying (10) are accurate.

Another reason for the effectiveness of single–factor risk management strategies in the U. S. is that the estimated factor sensitivity matrix Λ in equation (9) has at times been such that λ_{s1} and λ_{s2} are approximately proportional over a wide range of maturities when the first two factors are assumed to be *level* and *slope* (Schaefer 1984). In this case, the ω that satisfies (4) for the *level* factor also approximately satisfies this equation for the *slope* factor. That is, one– and two–factor hedges are nearly identical for some maturities. As such, duration–based hedging has sometimes worked reliably for the U. S. Treasury market. This relation among factor sensitivities is clearly special and may not hold under all economic conditions in the U. S. As we will see, it does not hold for other countries.

Among the world's bond markets, the U. S. Treasury market is exceptional for the limited role of institutional frictions on the properties of zero–coupon bond yields. Regulatory restrictions and accounting conventions in Japan are such that certain investors have a strong preference for high–coupon JGBs. Moreover, because the shortest-maturity new issue has until recently had a ten–year maturity and accounting conventions have encouraged "buy and hold" investment strategies, certain parts of the JGB market have been relatively illiquid.

As such, bonds with different coupons that are otherwise virtually identical often trade several basis points apart in yield. These differences in yields are sufficiently large to invalidate an assumption that the same discount function prices the cashflows of both high– and low–coupon bonds. That is, for institutional reasons, the market effectively uses more than one zero–coupon bond yield curve to price JGBs. Thus, reliance on a fitted zero–coupon bond yield curve for risk management in the JGB market has significant limitations.

The structure of the German government bond market lies in between that of the U. S. and Japan in terms of the importance of institutional factors for bond pricing. Federal government bonds (BUNDs) are typically issued with 10 years to maturity. In addition, several other types of shorter–term federal government notes are issued. Thus, there are more on–the–run securities along the yield curve than in Japan, for example. Also, 10– and 5–year futures contracts, useful for price discovery and hedging, are traded in Germany. In particular, these contracts enhance the liquidity of deliverable bonds in the 5– and 10–year sectors.[5] At the same time, withholding taxes and accounting conventions often lead low–coupon bonds to trade at substantial premiums in price compared to high–coupon notes.

To avoid computing zero–coupon bond yields while preserving the tractability of linear models, immunization of government bond portfolios can be based directly on the BEYs of the coupon–paying bonds. As with the second strategy, the price changes are linearized as functions of yield changes, only this time in terms of their own yields, y_t^n:

$$\Delta P_t^n = \$D\left(n,c^n\right) \times \Delta y_t^n. \tag{12}$$

Next, changes in the N BEYs, Δy_t, are assumed to be determined as a linear function of changes in K risk factors

$$\Delta y_t = \Lambda \Delta f_t, \tag{13}$$

where Λ is now an $N \times K$ matrix of factor sensitivities. Combining (11) and (12) and letting ΔP_t denote the vector of price changes for the N bonds and D the $N \times N$ diagonal matrix with the dollar durations of the N bonds along the diagonal gives

$$\Delta P_t = D \times \Lambda \Delta f_t. \tag{14}$$

Under these assumptions, immunization against the risks associated with the K factors is accomplished by finding an ω that minimizes

$$\text{var}\left[\sum_{k=1}^{K} \omega' D \lambda_k \Delta f_{kt}\right], \tag{15}$$

where λ_k denotes the kth column of the matrix Λ.

Though much simpler to implement than the first two approaches to risk management, the tractability of using yields on coupon–paying bonds carries several potentially serious limitations. Most notably, the durations of the coupon–paying bonds change over time as the bonds approach maturity and as interest rates vary. Therefore, if bond yields are used for the factors, then the risk characteristics of the factors change over time and one might find greater instability in the estimates of the risk weights Λ over different sample periods. In contrast, the durations of current zero–coupon bonds are fixed at their maturities. This limitation of (13) must be weighed against the potentially greater explanatory power from regressing BEYs on market–determined yields on coupon bonds (versus on fitted zero yields that may poorly replicate the coupon bond prices). An intermediate strategy that may reduce "duration drift" would be to use a "constant maturity" BEY series, calculated using the market–determined BEY with maturity closest to the one of interest. Subsequently, to make international comparisons of the hedges for markets where zero–coupon bond calculations may be unreliable, we focus on (13)–(15) using constant–maturity series where available.

Factor Models for Government Bond Yields

As a first step toward implementing the risk management schemes discussed earlier, we estimate the parameters of the factor coefficient matrix Λ in (13). Suppose that one common factor underlies changes in bond yields in a country so that K is unity. Table 1 presents the estimates of the vector λ_1 for Japan, Germany, and the U. S. Two different samples of daily data were examined: June 8, 1992 through November 30, 1992 and December 1, 1992 through April 30, 1993. The data thus provide evidence on the stability of the risk coefficients λ_1 over time. We note that a currency crisis occurred in Europe during September 1992 when the United Kingdom and Italy left the ERM.

Table 1
Estimates of One–Factor Models

| | | Japan | | | | | | | |
| | | June 8, 1992 – Nov. 30, 1992 | | | | Dec. 1, 1992 – April 30, 1993 | | | |
Bond	[mat.]	λ_1	[s.e.]*	R^2	s.e.e.	λ_1	[s.e.]	R^2	s.e.e.
78	[2.6]	0.657	[.06]	0.57	.026	0.690	[.04]	0.71	.021
99	[4.6]	0.771	[.06]	0.64	.023	0.733	[.04]	0.77	.019
111	[5.6]	0.782	[.04]	0.76	.017	0.748	[.04]	0.82	.016
119	[6.6]	0.801	[.03]	0.83	.014	0.766	[.03]	0.89	.012
133	[7.9]	1.000	[.00]	1.00	.000	1.000	[.00]	1.00	.000
140	[8.6]	0.934	[.01]	0.99	.002	0.935	[.01]	0.98	.006

| | Germany | | | | | | | |
| | June 8, 1992 – Nov. 30, 1992 | | | | Dec. 1, 1992 – April 30, 1993 | | | |
Maturity	λ_1	[s.e.]	R^2	s.e.e.	λ_1	[s.e.]	R^2	s.e.e.
2	1.464	[.11]	0.62	.042	1.313	[.10]	0.64	.040
3	1.254	[.09]	0.61	.037	1.220	[.08]	0.72	.031
4	1.202	[.08]	0.65	.033	1.163	[.06]	0.80	.023
5	1.084	[.07]	0.67	.028	1.136	[.06]	0.81	.022
7	0.975	[.05]	0.78	.019	1.032	[.04]	0.86	.016
10	1.000	[.00]	1.00	.000	1.000	[.00]	1.00	.000

| | United States | | | | | | | |
| | June 8, 1992 – Nov. 30, 1992 | | | | Dec. 1, 1992 – April 30, 1993 | | | |
Maturity	λ_1	[s.e.]	R^2	s.e.e.	λ_1	[s.e.]	R^2	s.e.e.
2	1.027	[.05]	0.74	.037	.936	[.07]	0.65	.037
3	1.146	[.06]	0.77	.037	1.004	[.06]	0.73	.032
4	1.147	[.04]	0.87	.026	1.003	[.04]	0.83	.024
5	1.167	[.04]	0.90	.023	1.069	[.04]	0.88	.021
7	1.125	[.02]	0.96	.012	1.054	[.02]	0.96	.011
10	1.000	[.00]	1.00	.000	1.000	[.00]	1.00	.000

*Standard errors of the estimates are displayed in square brackets; s.e.e. is the standard error of the estimated residuals.

In Japan, JGBs with maturities under 10 years are seasoned bonds with initial maturities of 10 years. Relative to the newly issued and benchmark bond, seasoned issues are illiquid. Since there are no "on–the–run" bonds along the yield curve, we examine a subset of ex–benchmark bonds. These bonds were once the most liquid bonds traded. Recently they have traded with greater liquidity and depth than nearby nonbenchmark JGBs. Indeed, these bonds serve in part as "benchmark" reference bonds for comparably maturing bonds even though they are seasoned.

We study constant–maturity bond yields for Germany and the U. S. Regular issuance of U. S. Treasury bonds makes calculation of the constant–maturity series for the U. S. straightforward. The German government regularly issues federal government bonds at all maturities except the 7–year maturity, so we must interpolate the constant–maturity yields for this maturity.

Long-term bond yields generally fell in all three countries during this period; however, in the U. S., rates rose during October 1992. At the same time, the slopes of the yield curves $\left(y_t^{10} - y_t^2\right)$ varied substantially, implying that the 2-year rates often behaved quite differently from their long-term counterparts. The slope of the U. S. Treasury curve drifted up slightly and back down during the early sample period and remained relatively unchanged over the later period. A similar pattern emerged in Japan although there was considerable fluctuation at a level near 100 basis points (bp) during the later period. In Germany, the yield curve noticeably flattened (disinversion) during September 1992 and continued to do so during the remainder of the sample period.

One–Factor Models: Level Risk

The factor f_1 is assumed to be observable and equal to the change in the BEY of a long–maturity bond. In other words, f_1 is the *level* of interest rates. In the case of Japan, the bond chosen is #133 since this bond was cheapest to deliver into the futures contract over much of the sample period. The 10–year futures contract in Japan is one of the most liquid instruments in the world, and market pricing of JGBs all along the curve is often closely tied to the level of the futures.[6] In the cases of the U. S. and Germany, changes in the BEYs of the constant–maturity 10–year bonds are used. Table 1 displays the results.

Consider the results for Japan. The estimated values of the factor weights λ_1 are relatively small (less than unity) for the shorter–maturity bonds. Then they increase to the value unity for #133 (this is an identity). To interpret this pattern relative to common hedging strategies, recall that all elements of λ_1 must be equal for *factor hedging* to be the same as *duration hedging*. And in this case, with f_1 set equal to the BEY on a specific bond, this common value must be unity. Clearly the pattern of weights implies that single–factor hedging is *not* equivalent to duration hedging. Duration hedging is suboptimal as a hedge against a single interest rate risk factor. This conclusion is not sensitive to the choice of sample period; the factor weights decline more rapidly with maturity in the second sample period.

Comparing Japan with Germany and the U. S. leads to a similar conclusion about the suboptimality of duration hedging for Germany. The case of the U. S. is more ambiguous. The 3– to 7–year sector of the U. S. Treasury curve during the early sample period has weights that exceed unity, but all of the weights are near unity in the second period.

Both macroeconomic and institutional considerations underlie the differences in the weight vectors λ_1 across countries. The tendency for the λ_1 to be larger for intermediate–maturity U. S. Treasuries during the early sample period reflects their superior performance over 10–year bonds. As the BEY on the 10– and 2–year bonds declined due to the weak U. S. economy, those on the intermediate–term bonds declined more. In other words, the curvature of the yield curve changed. In contrast, for the second sample period, the estimated weights suggest that changes in y^{10} induced approximately parallel shifts in the yield curve. This is reflected in the standard deviations of the yield and slope changes displayed in Table 2 along the diagonals of the matrices. The fluctuation in both the 2– and 10– year yield changes exceeds that of the slope of the yield curve.

Table 2

Correlations Among the Factors*

	Japan					
	Dec. 1, 1992 – April 30, 1993			June 8, 1992 – Nov. 20, 1992		
	Δy^{78}	Δy^{133}	SL	Δy^{78}	Δy^{133}	SL
Δy^{78}	.027			.034		
Δy^{133}	.682	.046		.723	.037	
SL	.133	.816	.034	.286	.455	.027

	Germany					
	Dec. 1, 1992 – April 30, 1993			June 8, 1992 – Nov. 20, 1992		
	Δy^2	Δy^{10}	SL	Δy^2	Δy^{10}	SL
Δy^2	.065			.068		
Δy^{10}	.790	.039		.781	.026	
SL	-.818	-.294	.042	-.868	-.369	.045

	United States					
	Dec. 1, 1992 – April 30, 1993			June 8, 1992 – Nov. 20, 1992		
	Δy^2	Δy^{10}	SL	Δy^2	Δy^{10}	SL
Δy^2	.061			.071		
Δy^{10}	.800	.052		.859	.060	
SL	-.525	.090	.037	-.548	-.044	.036

* Standard Errors of the series are on the diagonal and correlations are displayed in off–diagonal elements of the matrices.

The government yield curve in Germany was substantially inverted during this period as the Bundesbank ran a tight monetary policy with the goal of reducing domestic inflationary pressures. However, following the currency crisis in September 1992, the Bundesbank lowered short–term rates substantially, and the yield curve disinverted by over 100 bp. The much greater volatility of short– versus long–term rates (Table 2) is reflected in the relatively large factor weights for short–maturity bonds in Table 1 on the factor y^{10}.

In Japan, the factor weights also differ substantially from unity but in the opposite direction from Germany: the factor weights on short–maturity bonds are smaller than those for the long–term bonds. The explanation may lie less in the Bank of Japan's monetary policy and more in institutional features of the market. In 1992, the bond market in Japan experienced a sustained rally in the midst of Japan's worst postwar recession. At this time, there were few signs of an imminent cut in the discount rate and, hence, of a further rally at the short end of the yield curve. Furthermore, since short–term bonds are relatively illiquid compared to those deliverable into 10–year futures, short–term trading concentrated in the liquid futures; and market rallies and selloffs were futures driven. Consequently, the variation in Δy^{133} significantly exceeded that of Δy^{78} (Table 2), and the factor weights in the deliverable sector exceeded those on short–term bonds.

Another important consideration in evaluating hedges is the extent to which shifts in the yield on one bond explain the variation in other bonds; that is, the magnitudes of the coefficient of determination (R^2). Exposure to this residual risk may be desired; if not, then additional common risk factors should be explored.

Two–Factor Models: Level and Slope Risk

The slope of the yield curve is one important dimension of shape that is not captured by a single *level* factor. Table 2 shows that the variation in slope SL $\left(\equiv \Delta y^{10} - \Delta y^2 \right)$ was substantial relative to variation in the individual bonds, especially in Japan and Germany. Specifically, for the second period, the standard deviation of SL in Japan was comparable to that of SL for the U. S. Yet the steepness of the Japanese curve was less than half that of the U. S., so the coefficient of variation of the Japanese yield curve's slope was much larger. Moreover, SL was correlated with the long–term rate in Germany and Japan, and the magnitudes of these correlations changed over the sample periods, especially in Japan. This is precisely what should happen if the interpretations of the factor weights suggested above are correct. In the case of the U. S., the correlation between the level factor Δy^{10} and SL is close to zero.[7]

The failure of the key presumption of duration–based hedging—that yield curves only shift in a parallel manner—does not *per se* invalidate duration–based hedging. If changes in the shape of the yield curve are uncorrelated with level changes *and* the factor weights on the level factor are equal for all bonds, then duration–based hedging is valid so long as one is unconcerned with the other sources of interest rate risk. Both conditions were approximately satisfied for the U. S. during our sample periods. In contrast, Table 1 and 2 imply that neither was satisfied for Japan and Germany.

Table 3 displays the factor weights with SL included as a second factor. Two cases are presented: correlated and uncorrelated factors. The weights for the correlated case were obtained using Δy^{10} and SL as factors in linear regressions. The weights in the uncorrelated case were obtained by first calculating the component of Δy^{10} that is uncorrelated with SL and then using this component and SL as the two factors.[8] Considering explanatory power, the two approaches are equivalent, so only one measure of R^2 is presented.

Table 3

Estimates of Two–Factor Models*

December 1, 1992 – April 30, 1993

Japan

Bond	λ_1^c	[s.e.]	λ_2^c	[s.e.]	λ_1^u	[s.e.]	λ_2^u	[s.e.]	R^2	s.e.e.
78	1.000	[.00]	-1.000	[.00]	1.000	[.00]	0.105	[.00]	1.000	.000
89	1.103	[.06]	-0.686	[.08]	1.103	[.06]	0.534	[.05]	0.830	.016
99	1.061	[.06]	-0.544	[.08]	1.061	[.06]	0.628	[.04]	0.840	.015
111	1.024	[.05]	-0.458	[.07]	1.024	[.05]	0.673	[.04]	0.880	.013
119	0.982	[.04]	-0.359	[.05]	0.982	[.04]	0.727	[.03]	0.930	.010
133	1.000	[.00]	0.000	[.00]	1.000	[.00]	1.105	[.00]	1.000	.000
140	0.914	[.02]	0.036	[.03]	0.914	[.02]	1.046	[.02]	0.980	.006

Germany

Maturity	λ_1^c	[s.e.]	λ_2^c	[s.e.]	λ_1^u	[s.e.]	λ_2^u	[s.e.]	R^2	s.e.e.
2	1.000	[.00]	-1.000	[.00]	1.000	[.00]	-1.276	[.00]	1.000	.000
3	1.053	[.06]	-0.534	[.06]	1.053	[.06]	-0.825	[.05]	0.850	.022
4	1.042	[.05]	-0.388	[.04]	1.042	[.05]	-0.675	[.04]	0.880	.018
5	1.037	[.05]	-0.315	[.05]	1.037	[.05]	-0.601	[.04]	0.870	.018
7	1.020	[.05]	-0.038	[.04]	1.020	[.04]	-0.320	[.04]	0.860	.016
10	1.000	[.00]	0.000	[.00]	1.000	[.00]	-0.276	[.00]	1.000	.000

United States

Bond	λ_1^c	[s.e.]	λ_2^c	[s.e.]	λ_1^u	[s.e.]	λ_2^u	[s.e.]	R^2	s.e.e.
2	1.000	[.00]	-1.000	[.00]	1.000	[.00]	-0.872	[.00]	1.000	.000
3	1.047	[.04]	-0.664	[.06]	1.047	[.04]	-0.530	[.06]	0.880	.021
4	1.033	[.03]	-0.471	[.05]	1.033	[.03]	-0.338	[.05]	0.910	.017
5	1.097	[.02]	-0.445	[.03]	1.097	[.02]	-0.304	[.03]	0.950	.013
7	1.066	[.02]	-0.189	[.02]	1.066	[.02]	-0.052	[.02]	0.970	.009
10	1.000	[.00]	0.000	[.00]	1.000	[.00]	0.128	[.00]	1.000	.000

* λ^c and λ^u are the factor weights for correlated and uncorrelated factors, respectively. Standard errors are displayed in square brackets; s.e.e. is the standard error of the estimated residuals.

However, the two representations lend themselves to different interpretations. Using the representation in terms of uncorrelated factors simplifies the objective function to be minimized over ω. More importantly, hedging against a subset of risk factors and remaining intentionally exposed to others is not naturally implemented in the representation with correlated factors. The remaining factors will embody some of the risk that was to be eliminated. Thus, looking ahead to risk management and trade strategy, the representation with uncorrelated factors is often more convenient.

Perhaps the most striking feature of the factor weights is that in all cases, the weights on the first *level* factor are near unity. (However, in the representation with uncorrelated factors, the *level factor is* not equal to any particular bond yield.) Thus, the first factor captures parallel shifts in the yield curve, and the second factor represents changes in its slope. With uncorrelated factors, the weights on the second factor increase with maturity in Japan, but they decrease in absolute value in Germany and in the U. S. This implies that a yield curve steepening in Japan has a larger effect on the long than on the short end of the JGB yield curve. For Germany and the U. S., on the other hand, an increase in *SL* is associated with declining rates so that short rates decline by more than long rates. These patterns are consistent with the previous interpretations of the factor weights for the one–factor models.

For shorter–term bonds, the percentages of variation in the yield changes explained by the two–factor models are typically 10% to 20% larger than the corresponding percentages for the one–factor models. Hedges against both *level* and *slope* may therefore behave differently than hedges against a single factor for portfolios involving bonds at both ends of the maturity spectrum.

In summary, we see very different patterns of weights on the *level* and *slope* factors across countries and moderate changes across sample periods. These patterns can be explained by economic conditions and by investor trading patterns. The practical consequences of these differences will be explored after a brief discussion of a candidate third factor.

Yield Volatility as a Third Factor

There are many candidates for risk factors in bond portfolio risk management. While *level* and *slope* are natural choices, it is instructive to pursue the possibility suggested by Longstaff and Schwartz (1992) that short–rate volatility may adequately substitute for *SL* in a model of the term structure. As a measure of short–rate volatility, we use the fitted estimate of the conditional variance of y^2_{t+1} given information at date t, V_t, where V is measured using their model of variances.[9] Our analysis differs in the potentially important respect that it uses the variance of the 2–year rate on a coupon bond instead of the variance of a short–term zero–coupon (Treasury bill) yield. Nevertheless, we expect the findings to suggest a role for volatility as a risk factor.

Table 4 displays the results for the case of uncorrelated factors with all three factors (Δy^{10}, SL, and ΔV) included for the second sample period with Japanese data. Comparing Table 4 to the first panel in Table 3 shows that the estimates of λ^u_1 and λ^u_2 are very similar and that the R^2s increase only moderately. Thus, there is little incremental explanatory power from including ΔV. Furthermore, the correlation between ΔV and SL is negligible.[10] Thus, SL and ΔV do not represent the same sources of risk. In fact, when ΔV substitutes for SL in the two–factor regressions, the R^2s decline to approximately those in Table 1 for the one–factor models.

Table 4

**Estimates of Three–Factor Model
December 1, 1992 – April 30, 1993**

Bond	λ^u_1		λ^u_2		λ^u_3		R^2	s.e.e.
78	1.000	[.00]	.110	[.00]	-0.037	[.00]	1.00	.000
89	1.115	[.06]	.616	[.04]	-0.562	[.87]	.84	.015
99	1.118	[.05]	.727	[.05]	-2.310	[.81]	.87	.014
111	1.052	[.05]	.785	[.04]	-1.250	[.68]	.91	.012
119	.999	[.03]	.836	[.03]	-0.746	[.50]	.95	.008
133	1.000	[.00]	1.110	[.00]	-0.377	[.00]	1.00	.000
140	1.014	[.03]	1.218	[.02]	-0.315	[.41]	.98	.007

There is an interesting pattern to the factor weights for ΔV, however. Starting at the shortest maturity, the elements of λ^u_3 decline until the 5–year sector; then they increase monotonically with maturity. This suggests that volatility is acting like a *curvature* factor: an increase in the volatility of short–term rates leads to lower intermediate yields than short– and long–term yields and thereby reduces the usual convexity in the yield curve. This role for volatility is distinct from the findings of Litterman and Scheinkman (1988) for the U. S. Treasury yield curve since their volatility factor added convexity to the yield curve. Thus, the third factor for the U. S. Treasury curve induces curvature due to the conventional effect of convexity on the Treasury yield curve. In contrast, the JGB curve was bowed toward the origin in the intermediate sector during this sample period. This shape likely resulted from some domestic investors' shortening duration and others placing a 5–year maturity constraint on their JGB positions. As market volatility increased, these effects together led to a substantial richening of the intermediate sector in Japan.

Hedging in Practice for Japan and Germany

The differences in risk–factor sensitivities imply that hedge ratios will differ across one– and two–factor models and the conventional duration model. Suppose, for instance, that one is interested in hedging bond n_1 with a position in bond n_2. The optimal hedge is determined by the hedge ratio HR which minimizes

$$\text{var}\left[\Delta P^{n_1} - \text{HR}\Delta P^{n_2}\right]. \tag{16}$$

Assuming price changes follow a one–factor representation, (16) can be rewritten as

$$\text{var}\left[\$D\left(n_1,c^{n_1}\right)\lambda_{n_1 1}\Delta f_1 - \text{HR}\$D\left(n_2,c^{n_2}\right)\lambda_{n_2 1}\Delta f_1\right]. \tag{17}$$

The variance minimizing hedge ratio is given by

$$\text{HR}^{1f} = \frac{\lambda_{n_1 1}\$D\left(n_1,c^{n_1}\right)}{\lambda_{n_2 1}\$D\left(n_2,c^{n_2}\right)}. \tag{18}$$

If we assume parallel yield curve shifts (duration–based hedging), then $\lambda_{n_1 1} = \lambda_{n_2 1}$ and (18) simplifies to

$$\text{HR}^d = \frac{\$D\left(n_1,c^{n_1}\right)}{\$D\left(n_2,c^{n_2}\right)}. \tag{19}$$

Comparing (18) and (19) we see that

$$\text{HR}^{1f} = \frac{\lambda_{n_1 1}}{\lambda_{n_2 1}}\text{HR}^d. \tag{20}$$

For example, if $n_1 = 5$ and $n_2 = 10$, then the ratios of the λ's in (19) are .733 for Japan (bonds #99 and #133) and 1.136 for Germany using data from the later sample period. Thus the hedge ratios implied by the one–factor models differ from those implied by the standard duration model by about 27% and 14% for Japan and Germany, respectively.

To examine the sensitivity of portfolio value to the choice of hedge programs, we calculate the optimal hedge weights and performance information for a more complicated risk management problem: a portfolio of three bonds in which the portfolio manager is long 2– and 10–year bonds and short a 5–year bond. His goal is to immunize against changes in the risk factors. The three JGBs we examine are the #78, #99, and #140 (2.6–, 4.6–, and 8.6–year bonds as of the beginning of the first sample period). Without loss of generality, we assume that the par amount of #99 sold is ¥1. The risk management problem can thus be restated as finding the par weights ω_s and ω_l in the portfolio

$$\omega_s \times P^{78} + \omega_l \times P^{140} - P^{99} \tag{21}$$

that immunize this portfolio against small changes in the risk factors; i.e., the variance of changes in the portfolio value (21) due to changes in the factors is minimized.

For the one–factor model, the weights that solve (21) with $K = 1$ are those that solve the equation

$$\omega_s \times \lambda_1^{78} \times \$D^{78} + \omega_l \times \lambda_1^{140} \times \$D^{140} = \lambda_1^{99} \times \$D^{99} . \tag{22}$$

Since there are two unknown weights in (22), we impose an additional constraint on $\{\omega_1, \omega_2\}$ to obtain a unique solution. We impose the constraint that

$$P_t^{78} \omega_s + P_t^{140} \omega_l = P_t^{99} , \tag{23}$$

where t is the date that the hedge is put in place. Consequently, the proceeds from selling #99 equal the cost of long positions in #78 and #140. Equivalently, for every ¥1 par amount of #99 sold, ¥ ω_s and ¥ w_l par amounts of #78 and #140 are purchased.

For comparison, we also report the weights for a standard duration hedge. Specifically, the hedge weights are chosen to satisfy (23) and

$$\omega_s \times \$D^{78} + \omega_l \times \$D^{140} = \$D^{99} . \tag{24}$$

Clearly, the solutions to (23)–(24) and (22)–(23) are the same if the λ_1 are the same for all bonds in (22).[11]

These one–factor hedges eliminate the risk of shifts in the level of long–term rates but do not fully account for slope risk. To immunize the three–bond portfolio against both level and slope risk, we use the factor representation in terms of uncorrelated factors and solve the minimization problem (6). The first–order conditions to this minimum problem are equivalent to the following equations:[12]

$$\omega_s \times \lambda_1^{u78} \times \$D^{78} + \omega_l \times \lambda_1^{u140} \times \$D^{140} = \lambda_1^{u99} \times \$D^{99} \text{ , and} \qquad (25)$$

$$\omega_s \times \lambda_2^{u78} \times \$D^{78} + \omega_l \times \lambda_2^{u140} \times \$D^{140} = \lambda_2^{u99} \times \$D^{99} \text{ .} \qquad (26)$$

Since there are two unknowns and two equations, (25)–(26) uniquely determine the hedge weights ω_s and ω_l. As such, there is no constraint that the proceeds from selling #99 match the outlay for purchasing #78 and #140. In practice, then, it may be necessary to finance a portion of the hedge or invest the balance. We assume that in either case the transactions are made at London Interbank Offering Rate (LIBOR) as of the execution date.

The hedge interpretation of the portfolio weights ω starts with the premises that the portfolio manager wants to eliminate interest rate risk and that one– and two–factor weights represent different approaches to this goal. The two–factor hedge generally performs at least as well as the one–factor hedge. The tradeoff is that in the two–factor hedge, the portfolio manager gives up the proceeds–neutral feature of the one–factor hedge and therefore may have to manage a financing program.

An alternative motivation for one– and two–factor calculations relates to portfolio strategy. Specifically, a portfolio manager may care about changes in the *slope* of the yield curve but not about the future *level* of interest rates. In this case, a portfolio insensitive to changes in the first level factor but not to the second slope factor is intentionally exposed to *slope* risk. Similarly, solving for the weights that leave a portfolio insensitive to *level* and *slope* risk in (25) and (26) exposes the portfolio to the residual interest rate risk not explained by these two factors.

There is a subtle but potentially important difference between the calculations associated with these two motivations, however. Under the second motivation, the goal is a portfolio with exposure to some but not all sources of interest rate risk. If these sources are correlated, then the exposure may depend on the factor representation used. More precisely, if the goal is to generate a portfolio exposed to *slope* risk, then solving for the weights using (22) and (23) gives exposure to factors other than the level risk summarized by changes in y^{10}. But since *level* and *slope* changes may be correlated, the one–factor weights will embody aspects of both level and slope. In other words, this approach has eliminated part of the slope risk to which exposure is desired.

To maximize exposure to slope risk, one could instead estimate a two–factor representation with uncorrelated factors having a level and slope interpretation as was done earlier.[13] Then, instead of using the λ's from Table 1 in (22), we would use the weights λ_1^u on the level factor from Table 2 and solve (22) and (23). The weights calculated using the λ_1's from Table 1 versus Table 2 may differ significantly. Indeed, the weights λ_1^u from Table 2 lead to a proceeds–neutral and essentially zero–duration portfolio to gain *slope* risk exposure.

Returning to our focus on risk management, we see that the two–factor representation with uncorrelated factors clarifies the risks that portfolio managers face by using duration–based hedging instead of considering both *level* and *slope* risks. Namely, for the periods and countries considered, they are exposed to the risks of the second factor; and this clearly has significant consequences for portfolio risk given the increase in R^2s from Table 1 to Table 3.

Table 5 displays the hedge weights for the Japanese bond portfolios. The weights for the optimal one–factor hedge and those of the duration hedge are strikingly similar even though the λ_1's differ widely among the three bonds. This is a consequence of two characteristics. First, the product $\lambda_1^u \times \$D^n$ is approximately a linear function of $\$D^n$ as n varies across the nine bonds. Second, the sum $\omega_s + \omega_l$ is approximately unity. Hence, if we substitute the fitted values of the regression of $\lambda_1^u \times \$D^n$ on $\$D^n$ and a constant term (as n varies) for the $\lambda_1^u \times \$D^n$ in (22), then the weighted sum of the intercepts approximately cancel, leaving (24). That is, when (22) is satisfied, so approximately is (24), and vice versa. The second condition is a special feature of the bonds chosen, so the approximate equality of the duration and one–factor weights is not a general result.

Table 5

Estimated Hedge Weights for the Japanese Portfolio
June 8 – Nov. 30, 1992/Dec. 1, 1992 – April 30, 1993

	ω_s	ω_e	Financing Requirement
Duration	.58/.60	.35/.35	0.
1–Factor	.63/.61	.30/.33	0.
2–Factor	1.08/.100	.20/.29	36.5/36.0

Turning next to the two–factor hedges, note that much more weight is given to the short end of the yield curve (#78) than in the one–factor hedge. From (25) and (26), we express the weight ω_s as

$$\omega_s = \frac{\left[\lambda_1^{u99}/\lambda_1^{u140} - \lambda_2^{u99}/\lambda_2^{u140}\right] \$D^{99}}{\left[\lambda_1^{u78}/\lambda_1^{u140} - \lambda_2^{u78}/\lambda_2^{u140}\right] \$D^{78}} . \tag{27}$$

Heuristically, two considerations influence the allocation of duration of the intermediate bond between the long and short ends of the barbell position. First, for a shift in the level factor (parallel shift), the price of the long bond changes more than the prices of the short– and intermediate–term bonds. Investing a larger par amount in the short–term bond offsets this effect on value. This effect appears in (27) in the ratio $\$D^{99}/\$D^{78}$, which exceeds unity.

Second, since the estimated λ_1's are approximately unity, the first term in (27) is approximately

$$\left[\lambda_2^{u140} - \lambda_2^{u99}\right]/\left[\lambda_2^{u140} - \lambda_2^{u78}\right] .$$

Holding level fixed for a given change in slope SL, the larger the effect of SL on the intermediate–long than on the short–long bond yield spread, the more weight given to the short end of the barbell. This inverse weighting yields a portfolio with limited sensitivity to changes in the slope of the curve since the higher the volatility of the long–term wing of the butterfly, the more weight given to the short–versus the long–term wings. The last column of Table 5 gives the required amount to be financed per ¥100 face amount of #99 sold.

The relative performances of the optimal one–factor, optimal two–factor, and duration hedges have been analyzed. Specifically, we subtract the value of the portfolio at the time the hedge is executed from the value at the date on the horizontal axis. This gives the cumulative gain or loss on the position for each of the first 50 business days following the trade. For the first few days in December 1992, the two–factor hedge slightly underperformed the one–factor hedges in that its value deviated more from zero. Over longer periods of time, however, the two–factor hedge outperformed the one–factor hedges.

During the later period, all three hedges performed similarly and poorly because #140 sold off shortly after the portfolio was put in place (a futures lead selloff and steepening) while the other bond prices were relatively constant. The two–factor hedge partially neutralized the effects of the resulting steepening, but the most significant effect was on the curvature of the yield curve (for these three bonds). The two–factor model does not address this change in shape, so #140's declining price immediately affected the portfolio. In addition, the substantial change in market yields implies that the durations, prices, and hence optimal hedge weights change relatively rapidly.

Table 6 displays the corresponding hedge weights for two German portfolios.[14] Again the positions for the two–factor hedges require some financing—18 and 10.3 DM per 100 DM face amount of the 5–year note, respectively. For the early sample period, the three hedges all performed similarly. Drift in the hedge ratios implies that all three hedges deteriorated after 6 to 10 business days. During the second sample period, the optimal two–factor hedge behaved notably differently and better than the single–factor hedge for holding periods of 15 days. This may have resulted from the steepening of the German yield curve that is accommodated in the two–factor but not in the one–factor hedge. This illustrates the sensitivity of hedge results to the yield distributions over the hedge period.

Table 6

Estimated Hedge Weights for the German Portfolio
June 8 – Nov. 30, 1992/Dec. 1, 1992 – April 30, 1993

	ω_s	ω_e	Financing Requirement
Duration	.67/.63	.33/.26	0.
1–Factor	.79/.67	.20/.29	0.
2–Factor	.99/.83	.19/.21	18.1/10.3

Conclusion

The nature of yield curve risk over the past few years in Japan, Germany, and the U. S. reflects differing macroeconomic environments and institutional frictions. Consequently, the forms of optimal hedges against *level* and *slope* risks differ across countries and over time. Moreover, the commonly used duration model of risk management leads to suboptimal risk management, especially in Japan and Germany, which have substantial correlations between changes in the levels and slopes of the government yield curves. Calculations show that duration–based restructuring of portfolios may unintentionally and significantly alter the exposures to interest rate risk. This is particularly true of a portfolio's sensitivity to changes in the slope of the yield curve.

To explore the practical implications of different hedge strategies for changes in the yield curve, we computed the optimal hedge ratios for a portfolio of three bonds in which an investor was long a 2/10 barbell position and short a bond in the intermediate (5–year) sector. The weights for the two–factor hedges against both *level* and *slope* risks were greater for the short–term bond than for the one–factor hedges. Relatively larger weights on the short–term bond arose in the two–factor hedges to equalize the volatilities of the short and long wings of the barbell positions. This in turn reduced the sensitivity of the butterfly position to slope changes. Interestingly, in spite of the greater explanatory power of the two–factor compared to the one–factor models of yield changes, the optimal one–factor and duration hedges nearly matched the optimal two–factor hedge. This suggests that the changes in shapes of the yield curves during our sample periods were due more to curvature changes than to slope changes.

The tendency of portfolio values to drift away from zero is consistent with this conclusion. In most cases, the hedges were effective for only a few business days, after which changing market conditions required a rebalancing of the hedge. From the perspective of risk management, this finding highlights the dynamic nature of hedging. But from the perspective of trade strategy, this drift in the performance may have been desirable. Investors anticipating changes in the curvature of the yield curve could develop exposure to anticipated changes in shape using a butterfly position. However, the analysis presented earlier suggests that there are potential gains to using a three–factor model when the primary goal is exposure to curvature risk.

The notable differences in factor risk weights across countries suggest that the risk weights change with changing macroeconomic conditions. For best results, then, practical risk management must be forward looking in determining portfolio weights as retrospective calculations based on historical data may have limited effectiveness. Again, this finding applies particularly to *slope* risk. A next step in optimal risk management would therefore be to pursue ways of incorporating forecasts of yield curve slope over the horizon of typical holding periods. Future research will explore risk management strategies that depend on the investor's horizon and which incorporate such forecasts.

References

Asay, M., T. Kikugawa and K. Singleton. "Futures and Price Discovery in the Japanese Government Bond Market," Goldman Sachs Fixed Income Research Working Paper, 1993.

Bollerslev, T. "Generalized Autoregressive Conditional Heteroskedasticity." *Journal of Econometrics* 31 (1986): 307–327.

Chen, R. and L. Scott. "Maximum Likelihood Estimation for a Multi–factor Equilibrium Model of the Term Structure of Interest Rates." University of Georgia working paper, 1992.

Cox, J., J. Ingersoll and S. Ross. "A Theory of The Term Structure of Interest Rates." *Econometrica* 53 (1985): 385–408.

Duffie, D. and R. Kan. "A Yield–Factor Model of Interest Rates," Stanford University Working Paper, 1993.

Litterman, R. and J. Scheinkman. "Common Factors Affecting Bond Returns." Goldman Sachs Fixed Income Research, 1988.

Longstaff, F. and E. Schwartz. "Interest Rate Volatility and the Term Structure: A Two–Factor General Equilibrium Model." *Journal of Finance* 47 (1992):1259–1282.

Schaefer, S. "Immunization and Duration: A Review of Theory, Performance and Applications." *Midland Corporate Finance Journal* (Fall 1984): 41–57.

Shea, G. "Pitfalls in Smoothing Interest Rate Term Structure Data: Equilibrium Models and Spline Approximations." *Journal of Financial and Quantitative Analysis* 19 (1984): 253–269.

Singleton, K. "Regulatory and Institutional Restrictions and Price Discovery in Government Bond Markets." Stanford University manuscript, 1994.

Vasicek, O. and G. Fong. "Term Structure Modeling Using Exponential Splines." *Journal of Finance* 37 (1982): 339–348.

Notes

[1] I am grateful to Ayman Hindy for helpful discussions and to Daisuke Toriumi for helpful discussions and assistance in preparing the figures. Financial support from the Financial Services Research Initiative of the Graduate School of Business is gratefully acknowledged.

[2] See Chen and Scott (1992) for an empirical implementation of multi-factor versions of the Cox, Ingersoll, and Ross model.

[3] The normalization of the variances can be accomplished by redefining the factor sensitivities d_f.

[4] See, for example, Vasecek and Fong (1982) and Shea (1984).

[5] See Singleton (1994) for further discussion of the distributions of deliverable and nondeliverable BUNDs in Germany.

[6] See Asay, Kikugawa, and Singleton (1992) for further discussion of the role of futures in the setting of bond prices in Japan.

[7] The fact that SL and changes in the short-term rates have correlations that exceed -.5 for Germany and the U. S. is not a problem for single-factor hedging since the level factor is taken to be the long-term rate. In fact, as Schaefer (1984) notes, the orthogonality in U. S. data between the level and slope factors using the long-term rate as the level factor recommends the latter choice over a short rate.

[8] More precisely, Δy^{10} was regressed on SL, and the residuals from this regression

were used as the level factor. Note that, by construction, the weights on the level factor in the two representations are identical. This follows from a well-known result in linear regression. To compute the coefficient on x in a multiple regression of y on x and z, one can regress x on z, calculate the residuals e, and then regress y on e and z. The coefficient of e equals the coefficient on x in the original multiple regression.

[9] More precisely, the variance of y^2 was assumed to follow a GARCH model (Bollerslev 1986) augmented by the first lagged value of y^2. The fitted values of this variance process using within–sample estimates of the parameters served to approximate V. The third factor was ΔV_t.

[10] This finding is specific to this sample period. See the concluding section for further discussion.

[11] An alternative one-factor hedge is a *volatility* hedge in which the standard deviations of the price changes in the three bonds are substituted for duration in (24). This hedge is nearly identical to the duration hedge for both sample periods and countries.

[12] More precisely, when $\lambda_2^{u140}\lambda_2^{u78} \neq 0$, then the first-order conditions to the minimization problem (6) can be re-expressed as (25) and (26).

[13] The two-factor representation in terms of correlated factors is also not useful for isolating slope risk when slope and level are correlated.

[14] To compute these weights, we used the factor weights in Table 3 using constant maturity yield series and the durations and prices of specific bonds. During the early sample period, the three bonds were the BOBL 92 (8.75% of 7/20/95), the BOBL 100 (8.25% of 7/21/97), and the BUND (8.% of 7/22/02). During the later sample period, we used the BOBL 96 (8.5% of 4/22/96), Treuhand (6.125% of 3/26/98), and BUND (6.75% of 4/22/03).

The Internal Call Market:
A Clean, Well–Lighted Place to Trade

**Frederick L. A. Grauer, Global Chief Executive
        Officer, Wells Fargo Nikko Investment
        Advisors**

**Terrance Odean, Ph.D. Candidate, Haas School of
        Business, University of California, Berkeley**

Introduction[1]

> "The continuous trading market is an aberration from an
> economic viewpoint and generates a potentially permanent
> instability favoring fraud and manipulation of the market."
>
> — Maurice Allais, Nobel laureate, Economics

Herodotus tells us that in ancient Babylon, "Once in every year the
following course was pursued in every village; whatever maidens were
of marriageable age, they used to collect together and bring in a body to
one place; around them stood a crowd of men. Then a crier, having made
them stand up one by one, offered them for sale, beginning with the most
beautiful; and when she had been sold for a large sum, he put up another
who was next in beauty. ... They were sold on condition that they should
be married." In Herodotus's opinion, this was the wisest of all Babylonian
customs.

While the sale of human beings is abhorrent, this anecdote contains an
economic lesson. Perhaps what impressed Herodotus was that, by
convening an annual market, the Babylonians allowed the supply of and
demand for brides to aggregate over time. This increased the expected
matching ratio of brides and suitors and avoided the potentially permanent
social instability generated by a continuous market. In a continuous market
for brides, the supply of young women and demand for them would have

varied greatly. On days when many more brides were available than suitors, the most beautiful woman might have fetched a pittance. But when suitors greatly outnumbered brides, prices would have soared and fights would have broken out between successful and thwarted suitors. In a society where the price of a bride varied so widely, a young man saving for marriage would have faced great economic uncertainty.

Like the Babylonians, modern institutional investment funds can benefit from the temporal aggregation of a call market.[2] Imagine a large pension fund that is about to invest $100 million in large capitalization equities. How should it purchase these equities? Will it submit market orders to the New York Stock Exchange (NYSE)?

The motivation for this trade is to establish a long–term investment position; the trade is not prompted by any private information. The fund is concerned with the quality of trade execution, not immediacy. The exchanges offer immediate execution but at a cost of trading with informed traders who "cherry pick" market orders. Specialists fill the trades spurned by informed traders, but they quote a bid–ask spread to protect themselves from those same informed traders. Furthermore, with large trades, the specialists are likely to move the bid–ask spreads before completing the orders to compensate themselves for inventory risk. The floor of the exchange may be one of the worst places for an institution without private information to establish a new investment position. The pension fund would like to trade in a low–cost market with other informationless traders. Such traders come to the market frequently but not continuously. A call market can bring these traders together over time. A call market for composite assets (that is, baskets of securities) is an ideal market for passive institutional traders.[3]

In 1973, when Wells Fargo Bank established the first S&P 500 index fund, institutional investors had no alternatives to trading on the exchanges. Twenty years later they have a multitude. They have developed many techniques for managing risk. By investing in portfolios, they diversify and eliminate the idiosyncratic risks associated with individual stocks. By implementing buy and hold strategies, they diversify temporally and eliminate the risks of active trading in volatile markets. By investing in standardized indexed portfolios, implementing buy and hold strategies, and carefully choosing their trading venues, they minimize trading costs and thereby increase their ratio of expected return to risk. By trading in composite assets, they protect themselves from insiders.

This paper discusses various ways institutional investors control investment risk and trading costs. In particular, it describes the internal call markets of index–fund managers. In an internal market, the buy and sell orders of the index fund participants are first matched with each other.

Only unmatched orders are executed externally (e.g., on an exchange or on a crossing network). Although some of these internal markets are large, they have been ignored in the finance literature. A model of such call markets is presented. The paper is organized into the following topics: (1) recent figures on the growth and size of the indexing industry, trading mechanisms used to manage indexed portfolios, and marketplace alternatives to the traditional exchanges; (2) the internal markets of indexers; and (3) a model of these markets. Some of the mathematical calculations for the model are given in an appendix. Throughout the paper, the primary example of an internal call market is that of Wells Fargo Nikko Investment Advisors (WFNIA). The discussion generalizes to the internal call markets of other index fund managers.

Indexing, Trading Mechanisms and Alternative Marketplaces

Indexing has grown significantly since its introduction in the early 1970s. In 1973, domestic and international index funds offered by U.S. managers held $55 million. By the end of 1992, the indexed assets of U.S. managers stood at $389 billion (Figure 1), or 12% of all tax–exempt assets (Figure 2).[4]

Indexing is not confined to the U.S. At the end of 1992, $91.3 billion were invested in index funds offered by non–U.S. managers.[5]

Figure 1

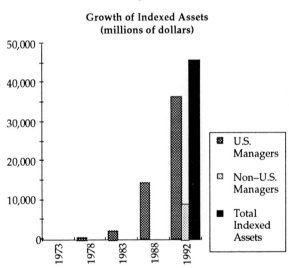

Growth of Indexed Assets (millions of dollars)

Legend:
- U.S. Managers
- Non–U.S. Managers
- Total Indexed Assets

Figure 2

Percentage of Tax–Exempt Assets That Are Indexed

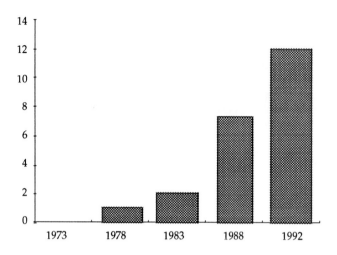

In the early years of indexing, a fund purchasing a complete cross–section of the S&P 500 filled out 500 buy tickets. These were bundled together and delivered to a brokerage firm. The orders were then executed, individually, on the exchange floor and in the over–the–counter market. The process was slow and expensive. Since then, indexing has been a driving force in the development of new trading mechanisms and new marketplaces that serve passive institutional investors. Today, index futures contracts, basis trades, and EFPs (exchange for physical) facilitate the trading of baskets of securities as composite assets. Upstairs block trading, the *rolodex market*, POSIT, Instinet, the NYSE's Crossing Session I, the Arizona Stock Exchange, and the internal call markets of index fund managers offer alternatives to the exchange floor. This section briefly describes each of these.

Composite assets are baskets of securities that can be traded as one asset.[6] Composite assets generally group together securities of a similar investment nature (e.g., high–capitalization stocks or long–term government bonds); thus the securities' essential investment quality is captured while the idiosyncratic risks of individual securities are reduced through diversification. Luskin (1987), Subrahmanyam (1991), and Gorton and Pennacchi (1993) argue that composite assets are well suited for passive investors. By trading in composite assets, passive investors signal the market that they are not trading on private information. Not only does trading in a composite asset signal a trader's lack of information, but also it offers the uninformed trader some protection from informed traders. For example, an informed trader with private information on IBM would not trade the S&P 500 on this information because it would have little impact on the overall index. Instead she would exploit her information by trading IBM stock or its derivatives. The lower adverse selection risks of trading in composite assets result in lower bid–ask spreads. Thus futures on the S&P 500 index have a much smaller bid–ask spread on average than do the individual underlying stocks.

But the smaller spread on the S&P 500 index futures is not only due to lower adverse selection risks. It also results from the great liquidity in S&P 500 index futures. While trading in composite assets mitigates adverse selection risks, only *standardized* composite assets, such as the S&P 500 index, concentrate liquidity (Grauer and Tiemann 1991). As an example, imagine a market with 1000 equity securities. The participants in this market agree that two composite assets, a high–cap 500 index and a low–cap 500 index, should be traded in this market. They further agree as to which 400 stocks are the largest cap and which 400 are the smallest cap. But they disagree as how to allocate the middle 200 stocks to two indexes. There are then $\binom{200}{100} = 9.0*10^{58}$ possible choices of the two composite assets. If each participant attempts to trade a particular choice of composite assets, a trading partner may never appear. Standardized composite assets are needed to obtain the concentration of liquidity found in S&P 500 index futures and in the internal markets of index fund providers.

In 1982, S&P 500 *index futures* were introduced on the Chicago Mercantile Exchange. The average daily trading volume of index futures contracts quickly surpassed the average daily trading volume in the equities underlying the index. Fleming, Ostdiek, and Whaley (1993) estimate that when bid–ask spreads, commissions, and exchange fees are considered, the transaction costs of buying the S&P 500 basket of stocks is 40 times higher than that of buying S&P 500 index futures. Salomon Brothers (1993) calculates the transaction costs of equities to be about 10 times that of futures. The liquidity of the futures market cements the role of the S&P 500 as the investment industry's large–capitalization portfolio standard.

Basis trades are a way for investors, who are restricted from investing in derivative assets, to take advantage of the liquidity of the futures markets. With a basis trade, an investor goes from a cash position to one in equities, or vice versa. The investor obtains futures market prices when they are more favorable than equity market prices without actually trading futures. For example, a pension fund may wish to purchase $100 million of S&P equities. The market impact of this purchase will be greater in the equities market than in the futures market, so a basis trade is arranged with a broker. The pension fund buys futures contracts in the broker's account, and the broker sells equities to the fund. The price of the equities is the average futures price minus an agreed–upon spread, or "basis." The basis is the difference between the futures price and the capitalization–weighted price of the S&P 500 securities minus the broker's implied commission. When the basis trade is complete, the fund owns equities and the broker has a perfectly hedged position: short equities and long futures.

An *EFP* is an exchange of index futures for an indexed basket of securities or vice versa. In 1992, $2.18 billion of S&P 500 EFPs traded on the Chicago Mercantile Exchange. An EFP allows an investor to take advantage of the liquidity in the futures market without changing equity exposure. When might an EFP be used? Suppose a pension fund has recently terminated a money manager. The pension fund does not want the terminated manager to sell the portfolio because he now lacks the incentive to get the best possible prices. The pension fund may bring the portfolio to a transaction management service for restructuring. If the pension fund has chosen to invest in S&P equities, then the part of the portfolio which is not already invested in such equities is sold. The cash proceeds are "equitized," as they are raised, through the purchase of S&P 500 futures contracts. When the pension fund can acquire an S&P 500 portfolio at acceptable transaction costs, the futures are exchanged for equities using an EFP.

Upstairs block trading was one of the first means adopted by institutional investors to cope with the lack of acceptably priced liquidity on the floor of the exchange. In a block trade, an investor wishing to buy or sell a large quantity of a particular security advises a block trader at a brokerage house of the size and desired price of the trade. The block trader finds investors to take the other side of the trade and negotiates a deal with both parties. The trade is then executed at an exchange. By finding and organizing both sides of a large trade, the block trader aggregates order flow that otherwise would not arrive simultaneously on the floor. The block trader earns a commission from both buyers and sellers.

Large institutional investors avoid the block trader's double commission by contacting each other directly through the *rolodex market*. This is a particularly appealing option for trading an entire basket of stocks, such as the S&P 500. When both buyer and seller are passive investors, they will usually agree to trade at some exogenously determined price (a price obtained from an external source such as an exchange) on the agreed–upon day. The trade will be brought to a broker and executed for a commission of about 1/2 cent per share.

POSIT, a crossing network operated by ITG and BARRA, is available to institutional traders but not to brokers, dealers, or specialists. In a crossing network, investors submit orders to buy or sell stocks at exogenously determined prices. The buy and sell orders are matched and executed without a bid–ask spread (that is, the orders are crossed). On POSIT, orders are crossed twice daily: at approximately 11:30 a.m. and 1:30 p.m. (Eastern Standard Time). Stocks are crossed at prices equal to either the midpoint between the National Market System bid–ask spread or that between the best NASDAQ quotes for a commission of 2¢ per share. In 1992, POSIT crossed $33 billion in equities (over 1.1 billion shares). ITG and BARRA now offer GLOBAL POSIT, a weekly crossing network for international securities. Trades on GLOBAL POSIT are executed at the local market close for a commission of 15 basis points (bp).

Instinet Crossing Services offers four crossing networks: The Crossing Network, Market Match, Yen Equities Network (YEN), and U. K. Crossing Network.[7] The Crossing Network matches buyers and sellers daily after the close. Listed issues trade at their closing price on their primary exchange, and over–the–counter (OTC) issues trade at the midpoint between the closing bid and ask quotes for a commission of 1¢ per share. The Crossing Network offers four tiers: passive traders, semi–passive traders, active traders, and broker/dealer/specialists. Traders in higher tiers can choose not to trade with those in lower tiers. For example, passive traders can stipulate that they wish to trade only with other passive traders and with semi–passive traders, but not with active traders and broker/dealer/specialists. In 1992, The Crossing Network crossed $15 billion in equities. Market Match matches buyers and sellers of U.S. equities each trading day before the NYSE opens. Trades cross at the day's volume–weighted average price. YEN is a weekly crossing network for Japanese equities. Trades are executed at the closing prices of the Tokyo Stock Exchange second session for a commission of 15 bp. The U.K. Crossing Network is a weekly crossing network with trades executed at the midpoint of the ISE (International

Stock Exchange) closing spread for a commission of 12.5 bp. The YEN and the U.K. Crossing Networks, as well as GLOBAL POSIT, are recent services with low but growing volumes.

The NYSE offers *Crossing Session I*, an after–hours crossing market.[8] The NYSE does not charge a fee for Crossing Session I; the session is available only through NYSE member firms, and the commissions they charge their clients are negotiated. The session starts following the regular day session and continues until 5:00 p.m. All trades are executed at the NYSE closing price. Crossing Session I accepts both two–sided and one–sided orders. The majority of orders are two–sided; that is, a buyer and seller have already been matched before the order is submitted. One–sided buy and sell orders are matched on a time–priority basis. In 1992, Crossing Session I's volume was $587 million.

The *Arizona Stock Exchange* (AZX) is an electronic call market that opens once a day after the close of the NYSE. Traders submit limit orders. An electronic, rule–based system determines the price that will best clear the market, and orders are crossed at that price. The AZX, unlike POSIT, The Crossing Network and Crossing Session I, has the potential for price discovery. In theory, traders can submit entire supply and demand schedules which, when matched, determine a market price. Most orders are submitted within 1/8 point of the close, and the exchange serves primarily as a crossing network. For the last nine months of 1992, volume on the AZX was $1.3 billion; for the first eight months of 1993, it was $2.0 billion.

Basis trades, EFPs, block trading, the rolodex market, Instinet, POSIT, NYSE after–hours trading, and the Arizona Stock Exchange all attempt to supply institutional investors with liquidity that is too highly priced on the exchange floor. Each is a useful tool for controlling market impact risk, but each has limitations. Basis trades and EFPs are suitable only in particular circumstances. Upstairs block trades can be "front run"[9] and include the risk of dealing with informed traders. The rolodex market is useful when it works, but it has a low success rate. The NYSE crossing sessions, POSIT, The Crossing Network, and the Arizona Stock Exchange all have relatively low matching ratios.[10] Furthermore, if an institution attempts to buy or sell an entire basket of equities through one of these, the basket is picked over; and the institution is forced to complete the unfilled—and most disadvantageous—parts of the trade on the exchange floor.

Passive institutional investors need a marketplace where great liquidity exists, entire baskets of portfolios can be traded, informed traders are excluded, and costs are minimal. Such a marketplace has developed. It is the internal market of large index fund managers.

Internal Call Markets

Though not discussed in the academic literature, the internal markets of index–fund managers facilitate more trading than the crossing networks. For example, in 1992, more than $44 billion in equities traded in WFNIA's internal market alone. Using fund opening days (the days on which the fund is open for contributions and withdrawals) to implement a call market, index fund managers temporally consolidate the supply and demand of their large customer bases. At WFNIA, this typically results in order–matching rates over of 70% for S&P 500 securities on fund opening days. Trades are crossed at market closing prices. Index fund participants bear no transaction costs for trading in this internal market.[11]

The potential savings are so significant that customers sometimes postpone a contribution to or withdrawal from an index fund until it can be matched in the internal market. Suppose a pension fund anticipates a need for cash at a future date. It wishes to maintain its exposure to equities until that date and still benefit from trading in the internal market. It may direct that its units of the index fund be sold only as internal crosses become available. As units are sold, equivalent index futures positions are purchased. When the time comes for the pension fund to withdraw its cash, the futures are sold. In this way, the cost savings of the internal markets are fully captured while an exposure to equities is maintained.

The cost savings of WFNIA's internal market is an estimated $230 million annually in commissions and bid–ask spread losses alone.[12] When foregone market impact is considered, the total savings on such potentially market–moving, large trades must be much greater.

The present structure of such an internal market results from a decision at the inception of the first S&P index fund. When Wells Fargo began this index fund in 1973, the Wells Fargo pension fund was its only customer. A few months later, Illinois Bell agreed to invest $300 million in the fund on the condition that Wells Fargo would first make an equal matching investment, which it did. However, it realized that if the index fund were run like a mutual fund, Wells Fargo would bear over half the transaction costs associated with the Illinois Bell contribution. This is because a mutual fund accepts cash contributions that are used to purchase stock. Since fundholders own a pro–rated share of the fund, they bear a pro–rated share of all trading costs. Early fund participants share the trading costs of subsequent participants, and, contrary to the spirit of passive investment, buy–and–hold investors are effectively punished for the trading of other investors. Wells Fargo rejected the mutual fund model and determined that investors would bear the costs of transactions made on their behalf but not the costs of transactions made for others. Thus, from an accounting standpoint, incoming investors first buy securities and then contribute them to the fund in exchange for units of the fund. When investors wish to sell their units, securities are sold on their behalf. On fund opening days, some investors buy units of a particular fund while others sell. To the best extent possible, these buy and sell orders are matched with one another. They constitute the largest part of the internal market: unit exchanges.

In 1987, WFNIA sought and obtained Department of Labor authorization to cross the orders of customers moving between funds provided that the crossing prices were exogenously determined. Like unit exchanges crosses, between–funds are done at market closing prices.

The New York Stock Exchange originally was organized as a call market, but by 1900 it had begun continuous trading.[13] In 1986, the Paris Bourse became the last of the world's major equity exchanges to switch from a periodic call market to continuous trading. Some see the transition of exchanges from call to continuous trading as the natural triumph of a superior market structure. Huang and Stoll (1992) cite the case of the Bourse when advising stock exchanges to "adopt a continuous trading system for active markets." Perhaps this advice should be changed to "adopt a continuous trading system for active traders." Evidence indicates that passive traders may be better served by call markets.

Passive investors have different needs from informed traders. Passive investors make diversified, long–term investments. Since their investment choices are not based on rapidly changing beliefs or short–lived information, they do not need the ability to trade every second of the day— or even every day. While immediacy of trade execution is not important to the passive trader, quality of execution is. Institutional passive investors often make large trades that can temporarily move markets and thereby reduce anticipated returns. Controlling trading costs and risks is an important part of passive trading. Informed traders, on the other hand, commonly make shorter horizon investments in specific stocks about which they have information. If their information is short lived, they willingly pay larger commissions, bid–ask spreads, and market–impact costs to facilitate immediate trades. With such disparate trading requirements, it is not surprising that passive investors and informed traders are best served by different market structures.

Schwartz (1992) writes, "Thus far, the assumption that participants demand transactional immediacy has gone practically unquestioned. Would some asset managers choose not to pay the price of immediacy if they truly understood the cost of the service and if they had an alternative?" We believe that passive institutional investors have come to understand the cost of continuous trading and that they are not willing to pay it. The world's exchanges may be switching to continuous trading, but many of its institutional investors are leaving the exchanges for the call trading found in crossing networks and the internal markets of index fund managers.

Grossman and Stiglitz (1980) show that, when information is costly, it is optimal for a subset of investors to collect information and for the rest to "free ride" on the information in the price. We contend that, by free riding on the price discovery of others, institutional passive investors may actually improve the quality of price discovery. The non–synchronous arrival on the exchange floor of large orders strains the specialist's ability to provide liquidity. Even when such trades are clearly identified as informationless, the specialist may not be willing to take on large inventory risk for fear that the market will move against her before she has had a chance to trade out of the inventory. Such large, informationless trades may move the market and increase the volatility of prices without revealing more information. They are better executed in a market that aggregates sufficient liquidity to accommodate large, informationless trades.[14] A simple model shows how call markets create liquidity for informationless trades.

A Model of Internal Call Markets

With the growth of crossing networks and of the internal markets of index fund providers, call markets without price discovery have become economically important. Our model is of an internal market provided

---

by the manager of a single index fund. The model applies also to a noncontinuous crossing network in one security.[15] The index fund in our model holds shares in the basket of stocks that comprise the index. This basket of stocks constitutes a single composite asset. On fund openings, participants place orders to buy or sell the composite asset. Buy and sell orders are first matched in the internal market, where there are no trading costs. Unmatched orders are filled on a pro–rated basis in the external market, where there are positive trading costs. We assume that, at fund openings, participants choose investment levels in the composite asset which optimize their utility functions. Participants have liquidity needs that change continuously, so their optimal investment levels also change continuously. However, they must wait until the next fund opening before trading to meet their liquidity needs and returning to optimal investment positions. Thus, participants bear an opportunity cost in waiting for fund openings.

Price discovery plays no role in the model; buy and sell orders are not contingent on some reservation price. Price is assumed to be fixed and exogenously determined. All trading is informationless and motivated solely by liquidity needs.

Other researchers have studied call markets in the context of price discovery. Gresik and Satterthwaite (1989) find that, in an economy where agents have privately known reservation prices, the expected inefficiency of optimally designed market mechanisms decreases almost quadratically as the number of agents increases. Bhattacharaya and Majumdar (1973) derive a bound on how well excess demand can be approximated by a normal distribution; this bound is inversely proportional to the square root of the number of agents in the economy. Our measure of efficiency—one minus the ratio of the expected costs when an internal market is available to the expected costs when it is not—increases as number of market participants grows.

In a partially informed economy, Goldman and Sosin (1979) show that "if sufficient uncertainty surrounds the dissemination of information, frequent transacting may be deleterious to market efficiency." They prove the existence of a unique optimal time interval between market openings. Garbade and Silber (1979) model a market where investors enter at a constant rate and in which clearing occurs periodically. The clearing price is determined by investors' demand functions. Garbade and Silber derive the period between market clearings that minimizes the variances of the difference between the clearing price and the equilibrium price. They find that this optimal period is inversely proportional to the square root of the entry rate. We look at total cost as a function of the number of fund participants and the time between fund openings. We derive closed–form solutions for the optimal time between fund openings for risk–neutral participants and for a class of risk–averse participants. Like Goldman and Sosin, we find a unique, non–zero optimal period between market openings.

Mendelson (1982) and Harris (1990) model call markets in which traders submit limit orders reflecting their demand curves. In our model, trades are neither motivated by nor contingent on prices.

Cohen, Maier, Schwartz, and Whitcolm (1982) examine two possible structures of a limit–order market that is run in–house by a brokerage firm. Like our model, theirs is of an in–house, or internal, market. In our market, prices are determined exogenously and execution is determined internally. In theirs, customers set prices with limit orders but execution depends on external prices. Their market, unlike ours, is continuous. Cohen, Maier, Schwartz and Whitcolm find, as do we, that the effectiveness of an internal market increases with its size.

Our model is from one fund opening at $t = 0$ to the next fund opening at $t = T$. There are N index fund participants. (A prototypical participant would be a pension fund.) At $t = 0$, each participant determines and makes an optimal investment in the index fund. Each participant has an exogenously driven liquidity process, $L_{i,t}$, that follows a Wiener process with mean zero and variance $\sigma^2 t$. The liquidity processes are independent of each other (and can be thought of as the flow of money into and out of a pension fund). When that flow is positive, cash reserves build up which the participants want to invest in the index fund. When the cashflow is negative, the participants want to sell shares of the index fund to meet cash needs. By waiting to trade at fund openings, participants incur an opportunity cost. For example, a participant's borrowing interest rate may be higher than her risk–free lending rate, and her risk–adjusted expected return from the fund may lie between them. When she has an inflow of cash, she would like to invest it immediately in the index fund; but she must settle for the lower return from lending the cash while she waits for a fund opening. As another example, the manager of a pension fund has guidelines regarding the amount of cash held by the fund. If too much cash (or too much borrowing) accumulates in the fund, he violates the guidelines and appears to be managing poorly. In waiting for the opportunity to rebalance at a fund opening, he bears a cost. The model assumes that the opportunity cost is proportional to the absolute value of L_t by a factor of C_2.[16]

At $t = T$, each participant trades $L_{i,T}$ to return to his optimal holding in the index fund.[17] His trading needs are first matched internally with those of other participants. Unmatched orders are traded externally. We assume that demands crossed in the internal market incur no trading costs. External trading costs are proportional to the amount traded and are the same for buying and selling. The cost of external trading is a constant, C_1, times the absolute value of the unmatched portion of the liquidity needs.

Thus, participants have two different types of costs: opportunity costs and external trading costs.

If the fund has only one participant, $(N = 1)$, all trades will be external and expected trading costs are:

$$C_1 \cdot E\big(|L_T|\big) = C_1 \cdot \sigma \sqrt{\frac{2T}{\pi}} . \tag{1}$$

When $N > 1$, the expected trading costs per participant are the expected net trading needs after each participant's orders have been matched with each other, times the external trading cost constant, divided by the number of participants:

$$\frac{C_1}{N} \cdot E\Big(\Big|\sum_{i=1}^{N} L_{i,T}\Big|\Big)_{-} = C_1 \cdot \sigma \sqrt{\frac{2T}{N \cdot \pi}} \tag{2}$$

We compare the expected trading costs of internal market participants, for whom only unmatched orders are traded externally, to the expected trading costs of investors who have no internal market and must trade all orders externally. One minus the ratio of these expectations measures the cost savings of the internal market.[18]

$$1 - \frac{E\big[Trading\ costs\ with\ internal\ market\big]}{\big[Trading\ costs\ without\ internal\ market\big]} = 1 - \frac{1}{\sqrt{N}} . \tag{3}$$

Multiplied by 100, this measure can be expressed as a percentage.

Figure 3

Expected Savings of Internal Market

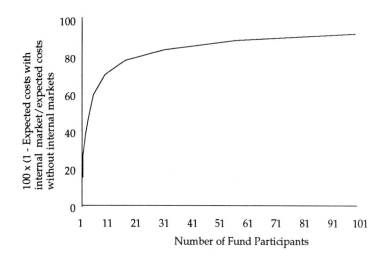

Number of Fund Participants

As the time between openings of the market increases, the amount of trading at any one opening increases with the square root of time. While this is a one–period model, we assume that participants remain in the fund period after period. Of primary interest to a participant is the expected amount of trading (external) per unit of time (e.g., one year) rather than the expected amount of trading at any one opening. Expected trading per unit of time is a decreasing function of period length, T :

$$E\left(\frac{trading}{T}\right) = \sigma\sqrt{\frac{2}{\pi \cdot T \cdot N}} \ . \tag{4}$$

Though the expected trading and expected trading costs per unit of time decrease asymptotically to 0 as the time between fund openings increases, fund participants cannot wait forever to trade. To find the optimal period between fund openings, participants must balance the lower trading costs of longer periods with increasing opportunity costs.

To derive the optimal period between fund openings, we first consider risk–neutral participants wishing to minimize expected total costs. Then we examine a class of risk–averse participants wishing to minimize risk–adjusted total costs.

Let $Q_1(N,T,\sigma)$ be a participant's external trading costs:

$$E[Q_1(N,T,\sigma)] = C_1 \cdot \sigma \sqrt{\frac{2T}{\pi \cdot N}}. \qquad (5)$$

Let $F_1(N,T,\sigma) = \dfrac{Q_1(N,T,\sigma)}{T}$, be a participant's trading costs per unit of time. Then

$$E[F_1(N,T,\sigma)] = \frac{k_1}{\sqrt{T}}, \text{ where } k_1 = C_1\sigma \cdot \sqrt{\frac{2}{\pi \cdot N}}. \qquad (6)$$

Opportunity costs are assumed to be proportional to the absolute value of L_t. (Compounding of opportunity costs is ignored.) The instantaneous opportunity cost is $C_2|L_t|dt$. Let

$$Q_2(T,\sigma) = \int_0^T C_2|L_t|dt$$

be a participant's cumulative opportunity costs over the non–trading period. Then

$$E[Q_2(T,\sigma)] = \frac{2C_2\sigma}{3}\sqrt{\frac{2}{\pi}} \cdot T^{\frac{3}{2}}. \qquad (7)$$

Let $F_2(T,\sigma) = \dfrac{Q_2(T,\sigma)}{T}$ be a participant's cumulative opportunity costs per unit of time. Then

$$E[F_2(T,\sigma)] = k_2\sqrt{T}, \text{ where } k_2 = \frac{2C_2\sigma}{3}\sqrt{\frac{2}{\pi}}, \qquad (8)$$

is the expected opportunity cost per unit of time.

To find the optimal period between fund openings, T^*, the expected total cost function $E[F_{total}] = E[F_1] + E[F_2]$ is differentiated with respect to T and set equal to zero:

$$T^* = \frac{k_1}{k_2} = \frac{3C_1}{2C_2\sqrt{N}} \qquad (9)$$

For risk–neutral participants, T^* is unaffected by the rate of diffusion in the liquidity process (σ). T^* is decreasing as opportunity costs (C_2) go up, decreasing as the number of participants in the fund (N) grows, and increasing as external trading costs (C_1) increase. Consistent with these last two findings are the observations that (1) WFNIA's S&P 500 index funds (which have many participants and lower trading costs) open weekly; (2) intermediate capitalization equity index funds (which have fewer participants and higher external trading costs) open every other week; and (3) the Russell 1000 and Russell 3000 index funds (which have yet higher external trading costs) open monthly.[19] Similarly, POSIT and The Crossing Network offer domestic equity crossing sessions once or twice daily; these sessions have high volume and low trading costs. But GLOBAL POSIT, YEN, and the U. K. Crossing Network offer international crossing sessions only once a week; these sessions have lower volume and higher trading costs than their domestic counterparts. Our model predicts that as volume builds on GLOBAL POSIT, YEN and the U. K. Crossing Network (or as trading costs drop), crossing sessions will be held more frequently.

Figure 4

Expected Trading Costs per Unit of Time

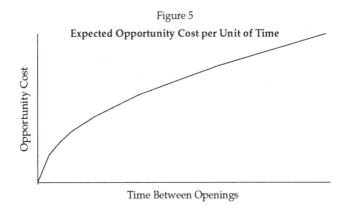

Figure 5

Expected Opportunity Cost per Unit of Time

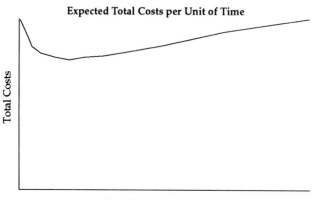

Figure 6

Expected Total Costs per Unit of Time

Total Costs

Time Between Openings

Next, consider a class of risk–averse participants wishing to minimize risk–adjusted total costs. Each participant wishes to minimize the function,

$$V = \frac{E(Q_1)}{T} + \frac{E(Q_2)}{T} + \frac{VAR(Q_1)}{T \cdot \rho} + \frac{\int_0^T E(C_2|L_2)^2 \, dt}{T \cdot \upsilon}, \tag{10}$$

where Q_1 and Q_2 are defined as before, and ρ and υ are the same for each participant.[20] To find the optimal period between fund openings, T^*, V is differentiated with respect to T and set equal to 0. (This is done in the appendix.)

For risk–averse participants, unlike risk–neutral participants, T^* changes as the rate of diffusion in the liquidity process (σ) changes; the direction of change depends on other parameter values. As in the risk–neutral case, T^* decreases as opportunity costs (C_2) go up and as the number of participants in the fund (N) grows. It increases as external trading costs (C_1) increase. T^* increases as the measures of risk tolerance, ρ and υ, increase.

Figure 7

Expected Total Risk–Adjusted Costs per Unit of Time

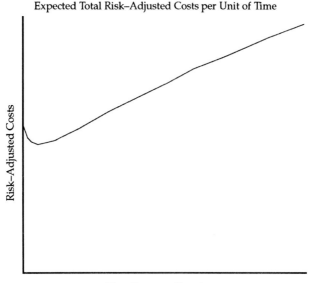

The model assumes that the liquidity processes for all fund participants have zero drift, i.e., at the beginning of a period, participants do not know whether they are more likely to be buyers or sellers at the end of the period. Relaxing this assumption, we allow for participants who plan to increase or decrease their investment level over the next period in addition to meeting their normal liquidity needs. This can be represented by assigning each participant's liquidity process a randomly determined drift component $\mu_1 \sim N(0, \sigma_\mu)$. The drift components are independent and are identically distributed. At the beginning of the period, each participant knows his own drift component but not those of other participants. More important, the index fund provider does not know the individual drift components; he only knows their distributions. The fund provider must determine the fund opening period that is optimal for the participants.

From the fund provider's point of view, each participant's liquidity process now has two random components: the drift component and the diffusion component. As before, the diffusion component, $L_{\sigma,t}$, is distributed $N(0, \sigma^2 \cdot t)$. The drift component, $L_{\mu,t}, = \mu \cdot t$, is distributed $N(0, \sigma_\mu^2 \cdot t)$. Thus, from the fund provider's point of view at $t = 0$, the total liquidity

$L_t = L_{\mu,t} + L_{\sigma,t}$ is distributed $N\left(0,\left(\sigma^2 + \sigma_\mu^2\right) \cdot t\right)$, at any $t,(0 <= t <= T)$. Although the individual liquidity processes are not $\left(0, \sigma^2 + \sigma_\mu^2\right)$ Wiener processes, the fund provider can nevertheless substitute $\left(\sigma^2 + \sigma_\mu^2\right) \cdot t$ for the variance of the liquidity process in the previous calculations of T^*. As noted above for risk–neutral investors (but not for risk–averse investors), the optimal period between fund openings will be unaffected by the increased variance of the liquidity process.

Our model simplifies the reality of an index fund provider's internal market. It makes no provision for new participants entering the market. In the last 20 years, indexing has grown steadily. On average, more money has flowed into rather than out of funds. With such a positive trend incorporated into the model, transaction costs savings will still increase as fund participants grow, but the increase will be slower. So too, if the model's participants have positively correlated liquidity processes, transaction costs savings will increase more slowly as a function of N.

In the model, participants meet their liquidity needs by trading in only one composite asset. In reality, participants may invest in several index funds and choose among them to meet liquidity demands. This too lowers the savings of transaction costs. The low matching rates on POSIT, The Crossing Network, and the Arizona Stock Exchange may be partially due to the fragmentation of liquidity among the many securities traded in these markets.

Conclusion

The marketplace constantly evolves to meet the needs of its many participants. Twenty years ago, Wells Fargo introduced the first S&P 500 index fund to meet the needs of institutional investors who wished to make long–term, well–diversified investments at a low cost. The growth of indexing has been accompanied by the growth of index fund managers' internal markets. Trading within these markets is done without bid–ask spread, commissions, or market impact; it is virtually free of transaction costs. We have seen how these internal markets achieve cost savings by bringing together many investors, aggregating liquidity through call trading, and concentrating trading on composite assets. Composite assets, like the internal markets, have evolved with indexing. Composite assets diversify away idiosyncratic risk, protect investors from traders with inside information, and facilitate low–cost trading in the internal markets of index fund managers. They are excellent vehicles for long–term investment strategies, and the internal markets are an ideal place to trade them.

Appendix

To calculate equation (3) we observe that $\left|\sum_{i=1}^{N} L_{i,T}\right|$ and $\left|L_{i,T}\right|$ have half–normal distributions:

$$1 - \frac{E[\text{Trading costs with internal market}]}{E[\text{Trading costs without internal market}]} =$$

$$1 - \frac{C_1 E\left[\left|\sum_{i=1}^{N} L_{i,T}\right|\right]}{C_1 E\left[\left|\sum_{i=1}^{N} L_{i,t}\right|\right]} = \tag{11}$$

$$1 - \frac{N C_1 \sigma \sqrt{\dfrac{2T}{N \cdot \pi}}}{N C_1 \sigma \sqrt{\dfrac{2T}{\pi}}} = 1 - \frac{1}{\sqrt{N}}$$

To derive equation (7), we integrate the expected instantaneous opportunity costs from 0 to T:

$$E\left[Q_2(T,\sigma)\right] = \int_{0}^{T} \int_{-\infty}^{\infty} \frac{C_2 \cdot |L_t|}{\sqrt{2\pi\sigma^2 t}} e^{-\frac{L_t^2}{2\sigma^2 t}} dL_t \, dt =$$

$$C_2 \cdot \int_{0}^{T} \sigma \sqrt{\frac{2t}{\pi}} dt \ . \tag{12}$$

$$= \frac{2C_2 \sigma}{3} \sqrt{\frac{2}{\pi}} \cdot T^{\frac{3}{2}}$$

To find the optimal period between fund openings, T^*, the expected total cost function $E[F_{total}] = E[F_1] + E[F_2]$ is differentiated with respect to T and set equal to zero.

$$E[F_{total}(N,T,\sigma)] = \frac{k_1}{\sqrt{T}} + k_2 \cdot \sqrt{T} \tag{13}$$

$$\frac{dE[F_{total}(N,T,\sigma)]}{dT} = \frac{-k_1}{2} \cdot T^{-\frac{3}{2}} + \frac{k_2}{2} T^{-\frac{1}{2}} = 0 \qquad (14)$$

and since $T > 0$,

$$T^* = \frac{k_1}{k_2} = \frac{3C_1}{2C_2\sqrt{N}} \qquad (15)$$

To solve for T^* in the risk–averse case, we first calculate

$$V = \frac{E(Q_1)}{T} + \frac{E(Q_2)}{T} + \frac{VAR(Q_1)}{T \cdot \rho} + \frac{\int_0^T E(C_2 L_2)^2 \, dt}{T \cdot \rho}. \qquad (10)$$

The first two terms of (12) are known from the risk–neutral case. To derive the third term of equation (12), $\dfrac{VAR(Q_1)}{T \cdot \rho}$, we use the expectation of the half–normal distributions of $\left| \sum_{i=1}^{N} L_{i,T} \right|$ and $\left| L_{i,T} \right|$, to calculate $var(Q_1)$:

$$\frac{VAR(Q_1)}{T \cdot \rho} = \frac{1}{T \cdot \rho} E \left[\left(\frac{C_1 \left| \sum_N L_T \right|}{N} \right)^2 - \left[E \left(\frac{C_1 \left| \sum_N L_T \right|}{N} \right) \right]^2 \right] =$$

$$\frac{1}{T \cdot \rho} \left[\frac{C_1^2 \sigma^2 T}{N} - \frac{2 C_1^2 \sigma^2 T}{\pi \cdot N} \right] = \qquad (16)$$

$$\frac{C_1^2 \sigma^2}{N \cdot \rho} \left(1 - \frac{2}{\pi} \right) = k_3$$

To calculate the fourth term in equation (12), $\dfrac{\int_0^T E(C_2 |L_2|)^2 \, dt}{T \cdot \rho}$, we integrate the expected instantaneous opportunity cost from 0 to T:

$$\frac{\int_0^T E\left(C_2|L_2|\right)^2 dt}{T \cdot \rho} = \frac{1}{T \cdot \rho} \cdot \int_0^T \int_{-\infty}^{\infty} C_2^2 \frac{L_t^2}{\sqrt{2\pi\sigma^2 t}} e^{-\frac{L_t^2}{2\sigma^2 t}} dL_t dt$$

$$= \frac{C_2^2}{T \cdot \rho} \cdot \int_0^T \sigma^2 t \, dt \qquad (17)$$

$$= k_4 T, \text{ where } k_4 = \frac{C_2^2 \sigma^2}{2\rho}$$

Thus

$$V = \frac{k_1}{\sqrt{T}} + k_2 \cdot \sqrt{T} + k_3 + k_4 T. \qquad (18)$$

Differentiating with respect to T, and setting equal to 0, we get:

$$\frac{dV}{dT} = \frac{-k_1}{2} \cdot T^{-\frac{3}{2}} + \frac{k_2}{2} T^{-\frac{1}{2}} + k_4 = 0 \qquad (19)$$

Bearing in mind that $T^* > 0$, (13) can be solved for T^*, the optimal time between fund openings for the given class of risk averse investors:

$$T^* = \frac{b^2}{3c^2} + 2^{\frac{1}{3}}$$

$$\left(b^4 + 6abc^2\right) \Big/ 3c^2 \left(2b^6 + 18ab^3c^2 + 27a^2c^4 + 3^{\frac{3}{2}} c^3 \sqrt{4a^3b^3 + 27a^4c^2}\right)^{\frac{1}{3}} \qquad (20)$$

$$+ \left(2b^6 + 18ab^3c^4 + 3^{\frac{3}{2}} c^3 \sqrt{4a^3b^3 + 27a^4c^2}\right)^{\frac{1}{3}} \Big/ 3 \cdot \sqrt[3]{2} \, c^2$$

where $a = \frac{-k_1}{2}$, $b = \frac{k_2}{2}$, and $c = k_4$.

Notes

1. We wish to thank Truman Clark, Jonathan Tiemann, and Klaus Toft for very helpful conversations and comments. We also wish to thank Eric Clothier, Patricia Dunn, Blake Grossman, Bertrand Jacquillat, Hayne Leland, Donald Luskin, Jim Ross, Mark Rubinstein, Jeff Skelton and Kathy Sonderby for their comments. All errors are ours.

2. In a call market, trading in a particular commodity takes place only at specific times when the market for that commodity is "called."

3. Passive traders and investors make long–term buy and hold investments. Their trades are motivated by liquidity needs—not by private information—and are termed "informationless." Trades made on the basis of private information are informed trades.

4. Assets indexed by U.S. managers are from a Rogers Casey survey of index fund providers. These figures are understated because not all index fund providers responded to the survey and because indexed assets managed internally by pensions funds are not included in totals. These totals are the numerator for the percentage of tax–exempt assets indexed. The denominator is the total U.S. tax–exempt assets from "The Money Market Directory of Pension Funds and their Investment Managers 1993" (Money Market Directories, Inc.: Charlottesville, VA). This includes all tax–exempt funds with assets over $1 million.

5. Intersec Research.

6. Two exchange–traded composite assets, Standard and Poor's Depository Receipts (SPY) and Index Super Units (ZIU), have recently been introduced on the American Stock Exchange. For discussions of a variety of composite asset alternatives, see Rubinstein (1989) and Harris (1990 JFM).

7. Instinet Corporation also runs the Instinet Real Time Trading System, an anonymous, negotiated, electronic trading system.

8. The NYSE also offers Crossing Session II for aggregate–priced multi–stock orders. All Crossing Session II orders are two–sided. Orders must be trades of at least 15 listed stocks with a value of at least $1 million. No order matching is done in Crossing Session II. Rather, previously agreed–upon trades are executed.

9. A block trade is front run when the broker, or some other trader who is aware of the pending trade, makes a trade before the block trade to profit from the price impact of the block trade. It is generally illegal for a broker to front run a customer.

10. The Crossing Network and AZX report share matching rates of 7% and 5%, respectively. These rates are not automatically comparable to each other or to matching rates on other crossing networks or exchanges. For both The Crossing Network and AZX, matching ratios are higher for liquid and high capitalization stocks, for unconstrained orders, and for orders matched than for shares matched. This is because large orders are completely filled less often than small orders. POSIT does not keep data on unfilled orders or on matching rates. Matching rates are not relevant for Crossing Session I since the majority of orders are two sided.

11. Transaction costs include commissions, bid–ask spread, and risk of market impact. Fund participants pay usual investment management fees but (at WFNIA) there are no additional charges when they trade in the internal market.

12. For domestic stocks, this estimate assumes commissions of 4¢ per share, 1/2 bid–offer spread of 23 bp for S&P 500 stocks, 90 bp for extended market stocks, and 168 bp for low–cap stocks; for international stocks an average of 101 bp in costs are assumed.

13. The NYSE still opens daily trading with a call market.

14. While removing large informationless trades may have benefits in a specialist–based exchange, removing all informationless trades would not be beneficial and could even result in no trading. Black (1991) suggests that an exchange should address the needs of its informationless traders so that they do not migrate to other trading venues.

15. We assume that the transaction costs in the internal market are zero. To model crossing

---

networks, a cost function should be added for internally crossed trades.

[16] The authors wish to thank Klaus Toft for discussions helpful to developing of the model.

[17] Hereafter, the subscript i in $L_{i,t}$ will be suppressed when it is possible to do so without ambiguity.

[18] Because C_1 appears in both the numerator and denominator of the ratio, we are in effect calculating

$$1-E\left[\left|\sum_{i=1}^{N}L_{i,T}\right|\right]\Bigg/E\left[\sum_{i=1}^{N}|L_{i,T}|\right].$$

This is not the same as the expected matching rate, which is:

$$1-E\left[\left|\sum_{i=1}^{N}L_{i,T}\right|\Bigg/\sum_{i=1}^{N}|L_{i,T}|\right].$$

The two are, however, approximately equal. Numerical estimation shows that

$$E\left[\left|\sum_{i=1}^{N}L_{i,T}\right|\Bigg/\sum_{i=1}^{N}|L_{i,T}|\right]\approx\frac{1}{\sqrt{N}},$$

and that for $N>10$, the approximation is within one per cent.

[19] While the majority of WFNIA's S&P 500 index funds open weekly, a few open daily.

[20] Implicit in the choice of risk–adjusted cost function is an assumption that the crossing rate and the realized opportunity costs are not correlated. For large N, the assumption is a good approximation; for very small N it is not.

The term ρ is a measure of a participant's tolerance for variation in transaction costs. The fourth term of

$$V,\ \int_{0}^{T}E\big(C_2|L_2|\big)^2\,dt\Big/T\cdot\upsilon,$$

emphasizes a participant's aversion to large temporary liquidity imbalances. (For example, a four–week period with three weeks of zero–liquidity imbalance and one week of $400,000 imbalance would be less desirable than a four–week period with a constant imbalance of $100,000.) The term υ measures a participant's tolerance for such temporary imbalances. An alternative risk–adjusted cost function would be to replace the fourth term of V with

$$\text{var}\left(\int_{0}^{T}C_2|L_t|dt\right)\Big/T\cdot\upsilon.$$

Such a specification emphasizes a participant's aversion to variation in cumulative opportunity costs.

References

Allais, M. *The Los Angeles Times* (October 26, 1989), D1.

Bhattacharya, R. N. and M. Majumdar. "Random Exchange Economies." *Journal of Economic Theory* 6 (1973): 37–67.

Black, F. "Exchanges and Equilibrium." Unpublished manuscript, Goldman Sachs, 1991.

Cassady, R. Jr. *Auctions and Auctioneering*. Berkeley, CA: University of California Press, 1967.

Cohen, K. J., S. F. Maier, R. A. Schwartz, and D. K. Whitcomb. "An Analysis of the Economic Justification for Consolidation in a Secondary Security Market." *Journal of Banking and Finance* 6 (1982): 117–136.

Fleming, J., B. Ostdiek and R. Whaley. "The Integration of Stock, Futures, and Options Markets: Evidence from the Index Derivatives." Unpublished manuscript, Duke University, 1993.

Goldman, M. B. and H. B. Sosin. "Information Dissemination, Market Efficiency and the Frequency of Transactions." *Journal of Financial Economics* 7 (1979): 29–61.

Gorton, G. B., and G. G. Pennacchi. "Security Baskets and Index–linked Securities." *Journal of Business* 66, 1 (1993): 1–27.

Grauer, F. L. A., and J. Tiemann. "The Economics of Passive Investing." In Grauer and Okamoto, eds., *Investment Strategy in the New Era: The Practical Use of Investment Technology*. Tokyo: Toyo Keizai Shinposha, 1991.

Gresik, T., and Satterthwaite. "The Rate at Which a Simple Market Converges to Efficiency as the Number of Traders Increases: An Asymptotic Result for Optimal Trading Mechanisms." *Journal of Economic Theory* 48 (1989): 304:332.

Grossman, S., and J. Stiglitz. "On the Impossibility of Informationally Efficient Markets." *American Economic Review* 70:3 (1980): 393–408.

Harris, L. E. "The Economics of Cash Index Alternatives." *The Journal of Futures Markets* 10:2 (1990): 179–194.

Harris, L. E. "Liquidity, Trading Rules, and Electronic Trading Systems." Monograph 1990-4, Stern School of Business, New York University, 1990.

Huang, R. and H. Stoll. "The Design of Trading Systems: Lessons from Abroad." *Financial Analysts Journal*, September–October (1992): 49–54.

Herodotus. *The Histories of Herodotus*. Trans. by Henry Cary. New York: D. Appleton and Co., 1899.

Luskin, D. L. "The Marketplace for 'Composite Assets'." *The Journal of Portfolio Management* (Fall 1987): 12–19.

Mendelson, H. "Market Behavior in a Clearing House." *Econometrica* 50:6 (1982): 1505–1524.

Rubenstein, M. 1989, "Market Basket Alternatives" *Financial Analysts Journal*, September–October 1989, 20–29, & 61.

Salomon Brothers (G. Gastineau). "A Framework for the Analysis of Portfolio Execution Costs—Stocks Versus Derivatives." Salomon Brothers Report, 1993.

Schwartz, R. A. "Competition and Efficiency." In Lehn, K. and R. Kamphuis, Jr., eds. *Modernizing U. S.Securities Regulation: Economic and Legal Perspectives*. Homewood, IL: Business One Irwin, 1992, 341–351.

Schwartz, R. A. *Reshaping the Equity Markets: A Guide for the 1990s*. New York,NY: Harper Business, 1991.

Subrahmanyam, A. "A Theory of Trading in Stock Index Futures." *The Review of Financial Studies* 4:1 (1991): 17–51.

The Future of Futures

Myron S. Scholes, Professor, Graduate School of Business, Stanford University; and Principal, Long–Term Capital Management

Introduction

This chapter describes the evolution of the financial infrastructure into the next century. We argue that derivative instruments are one of the foundations of this new infrastructure. We focus on the significant and expanding role that derivatives will play in reducing the frictions involved in providing financial services. This reduction in frictions will enable investors to do business more efficiently and profitably. Moreover, it will reduce the cost of capital to firms.

After an overview of recent developments in financial innovation and change, we discuss the ability of derivative instruments to reduce frictions. Derivatives break cashflows into finer gradients and thus provide investors and issuers with the particular cashflows they desire. We view derivatives as elemental building blocks in creating tailor–made investments that provide payoff patterns to match investors' demand. This customizing ability of derivatives is the basis for the evolution of the financial infrastructure. Subsequent sections of the paper address issues relating to this evolution from the viewpoints of financial institutions, regulators, and academic researchers.

Background

Over the last ten to fifteen years, we have witnessed an explosive growth in financial innovation and new financial products. For example, ten years ago, automatic teller machines were rarely used to facilitate transactions processing. Almost all entities now accept credit cards in a global economy. Financial intermediaries such as banks, insurance companies, and investment banks have created many new financing alternatives to facilitate large–scale projects by corporations and other entities on a global basis. The explosive growth of mutual funds in the U. S. and other investment programs abroad has provided vehicles for individuals to save either directly or indirectly through pension accounts. These vehicles allow individuals not only to transfer resources through time but also to allocate resources globally. New and innovative risk–sharing mechanisms have been developed over the last ten years to allow individuals and corporations to pool risks and to share them efficiently with other parties. For example, ten years ago corporations rarely used derivative contracts to hedge risks. Organized financial markets have experienced growth on a global scale. The Asian and European markets, along with the U. S., are active in trading bonds, stocks, and commodities. Listed futures and options exchanges have flourished around the world. Without the development of these markets in standardized contracts, many of the over–the–counter innovations fostered by financial institutions could not have been developed. These listed markets provide important price signals to investors and corporations as to how to allocate resources among competing ends.

Each of the above examples of financial innovation and change stresses the functions of a financial system. Merton (1993) and Sanford (1993), for example, emphasize that a focus on the functions of the financial system will provide a road map to future innovations in financial techniques, services and products. Financial infrastructures will develop that provide more efficient alternatives to (1) facilitate transactions, (2) supply funding for large–scale projects, (3) transfer savings into the future and across markets, (4) provide for more efficient risk–sharing and risk–pooling mechanisms, and (5) transmit more efficient price signals to market participants.

These developments are hindered by market frictions. Unfortunately, we live in a second–best world. Transaction costs are a necessary part of all financial interactions. These costs include asymmetric information costs, the hidden information and action costs of dealing with other entities. For example, an investment bank incurs expenses not only to design a new financial product but also to inform customers that the product provides the stated functions and that the price of the product is not too high. This is a hidden information cost. Investment fund managers and their investors incur dead–weight costs when fund mangers act as agents for investors. This is a hidden action cost.

New financial innovation tends to reduce the friction costs of providing financial services. The successful financial innovators are those that provide financial services at lower friction costs. Although the functions of a financial system have been fairly static for many generations, the nature and costs of financial services change over time.

Surprisingly, many practitioners and regulators focus not on the financial functions but on the institutions that serve market participants. The manner in which financial services are provided is less important than the types of financial services that financial institutions provide. In recent years, financial regulators have tried to save many financial institutions, e.g., the savings and loan industry in the U. S., even when other entities provided their products more efficiently. A whole new infrastructure had developed to repackage mortgage contracts, the former mainstay of the savings and loan industry. Mortgage buyers no longer needed to go to a full–service shop to secure a mortgage. Now it is just as likely that a mutual fund investor, a pension fund, a hedge fund, a bank, or any other entity buys and sells mortgage pools. Banks, mutual funds and other entities provide secure mechanisms for investors' savings.

Regulation has aimed to shore up financial institutions and to prolong the life of financial infrastructure by delaying the growth of more efficient competition. At times, these attempts have hindered the growth of the protected financial institutions. Regulators appear to compete with the financial institutions and markets that they regulate. To protect themselves, financial institutions prefer to select among several different regulatory options. Moreover, with competition, regulators expend more effort to understand the financial functions and the competitive forces faced by the entities that they regulate. For example, in the U. S., the Commodity Trading Commission regulates financial futures and options on futures, and the Securities and Exchange Commission regulates securities and options on securities. Yet functionally, these instruments prove to be close substitutes for one another.

Miller (1986, 1992) argues that all financial innovation results from a desire to mitigate the effects of regulations such as tax rules, accounting rules, or regulatory frictions imposed by government entities. Reducing the import of other frictions, however, plays a large role in fostering new financial innovations. Miller could be correct, however, if in a second–best world, regulations and frictions are not separable because inefficient regulations arise from other frictions.

Institutions change while financial functions remain relatively stable. The development of efficient infrastructure necessarily follows from the functions of a financial system—a need to satisfy investor and corporate demands for products and services—rather than to preserve particular institutions. The financial functions define institutional changes. Moreover, the functional approach is relatively culture free. Investors and institutions have the same demand for financial services and products around the world.

Telecommunications and computing technology have created more efficient channels through which entities can provide financial services. These new channels reduce the importance of particular financial institutions. As Sanford (1993) has argued, even without further technological advances, current computing and telecommunications technologies can completely transform the infrastructure through which financial institutions provide services in the next two decades. Further reduction of frictions and restrictions will enable investors and corporations to transact, to save, to shift and pool risks, and to reduce information asymmetries more efficiently. Although today's institutions will survive, the form in which they provide services will change dramatically.

To describe the evolution of financial infrastructure into the next century, it is appropriate to concentrate on how derivative instruments will play a large and expanding role in reducing frictions in providing financial services. In the next section, we turn to a description of derivative contracts. We then discuss the use of derivative contracts in the investment process and in corporate financial management. We then turn from the demanders of financial services to the providers, the financial institutions, and their concerns about managing the transformation. This leaves the last word to the regulators and to the academic research agenda.

Derivative Contracts

A derivative is an instrument whose payoff depends on the performance of an underlying asset, index or security. The payoff pattern can linearly depend on the performance of the underlying asset, as in the case of a futures or a forward contract. The payoff pattern can be nonlinear, as in the case of an option contract. These contracts are not new; they have existed in various forms for centuries. But their use

---

has exploded recently for many reasons: computing and telecommunication technology has made them less costly, regulators and monitors now understand their efficiency, their flexibility makes them attractive for business in a global economy, and the academic research has furthered understanding of their use and value.

Most financial instruments are derivative contracts in one form or another. Black and Scholes (1973) pointed out that the equityholders of a firm with debt in its capital structure have an option to buy back the firm from its debtholders on maturity of the debt. The high–yield bond (the so–called "junk bond") is a riskier option contract than more highly rated corporate debt. Corporate debt and equity contracts are derivative to the underlying investments. Researchers have pointed out that firms undertaking investment projects use option theory to decide whether to invest in new projects or to change the investment levels of existing projects.

It is easy to forget that a firm's capital structure is derivative to the underlying investments of the firm. Debt and equity are like boxes that provide particular cashflows to investors. They evolve over time as investors'demands change. Investors might prefer cashflow patterns that differ from those given by underlying investment instruments. Corporations might prefer to make payments based on patterns other than the standard boxes. This allows intermediaries to offer derivative contracts of various forms to more closely match the needs of demanders and suppliers of funds. Investment projects are coarse bundles of cashflows; corporations are combinations of these coarse bundles of cashflows. They issue securities to finance their activities, claims that represent bundles of coarse cashflows. As frictions are reduced or to reduce frictions, however, entities break cashflows into finer gradients through the use of derivatives. This process gives investors and issuers the cashflows they want. This in turn reduces the cost of capital to firms. Institutional boxes evolve and change their form and shape.

Alternative Ways to Invest in Contractuals: The Building Blocks

Table I illustrates four financial forms. The top panel depicts the performance of a standard, simple swap contract. In a swap contract, parties agree to exchange cashflows depending on various indices based on a notional or stated amount. Unlike a bond contract, the parties do not exchange any principal amounts. For example, Bank X might agree to pay Corporation Z a floating rate of interest based on LIBOR (the London Interbank Offering Rate in dollars, R) on $100 million notional amount, while Corporation Z in turn agrees to pay Bank X a fixed rate of interest on the same notional amount periodically for a set number of years. If the floating rate exceeds the fixed rate, when a cashflow should be exchanged, Bank X makes a payment to Corporation Z. For example, if at the end of the year, the floating rate is 7% and the fixed rate is 6%, the bank pays the corporation $1 million or 1% of $100 million.

In the top panel of Table 1, one party agrees to receive the change in value of a total–return Government Bond Index (such as a discount bond), $B^* - B$ on a notional amount B, and to pay at the LIBOR rate, R, on the same notional amount. If $B^* - B - RB$ is positive, the index will have appreciated by more than RB, and the party agreeing to receive the return on bonds receives the payment. If $B^* - B - RB$ is negative, that party must make this payment to the counterparty paying the return on bonds.

The second panel depicts a more conventional debt contract. An entity buys long–term bonds and finances its position. This is called a repurchase agreement. Although the illustration assumes that the borrower can attain financing of the entire position, in reality, financial intermediaries that finance these government bond positions require borrowers to post and maintain capital of approximately 2% to guard against default. The bond buyer realizes a gain or loss on the bond position and must repay the loan at the end of the period. The net payment received is $B^* - B - RB$, exactly the same as for the swap contract.

The third panel illustrates the investment returns from buying futures contacts on the total–return Government Bond Index. To prevent arbitrage, the futures price, F, generally sells above the spot price of a commodity by an amount equal to the interest on the notional amount but minus the present value of any carrying charges on the underlying instrument. Since, in this illustration, the futures contract has no carrying charges—the Index does not pay coupons—the futures price, F, will be equal to the current spot price of the Index, B, multiplied by one plus the interest rate.[1] The return on the futures contract is equal to $B^* - B - RB$, the same return as the swap and financed bond position.

TABLE 1

Alternative Ways to Invest in Contractuals–Building Blocks		
Illustration of a Swap Contract on Government Bond Index		
		RETURN
Receive:	Return on Bonds	B* - B
Pay:	LIBOR	-RB
	Total Payment	B* - B - RB

Illustration of a Leveraged Government Bond Investment		
		RETURN
Buy Bonds:	B	B + B* - B
Borrow	-B	-RB - B
	Total Payment	B* - B - RB

Illustration of a Futures Contract	
	RETURN
Buy Futures F= B(1 + R)	B* - F
Total Payment	B* - B - RB

Illustration of Option Contracts

Buy a Call Option and Sell a Put Option with Exercise Price (K) Equal to the
Forward Price; that is K = B(1 + R)

	RETURN	
	B* < K	B* > K
Buy Call: C	0	B* - B - RB
Sell Put -P	B* - B - RB	0
Total Payment	B* - B - RB	B* - B - RB

Conclusion: Without frictions, a swap contract is functionally equivalent to a leveraged contract, a futures contract and a long call and a short put option contract.

The final panel illustrates the investment returns available from buying call options and selling put options on the total–return Government Bond Index. The exercise price was selected to be the forward price of the underlying bond index to illustrate that the swap contract, financed bond position, futures contract and options positions can provide investors with exactly the same total payoff pattern. If B* - K is greater than zero, the call option will be exercised and the put option will expire unexercised. If B* - K is less than zero, the put option will be exercised and the call option will expire unexercised. Buying the call and selling the put are equivalent to holding a financed–bond position as in panel two.

Economically, these alternatives provide functionally equivalent payoffs in a world without frictions. There is no need for swap contracts and futures contracts. Investors participate in the returns on the bond index by either buying or selling a financed–bond position.[2] Option contracts are created to provide nonlinear payoff patterns. As Black and Scholes (1973) demonstrated, however, investors can create their own option by using financed–bond positions.

Once we move to the world of frictions, however, each of these contracts plays an important role in the evolution of the financial infrastructure. The swap or forward market is generally an over–the–counter market frequented by large financial institutions such as banks, investment dealers, insurance companies, and corporations. Here dealers fashion contracts that contain combinations of options and forwards to suit a counterparty's particular needs. Most likely, the contractual terms are idiosyncratic. Since the contract is generally tailored to the client, the dealer must take the other side of the contract. Dealers, however, tend to avoid general market risks. For example, they prefer not to hold the risk associated with a change in the value of the underlying bond index, a risk for which they have no comparative advantage. The dealer's risk of entering into a particular contract is partially offset by the risks of other contracts in the dealer's portfolio. Most dealers, however, enter the underlying market to hedge remaining risks. For example, they buy or sell to hedge the risks of promising to pay (receive) the returns on bonds to counterparties. Alternatively, the dealer might sell or buy futures (options) to hedge the inherent risks of the idiosyncratic contract's component pieces.

To stay competitive, the dealer is forced to select the least costly alternative to divide the cashflows on particular contracts. With well–functioning financing markets, futures markets, and options markets, dealers can provide idiosyncratic contracts to corporations and investors at lower cost than in the absence of these markets.

Dealers use the standard–form contracts in listed futures and options markets to hedge parts of the risk of idiosyncratic contracts. It is often too costly for dealers to hedge all of the contract risks involved; so they retain some risk, so–called "basis risk." Although corporations and investors cover the dealers' costs to provide these contracts, the dealers provide the payoff patterns at much lower cost than other alternatives.

The put–call relationship in the last panel of Table 1 brings out another important point about swap, financed bonds, and futures contracts. The buyer of a call option must rely on the seller of the call option to fulfill the obligation to pay the difference between the market price and the exercise price in the event that the buyer exercises the option. The buyer assumes the seller's credit risk. The buyer of options is exposed to the possibility of a seller's default on the contract. The seller, however, is not worried about the default risk of the buyer since the option is the buyer's asset in the event of bankruptcy.

Although each of these contracts is a zero–investment contract at inception—no money is exchanged—their value does change as the underlying asset value changes because the options are only settled periodically. Since these contracts involve the sale of put options in addition to the purchase of call options, each party is exposed to the other's credit risk. As the value of the bond index increases, the call option becomes more valuable and the put option less valuable. As a result, the receiver of the returns on the bond index has a receivable and is exposed to the credit risk of the writer of the call (the entity paying the return on bonds). As the value of the bond index falls, the put option becomes more valuable and the call becomes less valuable; the receiver of the returns on the bond index owes money on the contract. The credit risk has swung in the other direction.

It has become common practice to advertise the size of the market in these derivative contracts in terms of the notional amount outstanding. *Fortune* (March 7, 1994) and the General Accounting Office (1994) report that the size of the derivative market exceeds $15 trillion of notional amount outstanding. The notional amount, however, provides a meaningless estimate of market size. Although Chemical Bank and Bankers Trust each have over $2 trillion of outstanding notional contracts, this figure gives no indication of their credit exposure. The cash–settled value of their receivables is probably less than 3% of these stated amounts. (Remember that the dealer in swap contracts does not lose the value of the principal as is the case with a standard debt contract.)

Investment Process and Derivative Contracts

Observers often ask whether derivative contracts are a fad or the foundation of the new financial infrastructure. We have only seen the first steps in financial innovation using derivative contracts. With the elemental building blocks described in the last section, we will see financial intermediaries more clearly define the cashflow patterns demanded by investors and corporations. This will create more tailor–made investment products to suit investor needs.

Recent years have seen movements from individual securities to portfolios, to international diversification, and to broader classes of securities in investor portfolios. Investors have become willing to select from a broad class of mutual fund offerings. The entire mutual fund industry has grown dramatically in response to investor demand for alternative investment products and services.

This industry, however, is embryonic. It still does not efficiently address investor demands. Many investment managers attempt to outperform a number of benchmarks to provide enhanced returns. A few others, such as the various index funds, attempt to provide exposures to market factors. In the former case, investors assume extra risk to achieve the higher returns. Each fund group provides the inputs, the funds from which savers select. Many groups offer investors over one hundred different choices. Most savers cannot combine the inputs to provide the best expected returns for their selected risk level.

Applied financial theory and the requisite computing power now provide these portfolio choices. However, we have no delivery systems to provide investors with the tools to make allocation decisions. This generates dead–weight costs, which discourage savings and increase the cost of capital to corporations. Economic theory tells us that investors want to save for future consumption needs. They want to insure against contingencies. They want to control risks. Investment products will be developed that combine these mutual fund inputs efficiently to target investor needs over the life cycle.

Individuals reduce risk in three primary ways. In the 1960s and early 1970s, other than investments in a home and in human capital, individuals held a small number of stock issues and savings accounts of various kinds. To reduce their risk, they held more in savings accounts and less in stock. In the late 1970s through the present, investors learned that diversification reduces risk and does not sacrifice expected return. They moved away from individual stock selection to save through institutionalized diversified investments for both savings and retirement savings. The costs to provide these products have fallen dramatically over time.

A third way to reduce risk is to hedge. The hedge can be linear or non–linear in its payoff structure. For example, an investor who holds a portfolio of mutual funds might want to reduce his risk. He can sell his holdings, but this might be more costly than offsetting his risks by using futures

---

contracts or swap contracts. Individuals have acquired insurance against contingencies such as death and accident for many years. The financial infrastructure will develop to allow investors to buy financial insurance through contracts that provide nonlinear payoffs. For example, investors might prefer to participate in the appreciation in the underlying market at a reduced rate in exchange for a guaranteed floor[3].

Financial infrastructure will be built to provide investors with payoff patterns that match their risk tolerance level. Investment programs will insure investors against financial contingencies at extremely low cost through the use of derivative instruments. As long as the risks that the investor wants to hedge are highly correlated with a traded instrument, entities will provide financial insurance to meet that investor's idiosyncratic needs.

Derivatives are not a fad because they provide a less costly alternative to a direct investment. For example, many academics have argued that international diversification of investments provides higher returns for risk compared to domestic investments. Investors can expand their opportunity set through international diversification. The degree of international diversification in practice is far less than predicted by theory. The explanation is that the frictions associated with international investing have exceeded the benefits. The cost of learning how to invest internationally is quite high. Sophisticated entities incur substantial costs to invest internationally because of regulations, stamp duties, withholding taxes, brokerage and custodian fees. Even for institutional passive index accounts, these fees can approximate between .75% to 2.0% a year. Many institutions find it more efficient to invest the money that they would have invested abroad in home–country bonds (for example, at LIBOR) and enter into a swap contract with an intermediary to receive the returns on a foreign index in return for paying LIBOR.

Entities that are more efficient should make the foreign–country direct investment and then swap the returns on that direct investment with the entity that finds it more costly to invest abroad. Transportation costs are reduced. There may be considerable economies of scale because only a few entities need acquire the expertise to invest in these markets. The systematic returns to investing internationally can be transferred efficiently through swap (or other derivative) contracts. This reduction in costs improves global economic efficiency and more closely links the world economy. The use of derivatives allows for growth of efficient infrastructures to provide less expensive international investing.

It is inappropriate to limit the definition of derivatives to listed options and futures contracts or to swap and option contracts entered into with a financial intermediary. Investors can acquire equity–linked notes or structured bonds to achieve similar results. For example, a foreign investor who wants to invest in the U.S. market as represented by the Standard and Poor's 500 can (1) buy the stocks in the index, (2) buy a mutual fund that replicates the returns on the index, (3) invest in U.S. Treasury instruments and buy a futures contract on the index, (4) invest in U.S. Treasury instruments and receive the returns on the index though an over–the–counter swap contract, (5) buy an equity–linked note that provides this payoff structure, (6) buy a structured bond which provides for protection in case the market falls in value in return for only a partial participation in the index's growth, (7) buy a structured bond that provides for a truncated participation in the upside for more income in case the market falls in value, (8) buy put options to protect against a market decline in any of the above products, and (9) buy protection against currency price fluctuations. With frictions and restrictions, only a limited subset of these alternatives might be suitable for particular classes of investors.

Investors demand significantly higher returns for investing in illiquid investments. The bid–offer spreads are quite large; and since investors might be forced to sell quickly, they demand a premium in expected return to overcome the expected costs of the illiquid investment. Derivatives have been used to provide liquidity to the market, which attracts investors to these investment classes. For example, we have seen the transformation of a very illiquid market in mortgages into a much more liquid market through the securitization of mortgage pools. This "pool" concept revolutionized mortgage finance by improving liquidity. Securitization broadened the market and resulted in reduced costs of securing mortgages for many households. Emerging market investments provide another example. By pooling illiquid emerging–market securities into a fund, investment bankers have offered various tranches to different classes of investors. Investors in the upper–level tranches do not need to know the particular assets in the pool; they only need to know the value of the pool standing behind their claim. As a result, these derivatives trade with very low bid–offer spreads even though the underlying assets in the pool have high bid–offer spreads.

Investors might have expertise in a particular market. For example, a corporate bond manager at an insurance company might provide enhanced returns by constructing an optimal portfolio of corporate bonds for his firm. He might feel, however, that for a period of time, the general level of corporate bond yields will widen out relative to other asset classes such as mortgages. If this did occur, he would suffer an economic loss in returns relative to other investment classes. As a result, he prefers to invest in mortgages over the short term. One alternative is to sell his entire $2 billion corporate bond portfolio and buy mortgages. He would, however, lose the underlying superior portfolio that took considerable effort and cost to build. Moreover, he might not be able to find appropriate mortgage structures to replace the bonds. Under institutional rules, he might realize unwanted accounting or tax gains or losses. The costs might be too great to change the portfolio, and he could lose his opportunity.

Another alternative is for the corporate bond manager to retain the superior portfolio to earn enhanced returns and to hedge the systematic risks of corporate bonds. He may enter into a swap with another entity that is willing to receive the returns on corporate bonds in exchange for paying the returns on mortgages to his insurance company. The transfer of systematic risks provides a potentially lower–cost alternative to liquidating his portfolio. The corporate bond manager retains his portfolio; the manager retains flexibility to concentrate in areas of his expertise; and he can even swap for customized mortgage return characteristics. The use of derivatives might provide a low–cost alternative to a liquidation of the portfolio.

In the future, strategic investment management will evolve to combine the best of selectivity (market expertise) with risk reduction through derivatives. For example, if a bond manager can provide enhanced corporate bond returns, he can also become a superior stock manager. He concentrates his direct investment in particular corporate bonds to provide the enhanced returns. Then he enters into a swap contract: He agrees to pay the general level of corporate bond returns to another entity and to receive the return, say, on a stock market index. For example, assume that with his expertise in the bond market, he generates a return of 8% while corporate bonds, in general, produce a return of only 6%. He receives 8% on his specific bonds and pays 6% on his swap. His net return is 2% plus the return on the stock index. He has outperformed other index stock managers by 2%.

The current investment management process is geared to require managers to concentrate in specific investment regions or categories. For example, the manager is deemed to be a bond manger, money market manager, index manger, etc. Once a manager is an expert in any one area, however, he becomes superior in other areas as well though the indirect method of derivative contracts.

An investment hub is the investment area that provides superior returns. The investor, however, might not be well diversified by concentrating in the hub. To increase exposure to various markets, the investor can use derivative contracts.

Corporations and Financial Infrastructure

Some corporations use derivative contracts to hedge their exposures to interest rates, foreign currency price movements, and commodity price movements. Other companies use derivative contracts to attempt to beat the market; for example, *Fortune* (July 25, 1994) reported Procter and Gamble's $145–million loss.

During the 1990s, we will see a dramatic change in the way corporations manage their risks. The nature of bonds and stocks will also change with standard distinctions being blurred over time. The thrust will be towards a financial infrastructure to reduce the systematic risks of those parts of the business in which the corporation lacks expertise and to lever the returns on its core businesses for which it adds economic value.

In the past, equity capital and retained earnings have been the prime means by which corporations financed large projects. Equity capital has played another important role. It has served as assurance money against unforeseen events. By having enough assurance money or permanent financing, firms mitigate the dead–weight costs associated with reorganizing their businesses in the event of an unexpected downturn. Moreover, if a highly leveraged firm's debt–to–equity ratio increases because of market forces, it often cannot expand its business activities. To do so would most likely transfer its resources to debtholders at the expense of equityholders.

Equity is like a bucket, a reserve that guards against unforeseen downturns. The firm "dips" into the equity bucket to protect itself from reorganization costs that result from too heavy a debt load. If equity capital were costless, the firm would have a small amount of debt and a large amount of equity to finance its activities. By equity's being costless, we mean that there are no dead–weight financing costs to produce goods and services in corporate form. However, there are dead–weight costs. For example, equity has been taxed more heavily than debt. It would not be economic, for example, for a corporation to use the proceeds from equity issuance in order to pay for a portfolio of bonds. The returns on the bonds would be taxed once at the corporate level and the remainder taxed again at the shareholder level after the shareholder liquidated the position. It is expensive for corporations to hold cash reserves (assurance money) in the form of bonds.

When personal tax rates are far above corporate tax rates and capital gains tax rates are low, as was the case prior to the 1980s, the corporate form is tax advantageous compared to partnership form. In the 1980s, the reverse was true: personal tax rates were below corporate rates, and capital gains rates were quite high. More formally, as Scholes and Wolfson (1992) have shown, if t_c is the corporate rate, t_p is the personal rate, and t_s is the annualized capital gains rate,[4] then $1 earned in corporate form results in $1(1 - 1t_c)(1 - t_s)$ after both corporate– and shareholder–level taxes. Producing the same goods and services in partnership form results in $1(1 - 1t_p)$. If t_c is 40%, t_s is 20%, and t_s is 40%, the advantage of partnership form over corporate form is 25%. That is, the partner retains 25% more of the profits after all taxes than does the corporate shareholder producing the same goods and services. These tax rates are close to current U.S. tax rates. This encourages the firm to use more debt financing: Like partnership income, debt interest payments are tax deductible and taxed only once at the same rates as partnership income.

Moreover, to issue shares to the public involves other agency costs resulting from the separation of ownership and control. As Jensen (1989) argues, public shareholders demand higher returns to induce them to invest in corporate form. These agency costs increase the cost of capital to corporations. Those corporations that align shareholder and manger interests enhance value and reduce their cost of capital.

Since equity is expensive, firms will attempt to economize on using equity capital both to finance their activities and to provide assurance money for unforeseen events. The growth of derivative instruments has allowed firms to substitute debt for equity in their capital structures. If it were costless for firms to hedge such risks as interest rate risk, foreign exchange risk, and commodity price risk, all firms would hedge these risks. By hedging these risks, firms reduce the volatility of their earnings. Without the hedge, exogenous market price movements cause windfall gains and losses. Most firms add value by producing goods and services—not by forecasting the movements in interest rates, foreign exchange prices and commodity prices.

A firm that does not hedge these exogenous risks is forced to hold more equity to insure against the eventuality that random price movements might result in significant losses. Both equity and hedging activities are not costless. As the costs to hedge activities through the use of derivatives contracts and securities fall, however, the financial infrastructure will change. More and more entities will use hedging as part of their strategic financial activities.[5]

To remain competitive, corporations will be forced to hedge these exogenous risks. For example, if a utility can issue a bond whose interest rate is tied inversely to its fuel costs, it may be able to reduce its equity capital. As fuel costs increase, its interest costs decrease. Without the hedge, if profits were inversely related to fuel costs, the utility would need more equity capital to buffer the increase in fuel prices. A natural candidate to buy such a contract is the fuel supplier or producer.[6] These firms can offer contract terms that other corporate customers and direct customers want and then hedge systematic risks through derivative contracts.

The theory is simple. Reducing exogenous systematic risks reduces the need for equity. As a result, corporations substitute less expensive debt for equity in their capital structures. Shareholders bid up the stock prices of these firms because they will receive more valuable cashflows.

To use derivatives to hedge risks, corporations must understand the specific risks of the subparts of their businesses. This ties industrial organization more closely to the finance function. Derivatives allow corporations to separate various risks into those they understand and that add value for owners (such as supplying clients with power) and those that are exogenous and provide no excess value to owners. They can mitigate the risks that add no excess value to owners. The firm can "fine tune" its activities. Equity capital, however, does not fine tune activities: it is a coarse instrument providing many functions simultaneously.

Hedging allows many entities to remain private. Entering the public markets for shares provides many benefits in addition to financing activities. The functions include, among others: (1) the provision of an external valuation for shares, (2) liquidity for entrepreneurs to borrow against their holdings, (3) assurance money, and (4) a ready market to sell the company. But there are many costs to being a public corporation.[7] As these costs increase and the market for derivatives expands, many of the functions provided by the public issuance of shares will be provided by derivative contracts. Most of the regulatory infrastructure is based on the protection of small investors who buy shares. Derivatives are generally the province of large global investors.

Regulation and Financial Infrastructure

Technological improvements have reduced the costs to control risks. More tools to understand derivatives and to price risk have become available to investors, corporate managers, investment intermediaries, accountants, lawyers, rating agencies, and others. Financial institutions have developed sophisticated risk management reports and controls to manage risk. Accountants have become more familiar with control problems associated with derivatives. The rating agencies have increased their understanding of derivative instruments through their rating of structured bonds, collateralized mortgage obligations, contingent corporate debt, and myriad other contracts. In general, users of derivatives have become better educated.

As the market broadens, these instruments incur lower costs. More investors understand how to value and use them in their global activities. Investment intermediaries convert contracts from one form into another to satisfy demands. For them, the costs to produce these contracts fall as futures and options markets develop worldwide.

Because of the uncertainties associated with new infrastructure, there are regulatory implications. Do investors and corporations know how to price and hedge risks? Do banks and other intermediaries know how to price these contracts? Are they hedging their risks and providing proper risk controls? Do they have operational controls in place? Do these entities control and price the credit risk in the contracts?

The press, the public, and regulators fear derivatives because they are new and complex. Although pervasive and growing, derivatives are still mysterious to the general public. Many regulators argue that the growth of derivatives has led to an increase in the amount of systemic risk, the chance of a financial system meltdown at a great cost to taxpayers. Maybe the cost is the cost, not to taxpayers, but to regulators who must learn to understand the new financial infrastructure. It may be just as likely that derivatives have reduced the chance of a financial meltdown because they have reduced the need for banks and other entities to carry illiquid positions.

There is an important concern associated with the changing financial infrastructure. The speed of institutional change has increased in recent years. As new financial innovations have succeeded, regulatory conventions have become obsolete or lagged behind the new innovations. New finance does not easily fit into the old regulatory boxes. Tax laws have been strained. The definitions of securities and contracts have been tangled. The role of the various regulatory bodies has been changing.

Because of the dynamics of innovation, it has become very difficult for Congress to draft specific rules to regulate institutions. The half life of the regulations is very short. As a result, regulators must rely more on the industry in their own self interest to provide the appropriate economic level of risk controls and management.

Systemic risk is not well understood. What is the cost to taxpayers? Who should stand by to reduce systemic risk if not government agencies? If there is a chain reaction of some sort that leads to potential defaults, the government should provide liquidity to the system. What is the externality? The externality is that market chaos causes many bankruptcies and destroys valuable infrastructure that is costly to rebuild. The argument goes as follows: If market participants had had more time to sort out and incorporate information into new valuations, prices would rebound and society could have prevented these bankruptcies, avoiding their consequential dead–weight costs. On the other hand, even after the time needed to assess information had passed, if market prices did not rebound, businesses would fail at no further dead–weight cost to society.

The regulatory agencies can supply liquidity on a secured basis to financial entities. This provides only a short–term facility. The provision of secured financing does not create incentives for institutions to undertake activities that are subsidized by taxpayers—as is the case with specific banks or insurance companies being afforded government protection because they are "too big to fail." With secured financing, the loss, if any, resides with the stockholders of the financial entity.

Specific financial contracts do not necessarily increase systemic risk to the system. As we have seen, new innovations reduce the costs of providing financial services. As institutions develop many more ways to provide financial services to different entities more efficiently, no

---

The Future of Futures

one mechanism has as large an impact on the global market in financial services. As a result, we reduce systemic risk by reducing the import of any one mechanism in the provision of financial services.

Research Agenda and Conclusions

For many in economics and finance, the new strategic financial organization requires the answers to questions such as what should be hedged, how to decompose the cashflows of the firm, how a change in structure affects incentives within the organization, how much it costs to implement these changes, and how competitors, investors, regulators, rating agencies, customers and employees are affected.

The future research agenda is rich for financial institutions who must continue to understand how to provide products and services at lower friction costs to satisfy the functions of the financial system. On a micro level, they must build more efficient pricing mechanisms and risk control systems. They must model and price credit risk. There is an untapped research vein in the regulatory arena.

The remainder of this decade and decades beyond suggest exciting times for investment mangers to provide products and services. Corporate managers have an opportunity to go back to basics and determine an optimal investment and financial program. The new infrastructure allows corporations to design what they want for less. Corporations will change the ways in which they manage their economic balance sheets. The regulatory process can serve to attempt to monitor the divergence of innovation from infrastructure. As the pace of innovation accelerates, the gap between products and controls might widen. The system might be more vulnerable at these times. In response, regulators serve to warn the financial industry to develop controls.

Regulatory effort must be aimed at fostering the functions of the financial system and not on preserving its institutions. With global competition in the provision of goods and services, including financial services, it is not profitable for agencies to concentrate on narrow institutional definitions. The entity that provides services at lower cost and potentially in far different ways than anticipated will succeed despite the regulatory protection of other entities.

References

Benston, G. J. and C. Smith. "A Transaction Cost Approach to the Theory of Financial Intermediation." *Journal of Finance* 31 (May 1976): 215–231.

Black F. and M.S. Scholes. "From Theory to a New Financial Product." *Journal of Finance* 29 (May 1974): 399–412.

Fama, E. "Agency Problems and the Theory of the Firm." *Journal of Political Economy* 88 (April 1980): 288–307.

Finnerty, J. D. "An Overview of Corporate Securities Innovation." *Journal of Applied Corporate Finance* 4 (Winter 1992): 23–39.

Freeman, A. "A Survey of International Banking: New Tricks to Learn." *The Economist* (April 10, 1993): 1–37.

General Accounting Office. *Financial Derivatives*. Comptroller General of the United States, GAO/GGD, (1994): 94–133, Washington, DC.

Grossman, S. J. and O. D. Hart. "Corporate Financial Structure and Managerial Incentives." In J. J. McCall, ed., *The Economics of Information and Uncertainty*. Chicago: The University of Chicago Press, 1982.

Jensen, M. C., and W. Meckling. "Theory of the Firm: Managerial Behavior, Agency Costs and Ownership Structure." *Journal of Financial Economics* 3 (October 1976): 305–360.

_____, "Eclipse of the Public Corporation." *Harvard Business Review* 67 (September/October 1989): 61–74.

Litzenberger, R. H. "Swaps: Plain and Fanciful." *Journal of Finance* 47 (July 1992): 831–850.

Loomis, C. J. "A Whole New Way to Run a Bank." *Fortune* (September 7, 1992):76.

_____, "The Risk That Won't Go Away." *Fortune* (March 7, 1994): 78.

Merton, R. C. "Financial Innovation and Economic Performance." *Journal of Applied Corporate Finance* 4 (Winter 1992): 12–22.

_____, "Operation and Regulation in Financial Intermediation: A Functional Perspective." Working Paper 93–020, Harvard Business School, 1993.

Miller, M. H. "Financial Innovation: The Last Twenty Years and the Next." *Journal of Financial and Quantitative Analysis* 21 (December 1986): 459–471.

_____, "Financial Innovation: Achievements and Prospects." *Journal of Applied Corporate Finance* 4 (Winter 1992): 4–11.

Ross, S. A. "The Economic Theory of Agency: The Principal's Problem." *American Economic Review* 63 (May 1973): 134–139.

_____, "Institutional Markets, Financial Marketing, and Financial Innovation." *Journal of Finance* 44 (July 1989): 541–556.

Sanford, C. "Financial Innovation in the Year 2020." *Kansas Federal Reserve* (1993): 1–12.

Scholes, M.S. and M. A. Wolfson. *Taxes and Business Strategy: A Planning Approach*. Englewood Cliffs, NJ: Prentice–Hall, 1992.

Notes

[1]   As shown in the third panel of the illustration, if $F > B(1 + R)$ by an amount X, market participants would sell the future and hedge their position by buying government bonds (financed as in panel two). Market participants would receive $B^* - B - RB$ on their bonds and pay $B^* - B - RB - X$ on the future, realizing a sure profit of X. If futures were selling for a price of X below this amount, the market participant would follow the opposite strategy and make a sure profit of X.

[2]   It is not necessary to finance any of these positions at the 100% level. Any other fixed level of capital illustrates the same functional equivalence. A sale of bonds with a promise to repurchase them is a financing trade called a repurchase agreement. The seller receives the bond rate on the proceeds of the sale. A direct financing trade on a long position is sometimes called a reverse repurchase agreement.

[3]   Recently, the government of France has allowed individuals to invest up to the equivalent of approximately $100,000 in an equity account. The account allows French investors to buy French equity without paying any tax either at the corporate or shareholder level if they hold their funds in the account for five years. Although the account offers significant tax advantages to investors, many French investors fear the potential losses of investing in the market. To overcome this fear, many French banks have established programs which insure that the investor receives the maximum of the appreciation in a French market index and that he receives his money back at the end of five years. With this form of insurance, many French citizens have entered the program.

[4]   Shareholders pay taxes on dividends when received at ordinary rates and on realized capital gains when they sell shares. Therefore, t_s is an annualized equivalent shareholder–level tax rate that includes the investor's ability to defer payment of the tax on gains.

[5]   Many corporations use derivatives to attempt to add value for shareholders. Some treasury departments are able to add value because they do have expertise at forecasting the direction of interest rates or other prices more efficiently than other market participants. Derivative instruments are one way in which they can take directional risks (for example, Procter and Gamble's loss of $145 million). Unlike this tactical approach to the use of derivatives (and any other market instrument), a strategic approach uses derivatives as any other financial tool for long–term planning.

[6]   As an illustration of a change of financial infrastructure in natural gas distribution, see "Enron Gas Services," Harvard Business School, N9–294–076. For an application to the extraction industry, see "American Barrick Resources Corporation Managing Gold Price Risk," Harvard Business School, N9–293–128.

[7]   For example, corporations are subject to shareholder suits, constraints on their business activities, compliance costs, and disclosure costs.